Shojo Beat

From Me to You

Vol. 22
Story & Art by
Karuho Shiina

Volume 22

Contents

Story Thus Far

Sawako Kuronuma has always been a loner. Though not by choice, this optimistic 16-year-old girl can't seem to make any friends. Stuck with the unfortunate nickname "Sadako" after the haunting movie character, rumors about her summoning spirits have been greatly exaggerated. With her shy personality and scary looks, most of her classmates will barely talk to her, much less look into her eyes for more than three seconds lest they be cursed. Thanks to Kazehaya, who always treats her nicely, Sawako makes her first friends at school, Ayane and Chizu. Eventually, Sawako finds the courage to date Kazehaya.

The time has come for Sawako and her friends to think about their futures after high school. When Sawako chooses to attend the local college with Kazehaya, Pin encourages her to aim higher and attend "D" University of Education in Sapporo. Ryu decides to leave town and go to a college where he can continue playing baseball. Chizu feels lonely at the thought of everyone leaving, and Kento is confused by Yano's hot-cold behavior as she wavers over taking the easy road by going to a Sapporo college or risking everything to go to the school she really wants in Tokyo.

Episode 88: Don't Go

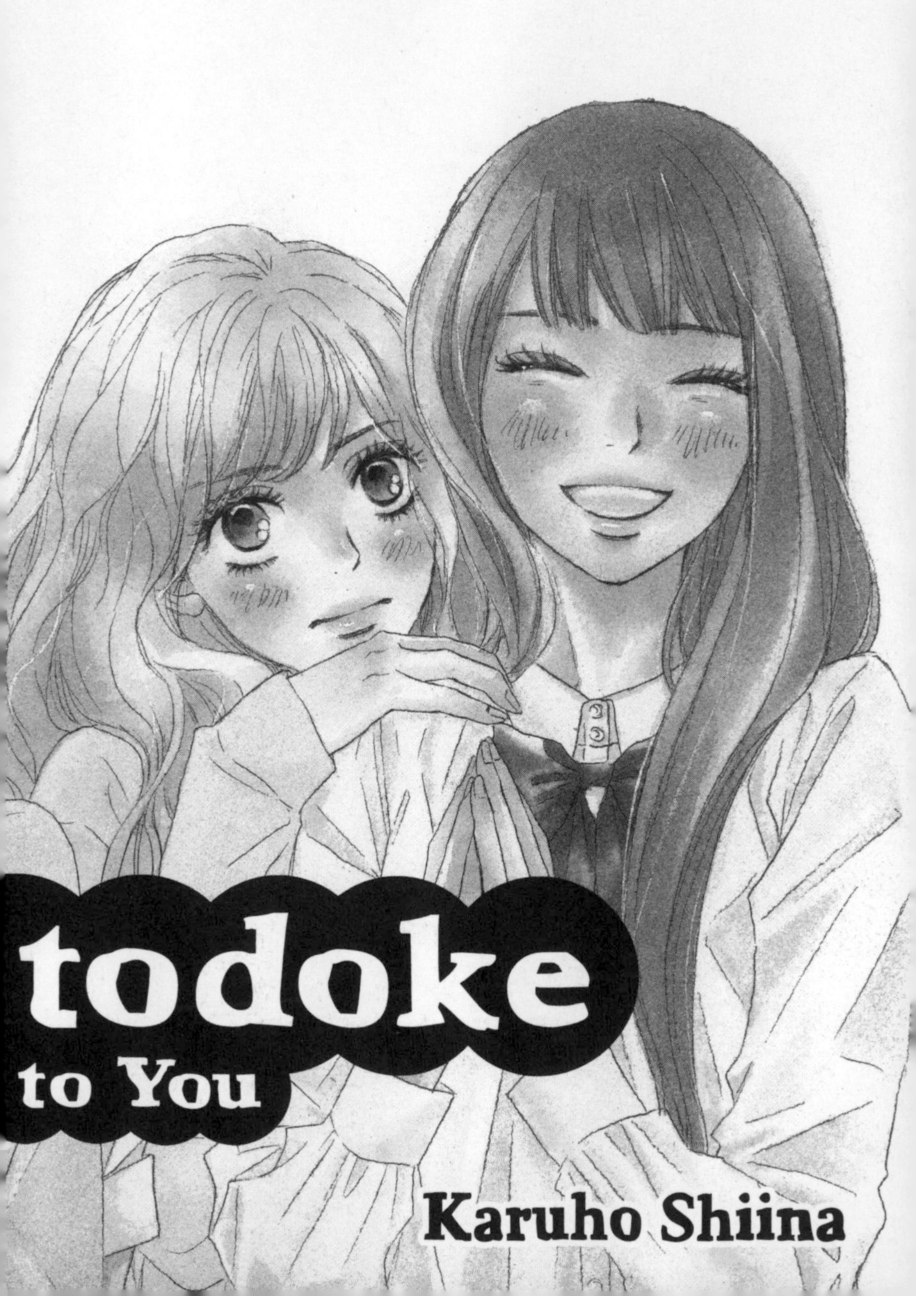
todoke
to You
Karuho Shiina

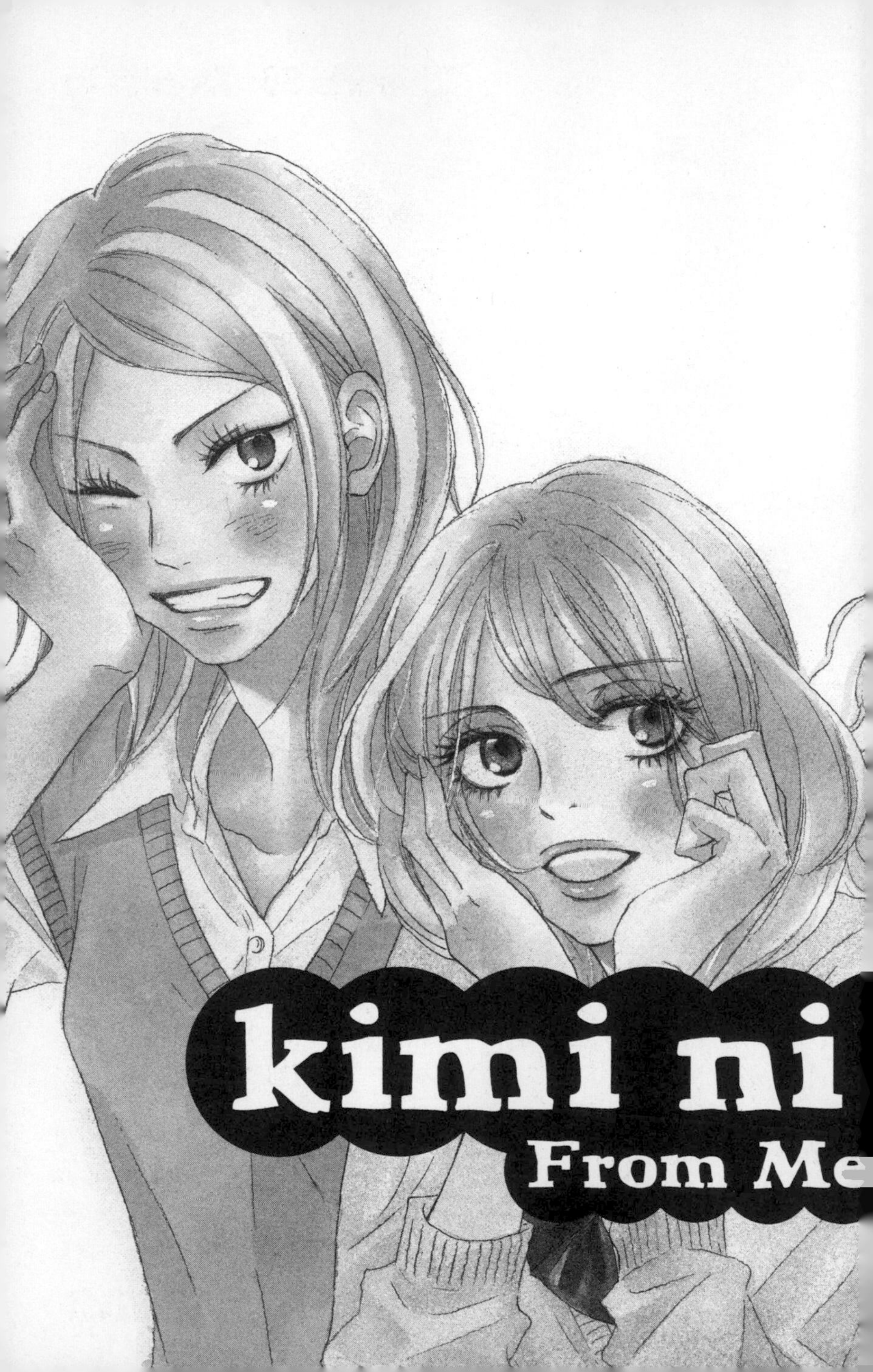
kimi ni
From Me

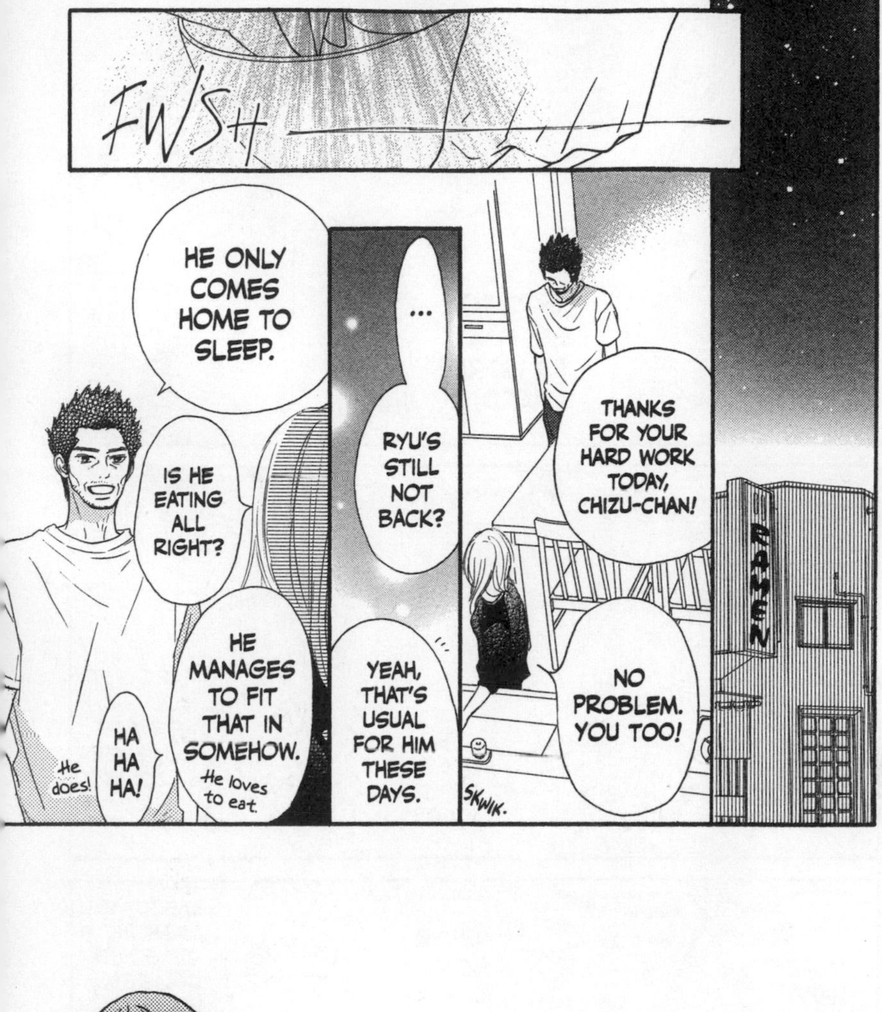
FWSH
THANKS FOR YOUR HARD WORK TODAY, CHIZU-CHAN!
RAMEN
NO PROBLEM. YOU TOO!
SKWIK.
...
RYU'S STILL NOT BACK?
YEAH, THAT'S USUAL FOR HIM THESE DAYS.
HE ONLY COMES HOME TO SLEEP.
IS HE EATING ALL RIGHT?
HE MANAGES TO FIT THAT IN SOMEHOW.
He loves to eat.
HA HA HA!
He does!

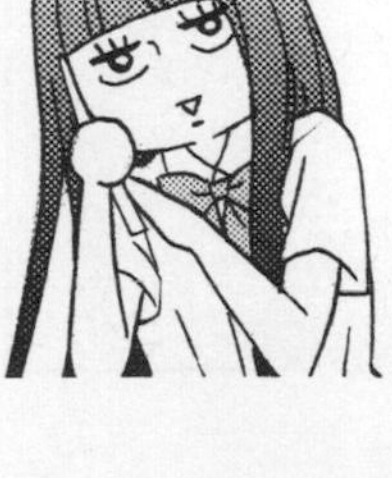

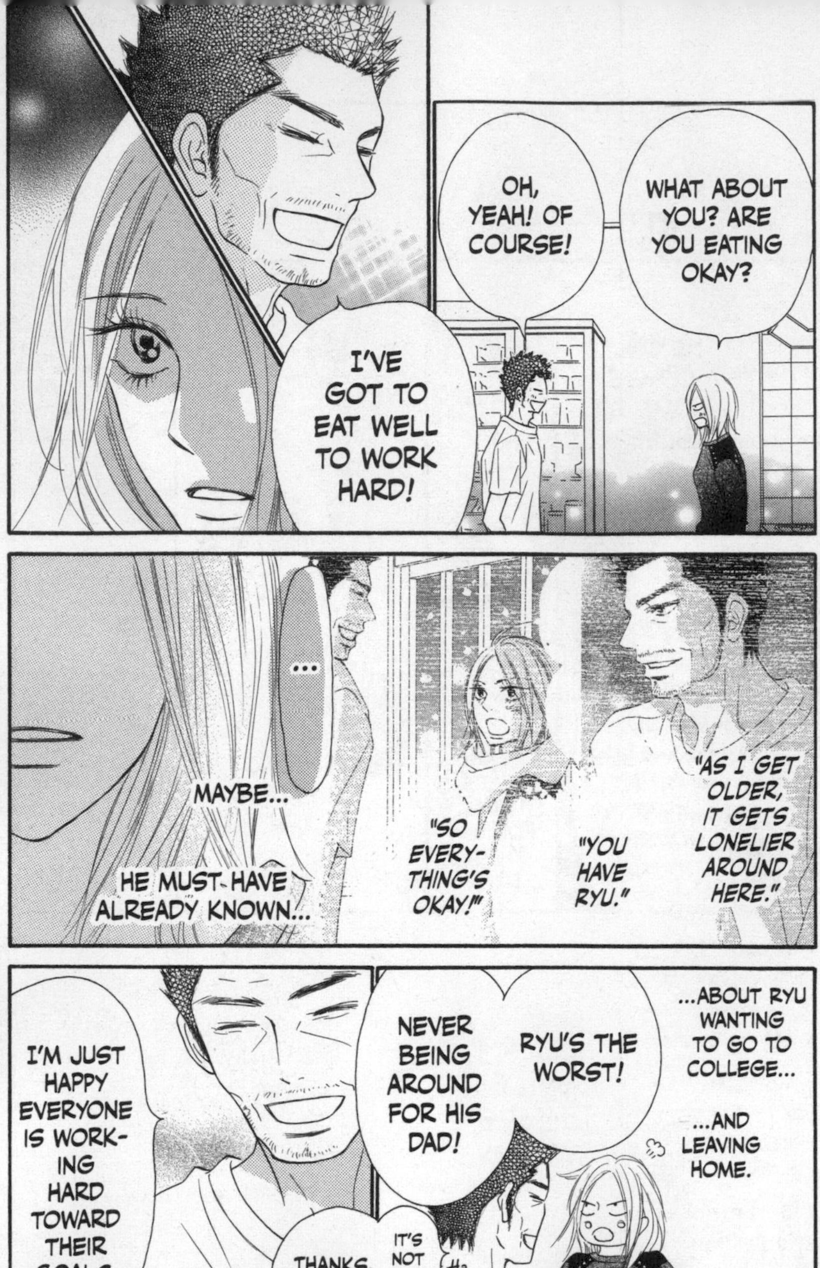
WHAT ABOUT YOU? ARE YOU EATING OKAY?
OH, YEAH! OF COURSE!
I'VE GOT TO EAT WELL TO WORK HARD!
"AS I GET OLDER, IT GETS LONELIER AROUND HERE."
"YOU HAVE RYU."
"SO EVERYTHING'S OKAY!"
...
MAYBE...
HE MUST HAVE ALREADY KNOWN...
...ABOUT RYU WANTING TO GO TO COLLEGE...
...AND LEAVING HOME.
RYU'S THE WORST!
NEVER BEING AROUND FOR HIS DAD!
Ha ha ha!
IT'S NOT LIKE THAT.
I'M JUST HAPPY EVERYONE IS WORKING HARD TOWARD THEIR GOALS.
THANKS, THOUGH.

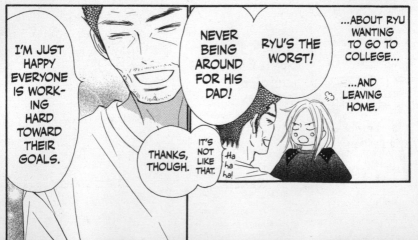

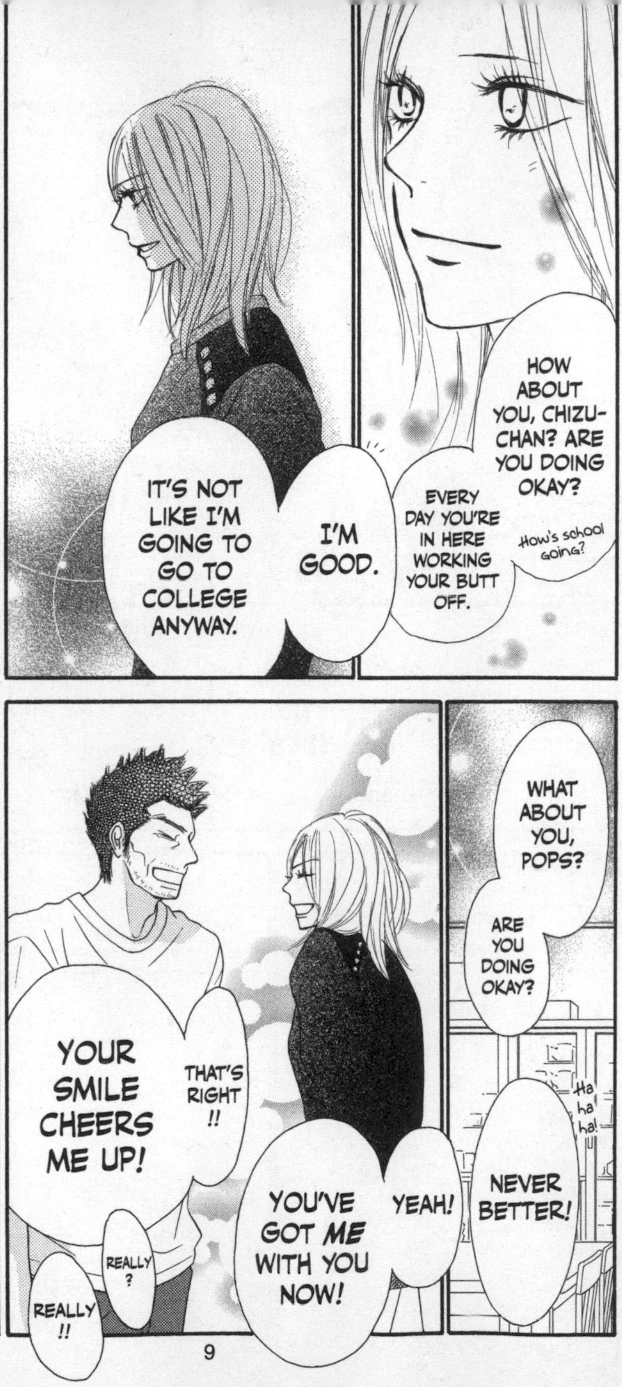
HOW ABOUT YOU, CHIZU-CHAN? ARE YOU DOING OKAY?
How's school going?
EVERY DAY YOU'RE IN HERE WORKING YOUR BUTT OFF.
I'M GOOD.
IT'S NOT LIKE I'M GOING TO GO TO COLLEGE ANYWAY.
WHAT ABOUT YOU, POPS?
ARE YOU DOING OKAY?
Ha ha ha!
NEVER BETTER!
YOUR SMILE CHEERS ME UP!
THAT'S RIGHT!!
YEAH!
YOU'VE GOT *ME* WITH YOU NOW!
REALLY?
REALLY!!

KARUPIN on JAPAN 1

Hello! How are you? I'm Shiina. Nice to meet you!

By the way, there were no sidebars in volume 21! I've been scribbling meaningless stuff in them since volume 1, but last time I just didn't have the time.

I feel like a graphic novel is easier to read without sidebars, but I felt like writing them again for volume 22!

My daily life is drama-free, so I don't have a lot that's fun to write about. Oh no... That sounds kinda grim!

Um... My favorite foods are basically every main and side dish!

(Information no one needed to know.)

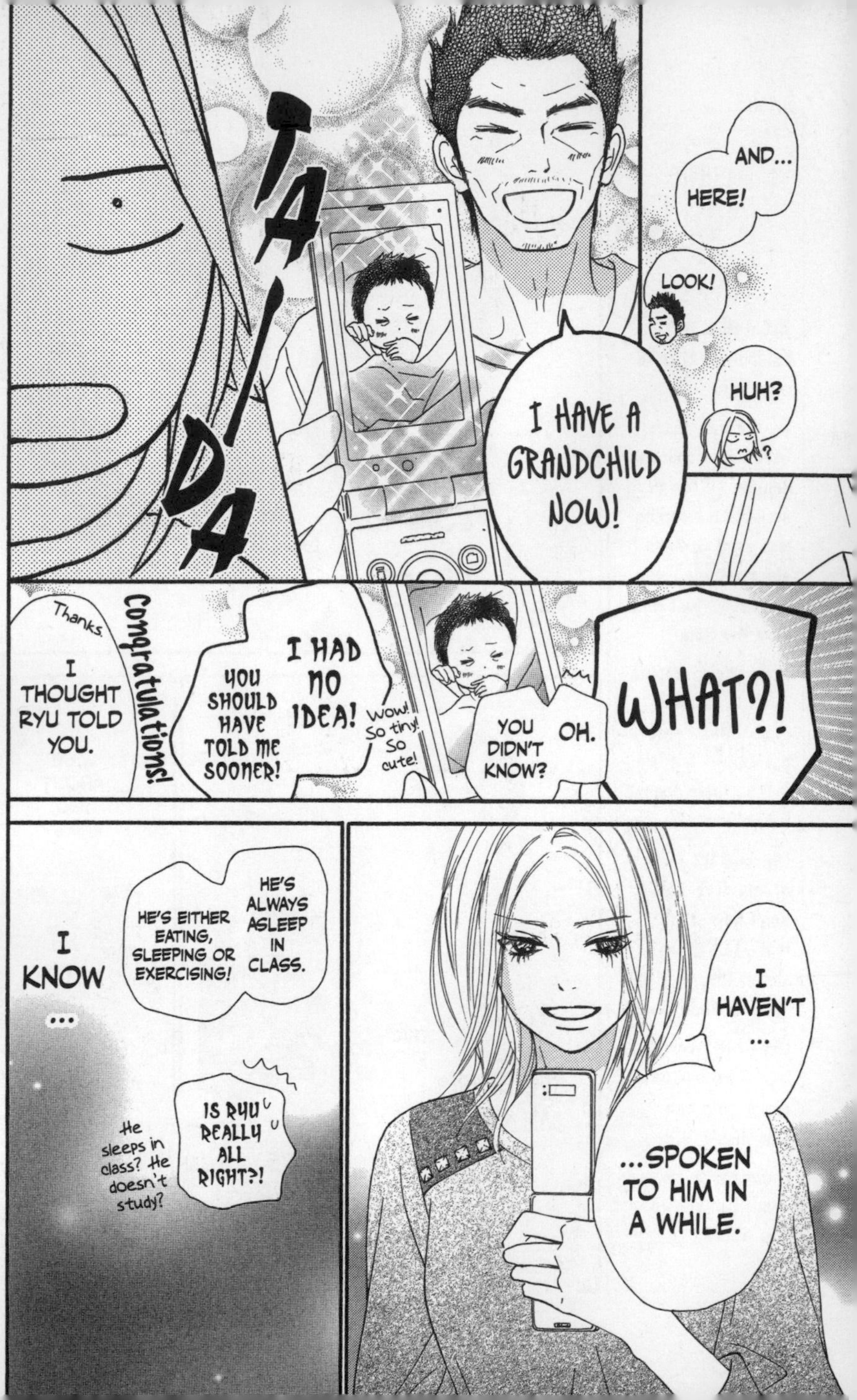
AND... HERE!
LOOK!
HUH?
I HAVE A GRANDCHILD NOW!
TA-DA
WHAT?!
OH.
YOU DIDN'T KNOW?
Wow! So tiny! So cute!
I HAD NO IDEA!
YOU SHOULD HAVE TOLD ME SOONER!
Congratulations!
Thanks.
I THOUGHT RYU TOLD YOU.
I HAVEN'T ...
...SPOKEN TO HIM IN A WHILE.
HE'S ALWAYS ASLEEP IN CLASS.
HE'S EITHER EATING, SLEEPING OR EXERCISING!
I KNOW ...
IS RYU REALLY ALL RIGHT?!
He sleeps in class? He doesn't study?

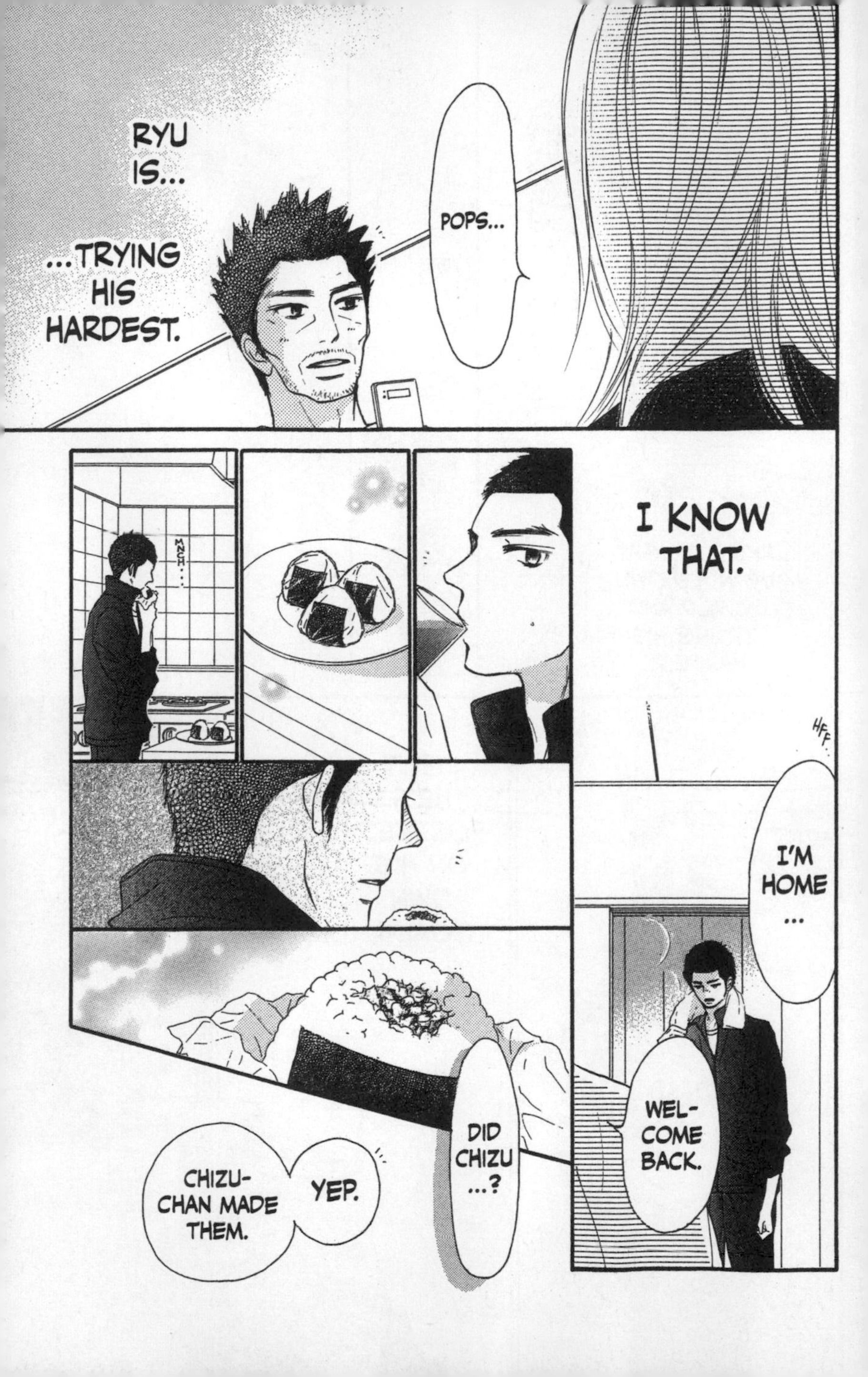
POPS...
RYU IS...
...TRYING HIS HARDEST.
I KNOW THAT.
MNCH...
HFF
I'M HOME ...
WEL-COME BACK.
DID CHIZU ...?
YEP.
CHIZU-CHAN MADE THEM.

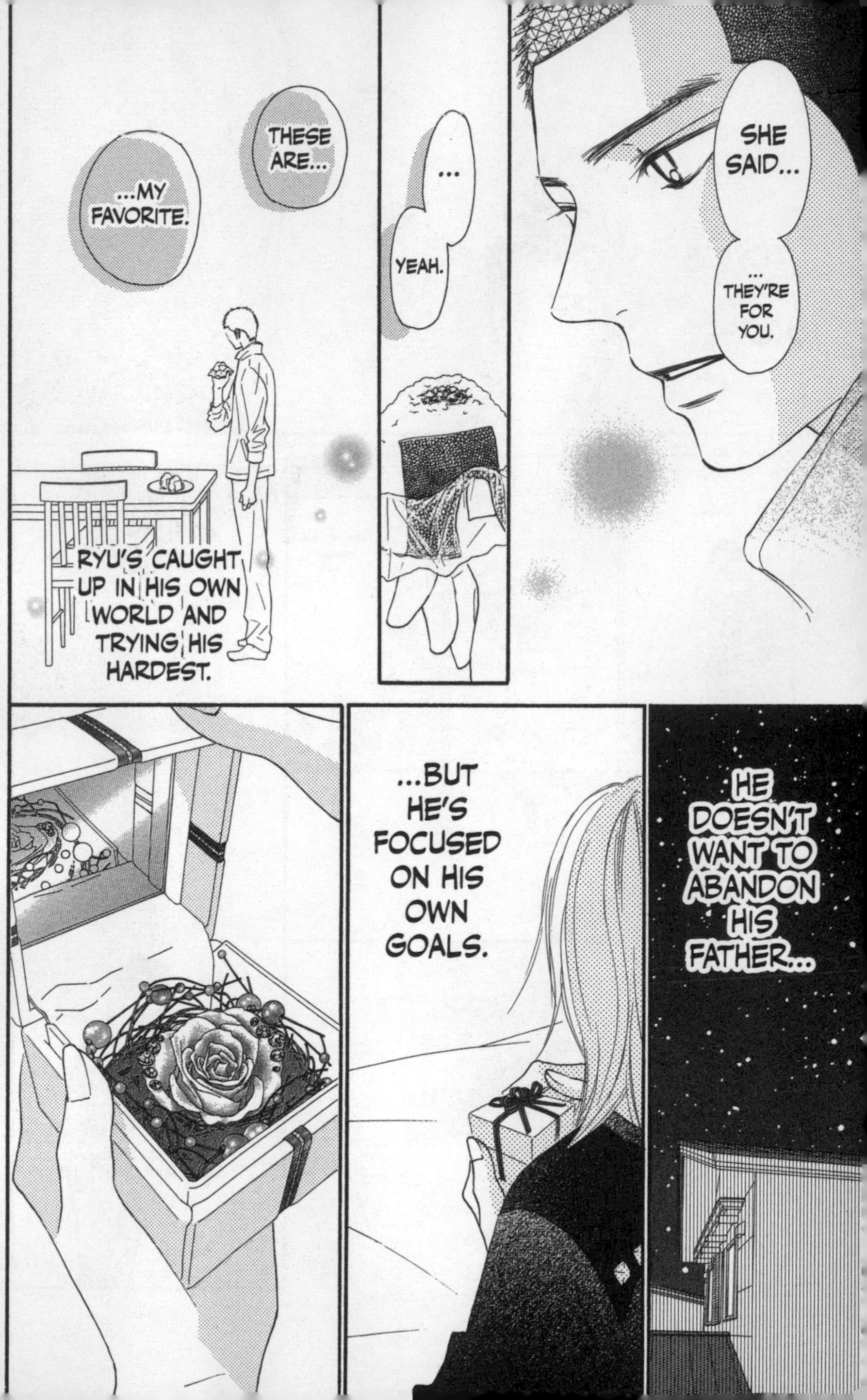
SHE SAID...
...THEY'RE FOR YOU.
...
YEAH.
THESE ARE...
...MY FAVORITE.
RYU'S CAUGHT UP IN HIS OWN WORLD AND TRYING HIS HARDEST.
HE DOESN'T WANT TO ABANDON HIS FATHER...
...BUT HE'S FOCUSED ON HIS OWN GOALS.

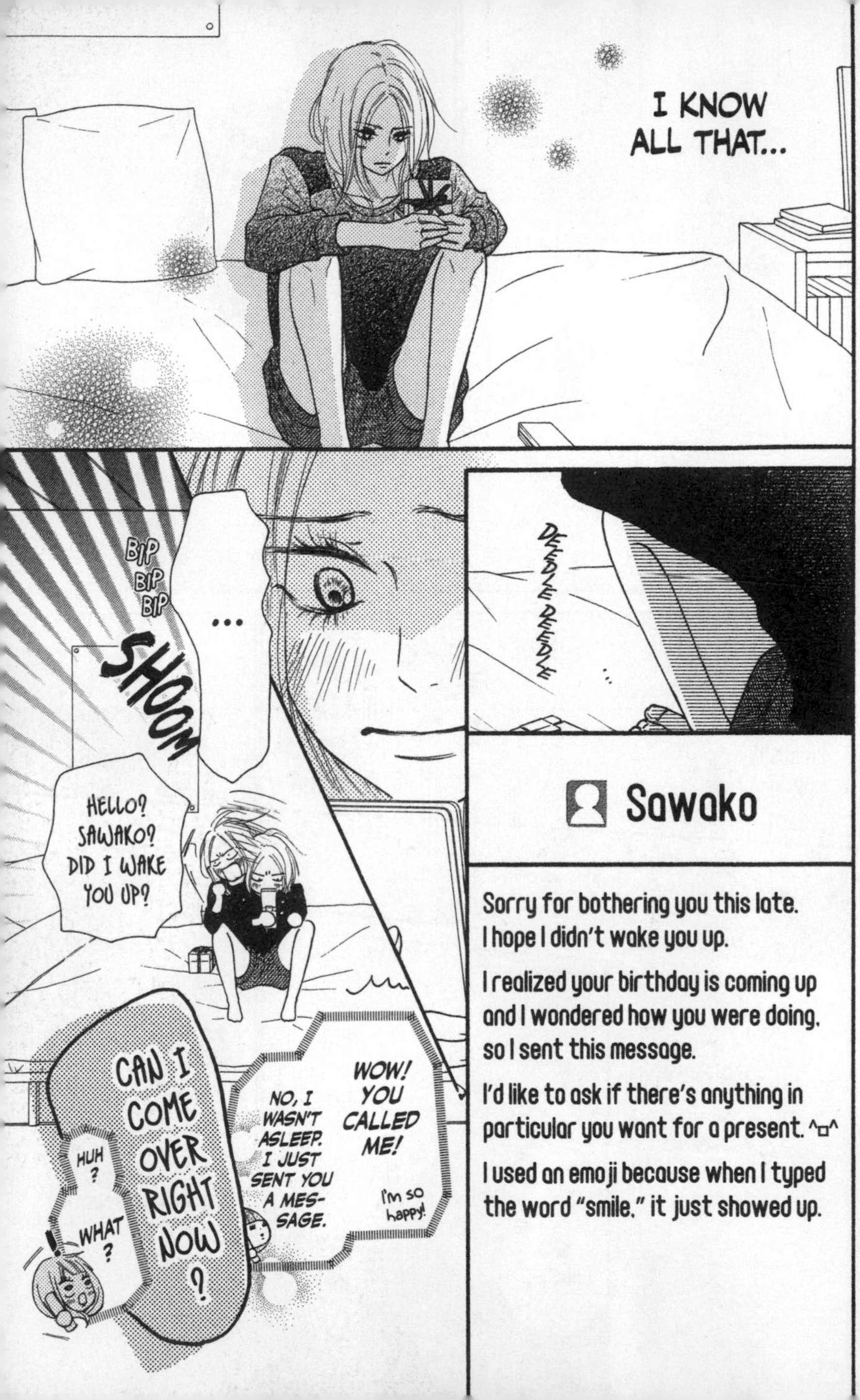
I KNOW ALL THAT...
DEEDLE DEEDLE DEEDLE
...
Sawako
Sorry for bothering you this late.
I hope I didn't wake you up.
I realized your birthday is coming up and I wondered how you were doing, so I sent this message.
I'd like to ask if there's anything in particular you want for a present. ^¤^
I used an emoji because when I typed the word "smile," it just showed up.
BIP BIP BIP
SHOOM
...
HELLO? SAWAKO? DID I WAKE YOU UP?
WOW! YOU CALLED ME!
I'm so happy!
NO, I WASN'T ASLEEP. I JUST SENT YOU A MES-SAGE.
CAN I COME OVER RIGHT NOW?
HUH?
WHAT?

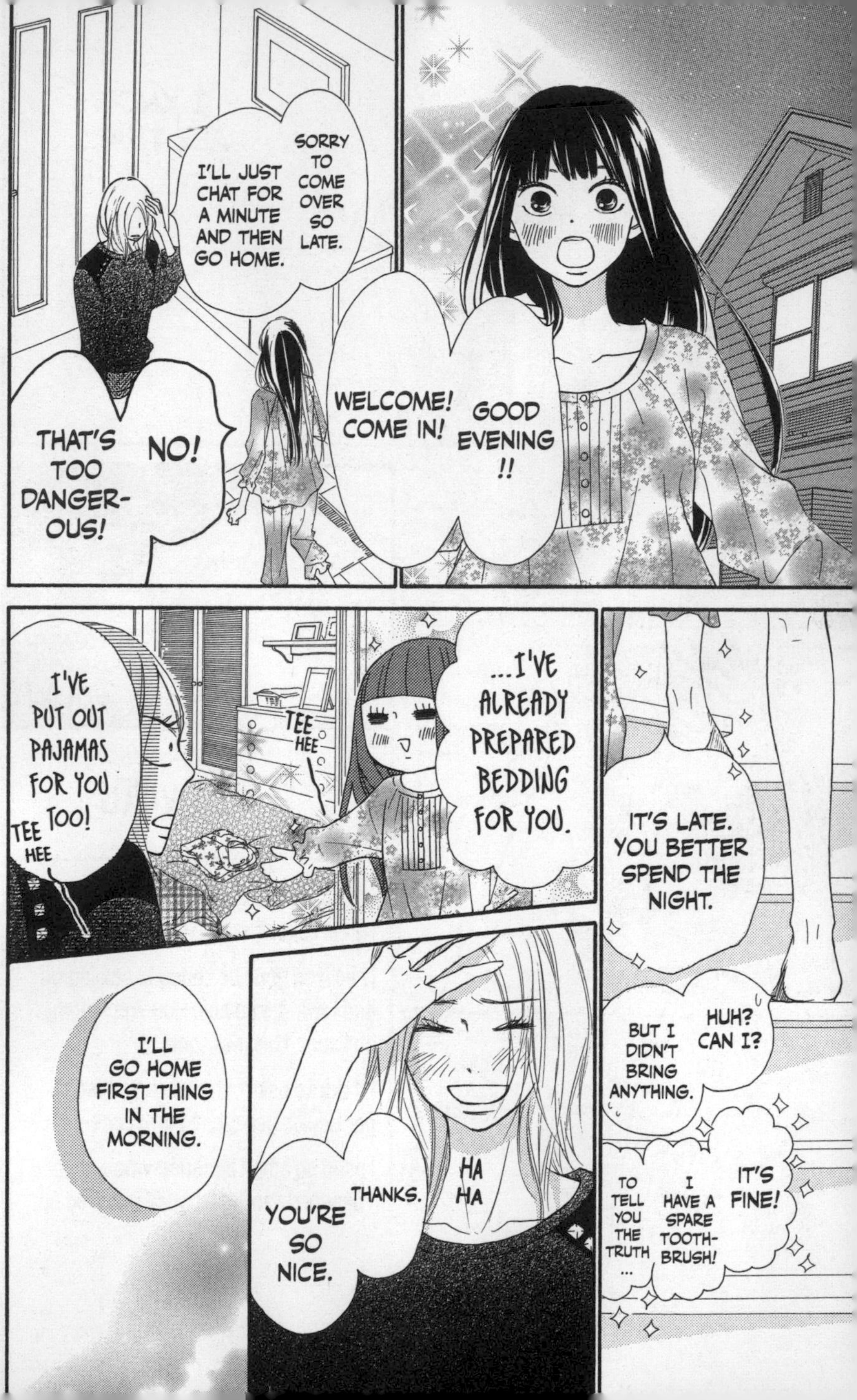
GOOD EVENING!!
WELCOME! COME IN!
SORRY TO COME OVER SO LATE.
I'LL JUST CHAT FOR A MINUTE AND THEN GO HOME.
NO!
THAT'S TOO DANGER-OUS!
IT'S LATE. YOU BETTER SPEND THE NIGHT.
HUH? CAN I?
BUT I DIDN'T BRING ANYTHING.
IT'S FINE!
I HAVE A SPARE TOOTH-BRUSH!
TO TELL YOU THE TRUTH...
...I'VE ALREADY PREPARED BEDDING FOR YOU.
TEE HEE
I'VE PUT OUT PAJAMAS FOR YOU TOO!
TEE HEE
HA HA
THANKS.
YOU'RE SO NICE.
I'LL GO HOME FIRST THING IN THE MORNING.

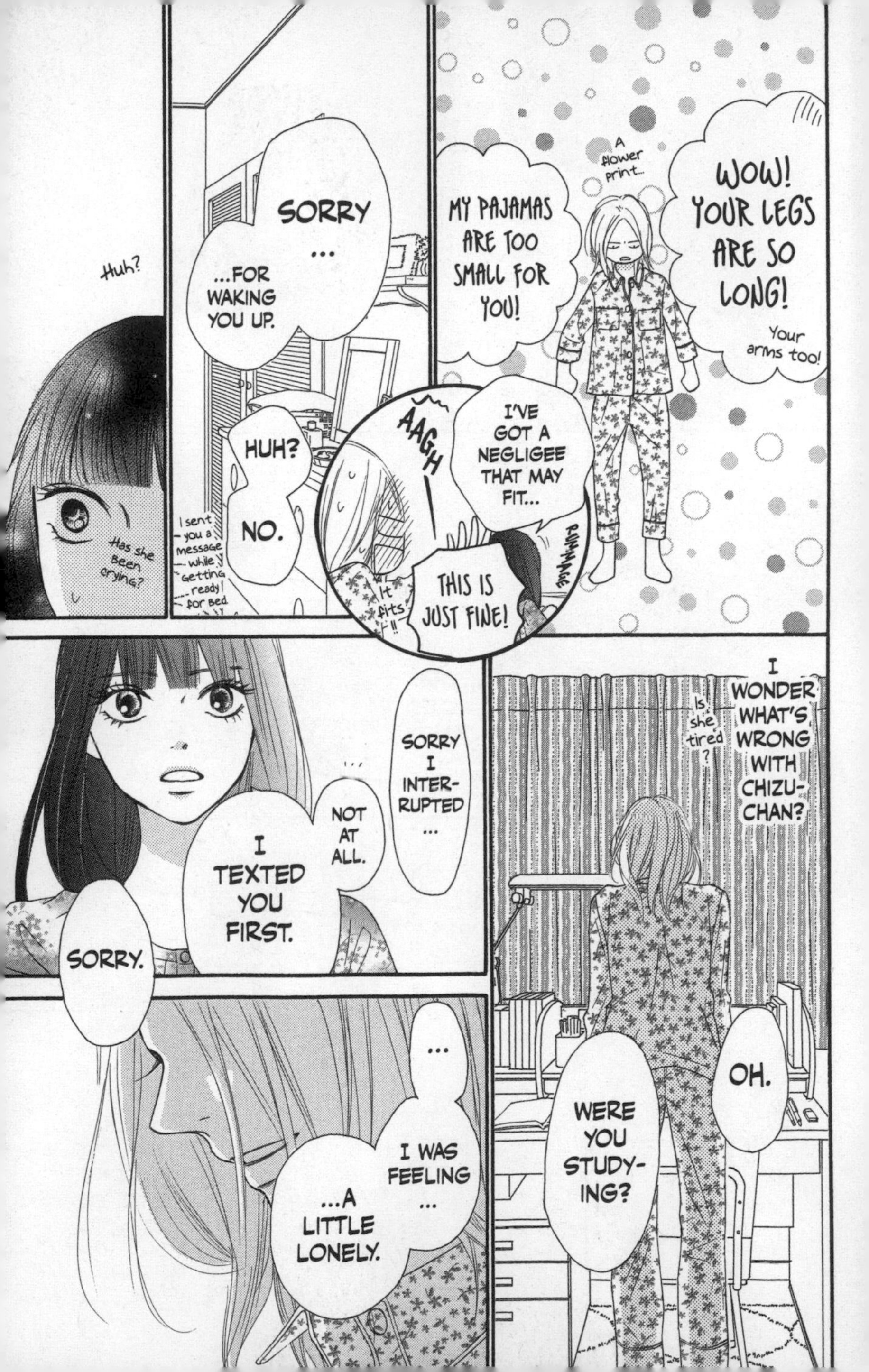
WOW! YOUR LEGS ARE SO LONG!
Your arms too!
A flower print...
MY PAJAMAS ARE TOO SMALL FOR YOU!
I'VE GOT A NEGLIGEE THAT MAY FIT...
AAGH
RUMMAGE
THIS IS JUST FINE!
It fits!!
SORRY ...
...FOR WAKING YOU UP.
HUH?
NO.
I sent you a message while getting ready for bed
Huh?
Has she been crying?
I WONDER WHAT'S WRONG WITH CHIZU-CHAN?
Is she tired?
OH.
WERE YOU STUDYING?
SORRY I INTER-RUPTED ...
...
NOT AT ALL.
I TEXTED YOU FIRST.
SORRY.
...
I WAS FEELING ...
...A LITTLE LONELY.

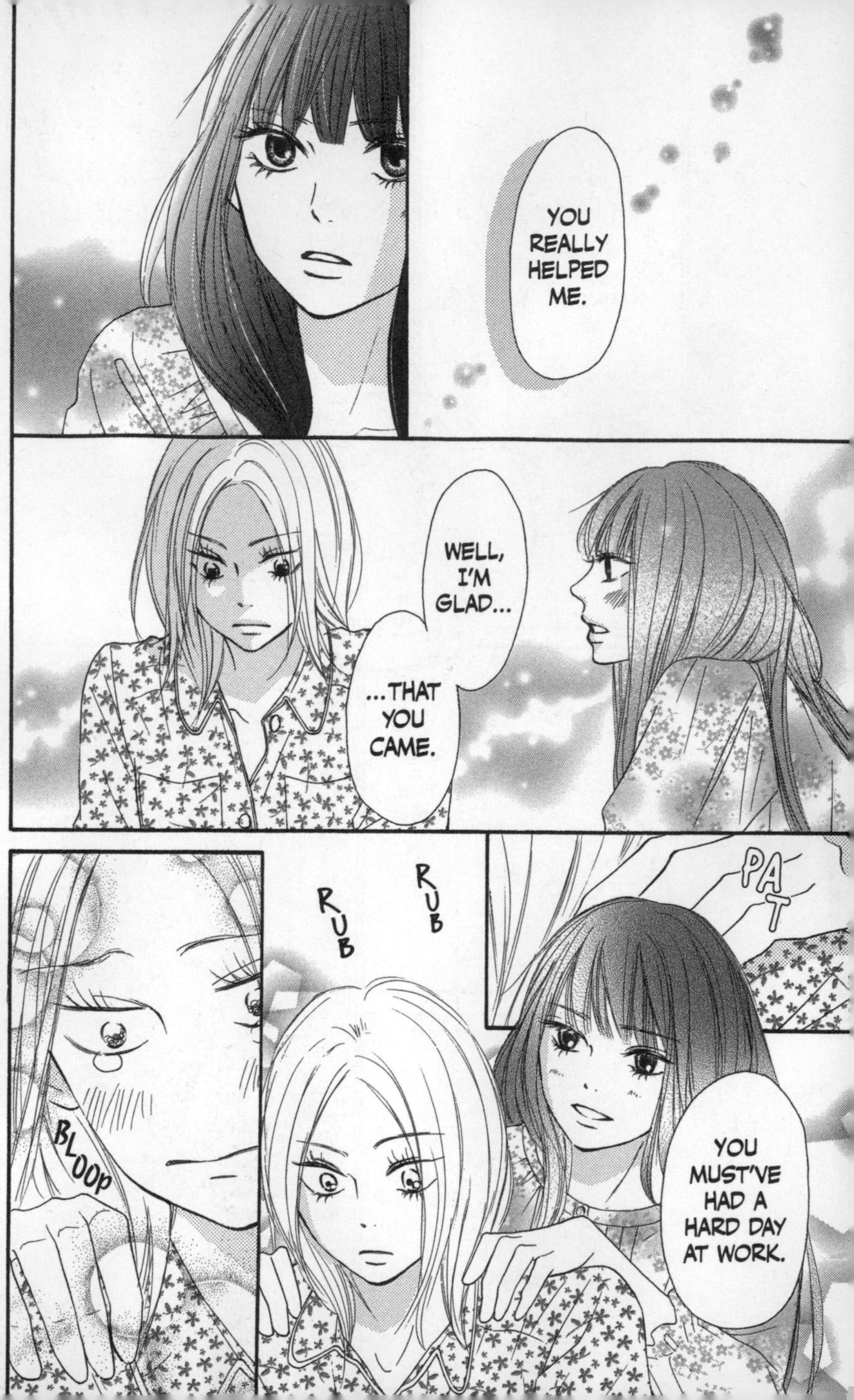
YOU REALLY HELPED ME.
WELL, I'M GLAD...
...THAT YOU CAME.
PAT
RUB
RUB
YOU MUST'VE HAD A HARD DAY AT WORK.
BLOOP

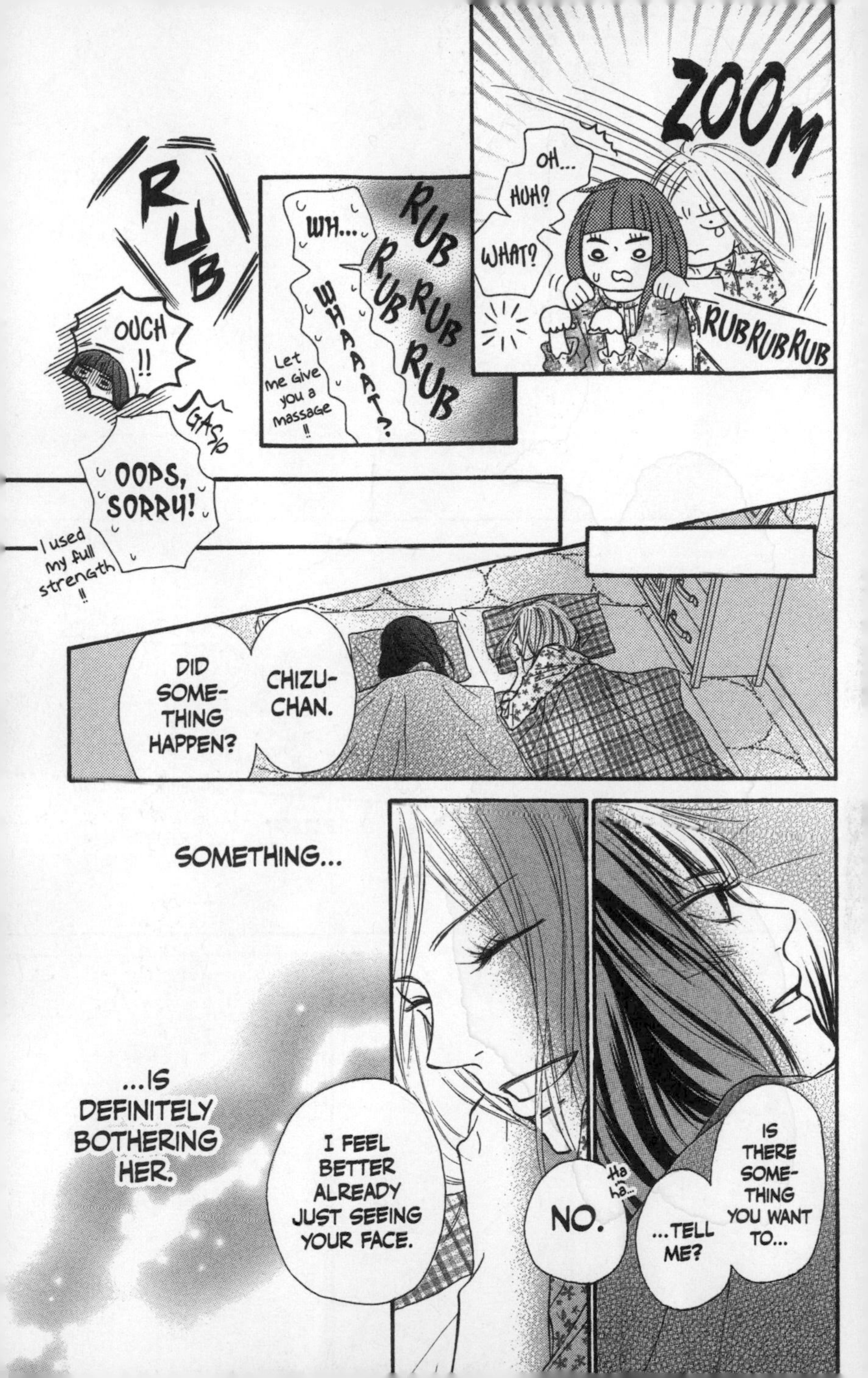
ZOOM
OH... HUH?
WHAT?
RUBRUBRUB
RUB RUB RUB RUB RUB
WH...
WHAAAAT?
Let me give you a massage !!
RUB
OUCH !!
OOPS, SORRY!
I used my full strength !!
CHIZU-CHAN.
DID SOMETHING HAPPEN?
IS THERE SOMETHING YOU WANT TO...
...TELL ME?
Ha ha...
NO.
I FEEL BETTER ALREADY JUST SEEING YOUR FACE.
SOMETHING...
...IS DEFINITELY BOTHERING HER.

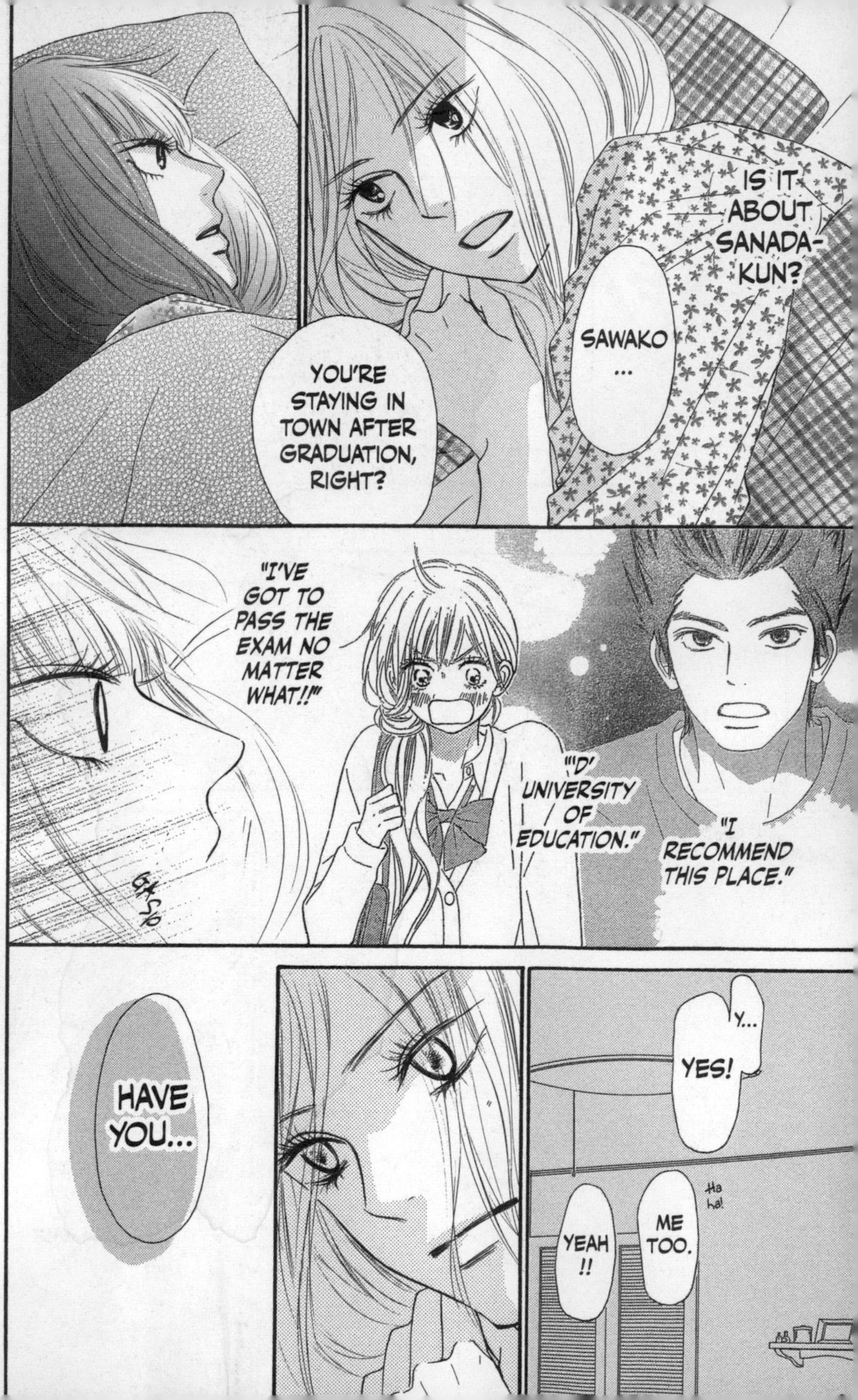
IS IT ABOUT SANADA-KUN?
SAWAKO ...
YOU'RE STAYING IN TOWN AFTER GRADUATION, RIGHT?
"I RECOMMEND THIS PLACE."
"'D' UNIVERSITY OF EDUCATION."
"I'VE GOT TO PASS THE EXAM NO MATTER WHAT!!"
GASP
Y... YES!
Ha ha!
ME TOO.
YEAH !!
HAVE YOU...

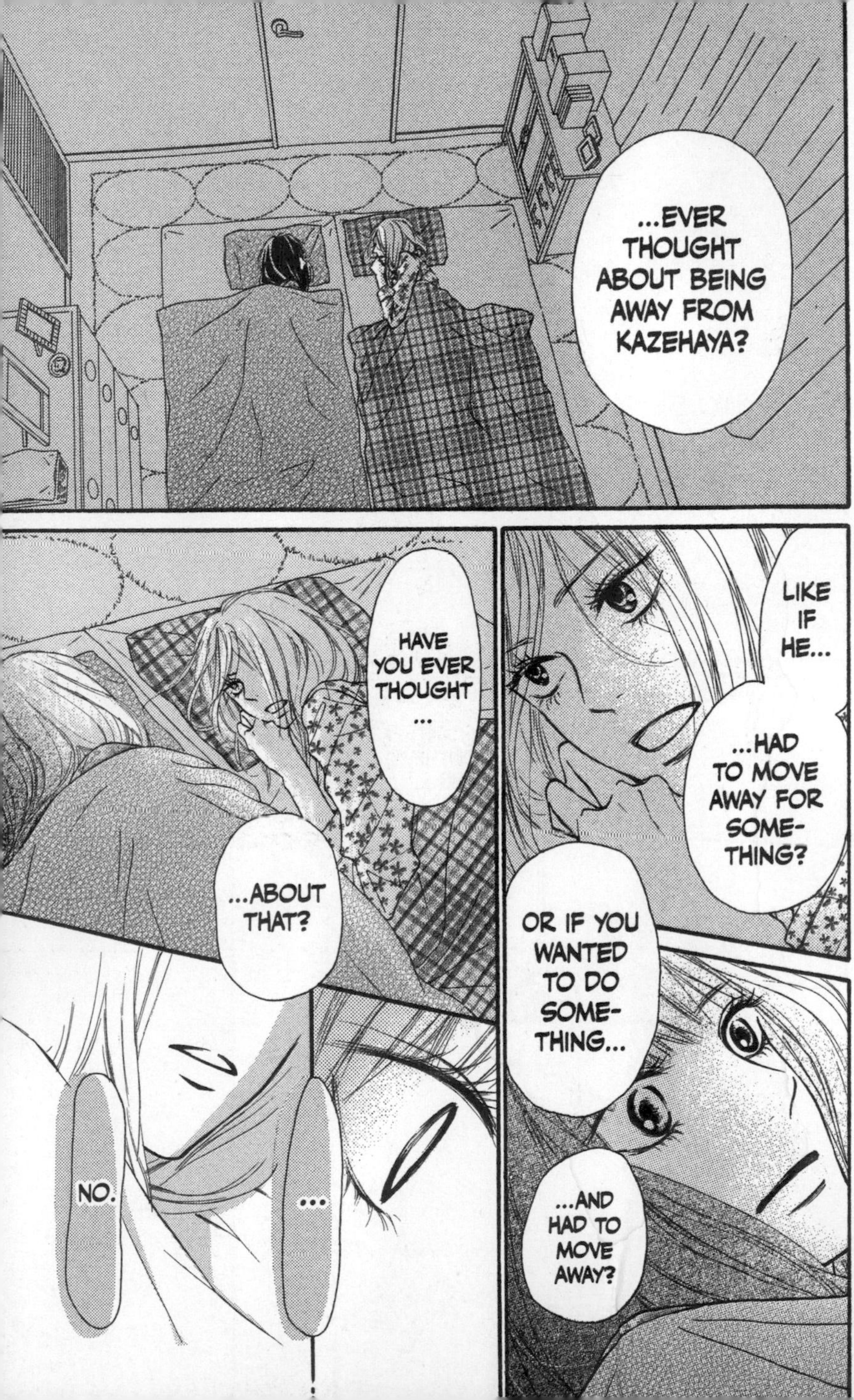

...EVER THOUGHT ABOUT BEING AWAY FROM KAZEHAYA?
LIKE IF HE...
...HAD TO MOVE AWAY FOR SOME-THING?
OR IF YOU WANTED TO DO SOME-THING...
...AND HAD TO MOVE AWAY?
HAVE YOU EVER THOUGHT...
...ABOUT THAT?
...
NO.

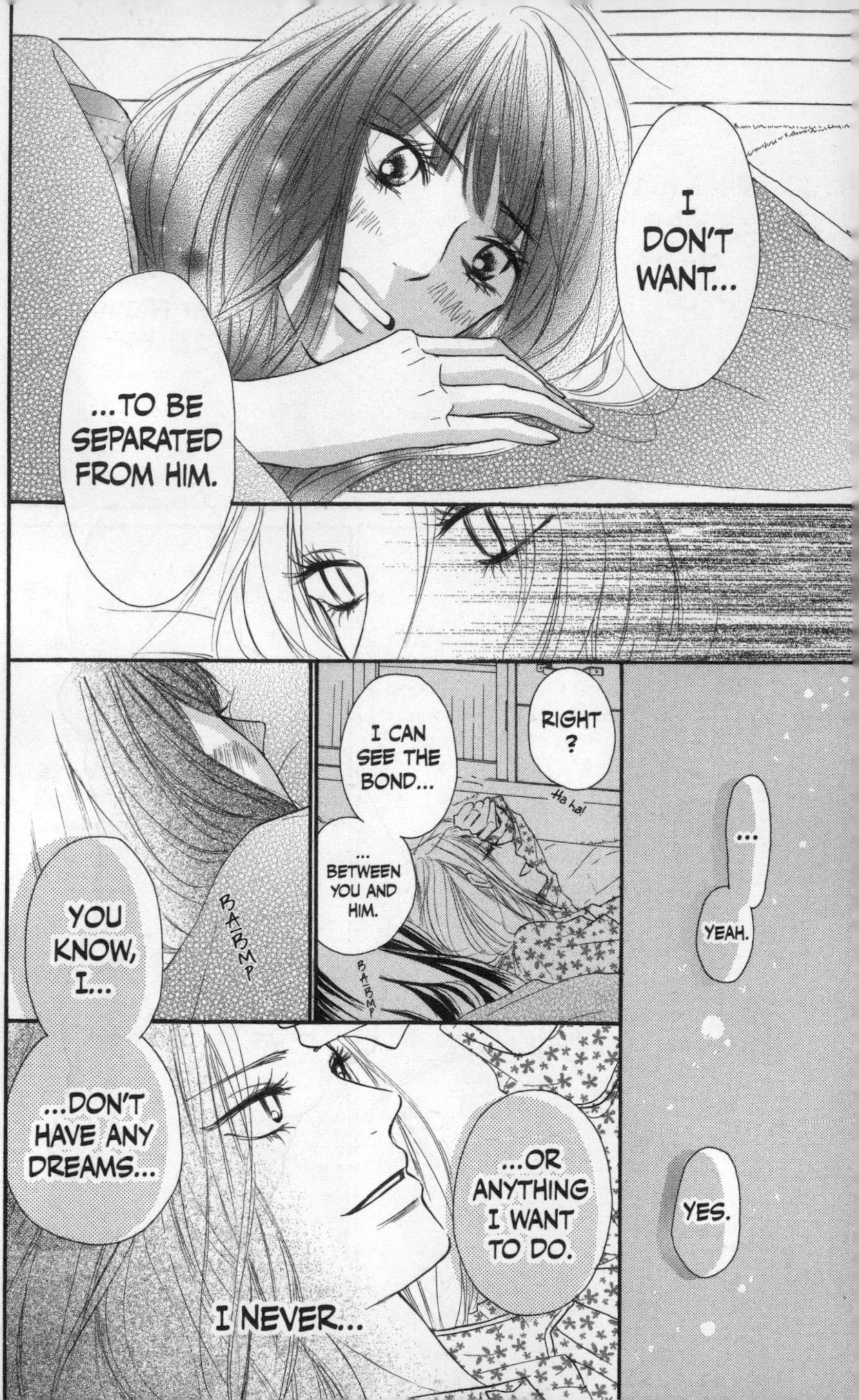
I DON'T WANT...
...TO BE SEPARATED FROM HIM.
...
YEAH.
YES.
RIGHT?
I CAN SEE THE BOND...
Ha ha!
... BETWEEN YOU AND HIM.
BA-BMP
YOU KNOW, I...
BA-BMP
...OR ANYTHING I WANT TO DO.
...DON'T HAVE ANY DREAMS...
I NEVER...

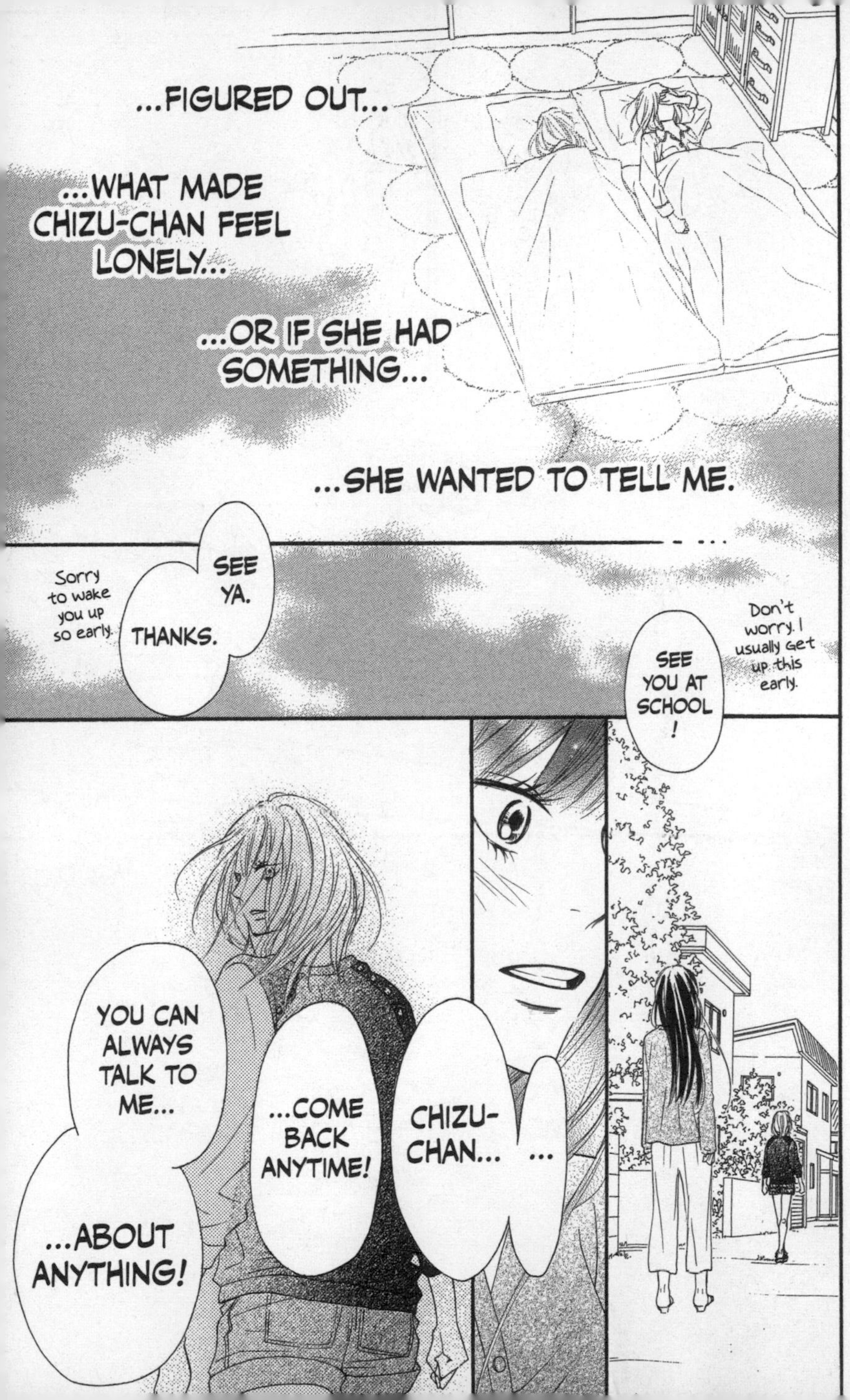
...FIGURED OUT...
...WHAT MADE CHIZU-CHAN FEEL LONELY...
...OR IF SHE HAD SOMETHING...
...SHE WANTED TO TELL ME.
SEE YOU AT SCHOOL!
Don't worry. I usually get up this early.
SEE YA.
THANKS.
Sorry to wake you up so early.
CHIZU-CHAN... ...
...COME BACK ANYTIME!
YOU CAN ALWAYS TALK TO ME...
...ABOUT ANYTHING!

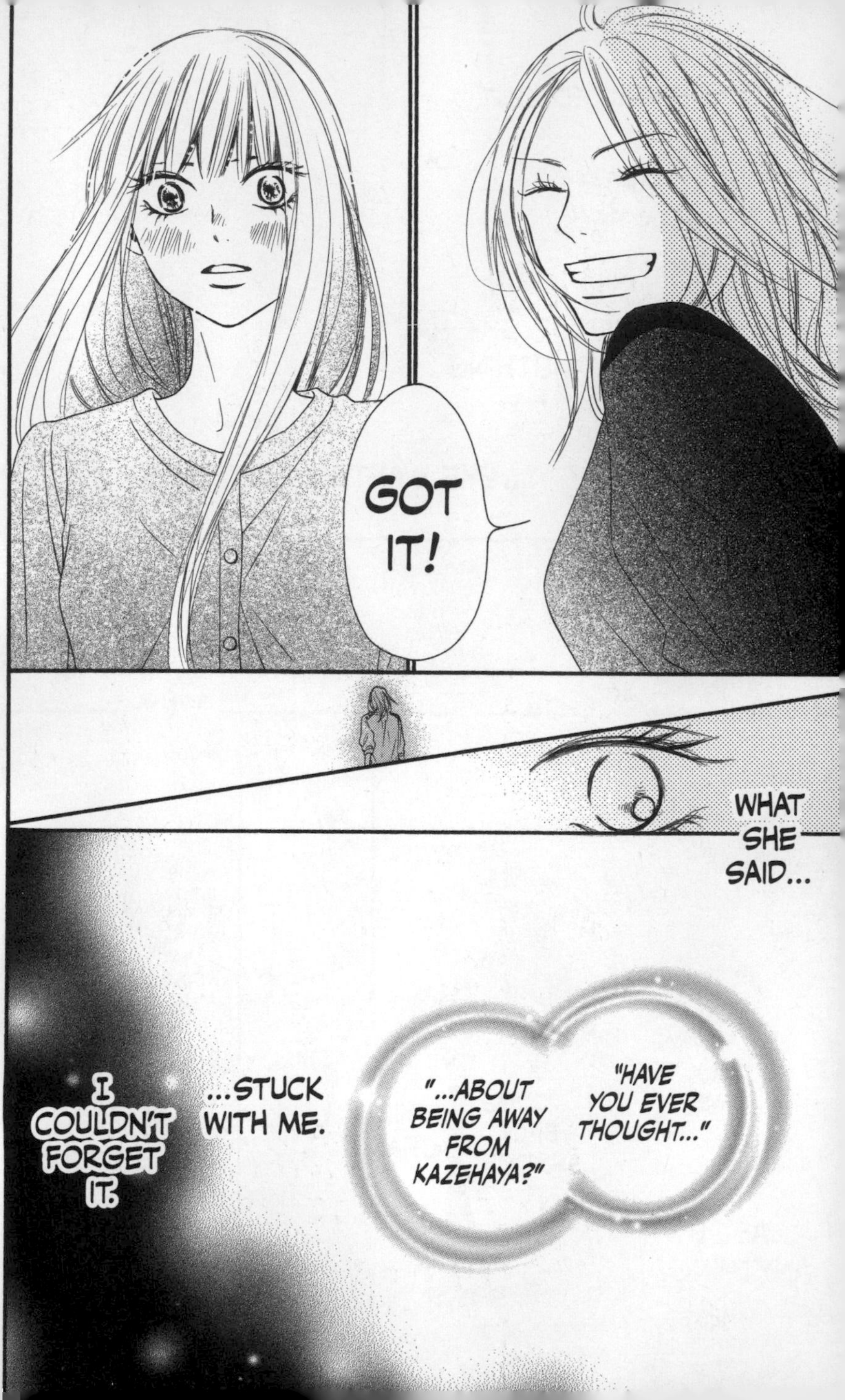
GOT IT!
WHAT SHE SAID...
"HAVE YOU EVER THOUGHT..."
"...ABOUT BEING AWAY FROM KAZEHAYA?"
...STUCK WITH ME.
I COULDN'T FORGET IT.

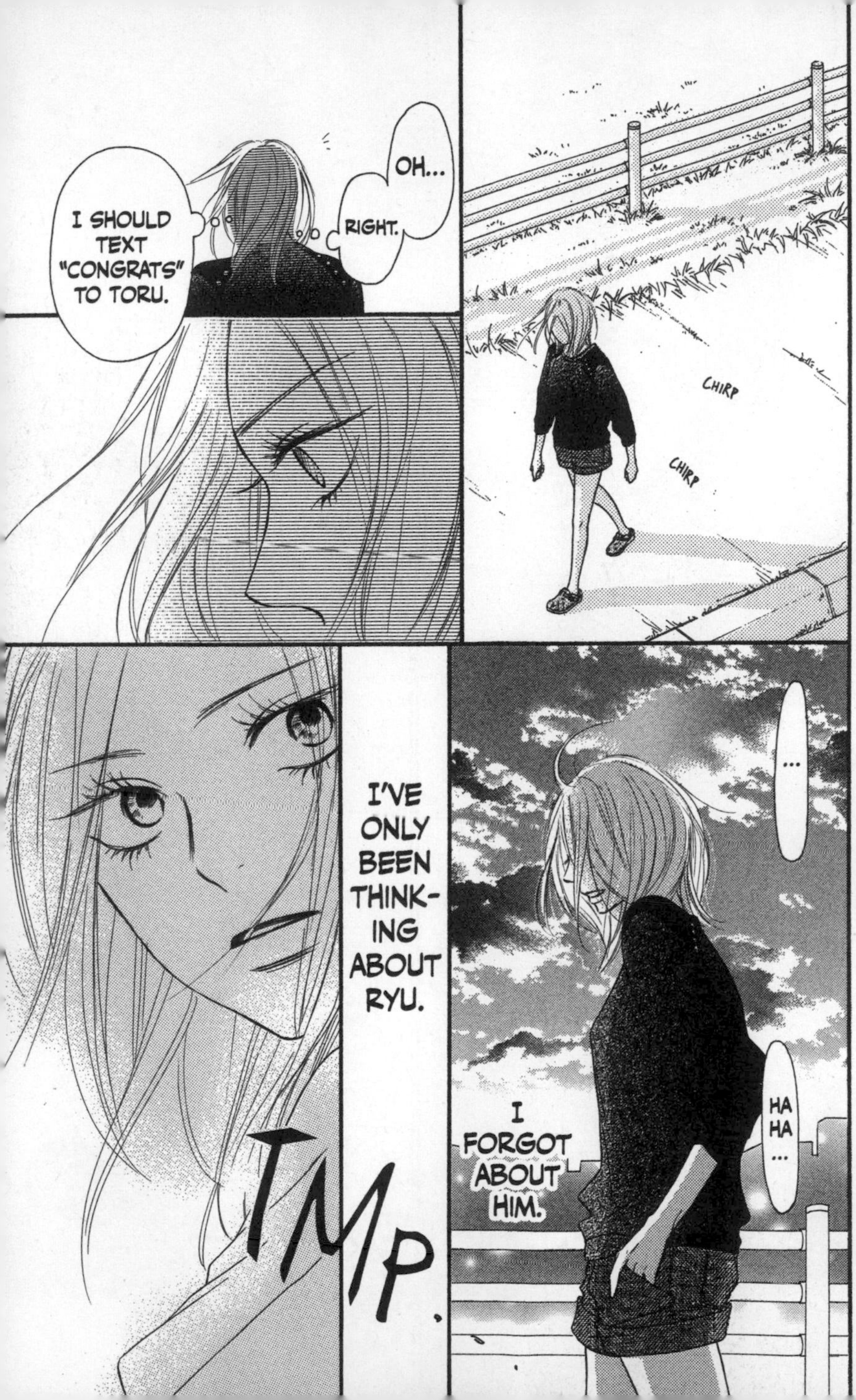
CHIRP
CHIRP
OH... RIGHT.
I SHOULD TEXT "CONGRATS" TO TORU.
...
HA HA ...
I FORGOT ABOUT HIM.
I'VE ONLY BEEN THINKING ABOUT RYU.
TMP.

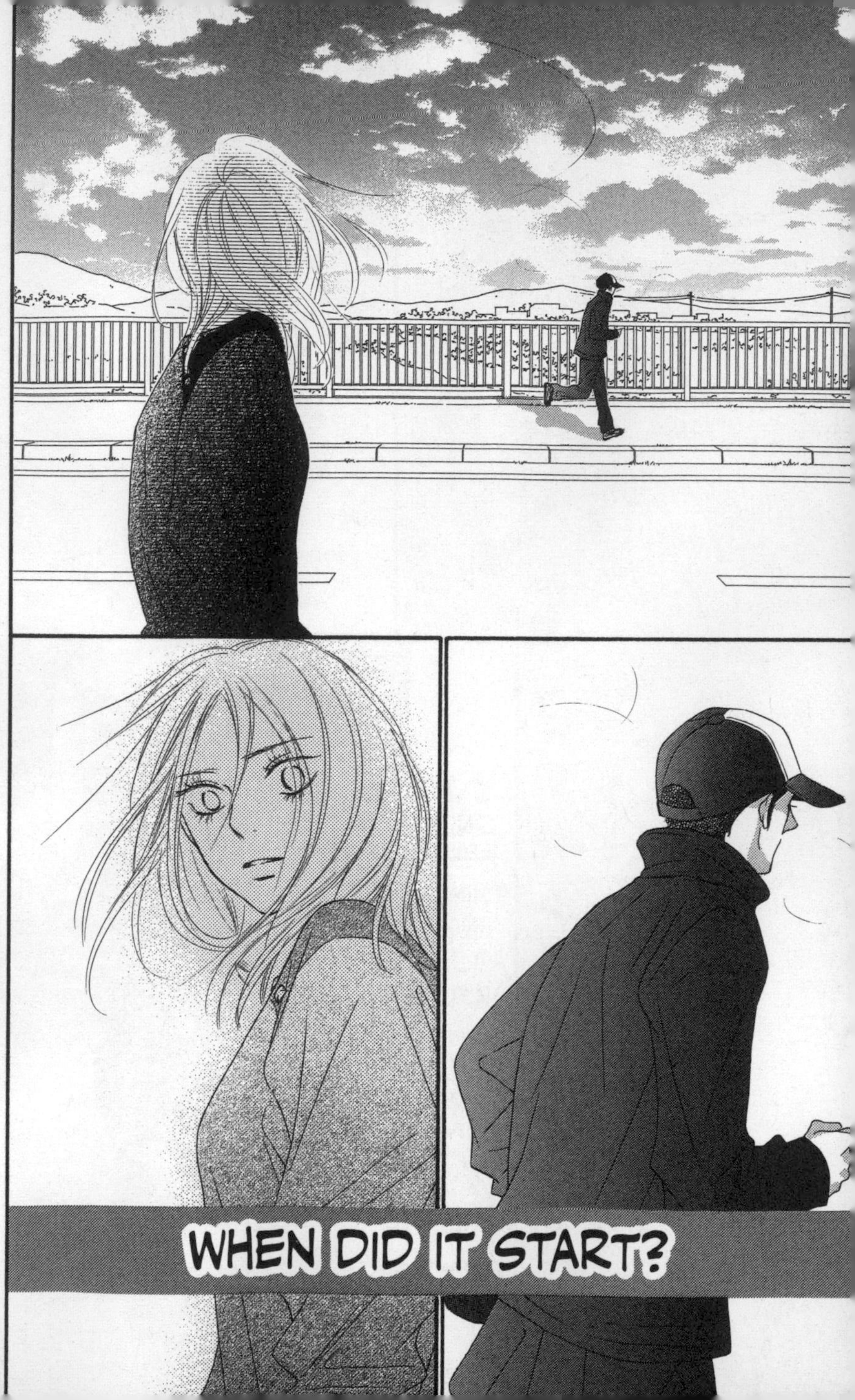
WHEN DID IT START?

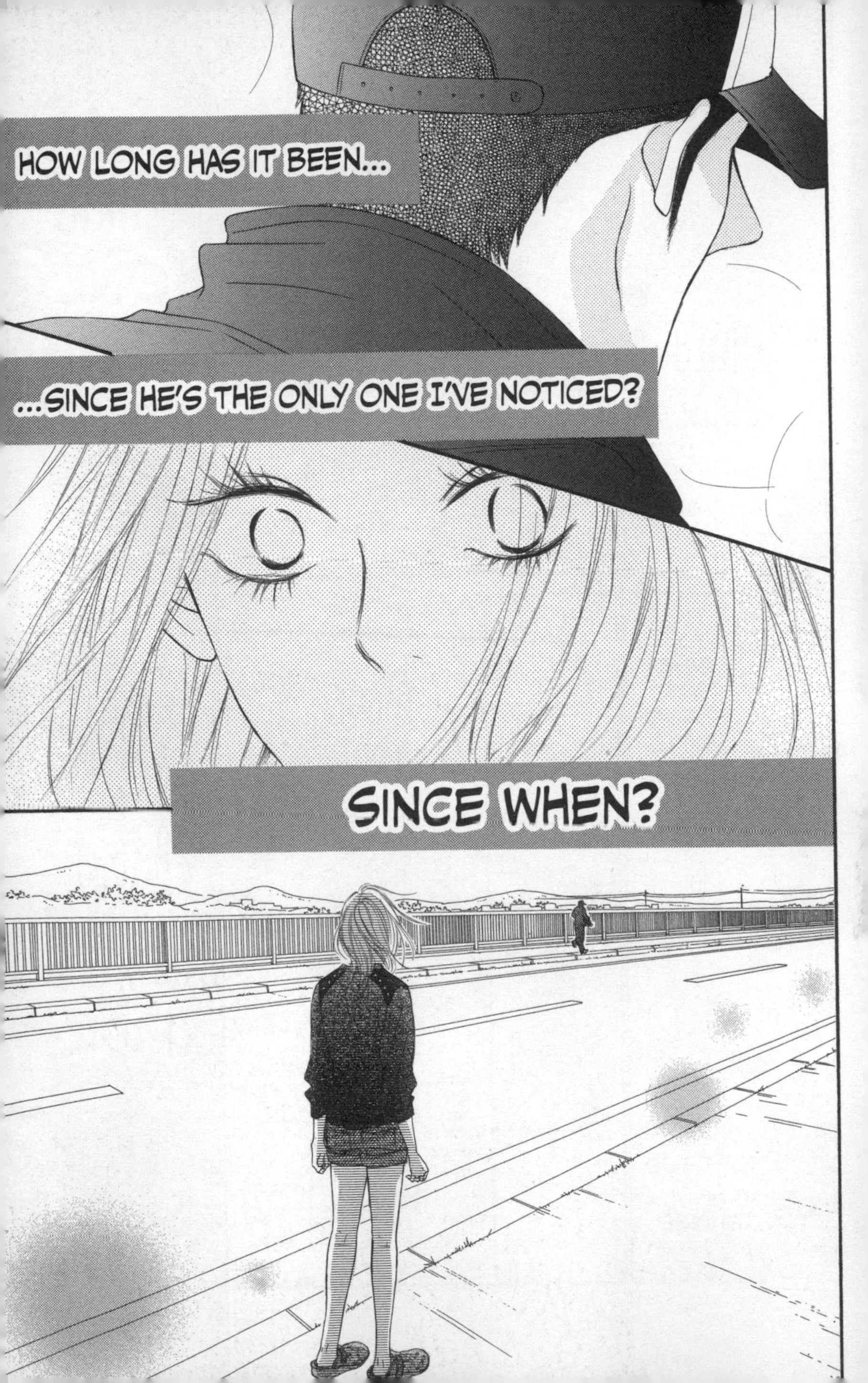
HOW LONG HAS IT BEEN...
...SINCE HE'S THE ONLY ONE I'VE NOTICED?
SINCE WHEN?

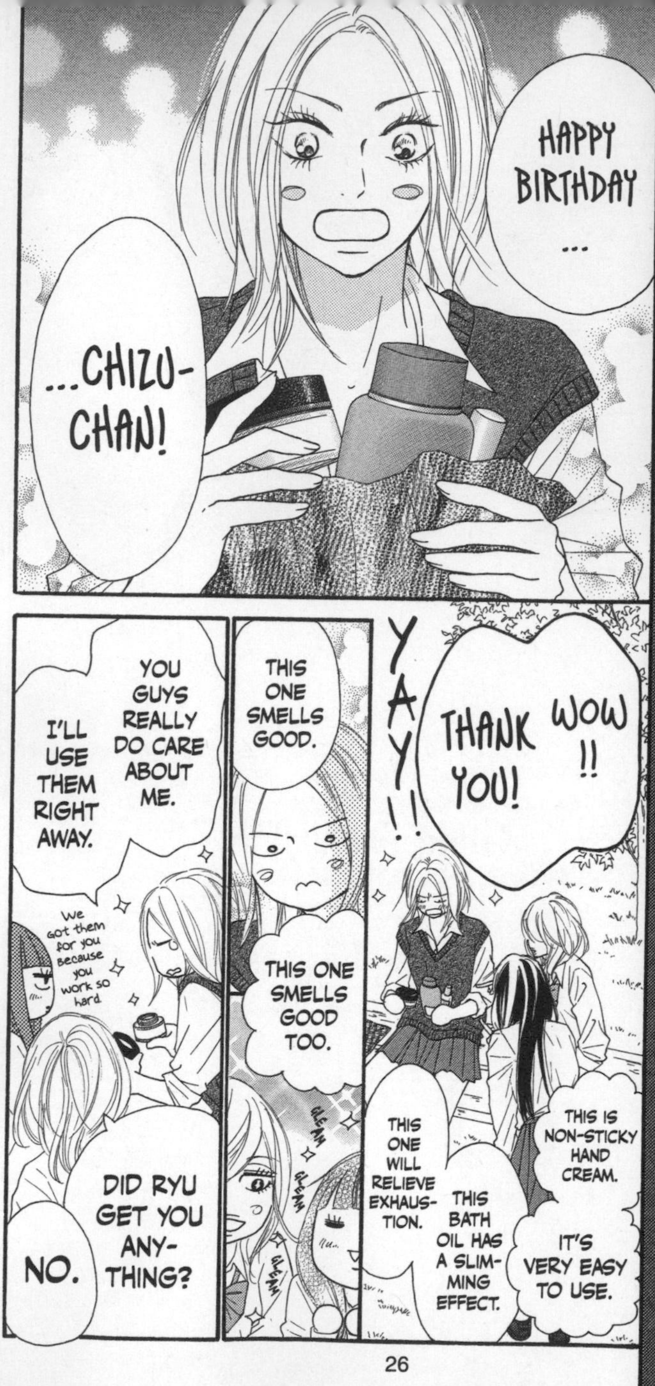
HAPPY BIRTHDAY ...
...CHIZU-CHAN!
WOW!!
THANK YOU!
YAY!!
THIS IS NON-STICKY HAND CREAM.
IT'S VERY EASY TO USE.
THIS ONE WILL RELIEVE EXHAUS-TION.
THIS BATH OIL HAS A SLIM-MING EFFECT.
THIS ONE SMELLS GOOD.
THIS ONE SMELLS GOOD TOO.
GLEAM GLEAM GLEAM
YOU GUYS REALLY DO CARE ABOUT ME.
I'LL USE THEM RIGHT AWAY.
We got them for you because you work so hard
DID RYU GET YOU ANY-THING?
NO.

HE'S THE ONLY ONE ...

...I HAVE EYES FOR.

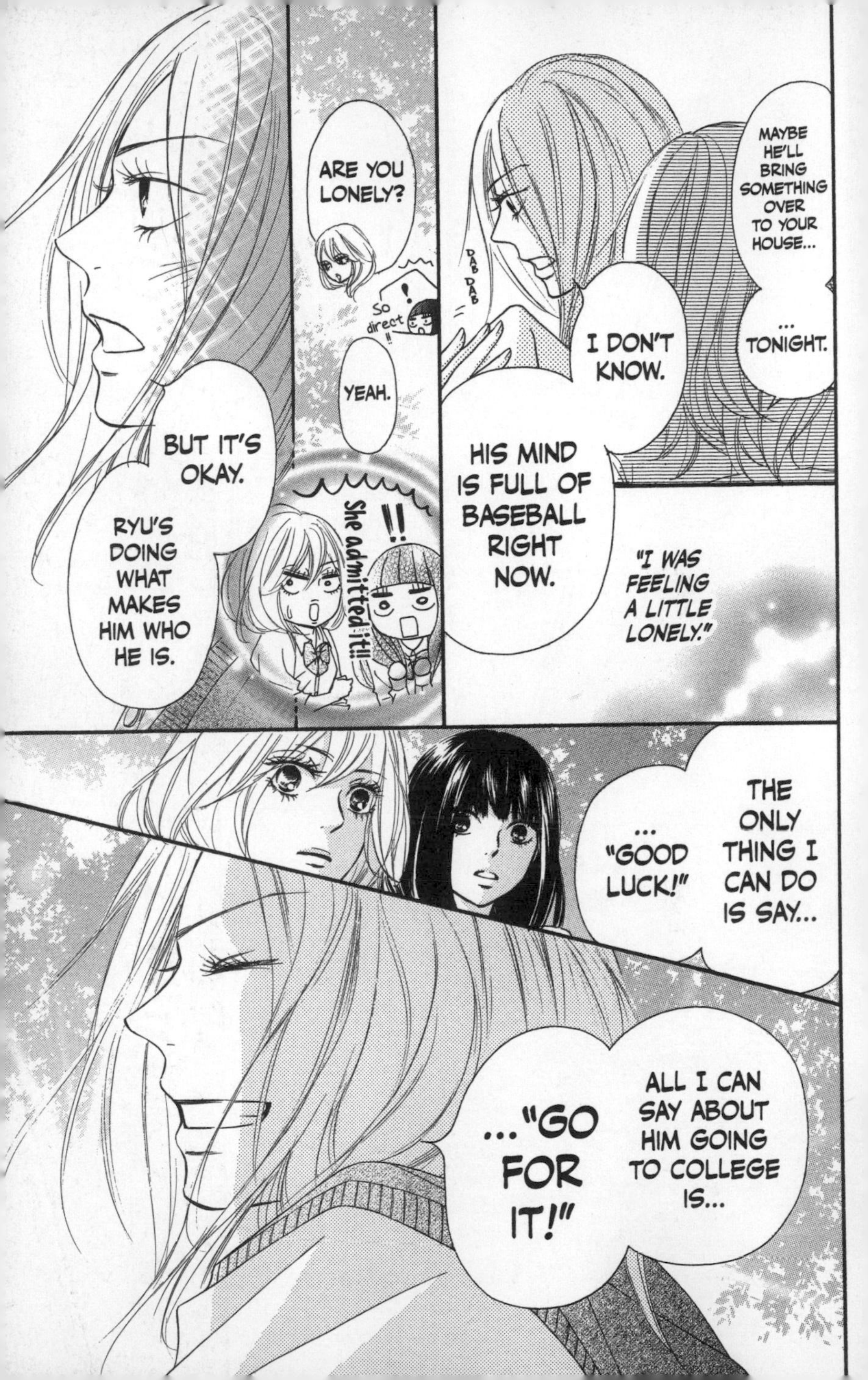
MAYBE HE'LL BRING SOMETHING OVER TO YOUR HOUSE...
...TONIGHT.
DAB DAB
I DON'T KNOW.
HIS MIND IS FULL OF BASEBALL RIGHT NOW.
"I WAS FEELING A LITTLE LONELY."
ARE YOU LONELY?
So direct!!
YEAH.
She admitted it!!
BUT IT'S OKAY.
RYU'S DOING WHAT MAKES HIM WHO HE IS.
THE ONLY THING I CAN DO IS SAY...
..."GOOD LUCK!"
ALL I CAN SAY ABOUT HIM GOING TO COLLEGE IS...
..."GO FOR IT!"

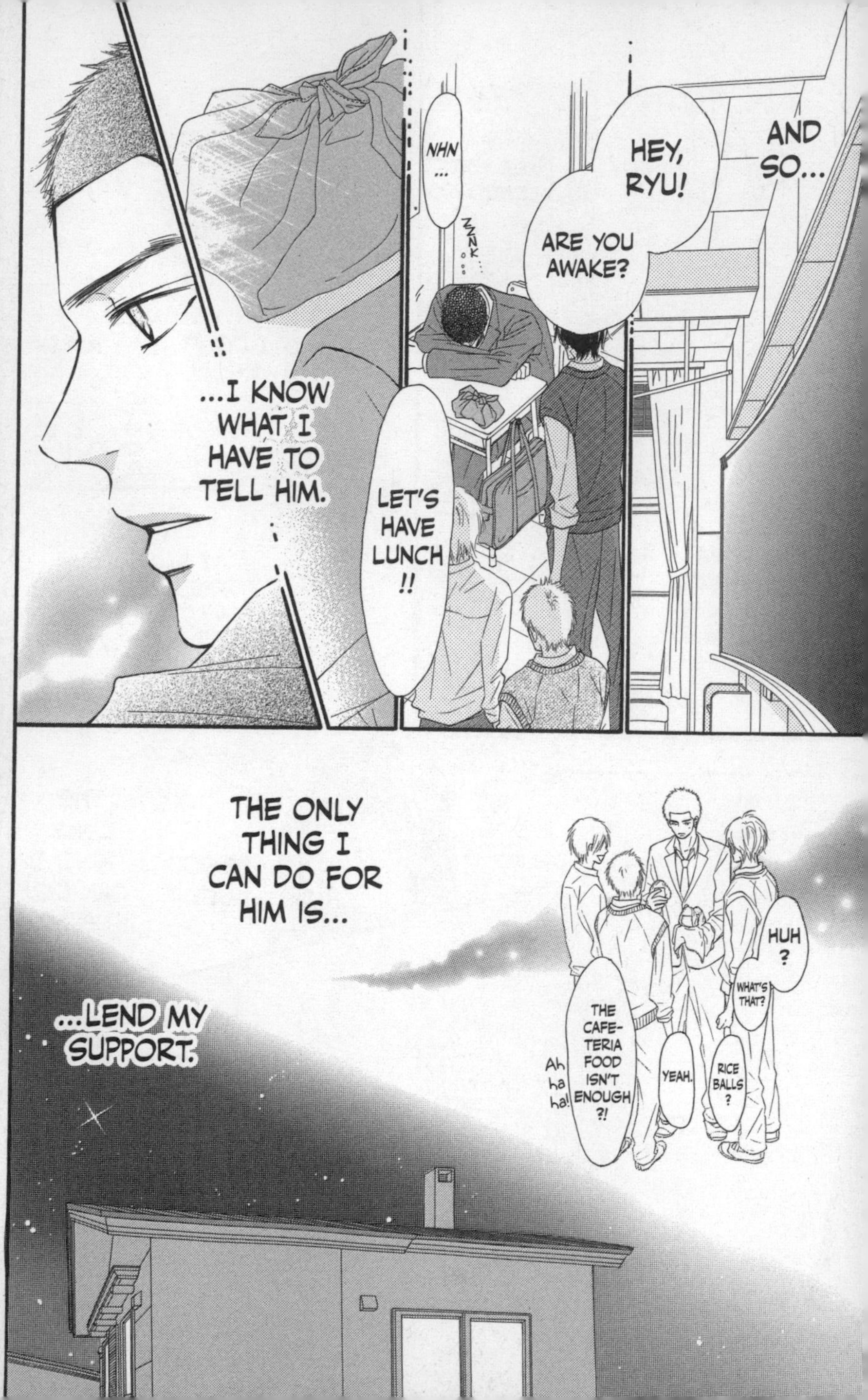
AND SO...
HEY, RYU!
ARE YOU AWAKE?
NHN...
ZZNK...
LET'S HAVE LUNCH!!
...I KNOW WHAT I HAVE TO TELL HIM.
THE ONLY THING I CAN DO FOR HIM IS...
HUH?
WHAT'S THAT?
RICE BALLS?
YEAH.
THE CAFETERIA FOOD ISN'T ENOUGH?!
Ah ha ha!
...LEND MY SUPPORT.

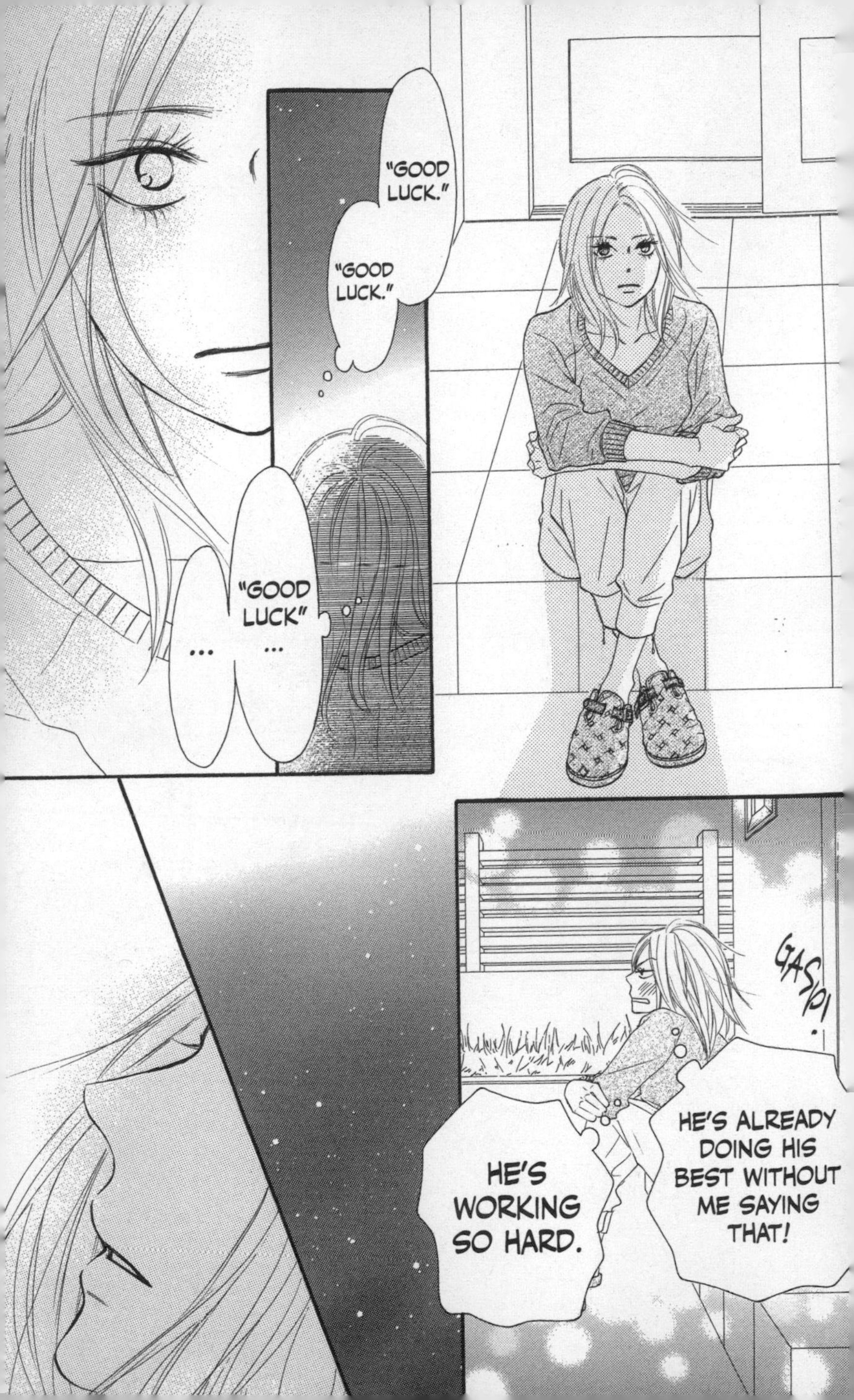

"GOOD LUCK."
"GOOD LUCK."
"GOOD LUCK"
...
...
GASP!
HE'S ALREADY DOING HIS BEST WITHOUT ME SAYING THAT!
HE'S WORKING SO HARD.

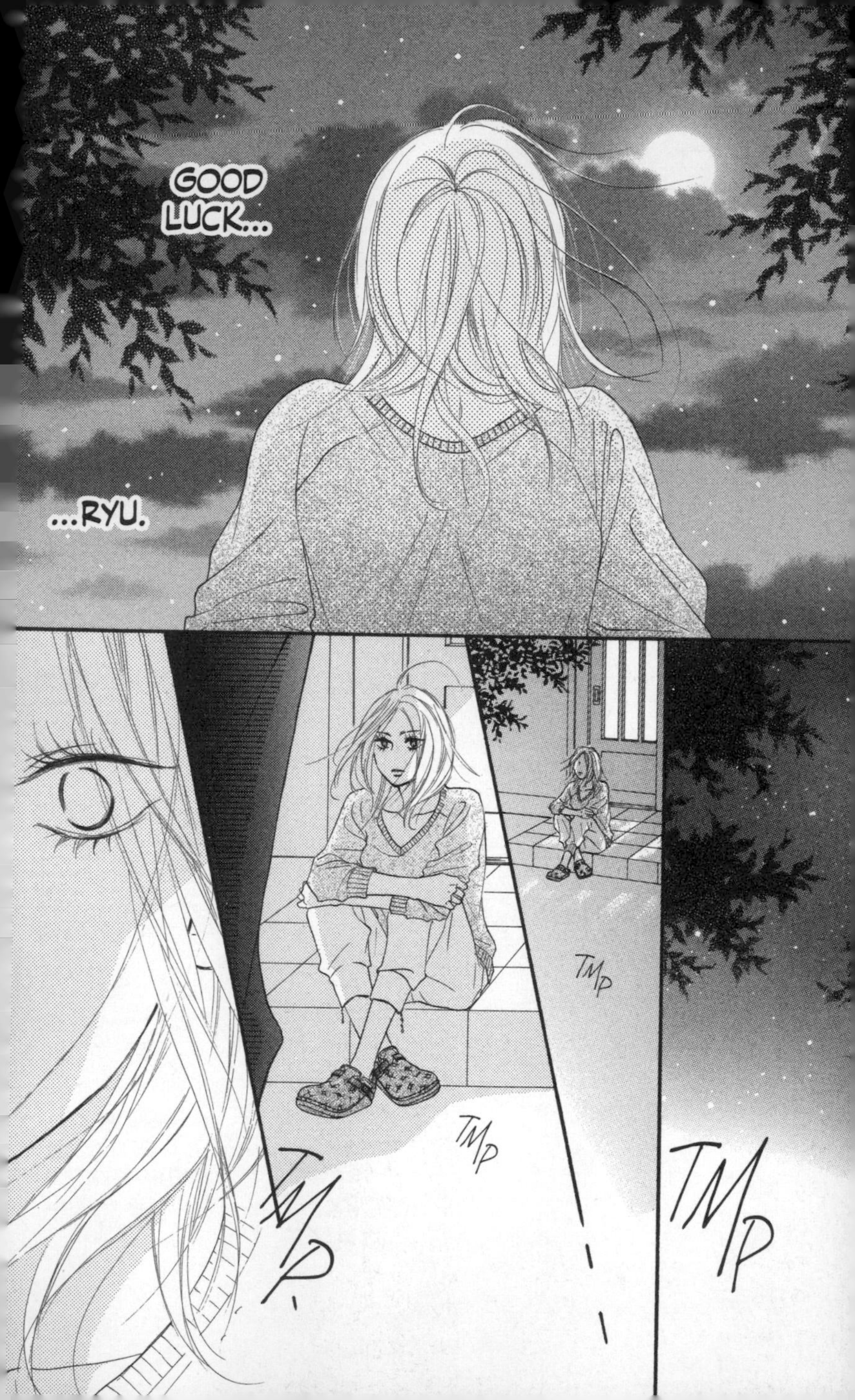

GOOD LUCK...
...RYU.
TMP
TMP
TMP
TMP

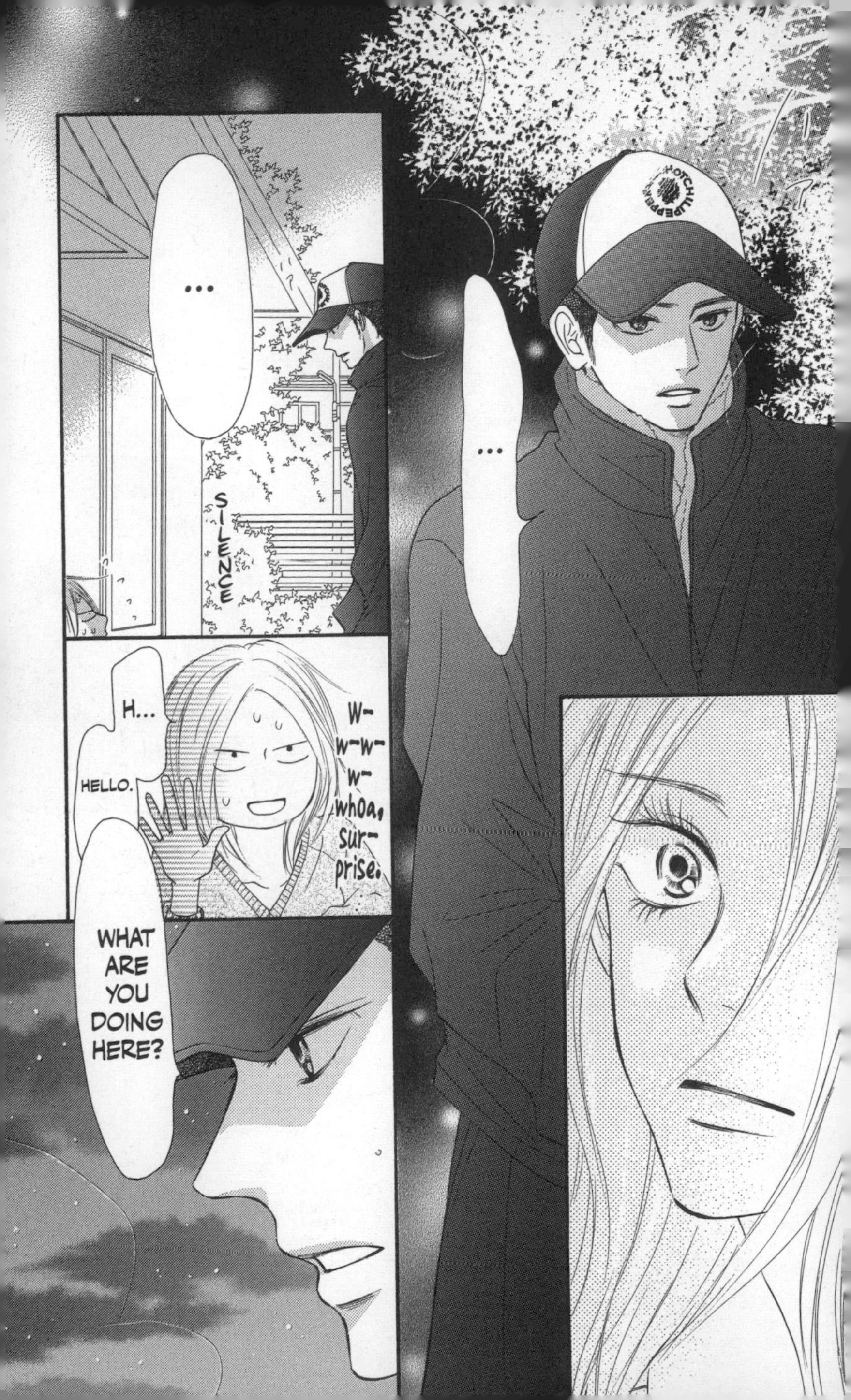
...
...
SILENCE
H... HELLO.
W-w-w-w-whoa, surprise.
WHAT ARE YOU DOING HERE?

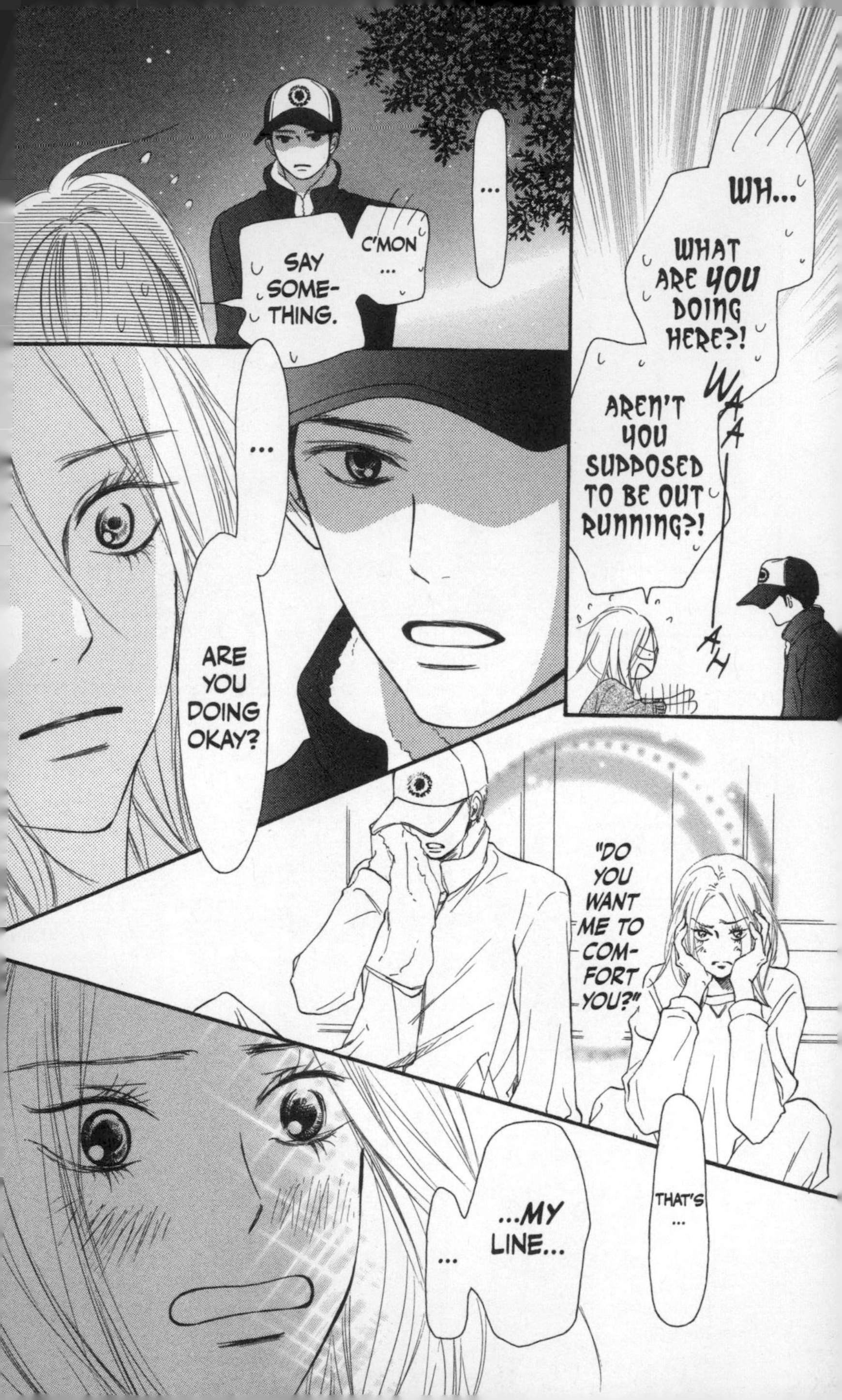
WH...
WHAT ARE YOU DOING HERE?!
AREN'T YOU SUPPOSED TO BE OUT RUNNING?!
WAAAH
...
C'MON ...
SAY SOME-THING.
...
ARE YOU DOING OKAY?
"DO YOU WANT ME TO COM-FORT YOU?"
THAT'S ...
...MY LINE...
...

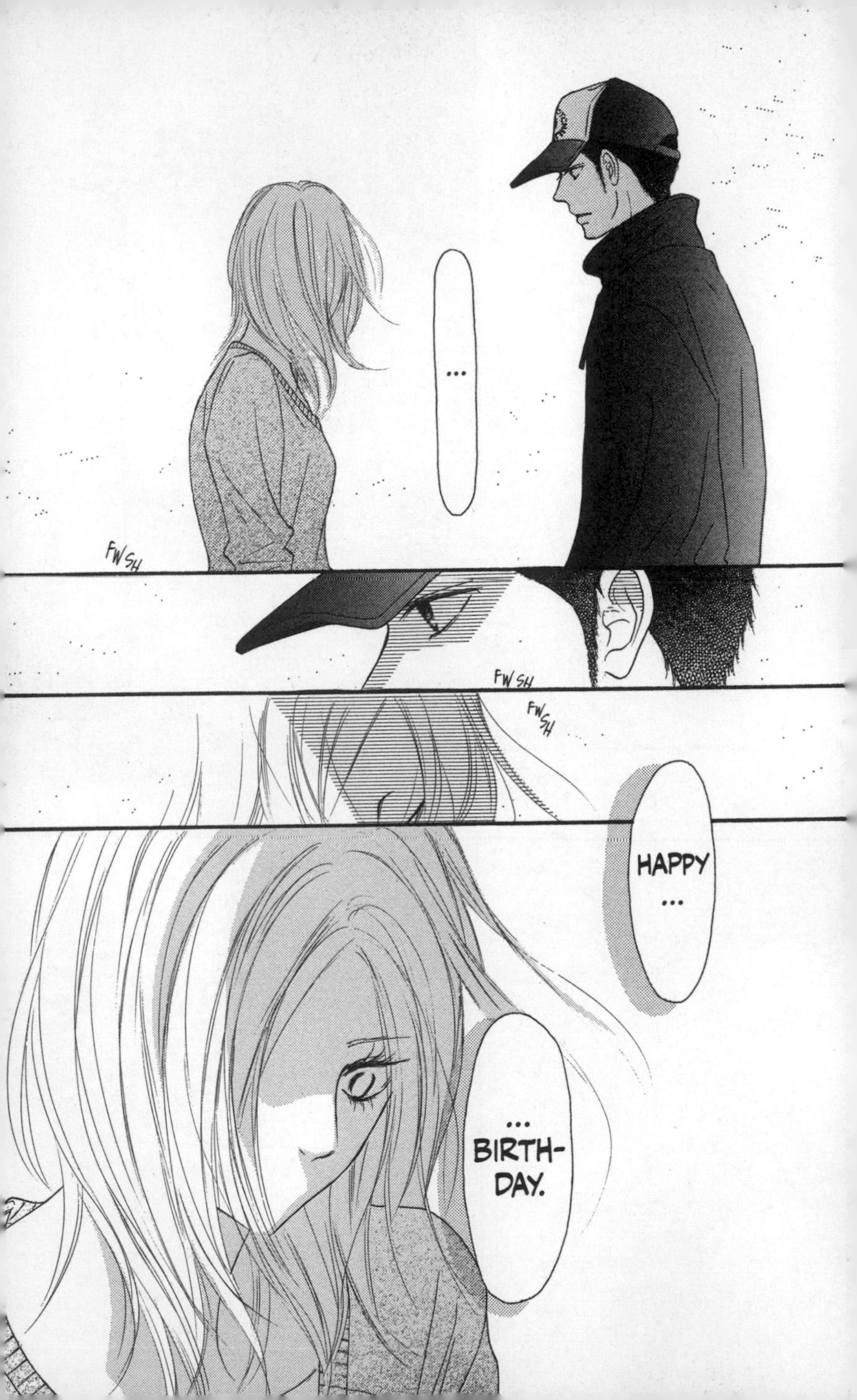
...
FWSH
FWSH
FWSH
HAPPY ...
... BIRTH-DAY.

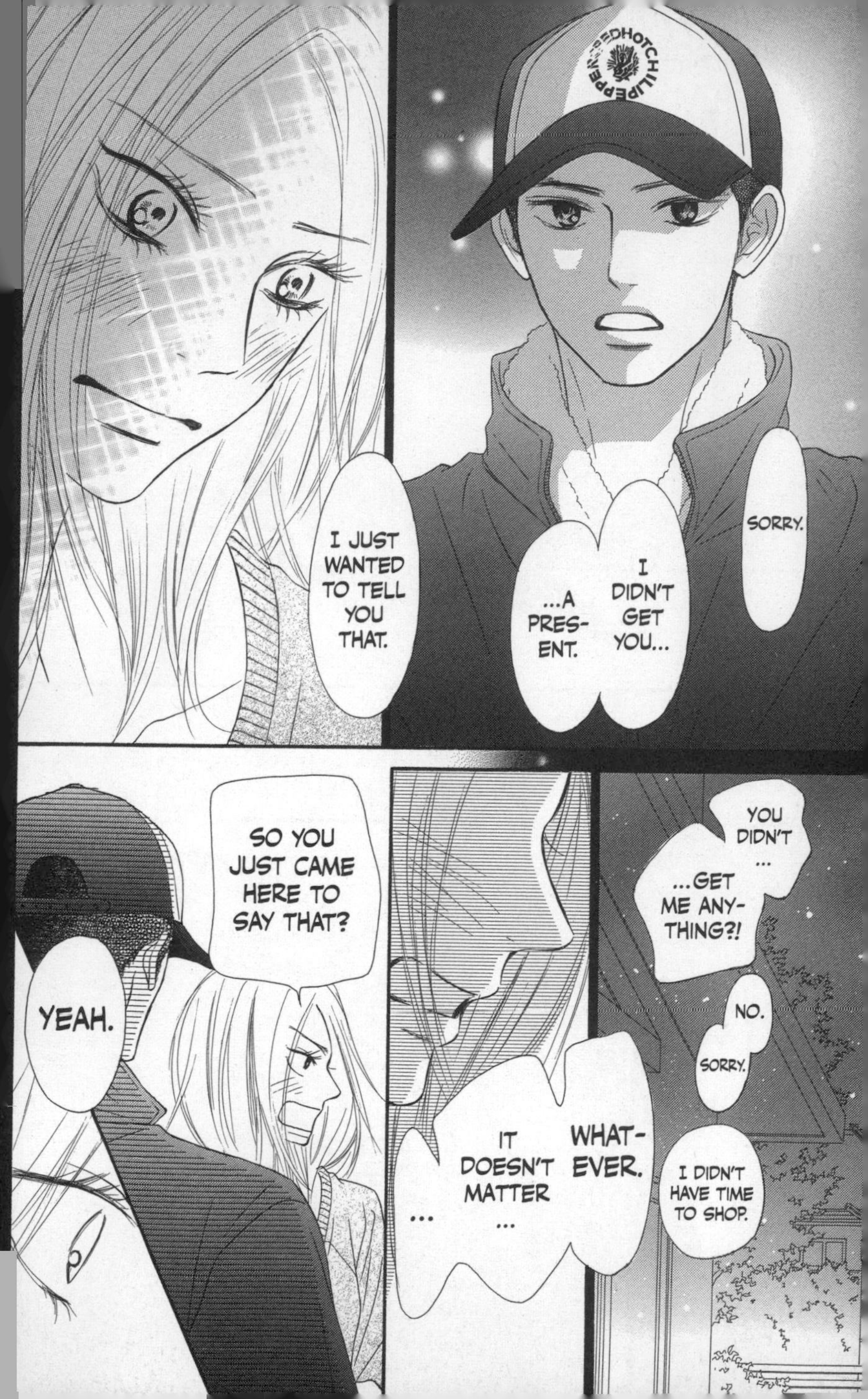
SORRY.
I DIDN'T GET YOU...
...A PRES-ENT.
I JUST WANTED TO TELL YOU THAT.
YOU DIDN'T ...
...GET ME ANY-THING?!
NO.
SORRY.
I DIDN'T HAVE TIME TO SHOP.
WHAT-EVER.
IT DOESN'T MATTER ...
...
SO YOU JUST CAME HERE TO SAY THAT?
YEAH.

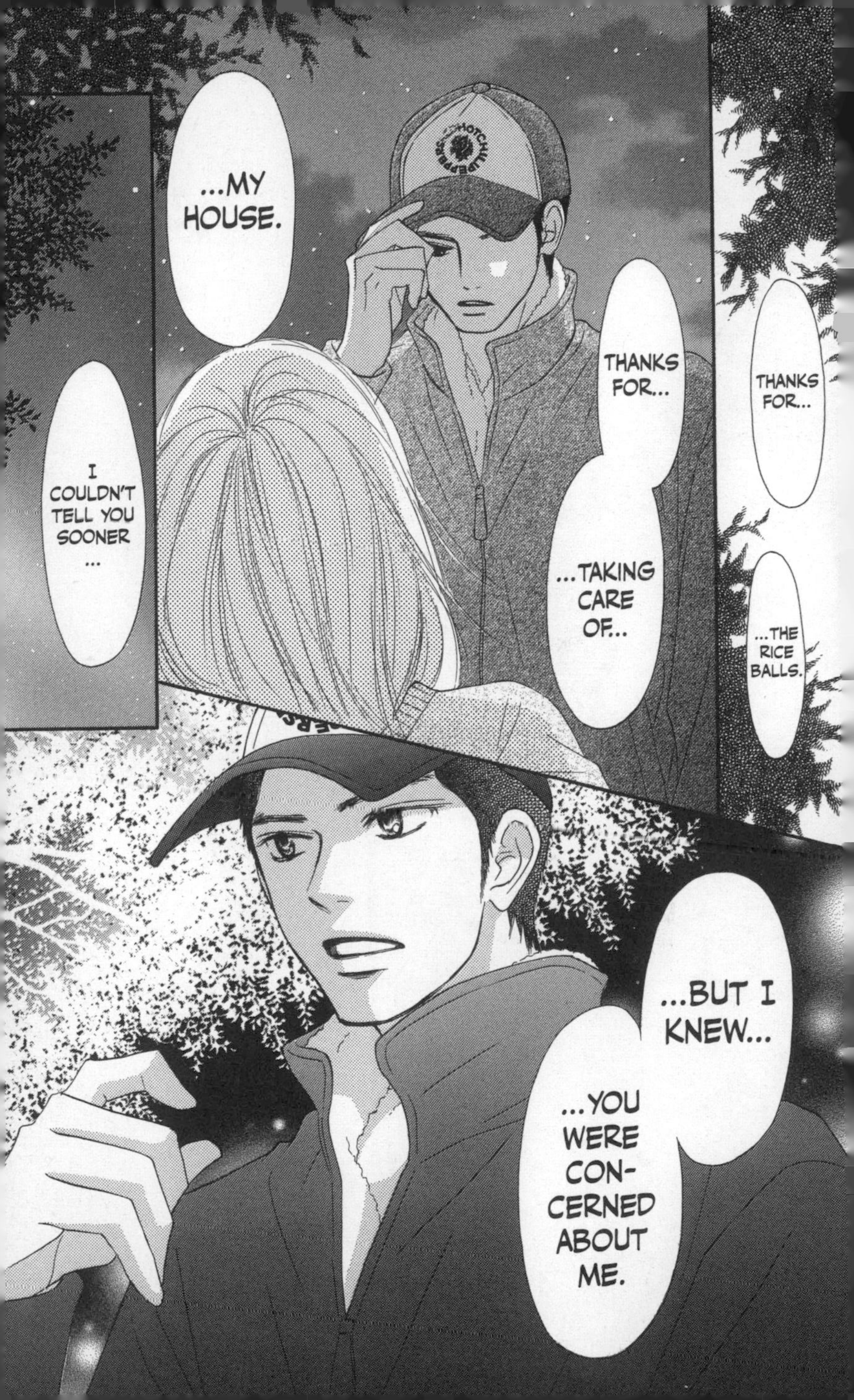
THANKS FOR...
...THE RICE BALLS.
THANKS FOR...
...TAKING CARE OF...
...MY HOUSE.
I COULDN'T TELL YOU SOONER ...
...BUT I KNEW...
...YOU WERE CON-CERNED ABOUT ME.

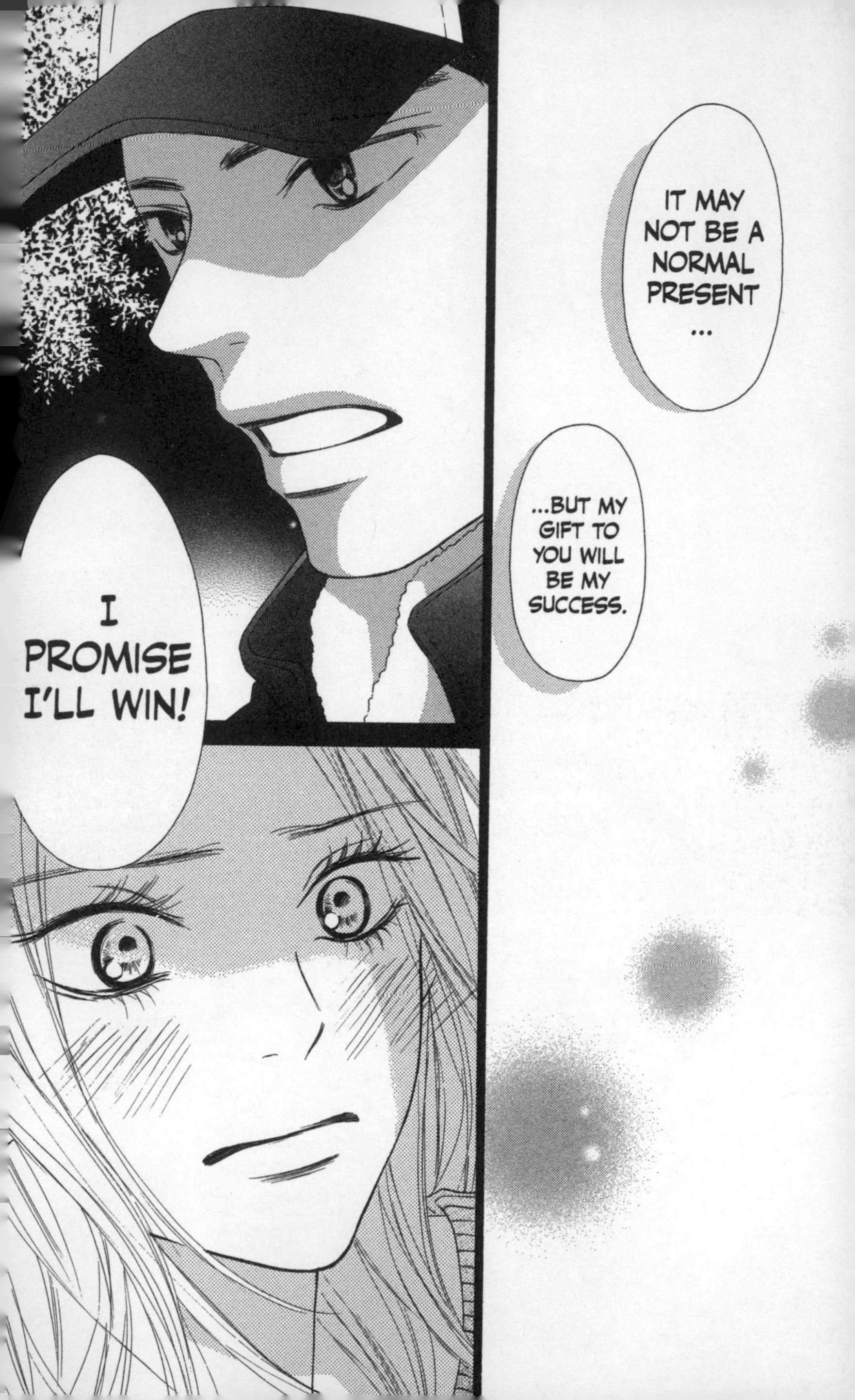
IT MAY NOT BE A NORMAL PRESENT ...
...BUT MY GIFT TO YOU WILL BE MY SUCCESS.
I PROMISE I'LL WIN!

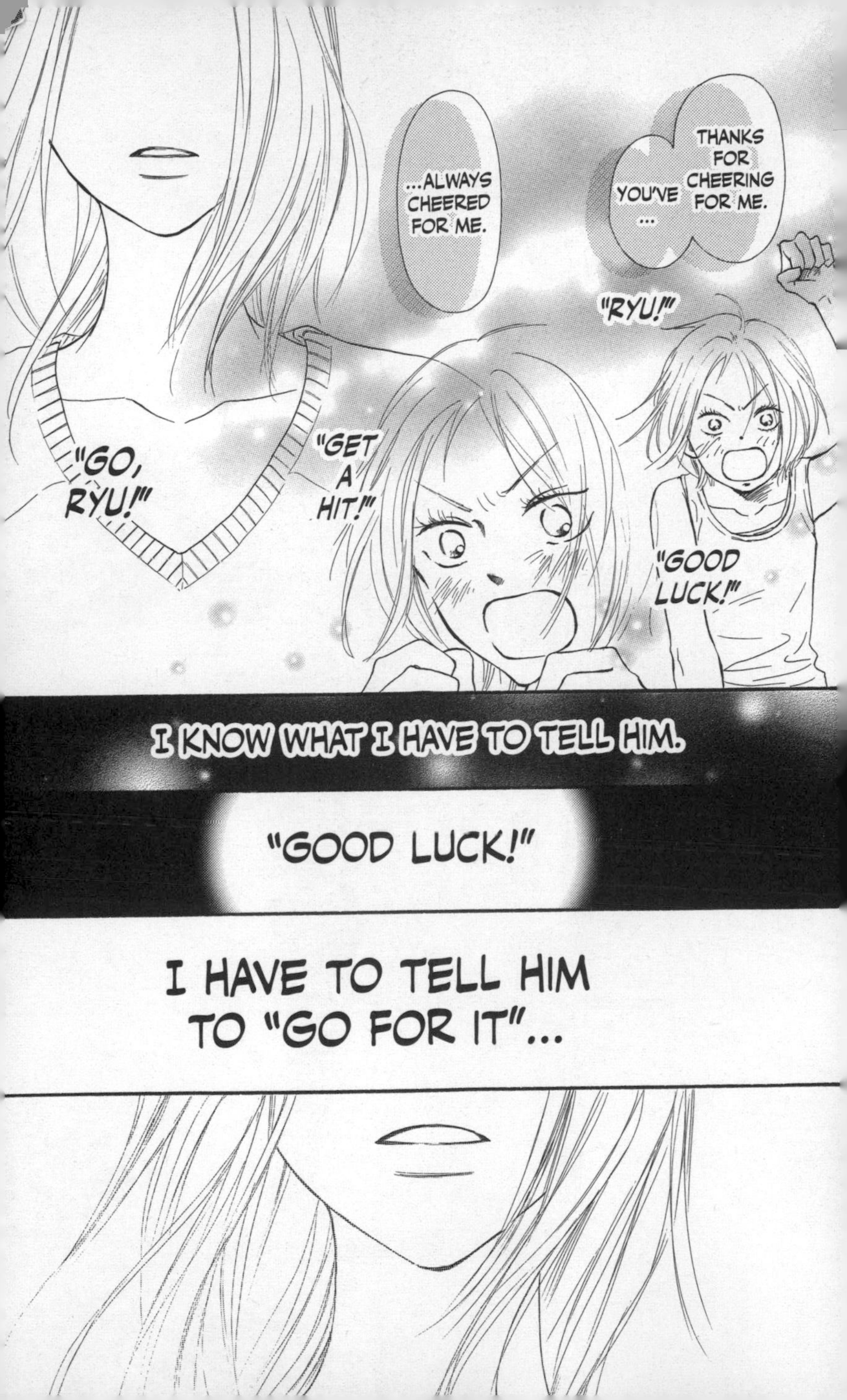
THANKS FOR CHEERING FOR ME.
YOU'VE ...
...ALWAYS CHEERED FOR ME.
"RYU!"
"GOOD LUCK!"
"GET A HIT!"
"GO, RYU!"
I KNOW WHAT I HAVE TO TELL HIM.
"GOOD LUCK!"
I HAVE TO TELL HIM TO "GO FOR IT"...

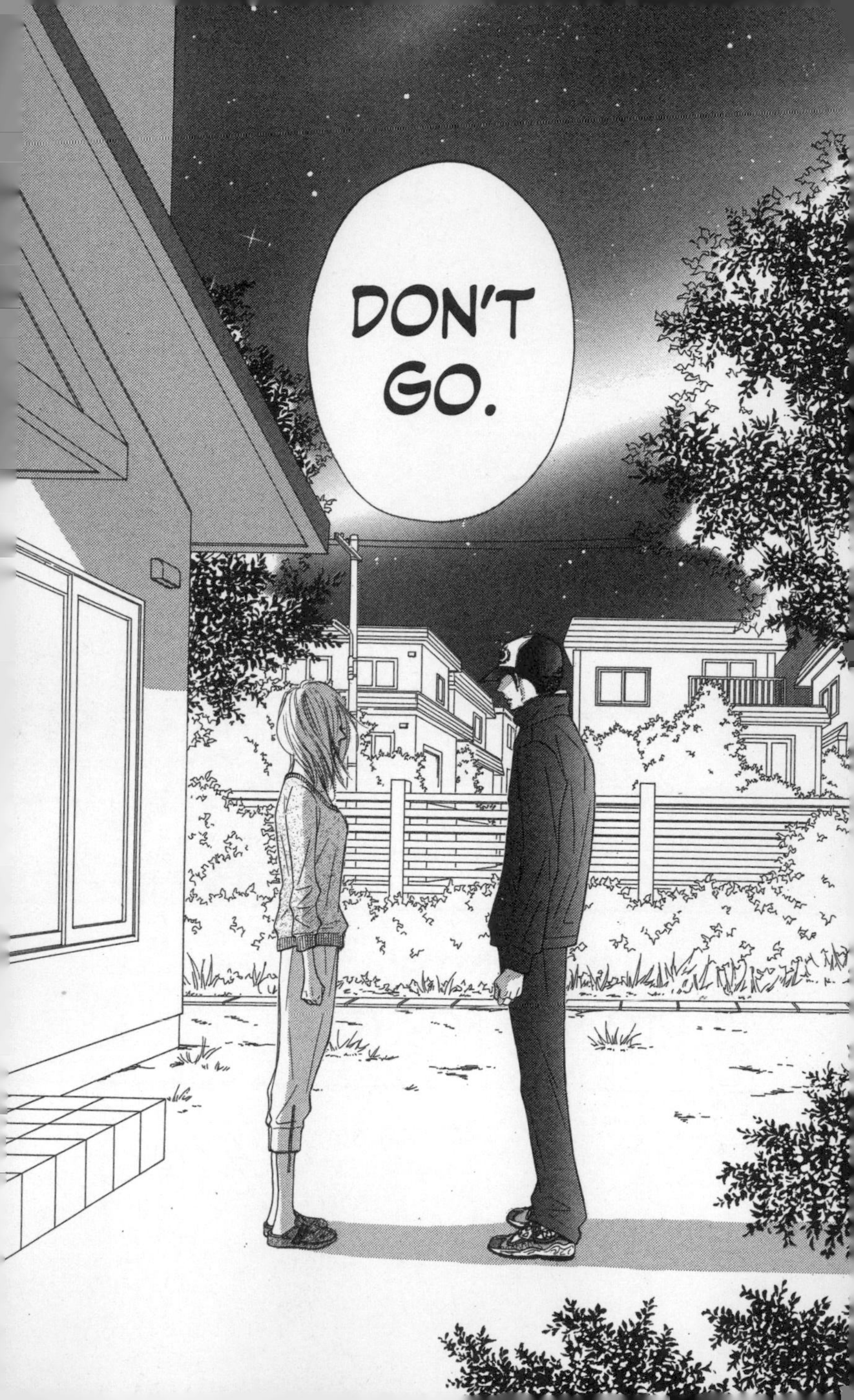
DON'T GO.

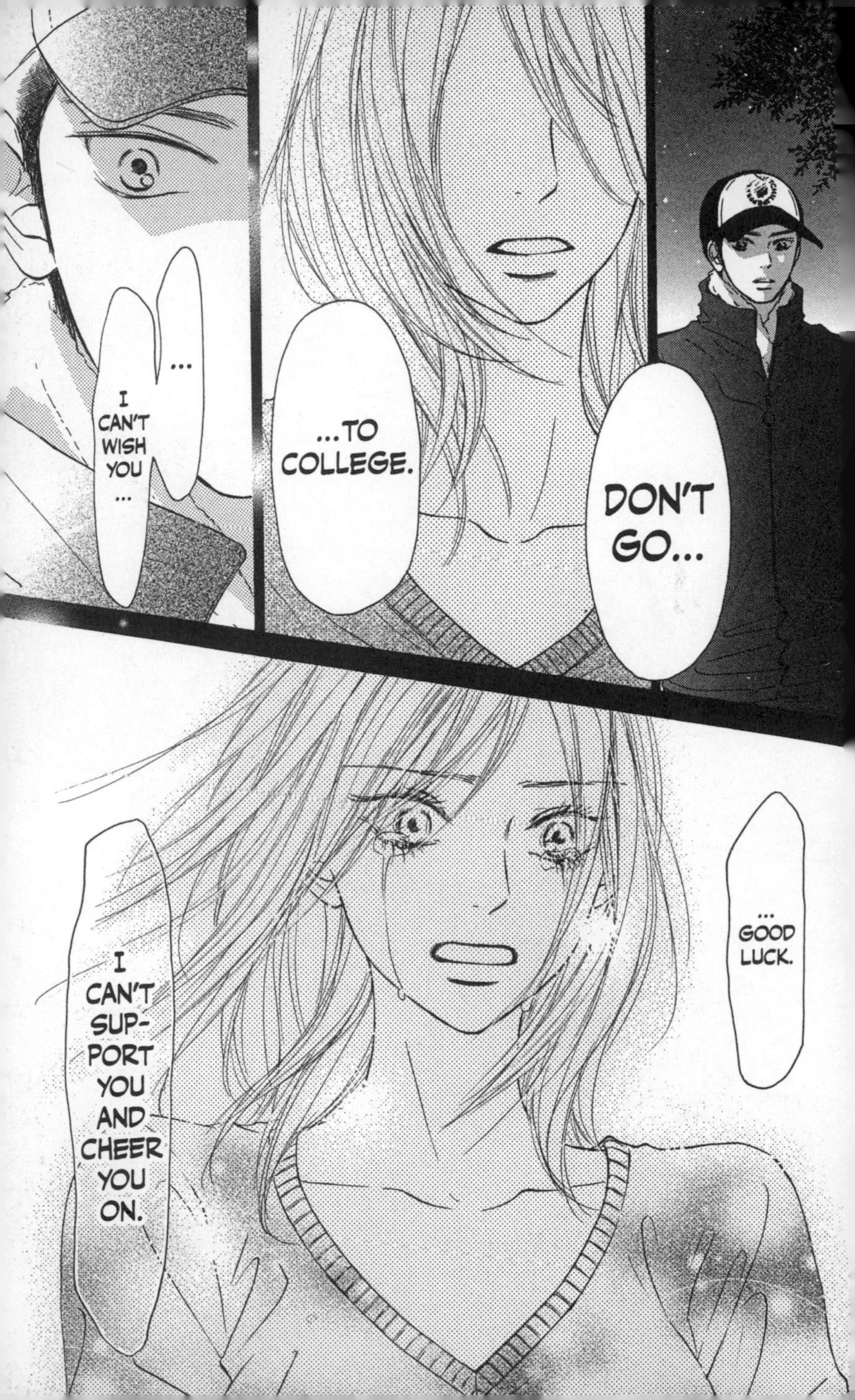
DON'T GO...
...TO COLLEGE.
...
I CAN'T WISH YOU ...
... GOOD LUCK.
I CAN'T SUP-PORT YOU AND CHEER YOU ON.

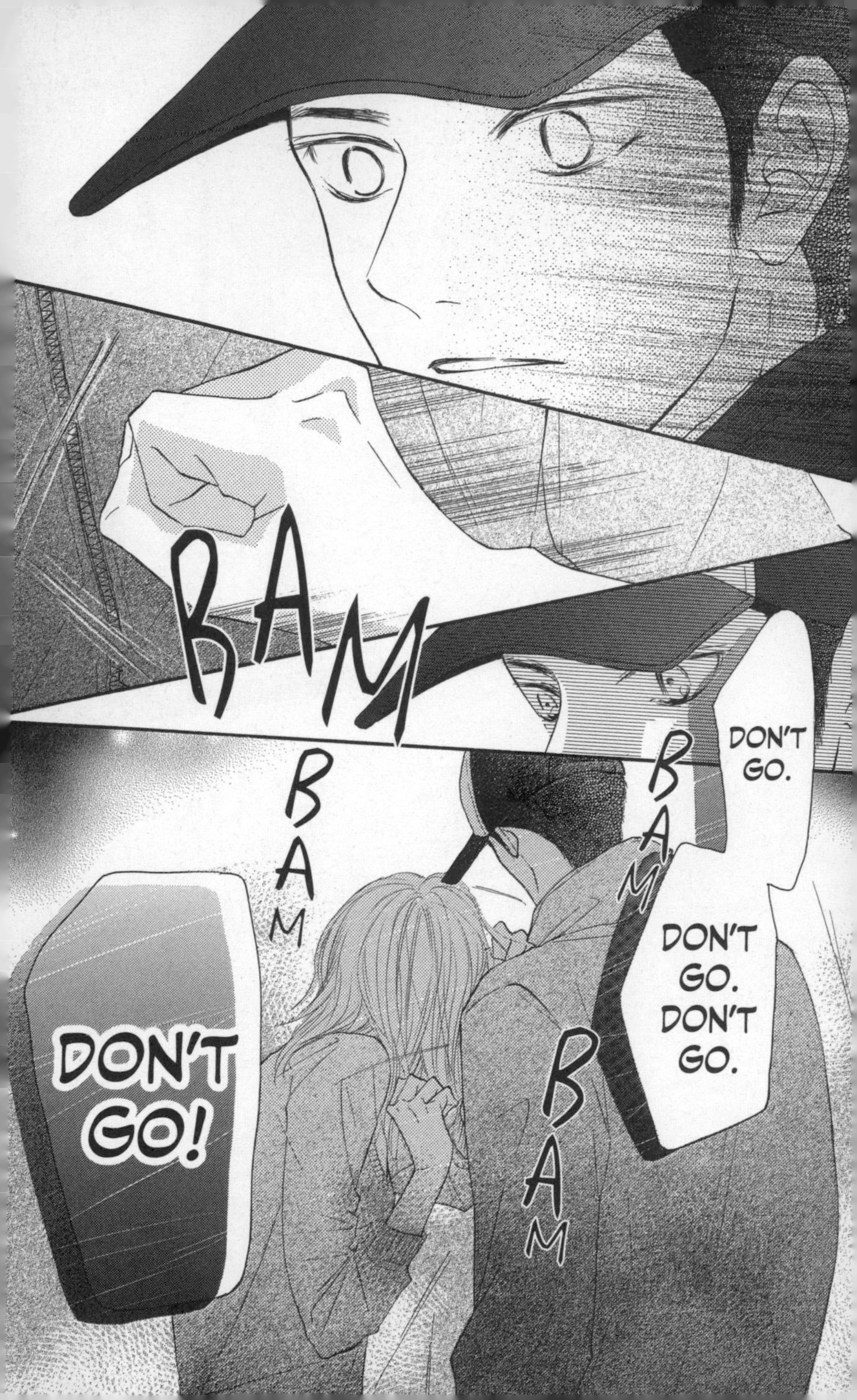
BAM
DON'T GO.
BAM
DON'T GO. DON'T GO.
BAM
BAM
DON'T GO!

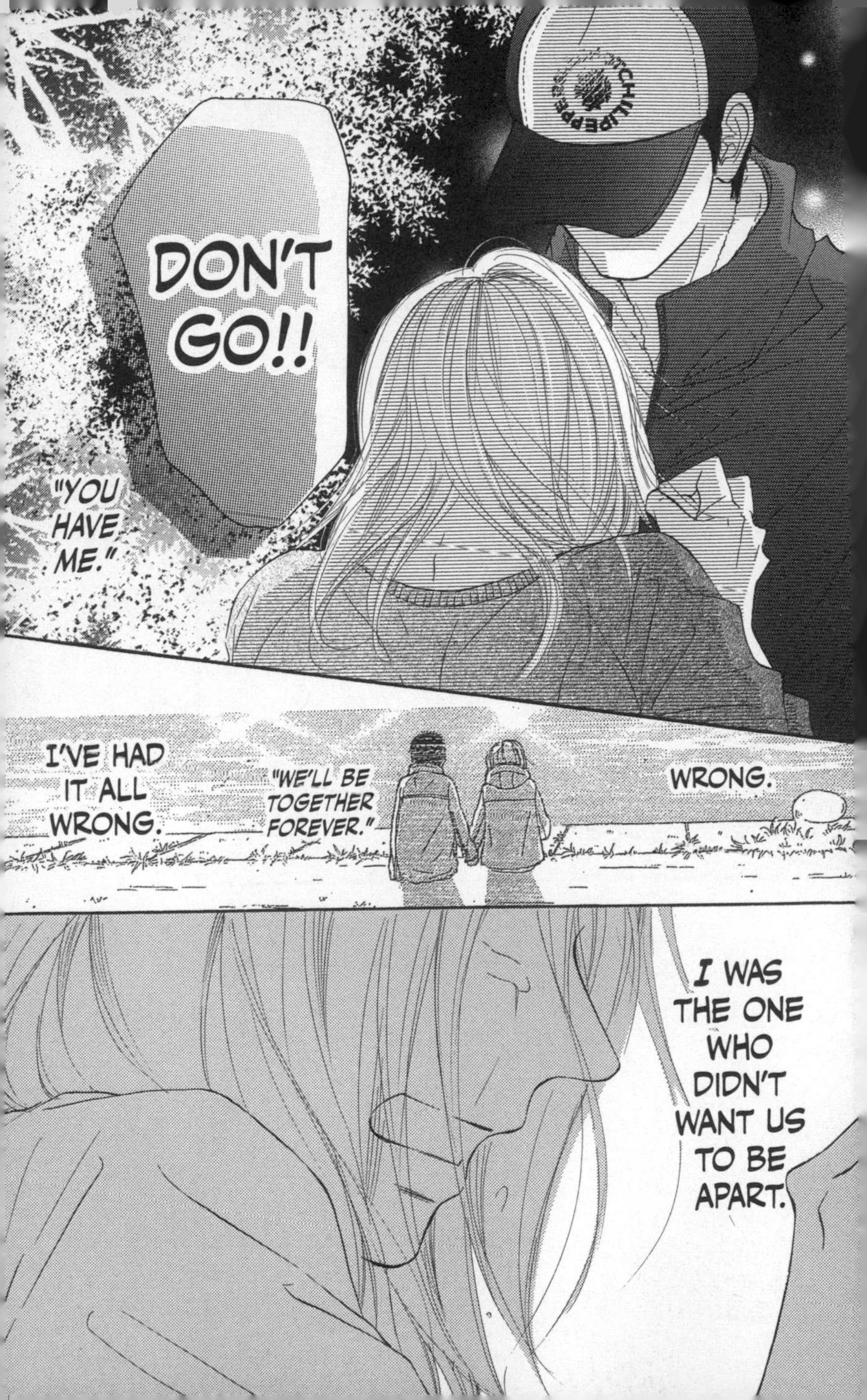

DON'T GO!!
"YOU HAVE ME."
WRONG.
"WE'LL BE TOGETHER FOREVER."
I'VE HAD IT ALL WRONG.
I WAS THE ONE WHO DIDN'T WANT US TO BE APART.

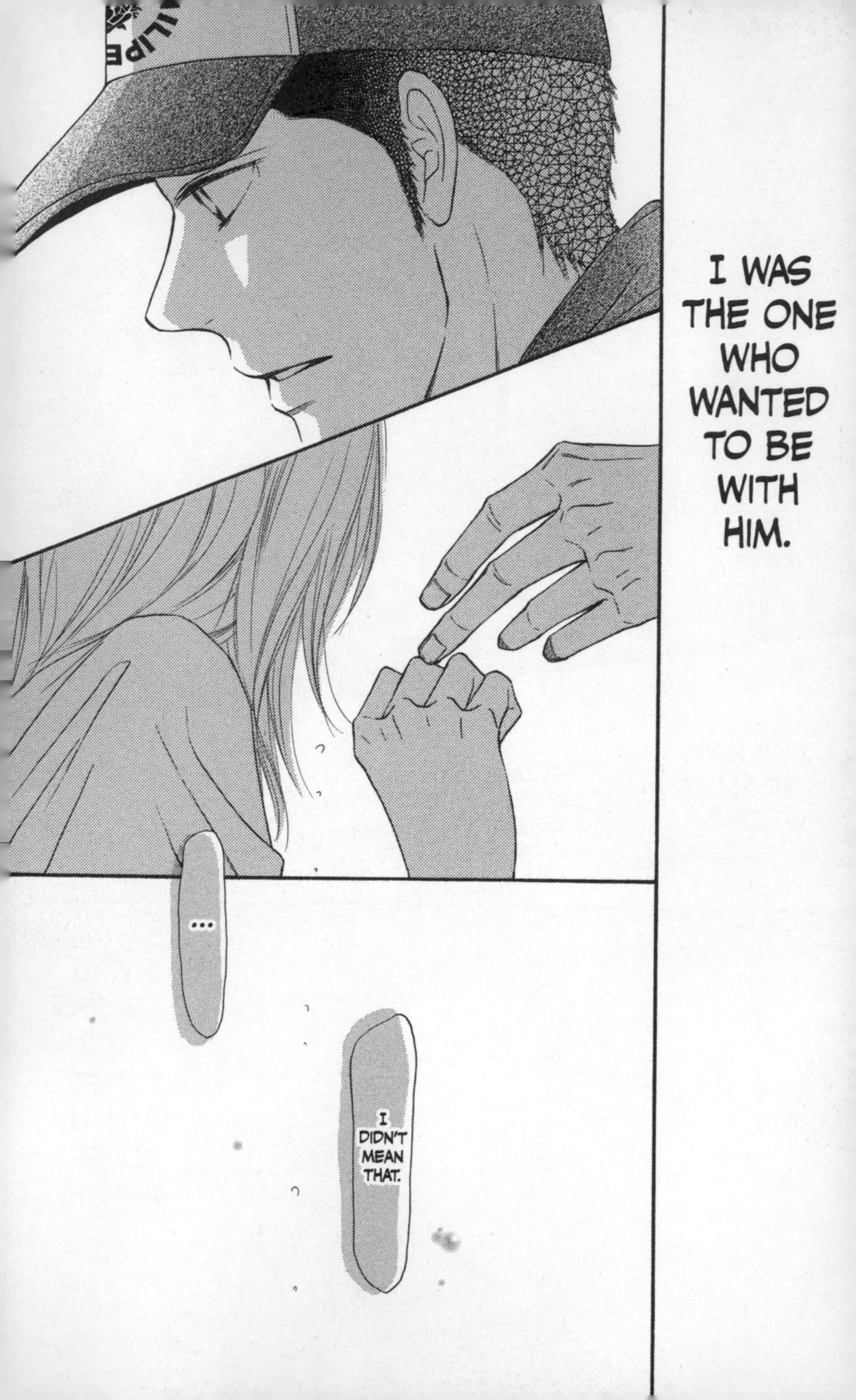
I WAS THE ONE WHO WANTED TO BE WITH HIM.
...
I DIDN'T MEAN THAT.

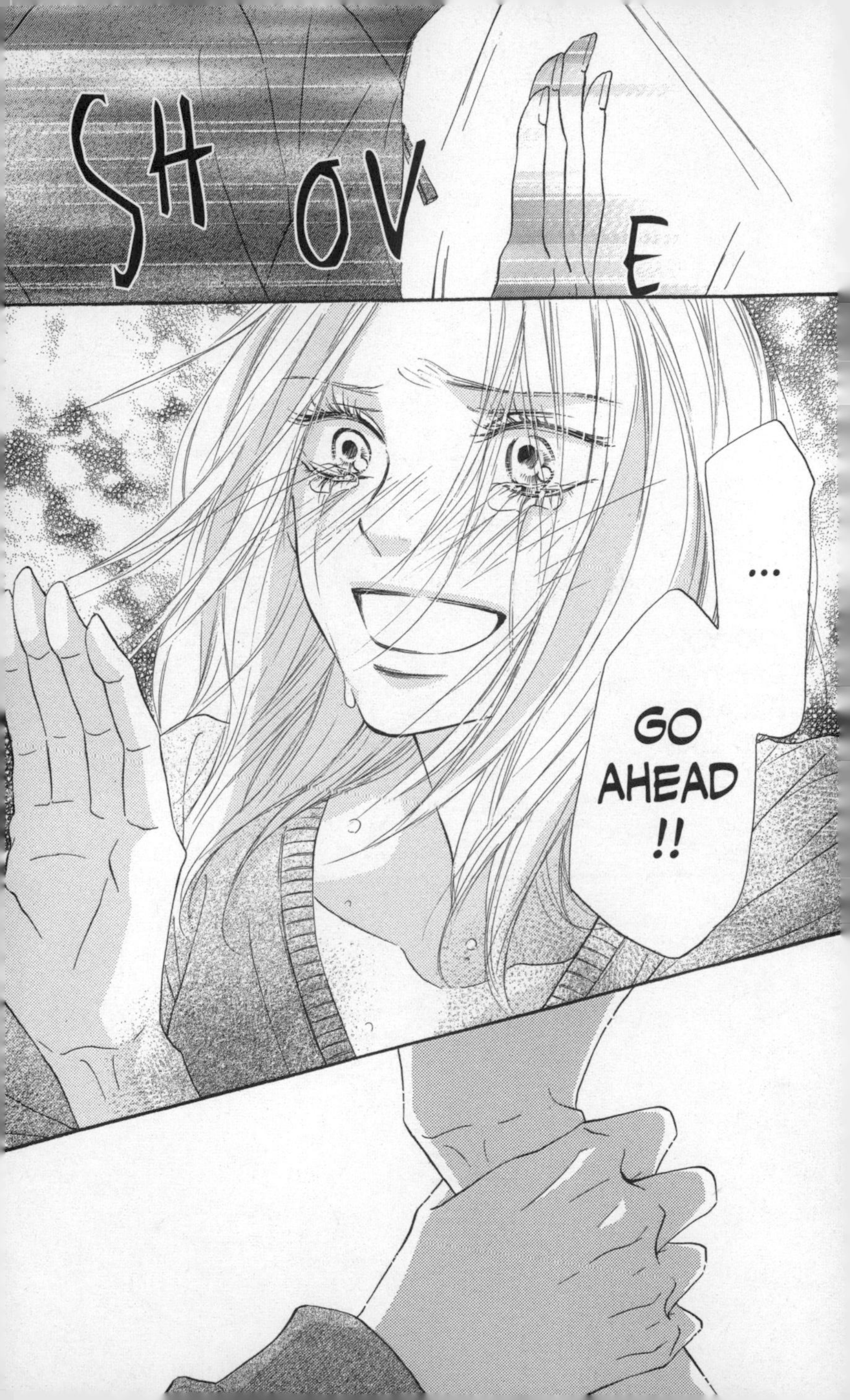
SHOVE
...
GO AHEAD !!

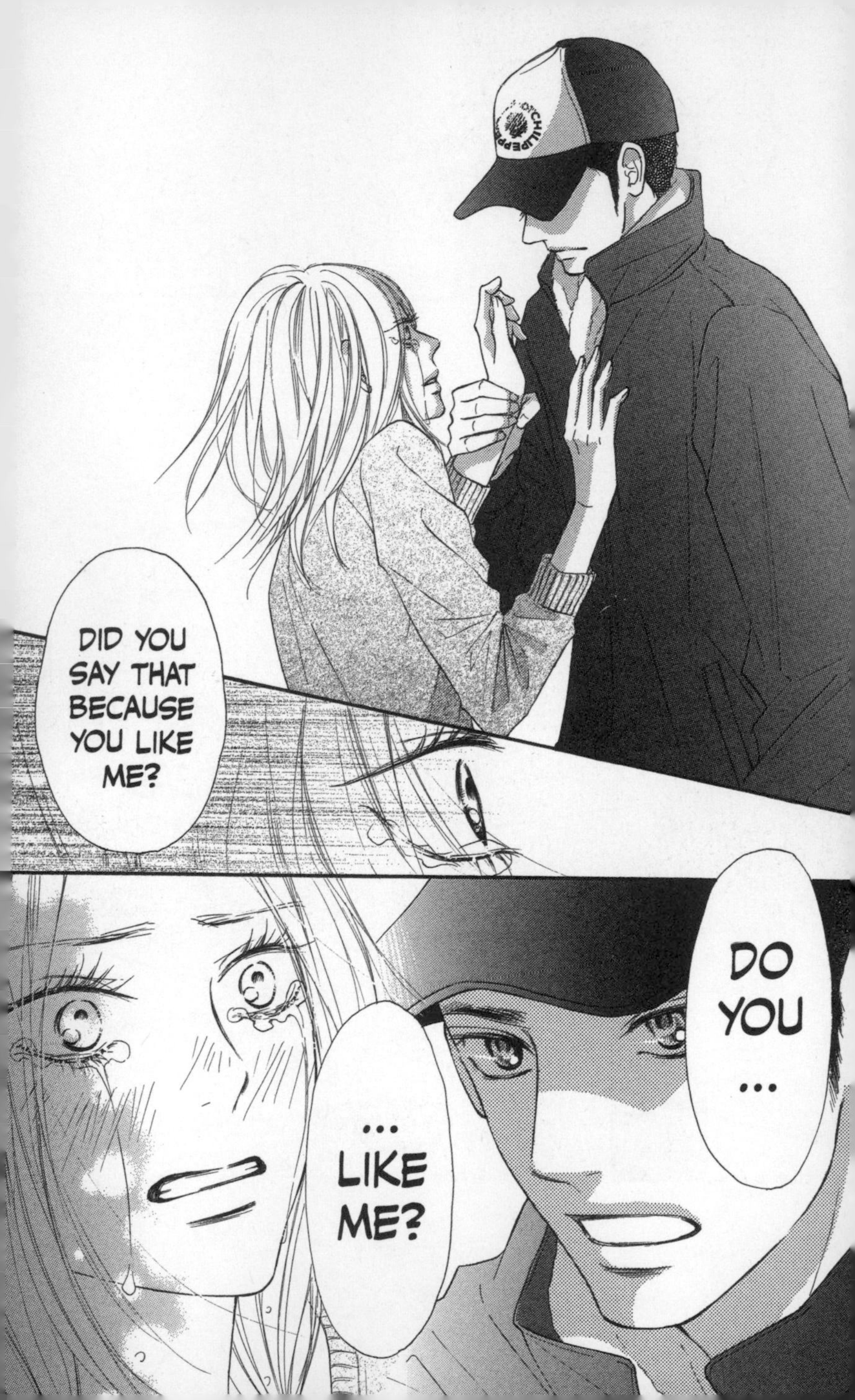
DID YOU SAY THAT BECAUSE YOU LIKE ME?
DO YOU ...
... LIKE ME?

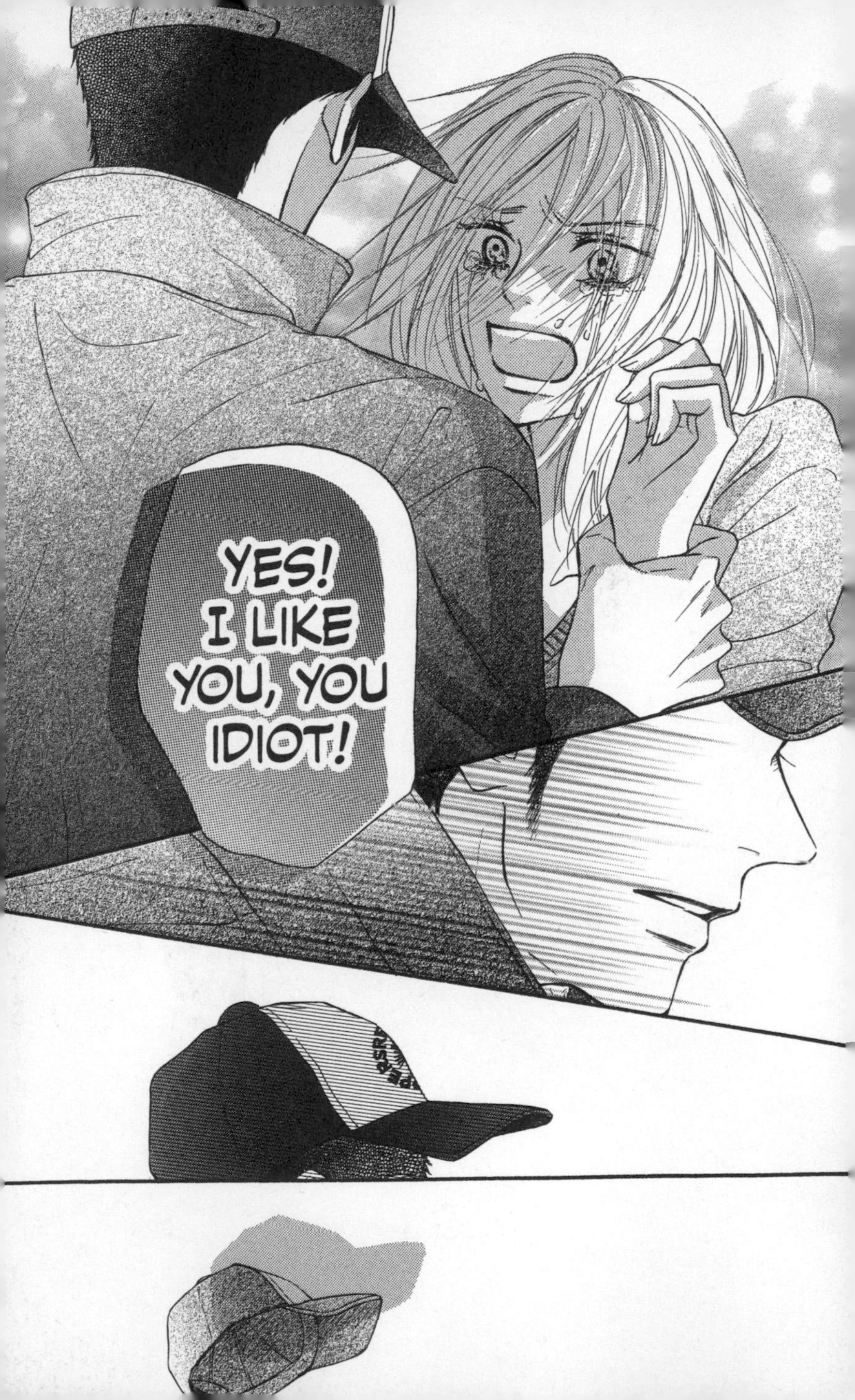
YES! I LIKE YOU, YOU IDIOT!

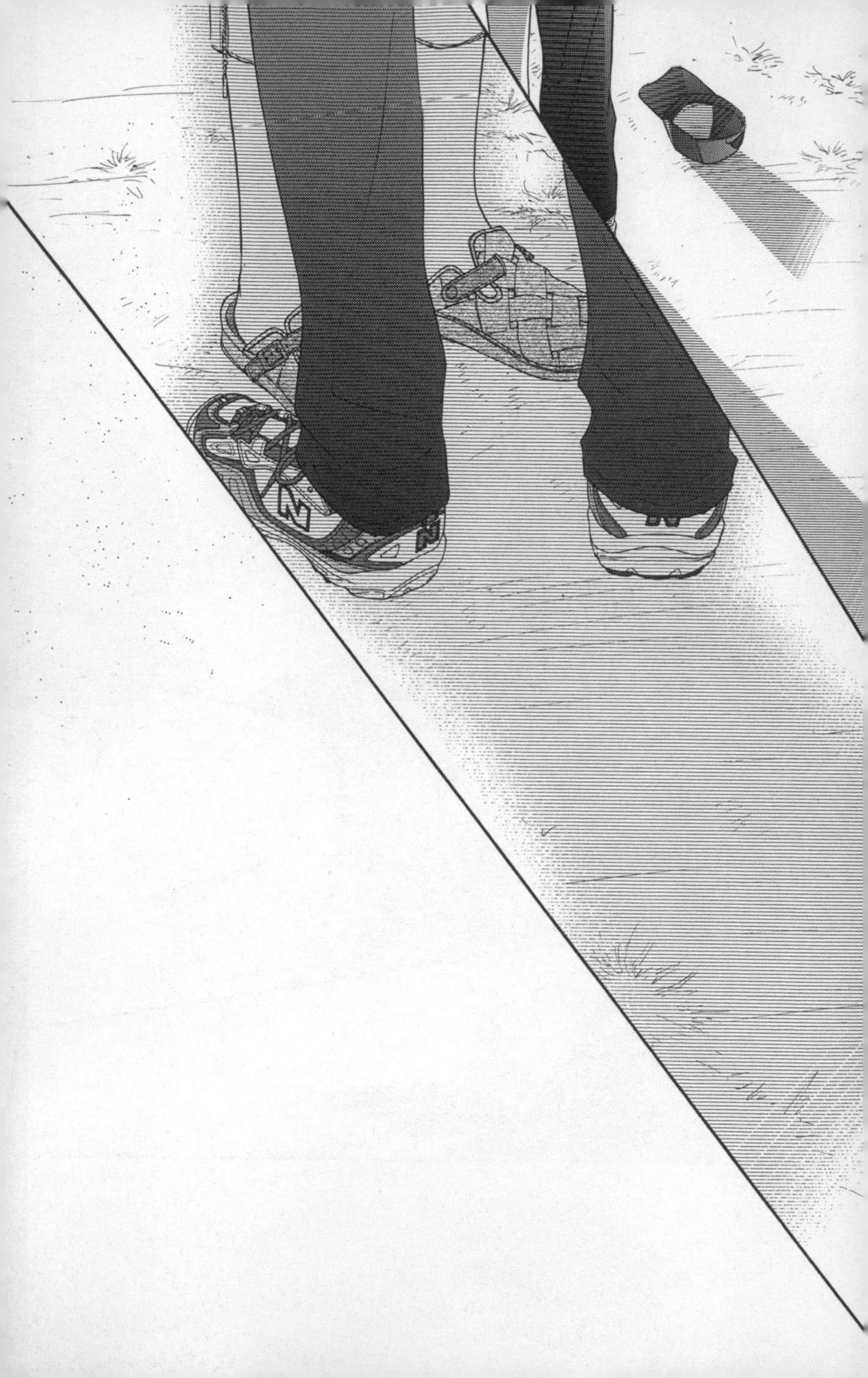

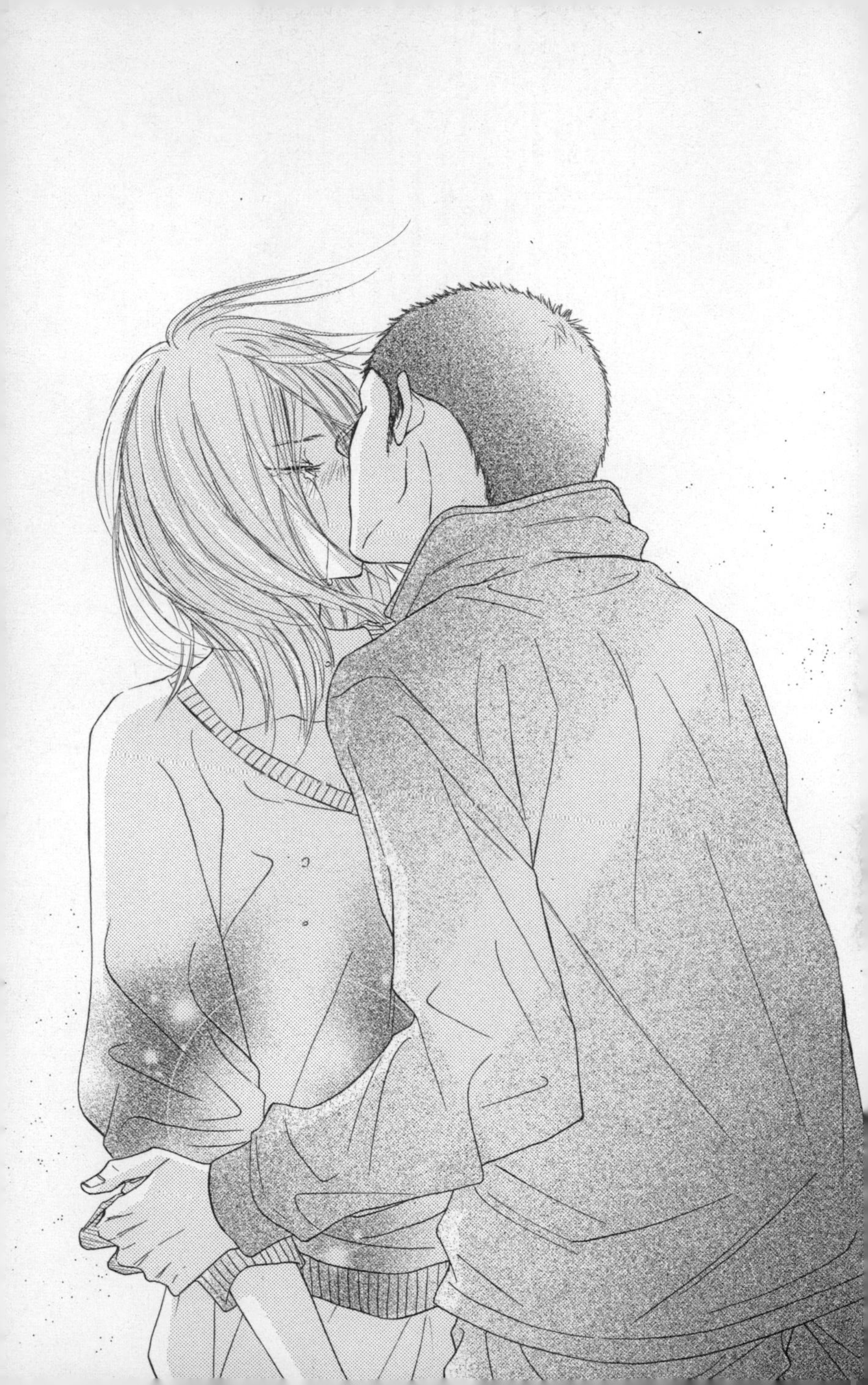

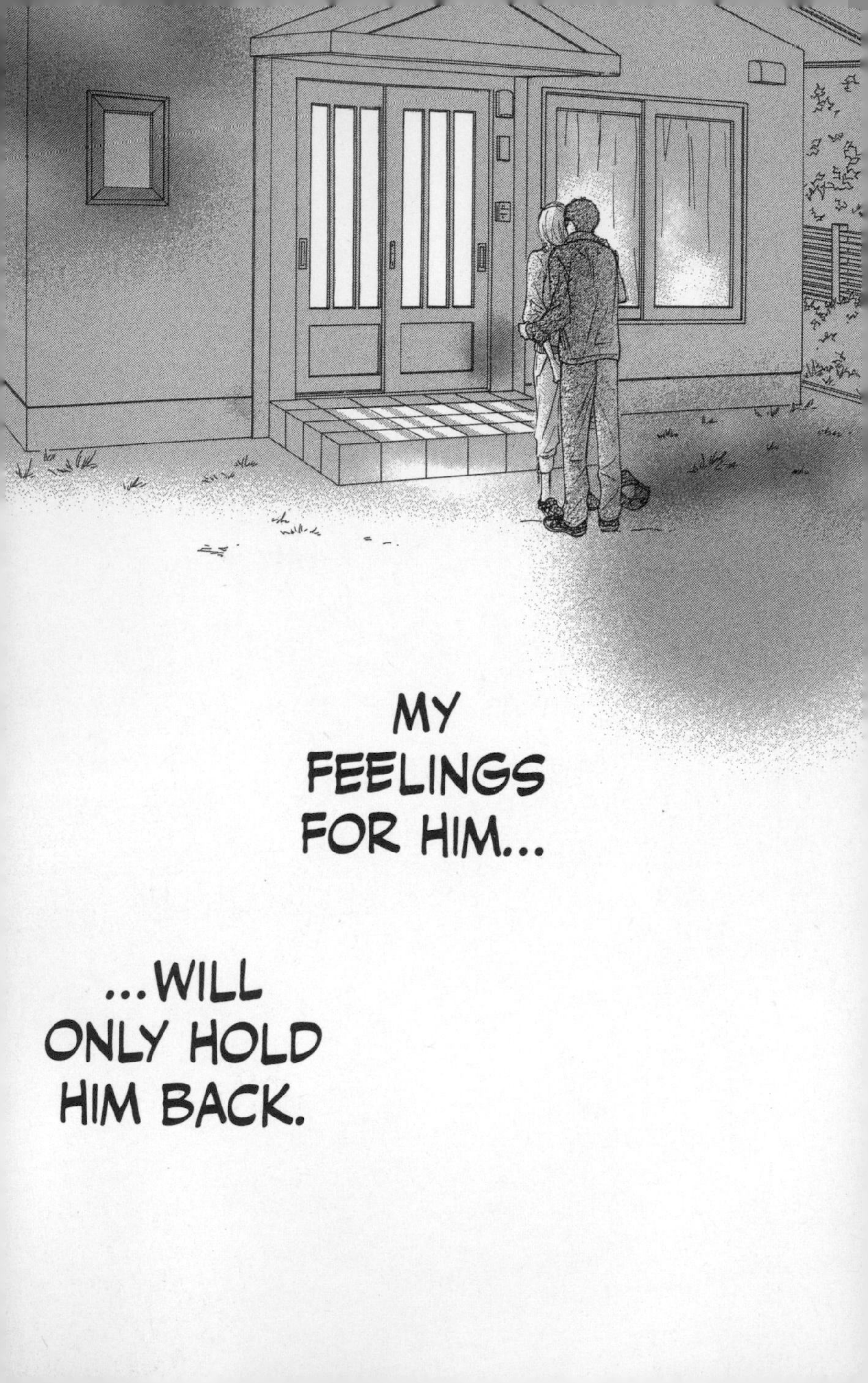
MY FEELINGS FOR HIM...
...WILL ONLY HOLD HIM BACK.

Episode 89: Proud of Myself

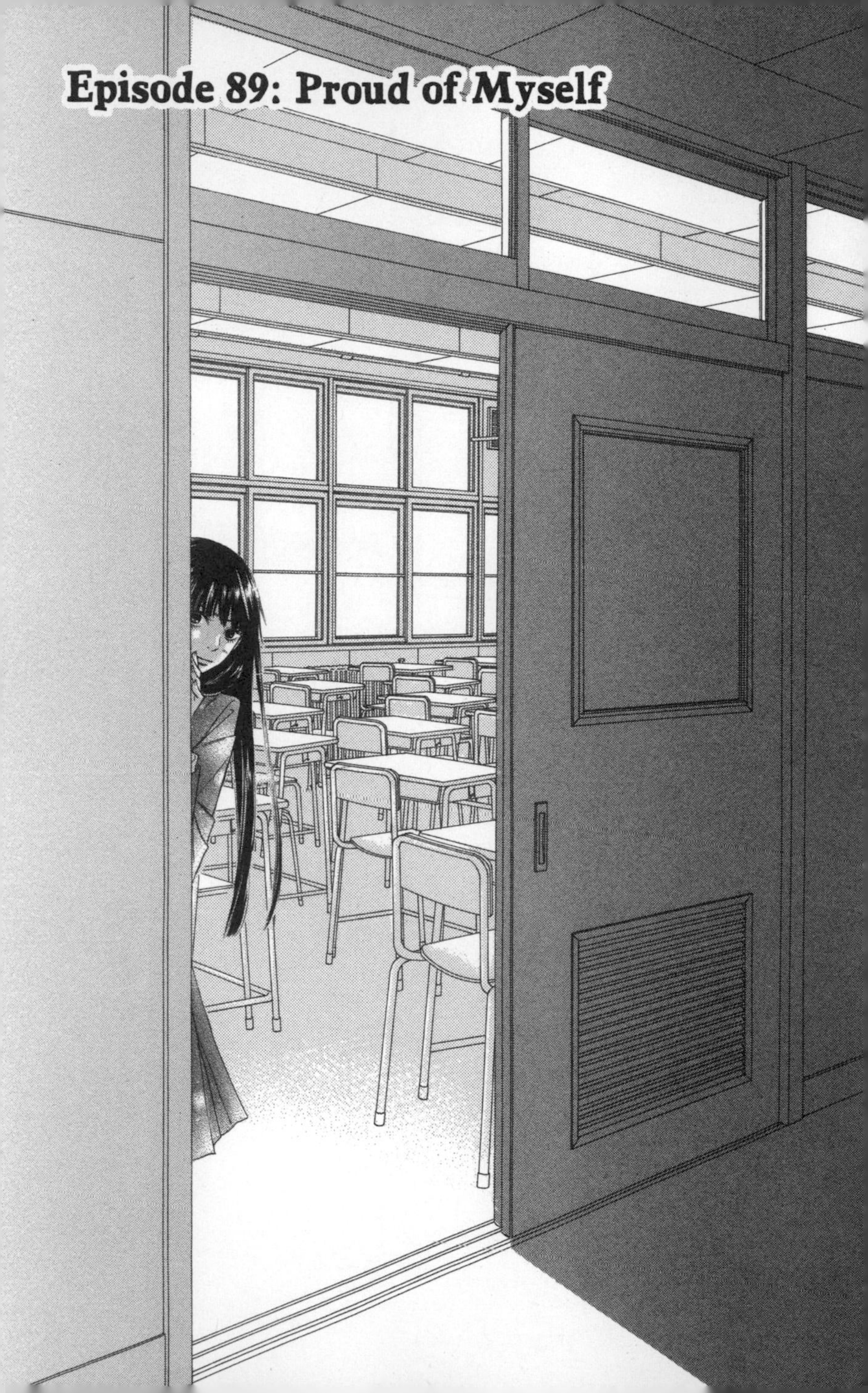

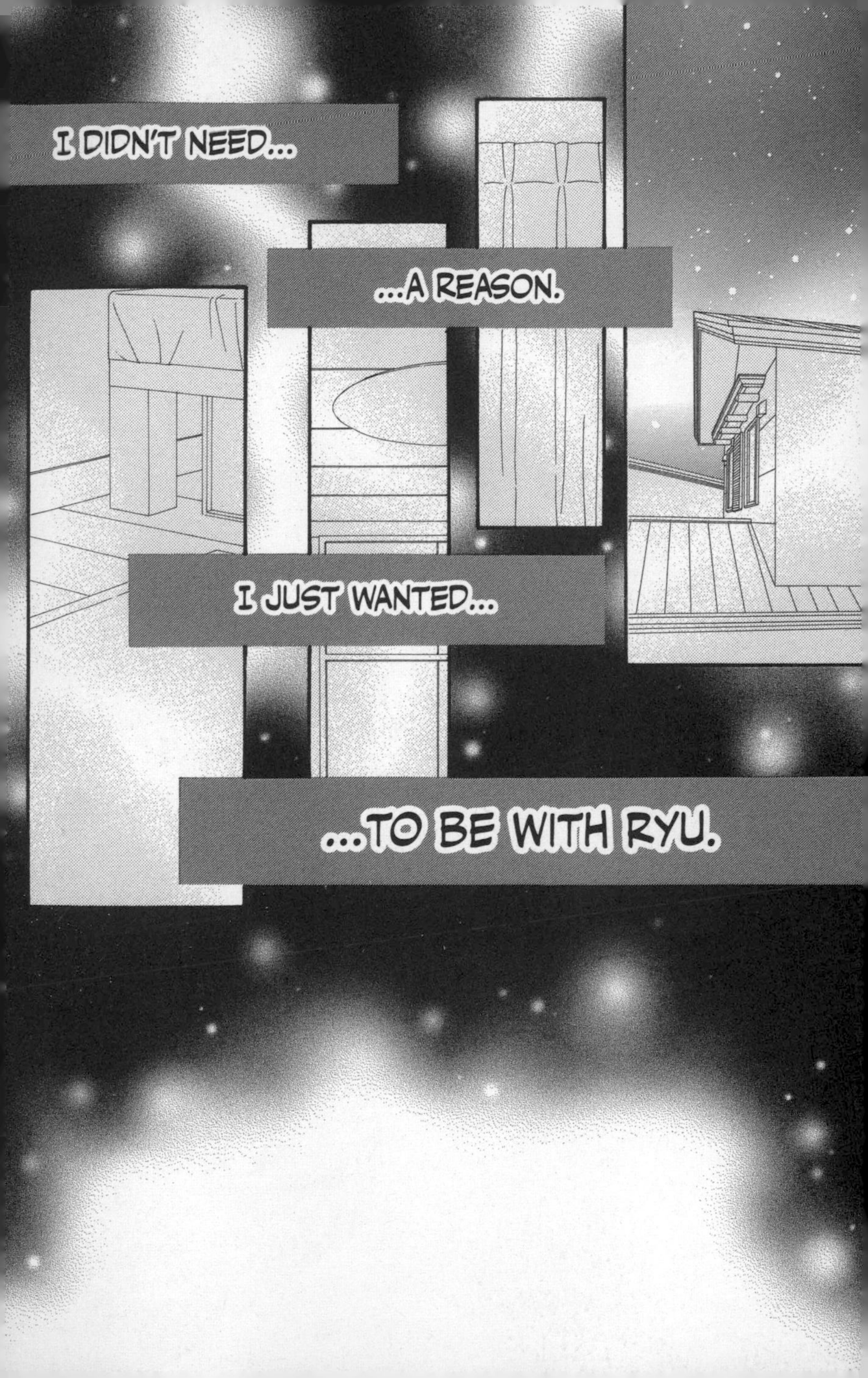
I DIDN'T NEED...
...A REASON.
I JUST WANTED...
...TO BE WITH RYU.

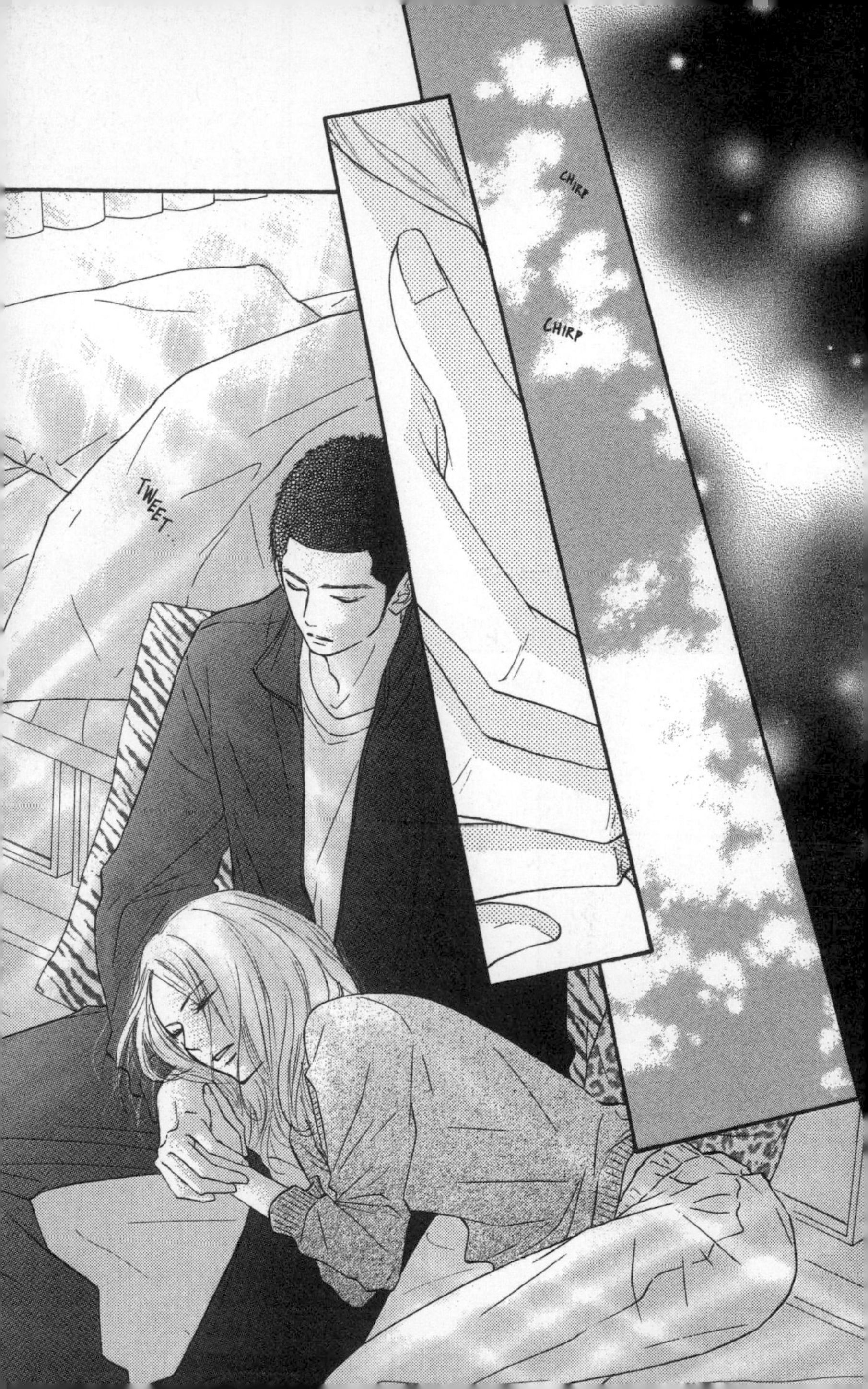
CHIRP
CHIRP
TWEET...

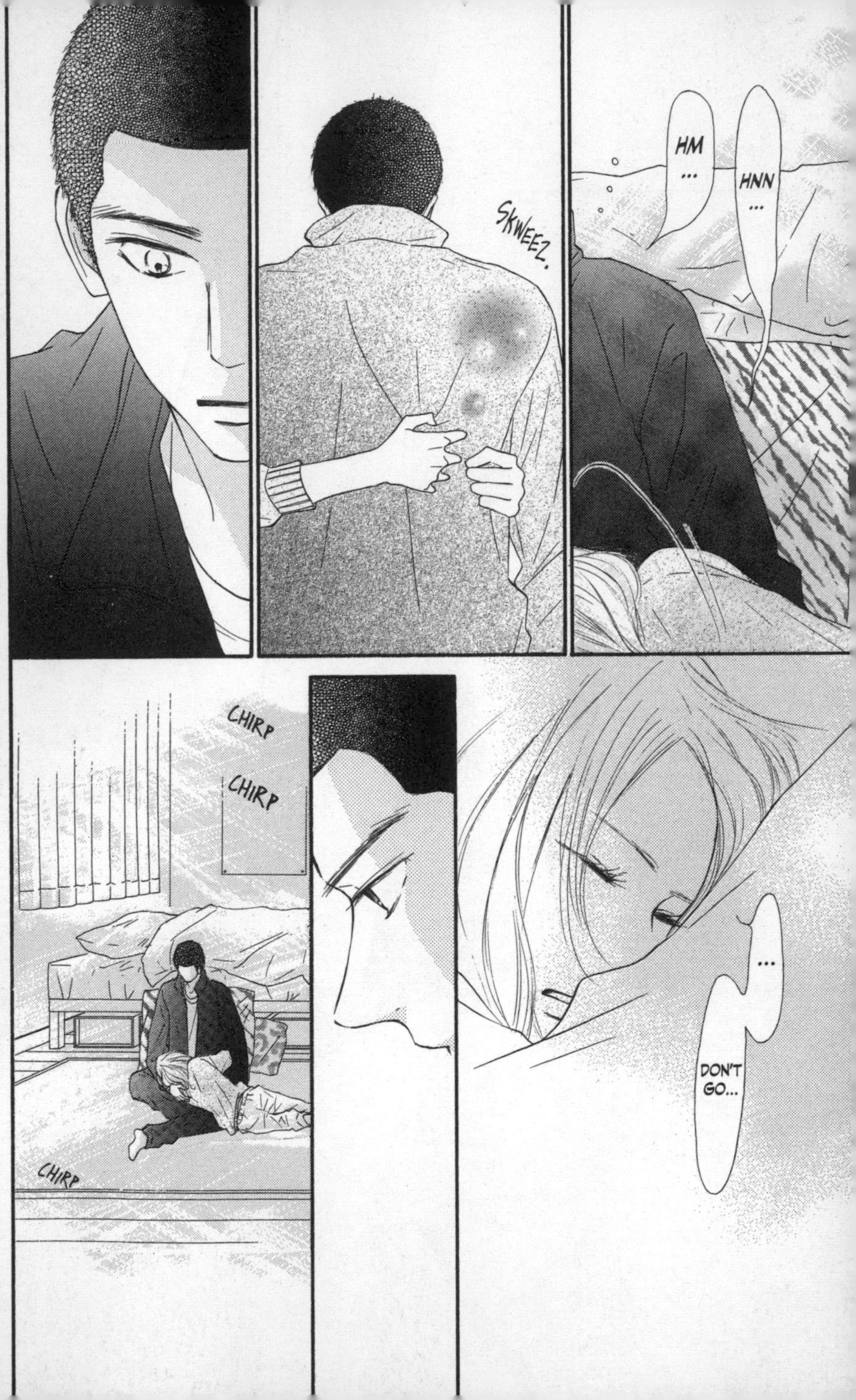
HM...
HNN...
SKWEEZ.
...
DON'T GO...
CHIRP
CHIRP
CHIRP

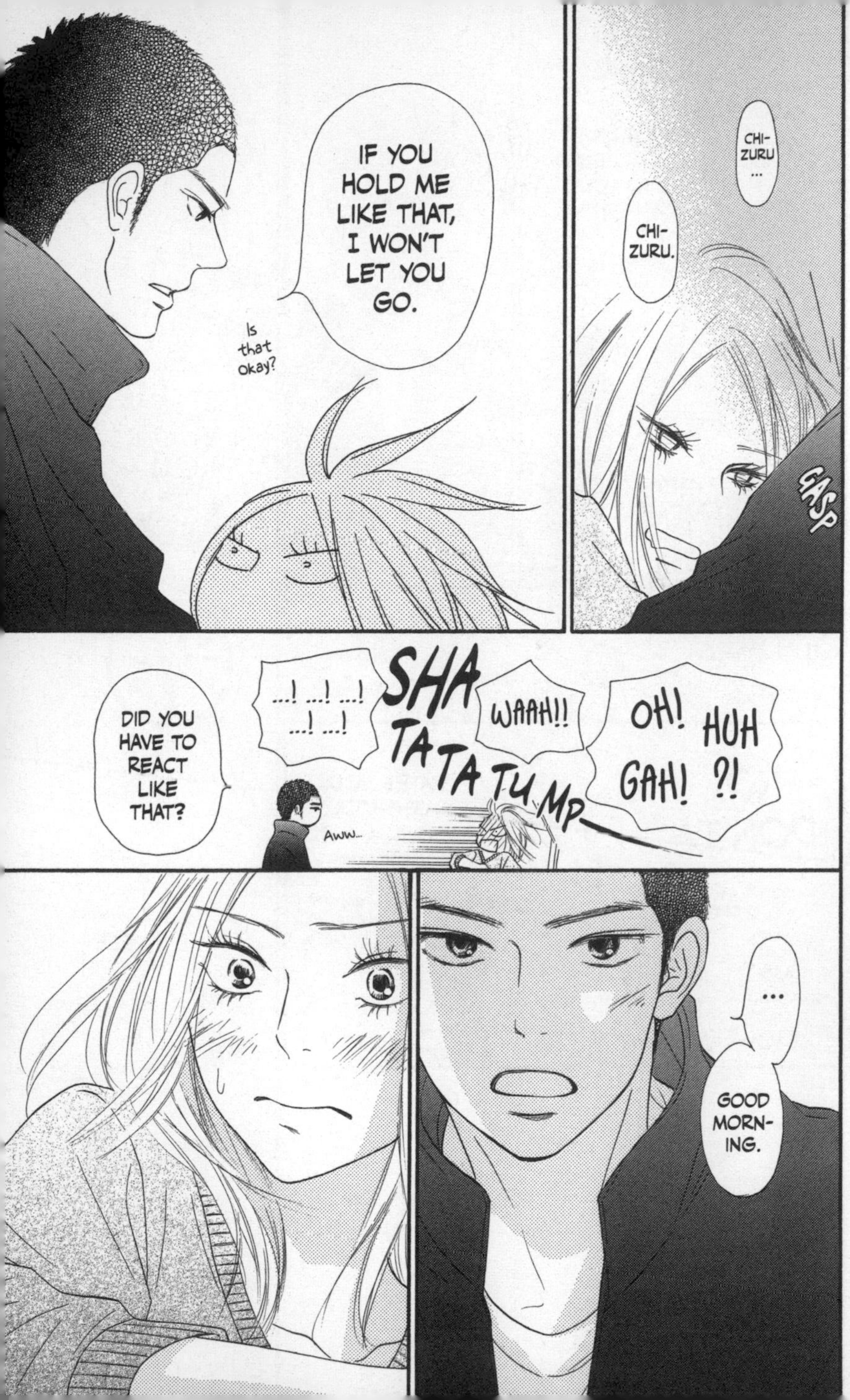
CHI-ZURU...
CHI-ZURU.
GASP
IF YOU HOLD ME LIKE THAT, I WON'T LET YOU GO.
Is that okay?
HUH?!
OH! GAH!
WAAH!!
SHA TATATA TUMP
...! ...! ...! ...! ...!
DID YOU HAVE TO REACT LIKE THAT?
Aww...
...
GOOD MORN-ING.

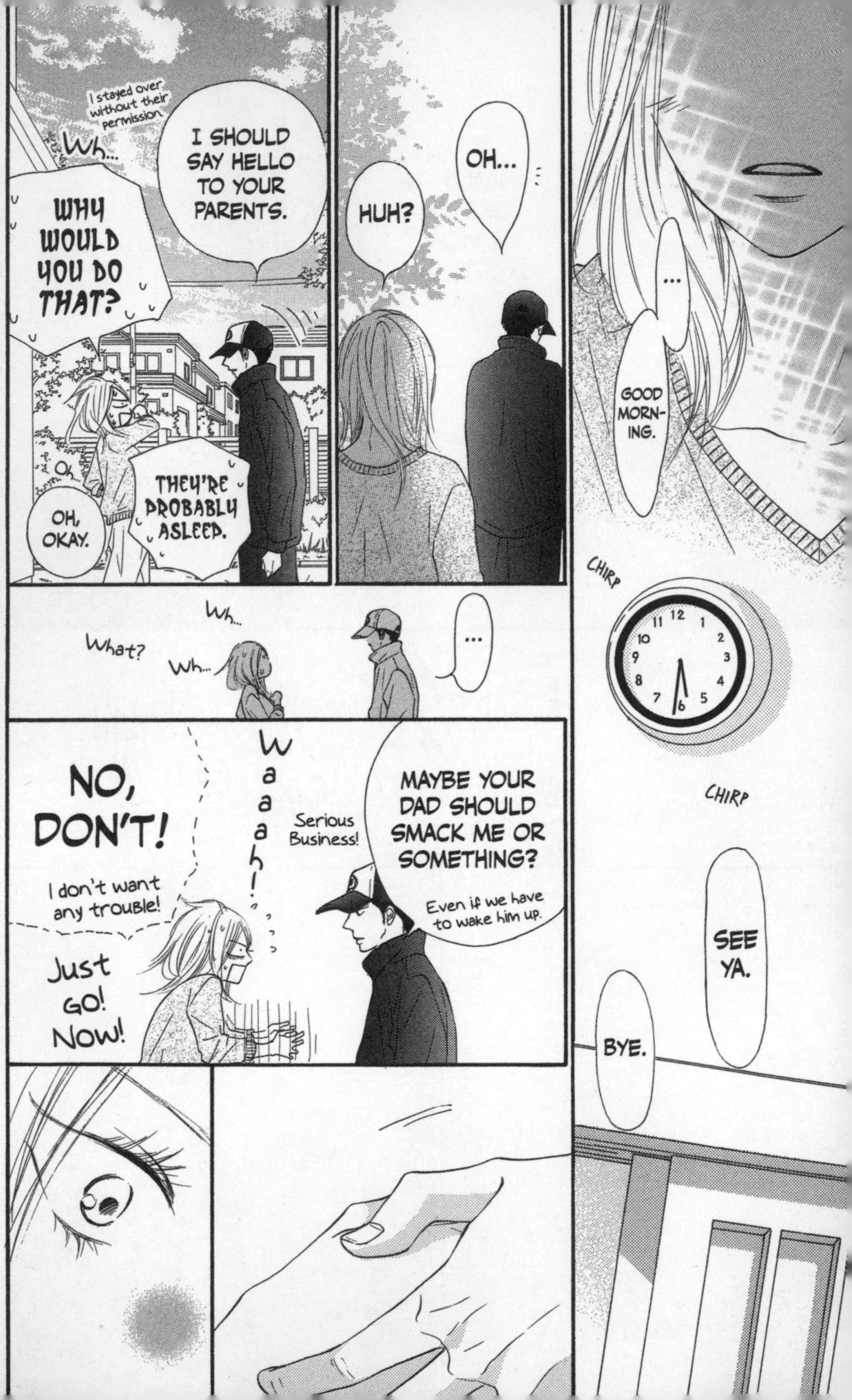
...
GOOD MORNING.
CHIRP
CHIRP
SEE YA.
BYE.
OH...
HUH?
I stayed over without their permission
I SHOULD SAY HELLO TO YOUR PARENTS.
Wh...
WHY WOULD YOU DO THAT?
THEY'RE PROBABLY ASLEEP.
Oh...
OH, OKAY.
...
Wh...
What?
Wh...
MAYBE YOUR DAD SHOULD SMACK ME OR SOMETHING?
Even if we have to wake him up.
Serious Business!
Waaah!
NO, DON'T!
I don't want any trouble!
Just GO! NOW!

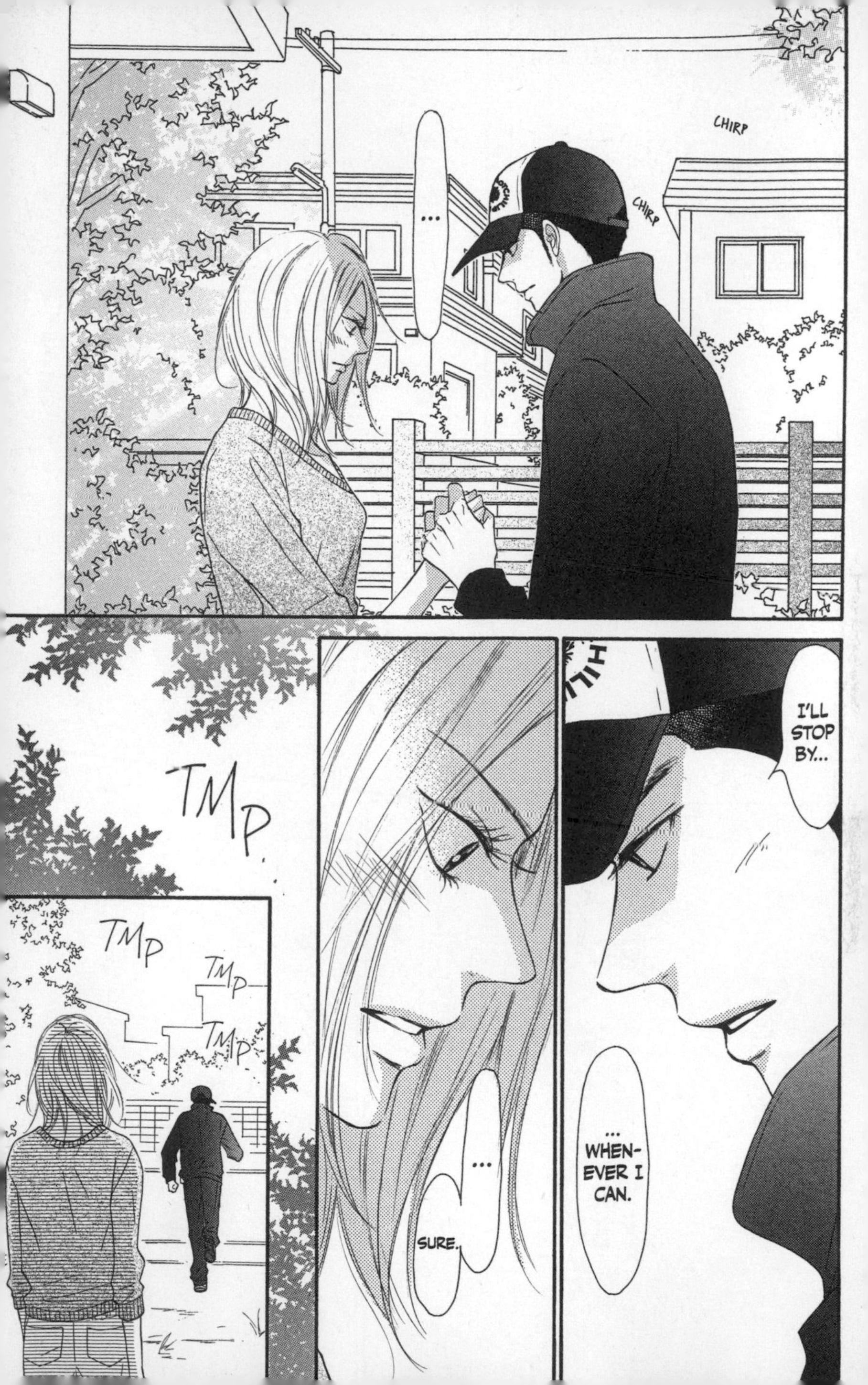
CHIRP
CHIRP
...
I'LL STOP BY...
... WHEN-EVER I CAN.
...
SURE.
TMP
TMP
TMP
TMP

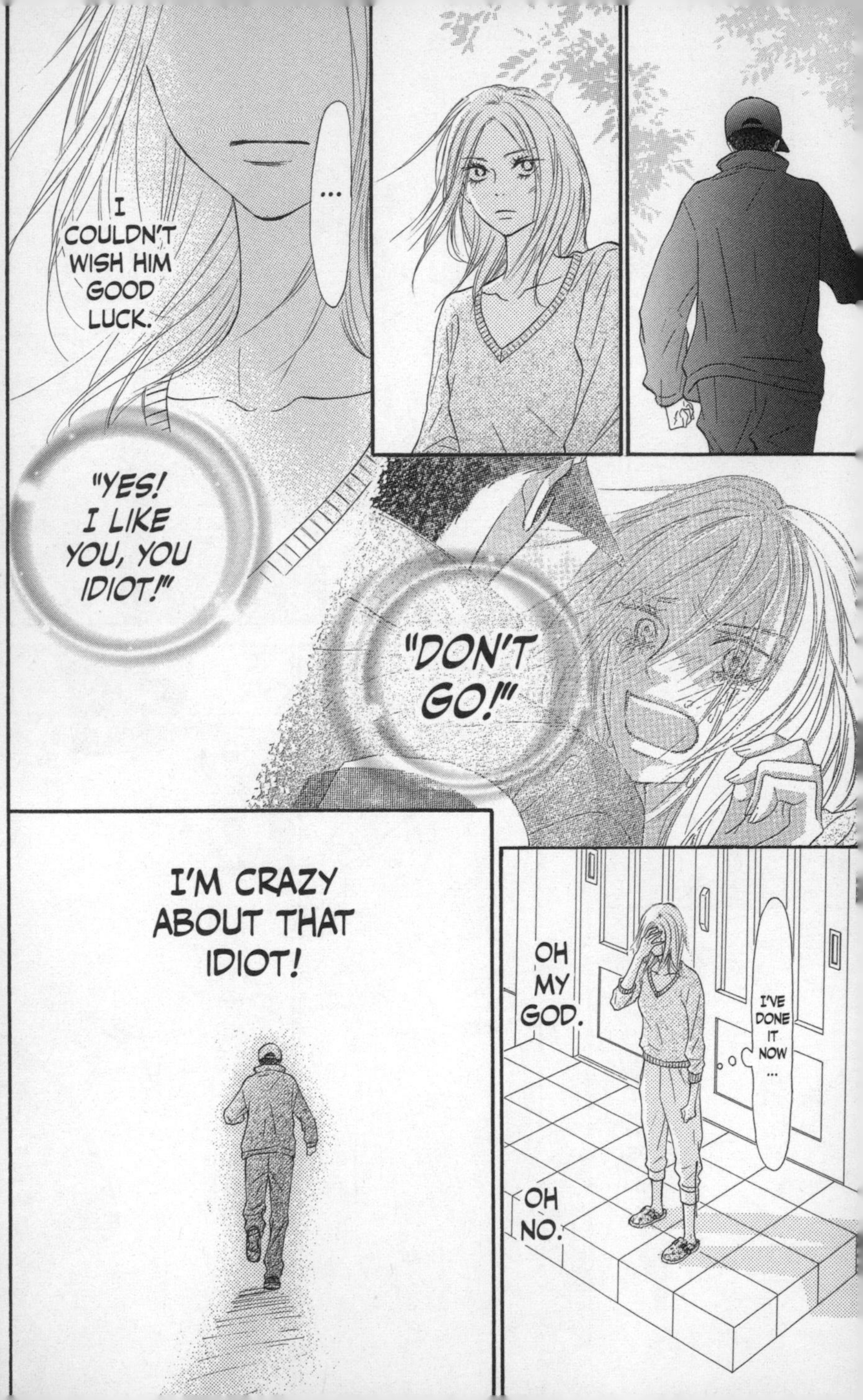
...
I COULDN'T WISH HIM GOOD LUCK.
"YES! I LIKE YOU, YOU IDIOT!"
"DON'T GO!"
I'VE DONE IT NOW ...
OH MY GOD.
OH NO.
I'M CRAZY ABOUT THAT IDIOT!

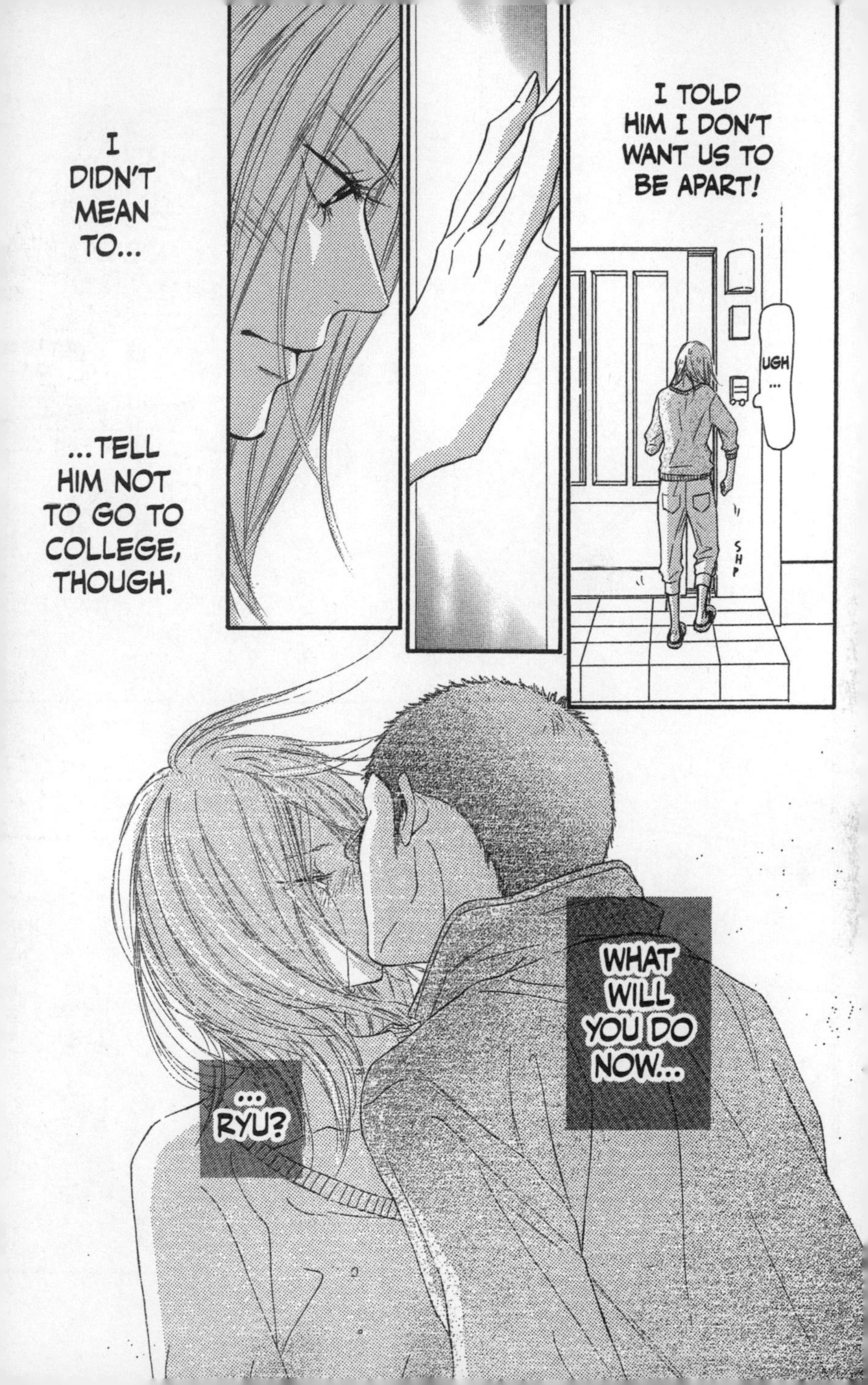
I TOLD HIM I DON'T WANT US TO BE APART!
UGH...
SHP
I DIDN'T MEAN TO...
...TELL HIM NOT TO GO TO COLLEGE, THOUGH.
WHAT WILL YOU DO NOW...
...RYU?

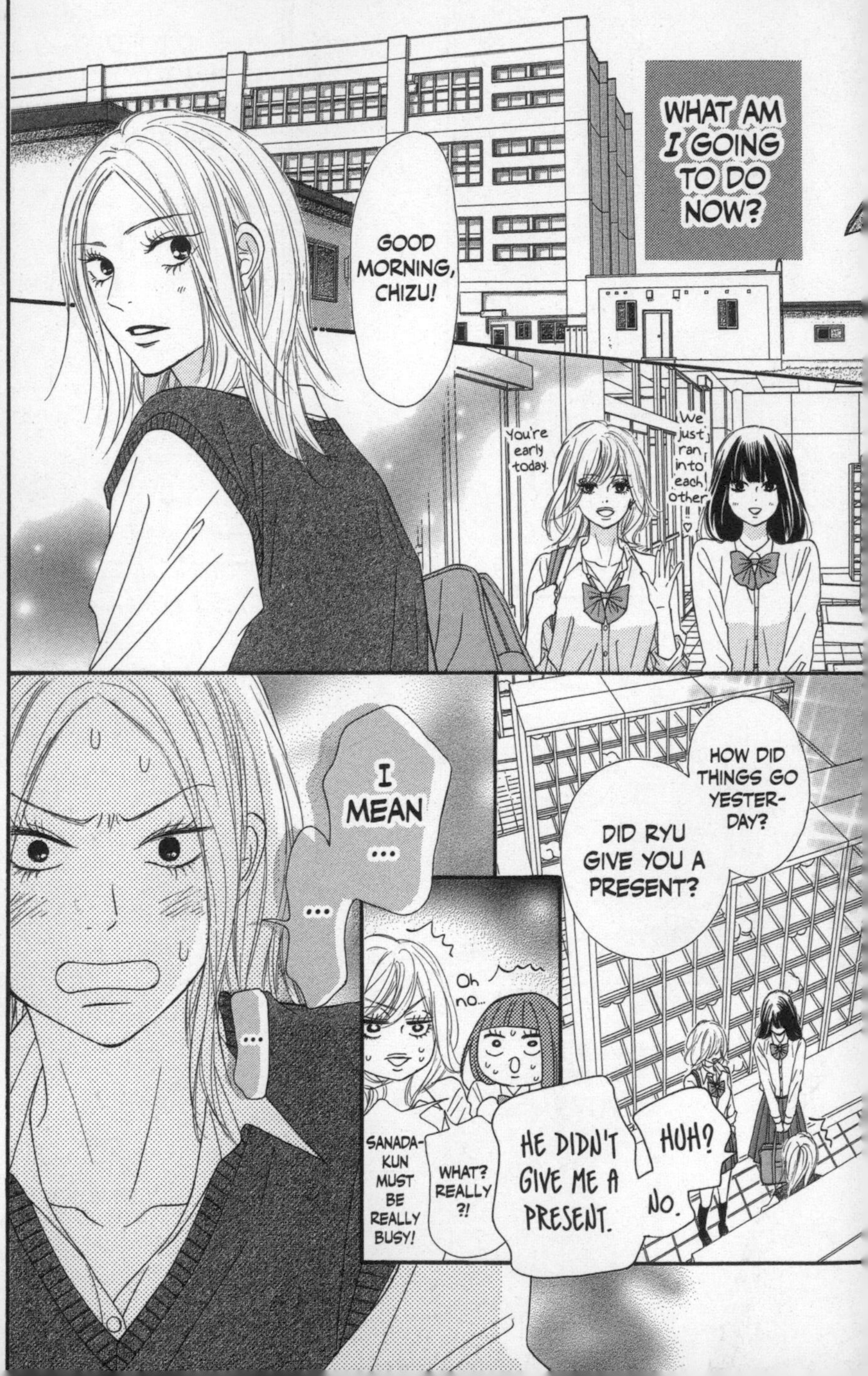
WHAT AM I GOING TO DO NOW?
GOOD MORNING, CHIZU!
We just ran into each other!! ♡
You're early today.
HOW DID THINGS GO YESTER-DAY?
DID RYU GIVE YOU A PRESENT?
HUH?
No.
HE DIDN'T GIVE ME A PRESENT.
WHAT? REALLY?!
SANADA-KUN MUST BE REALLY BUSY!
Oh no...
I MEAN...
...
...

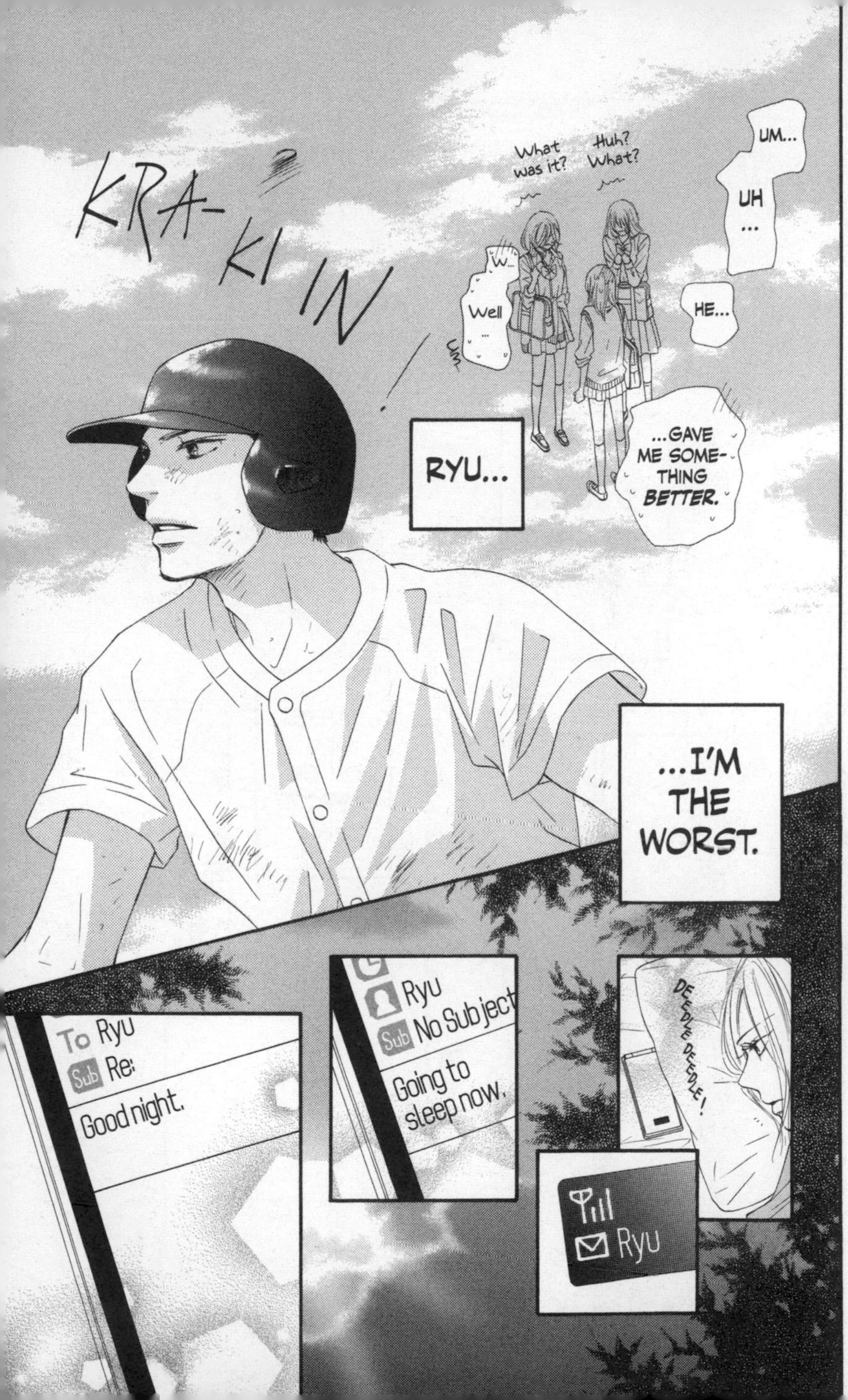
UM...
UH ...
HE...
...GAVE ME SOME-THING BETTER.
Huh? What?
What was it?
W... Well ... Um...
RYU...
KRA-KI IN
...I'M THE WORST.
DEEDLE DEEDLE DEEDLE!
Ryu
Ryu
No Subject
Going to sleep now.
To Ryu
Re:
Good night.

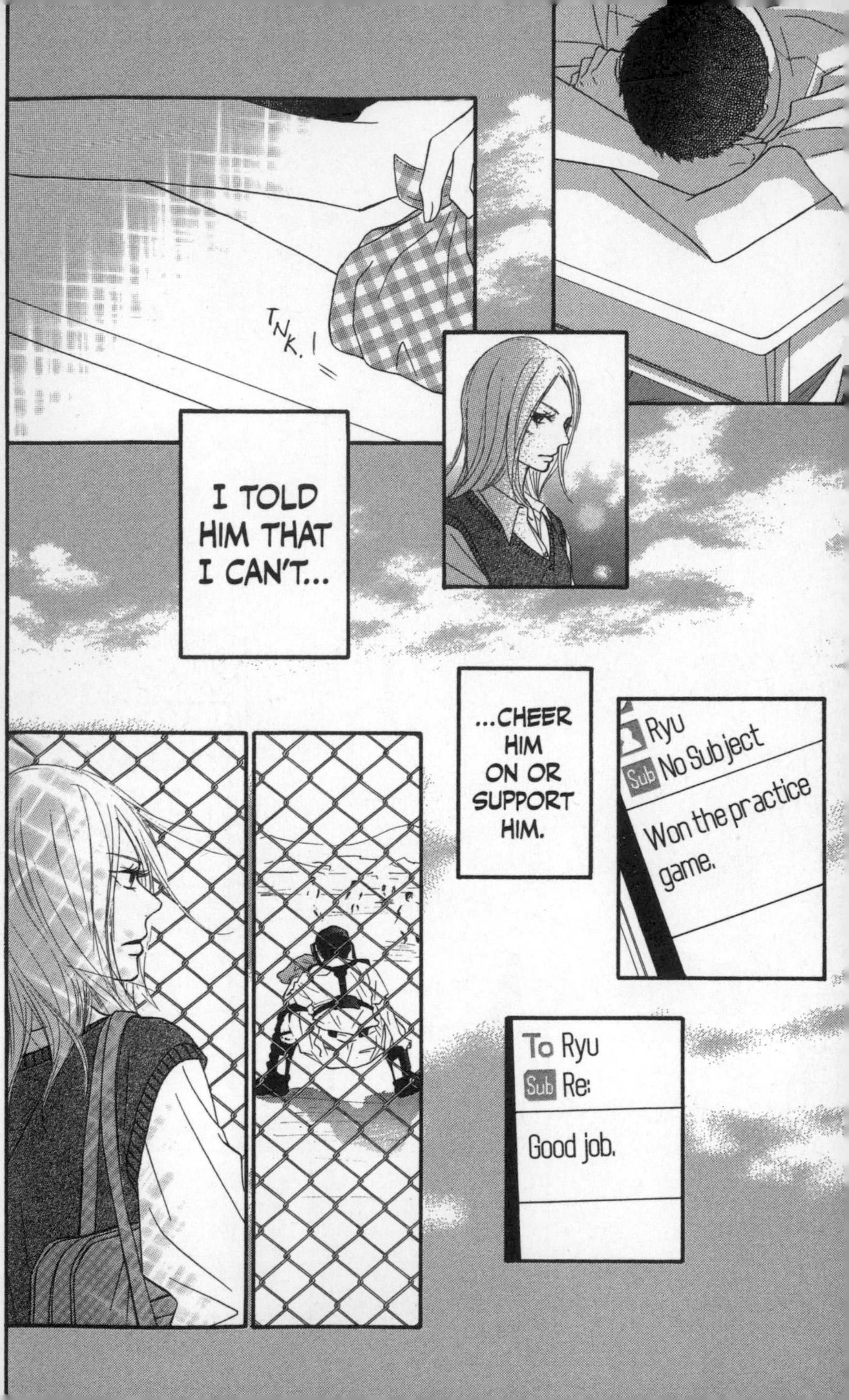
TNK!
I TOLD HIM THAT I CAN'T...
...CHEER HIM ON OR SUPPORT HIM.
Ryu
Sub No Subject
Won the practice game.
To Ryu
Sub Re:
Good job.

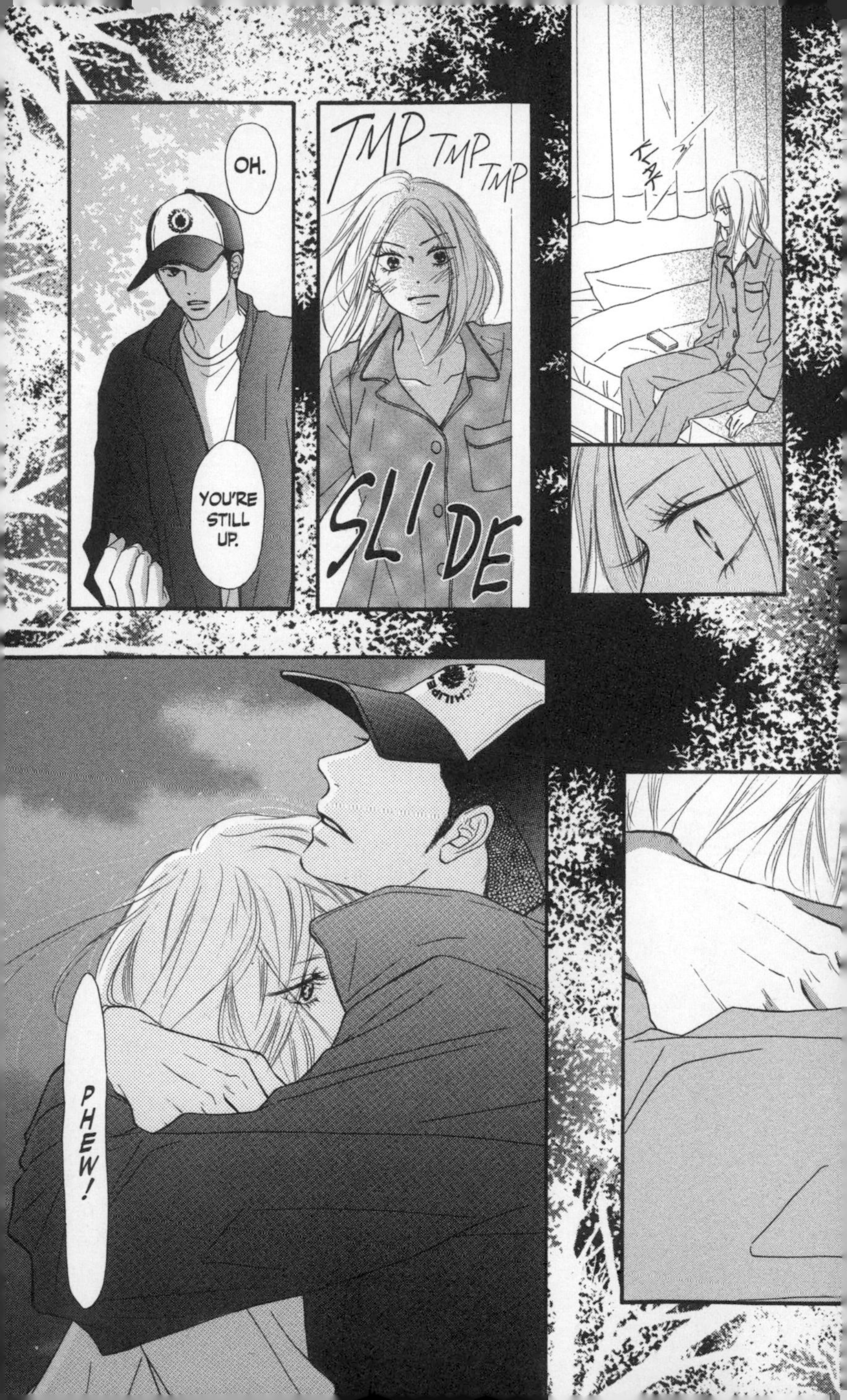
KLAK
TMP TMP TMP
SLIDE
OH.
YOU'RE STILL UP.
PHEW!

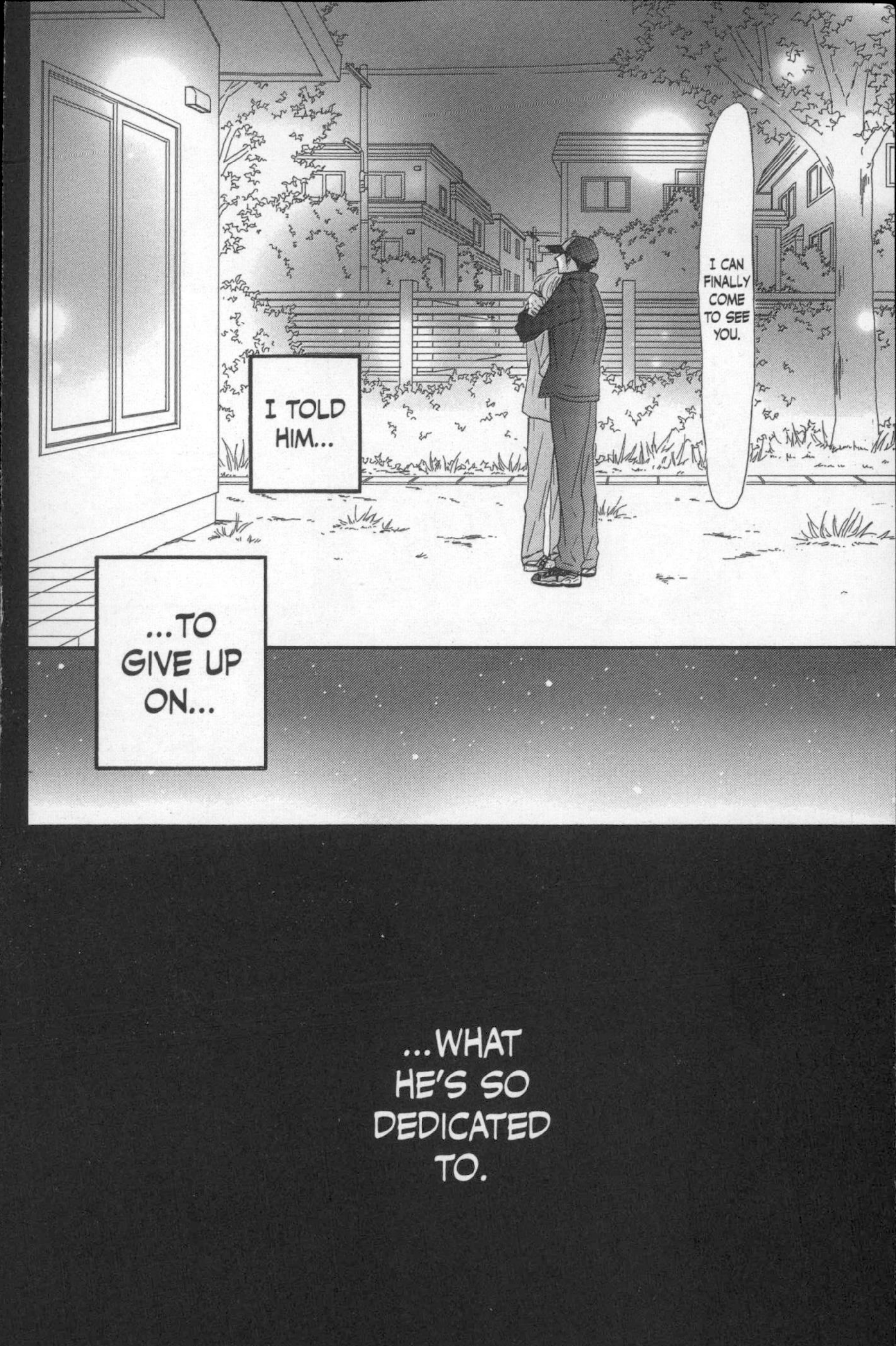
I CAN FINALLY COME TO SEE YOU.
I TOLD HIM...
...TO GIVE UP ON...
...WHAT HE'S SO DEDICATED TO.

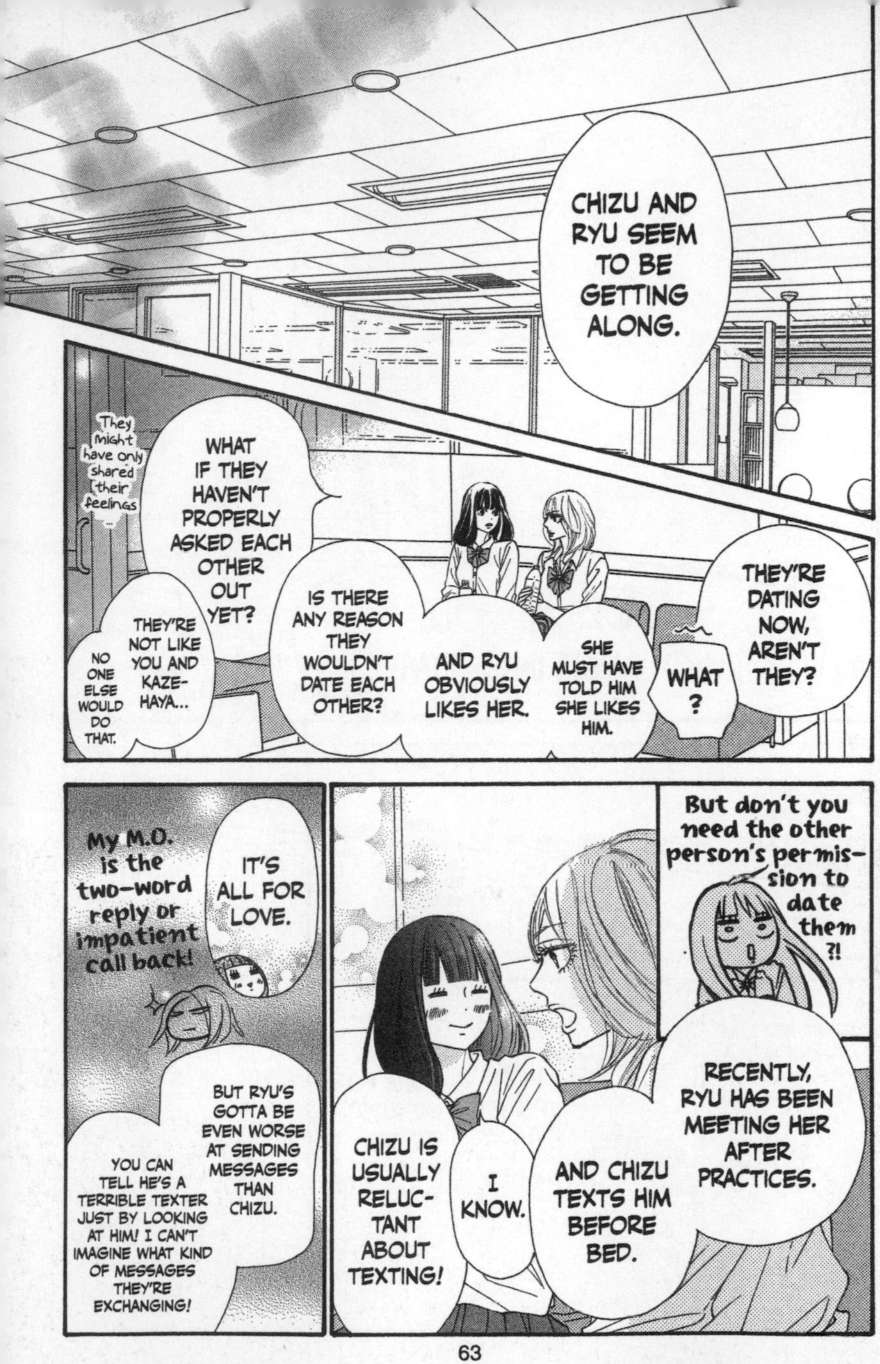
CHIZU AND RYU SEEM TO BE GETTING ALONG.
THEY'RE DATING NOW, AREN'T THEY?
WHAT?
SHE MUST HAVE TOLD HIM SHE LIKES HIM.
AND RYU OBVIOUSLY LIKES HER.
IS THERE ANY REASON THEY WOULDN'T DATE EACH OTHER?
WHAT IF THEY HAVEN'T PROPERLY ASKED EACH OTHER OUT YET?
They might have only shared their feelings...
THEY'RE NOT LIKE YOU AND KAZE-HAYA...
NO ONE ELSE WOULD DO THAT.
But don't you need the other person's permission to date them?!
RECENTLY, RYU HAS BEEN MEETING HER AFTER PRACTICES.
AND CHIZU TEXTS HIM BEFORE BED.
I KNOW.
CHIZU IS USUALLY RELUCTANT ABOUT TEXTING!
IT'S ALL FOR LOVE.
My M.O. is the two-word reply or impatient call back!
BUT RYU'S GOTTA BE EVEN WORSE AT SENDING MESSAGES THAN CHIZU.
YOU CAN TELL HE'S A TERRIBLE TEXTER JUST BY LOOKING AT HIM! I CAN'T IMAGINE WHAT KIND OF MESSAGES THEY'RE EXCHANGING!

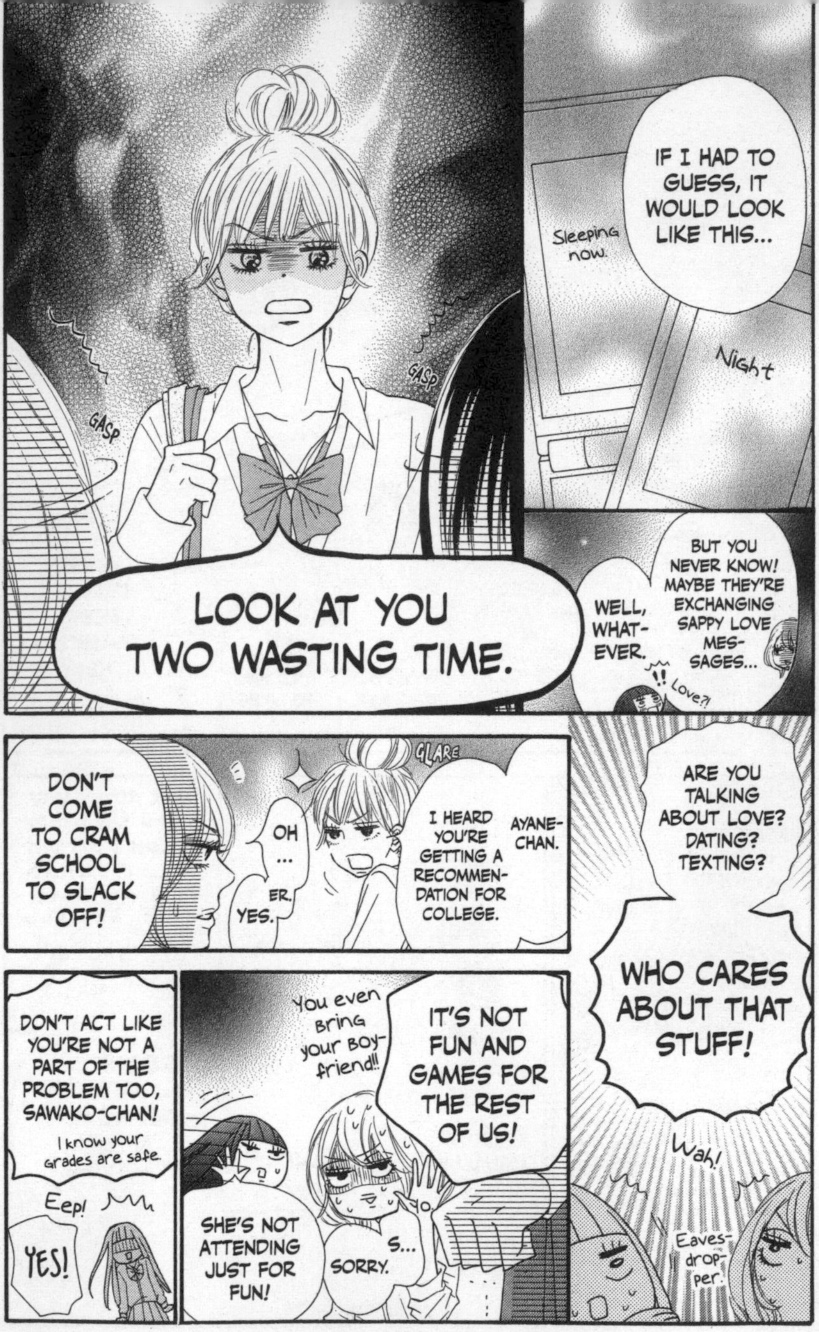
IF I HAD TO GUESS, IT WOULD LOOK LIKE THIS...
Sleeping now.
Night
BUT YOU NEVER KNOW! MAYBE THEY'RE EXCHANGING SAPPY LOVE MES-SAGES...
WELL, WHAT-EVER.
!! Love?!
GASP
GASP
LOOK AT YOU TWO WASTING TIME.
ARE YOU TALKING ABOUT LOVE? DATING? TEXTING?
WHO CARES ABOUT THAT STUFF!
Wah!
Eaves-drop-per.
GLARE
AYANE-CHAN.
I HEARD YOU'RE GETTING A RECOMMEN-DATION FOR COLLEGE.
OH ...
ER. YES.
DON'T COME TO CRAM SCHOOL TO SLACK OFF!
IT'S NOT FUN AND GAMES FOR THE REST OF US!
You even bring your boy-friend!!
Yo.
S... SORRY.
SHE'S NOT ATTENDING JUST FOR FUN!
DON'T ACT LIKE YOU'RE NOT A PART OF THE PROBLEM TOO, SAWAKO-CHAN!
I know your grades are safe.
Eep!
YES!

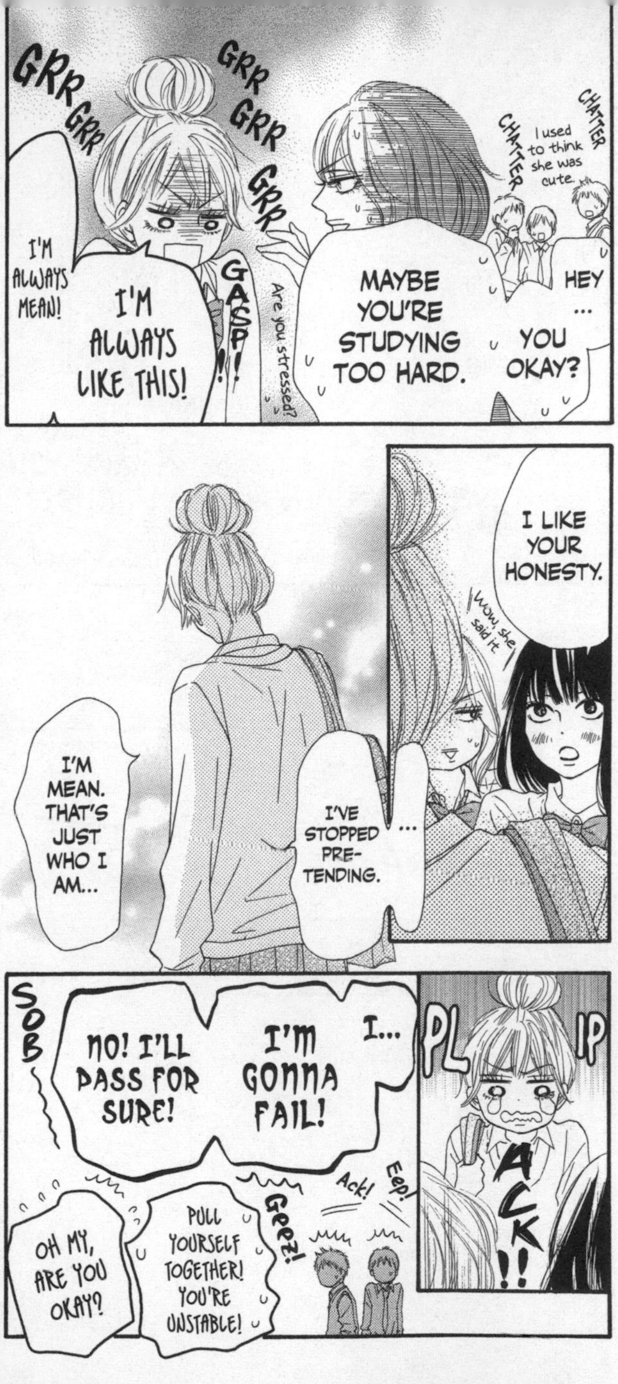
CHATTER
CHATTER
I used to think she was cute.
HEY ... YOU OKAY?
MAYBE YOU'RE STUDYING TOO HARD.
Are you stressed?
GRR
GRR
GRR
GRR
GRR
GASP!!
I'M ALWAYS LIKE THIS!
I'M ALWAYS MEAN!
I LIKE YOUR HONESTY.
Wow, she said it.
I'VE STOPPED PRE-TENDING. ...
I'M MEAN. THAT'S JUST WHO I AM...
PLIP
ACK!!
I...
I'M GONNA FAIL!
NO! I'LL PASS FOR SURE!
SOB
Eep!
Ack!
Geez!
PULL YOURSELF TOGETHER! YOU'RE UNSTABLE!
OH MY, ARE YOU OKAY?

KARUPIN on JAPAN 2

Recently (well, not that recently...), I went to get a health checkup. I'd never seriously gotten one before, but this time I did. My assistants did too.

There were some difficult tests like the stomach camera (it's hard because of the gagging) and another one that was challenging because you could only drink liquids the day before. I thought it would be easy, but...

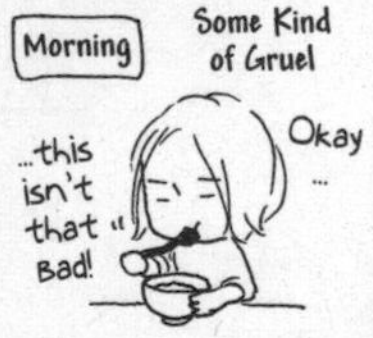
Morning
Some Kind of Gruel
...this isn't that bad!
Okay ...

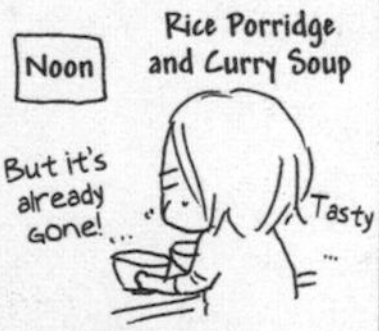
Noon
Rice Porridge and Curry Soup
But it's already gone!
Tasty ...

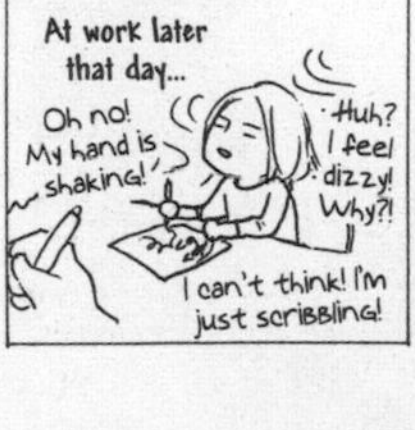
At work later that day...
Oh no! My hand is shaking!
Huh? I feel dizzy! Why?!
I can't think! I'm just scribbling!

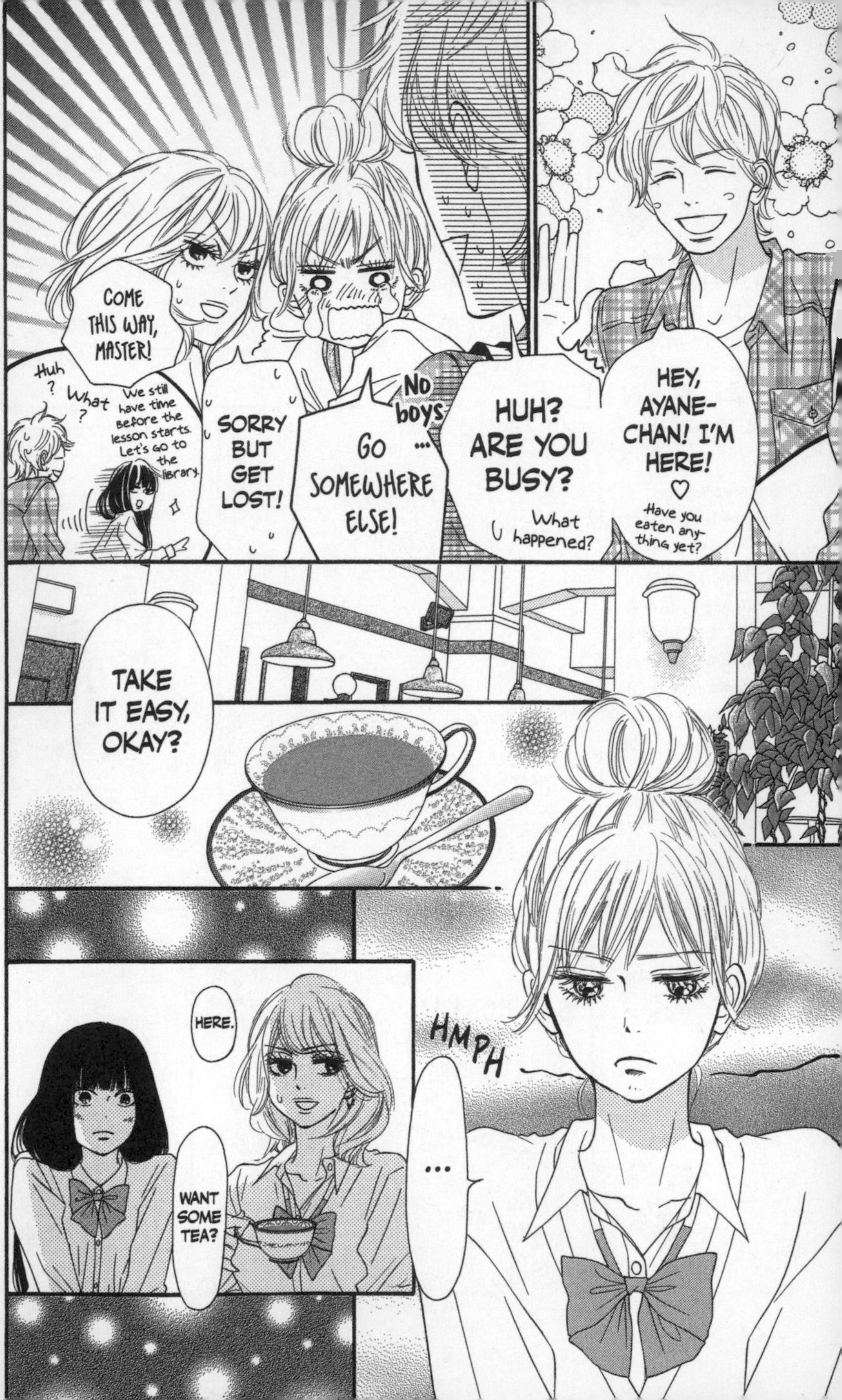
HEY, AYANE-CHAN! I'M HERE! ♡
Have you eaten anything yet?
HUH? ARE YOU BUSY?
What happened?
No boys...
GO SOMEWHERE ELSE!
SORRY BUT GET LOST!
COME THIS WAY, MASTER!
We still have time before the lesson starts. Let's go to the library.
Huh?
What?
TAKE IT EASY, OKAY?
HMPH
...
HERE.
WANT SOME TEA?

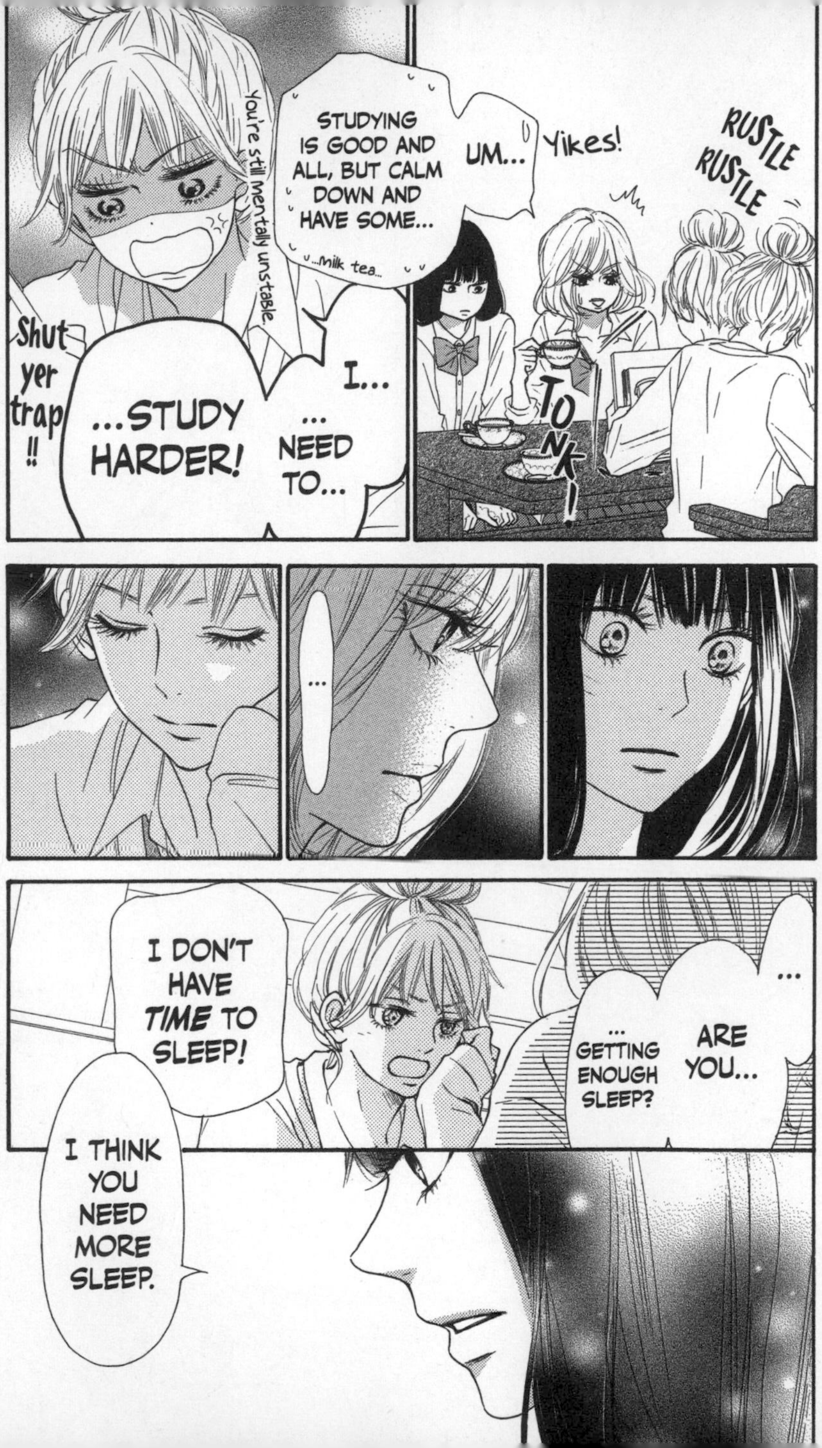
RUSTLE
RUSTLE
Yikes!
UM...
STUDYING IS GOOD AND ALL, BUT CALM DOWN AND HAVE SOME...
...milk tea...
TONK!
You're still mentally unstable.
I...
... NEED TO...
...STUDY HARDER!
Shut yer trap!!
...
...
ARE YOU...
... GETTING ENOUGH SLEEP?
I DON'T HAVE *TIME* TO SLEEP!
I THINK YOU NEED MORE SLEEP.

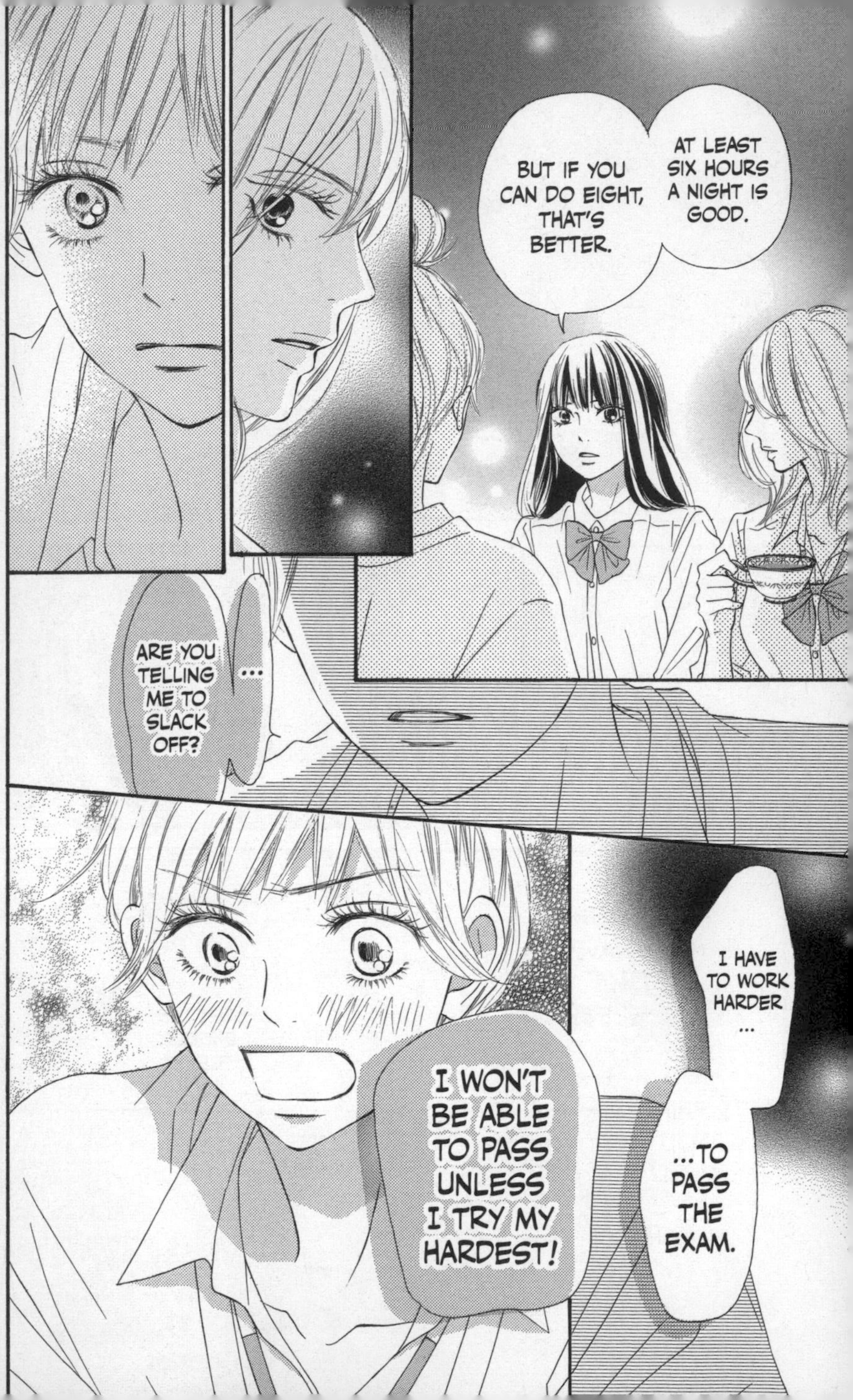
AT LEAST SIX HOURS A NIGHT IS GOOD.
BUT IF YOU CAN DO EIGHT, THAT'S BETTER.
...
ARE YOU TELLING ME TO SLACK OFF?
I HAVE TO WORK HARDER ...
...TO PASS THE EXAM.
I WON'T BE ABLE TO PASS UNLESS I TRY MY HARDEST!

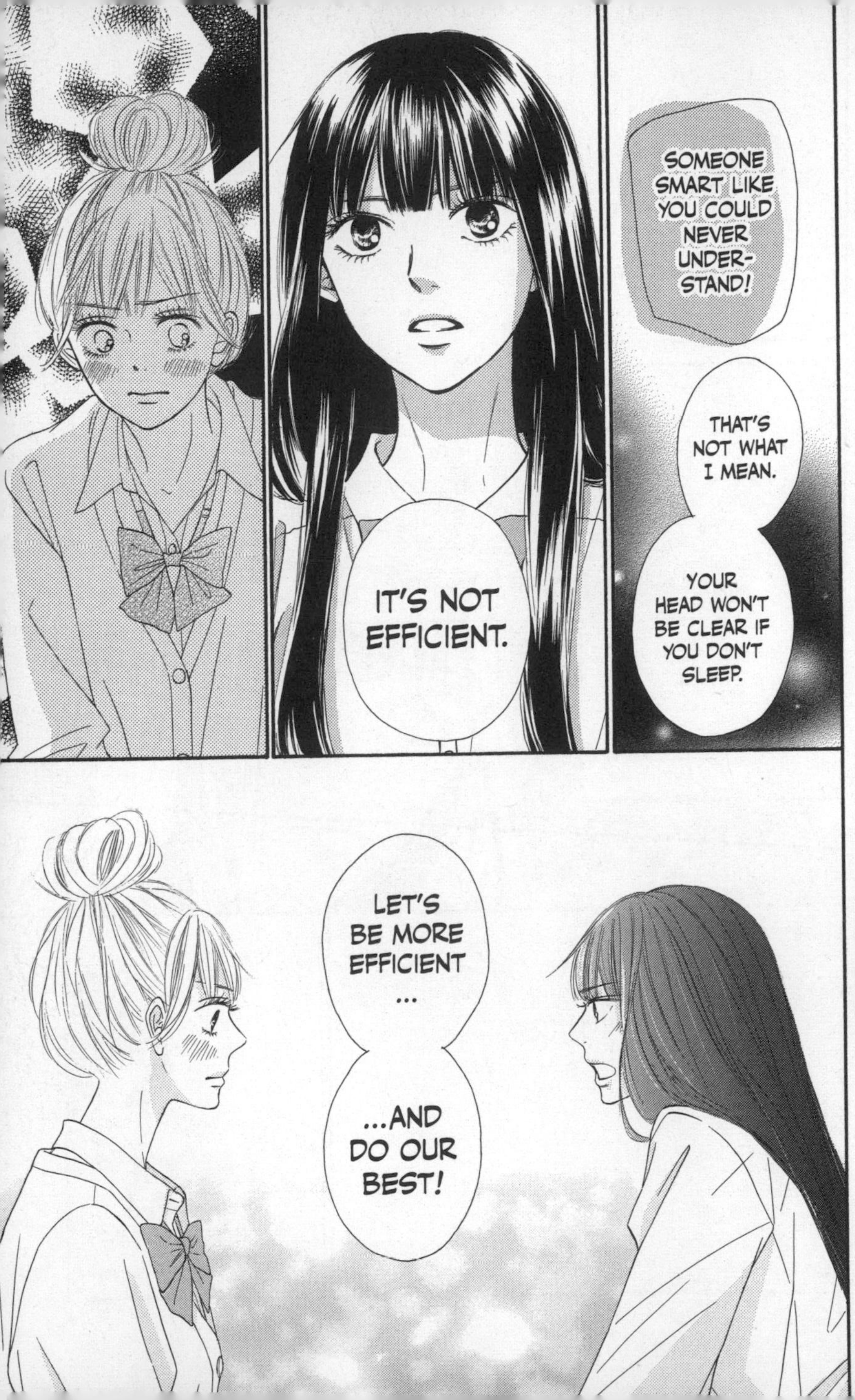
SOMEONE SMART LIKE YOU COULD NEVER UNDER-STAND!
THAT'S NOT WHAT I MEAN.
YOUR HEAD WON'T BE CLEAR IF YOU DON'T SLEEP.
IT'S NOT EFFICIENT.
LET'S BE MORE EFFICIENT ...
...AND DO OUR BEST!

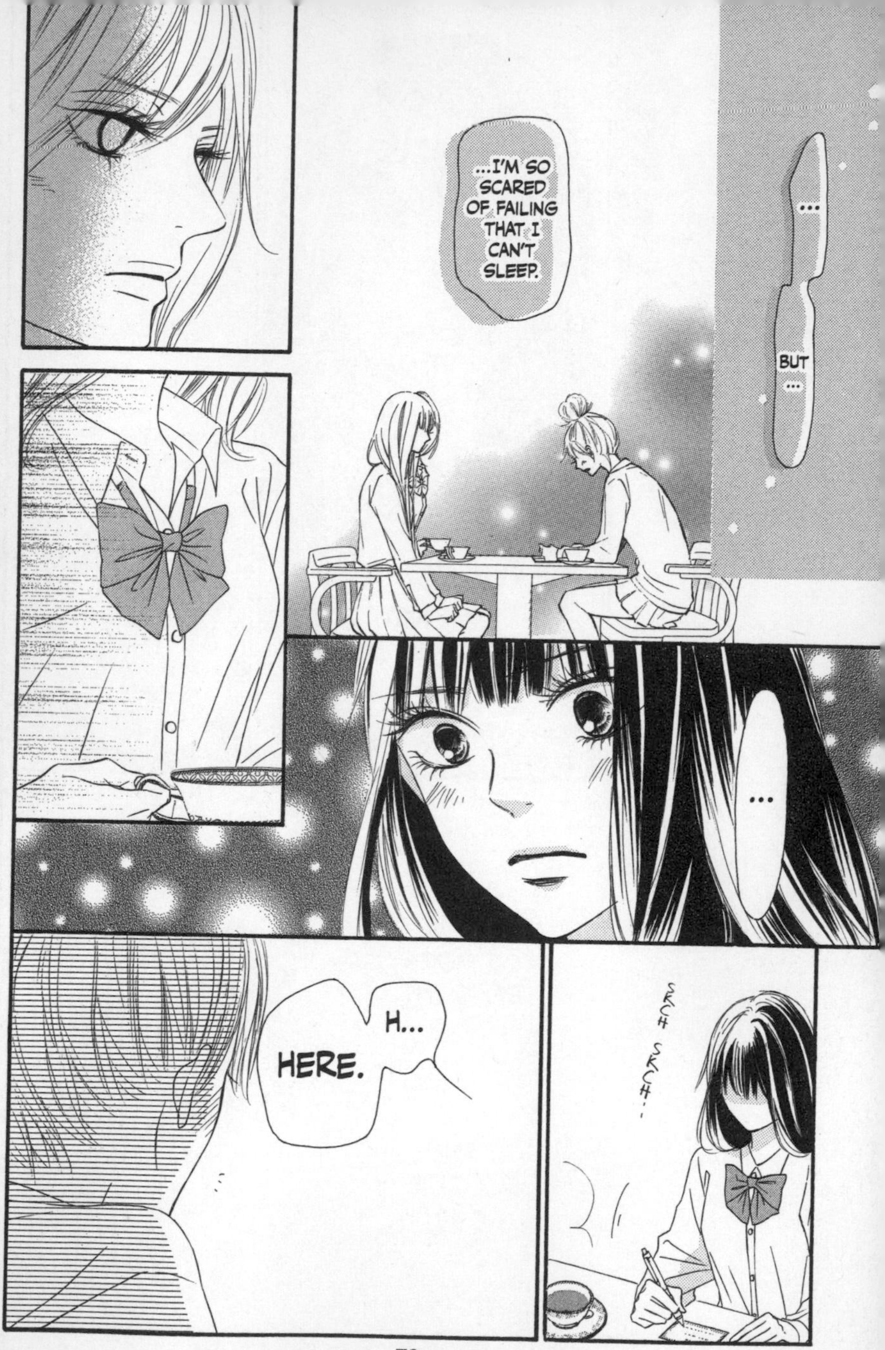
...
BUT ...
...I'M SO SCARED OF FAILING THAT I CAN'T SLEEP.
...
SKCH SKCH..
H...
HERE.

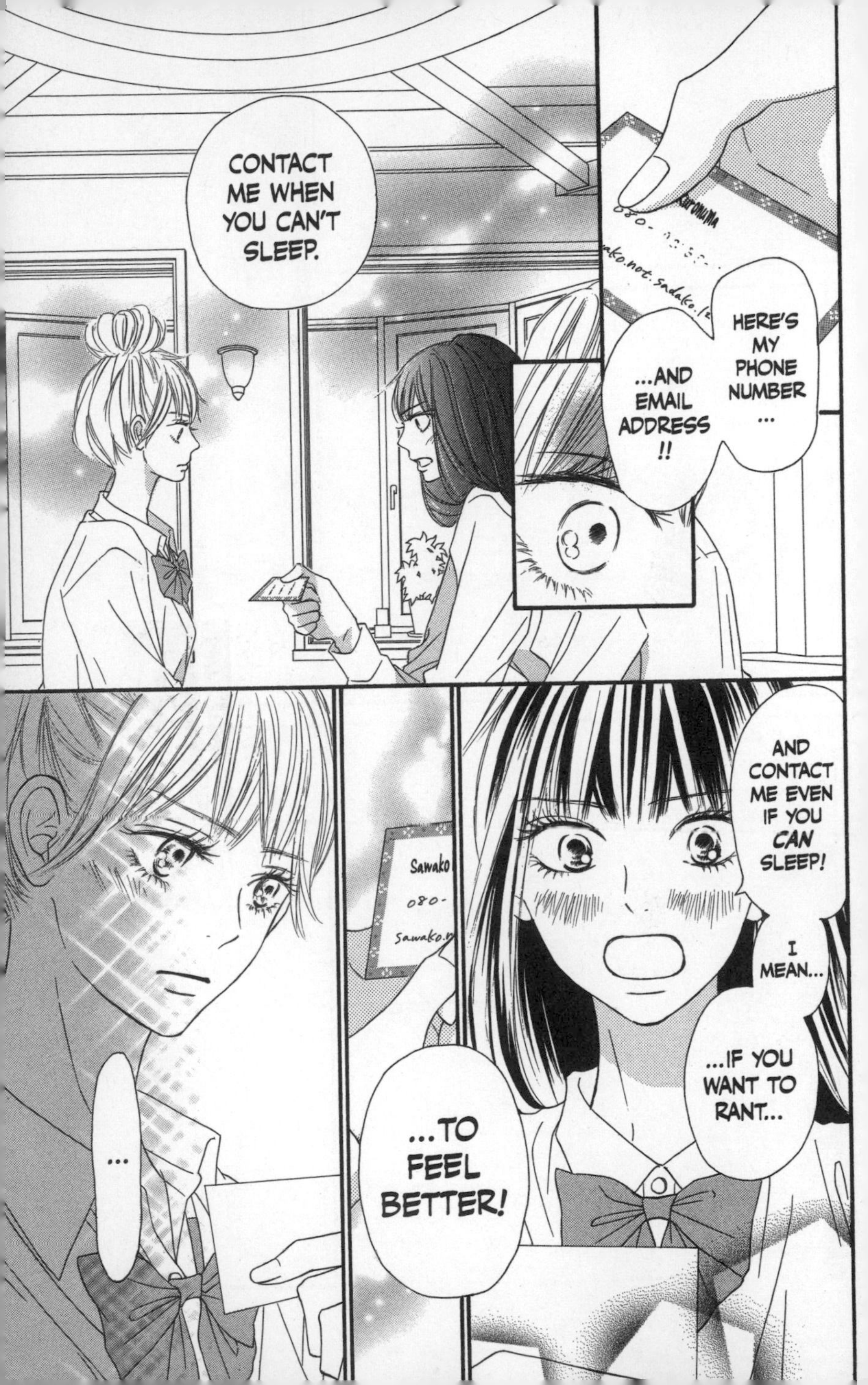
HERE'S MY PHONE NUMBER ...
...AND EMAIL ADDRESS !!
CONTACT ME WHEN YOU CAN'T SLEEP.
AND CONTACT ME EVEN IF YOU *CAN* SLEEP!
I MEAN...
...IF YOU WANT TO RANT...
...TO FEEL BETTER!
...

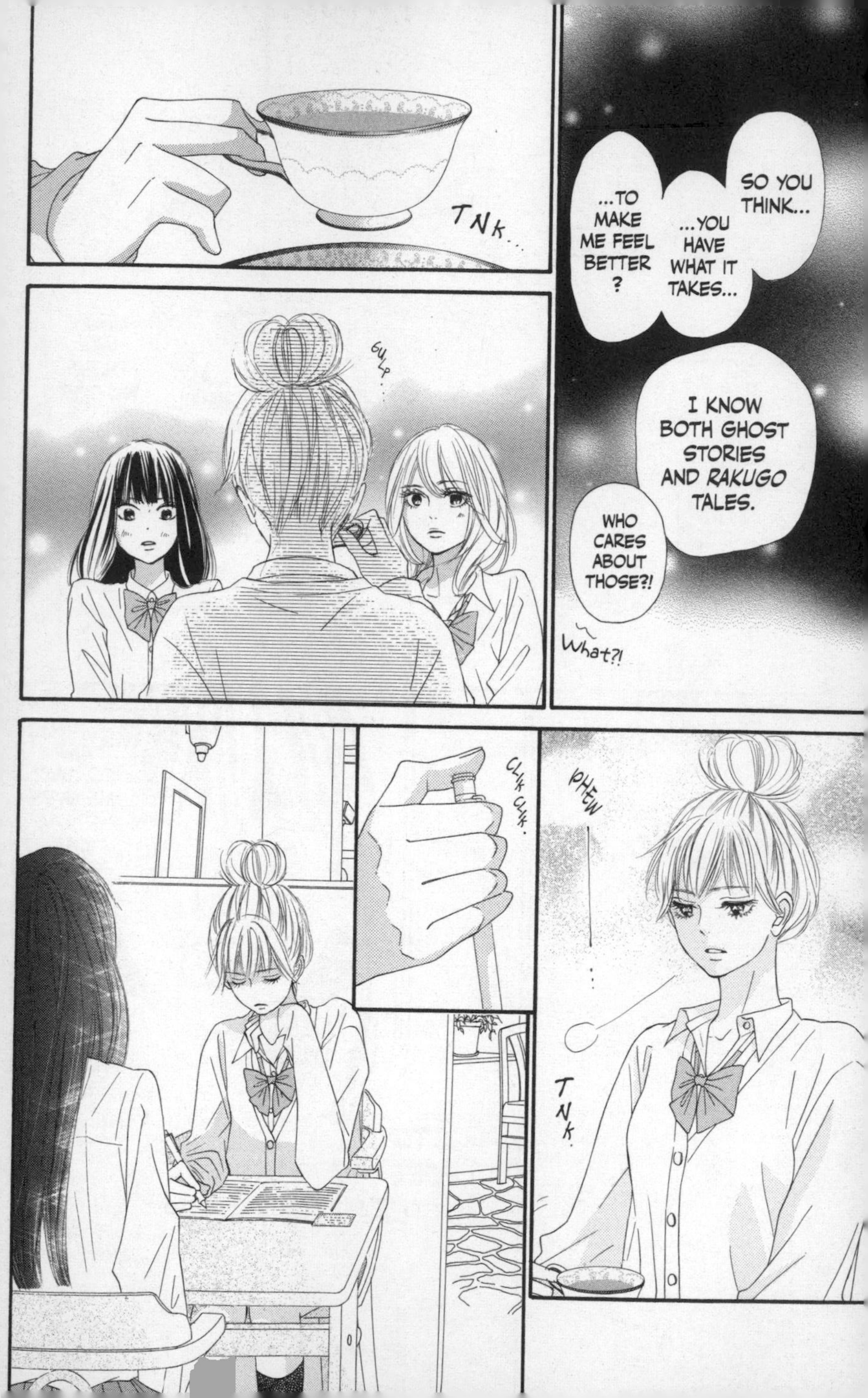
SO YOU THINK...
...YOU HAVE WHAT IT TAKES...
...TO MAKE ME FEEL BETTER ?
I KNOW BOTH GHOST STORIES AND RAKUGO TALES.
WHO CARES ABOUT THOSE?!
What?!
TNk...
GULP
PHEW
TNk.
CLIK CLIK.

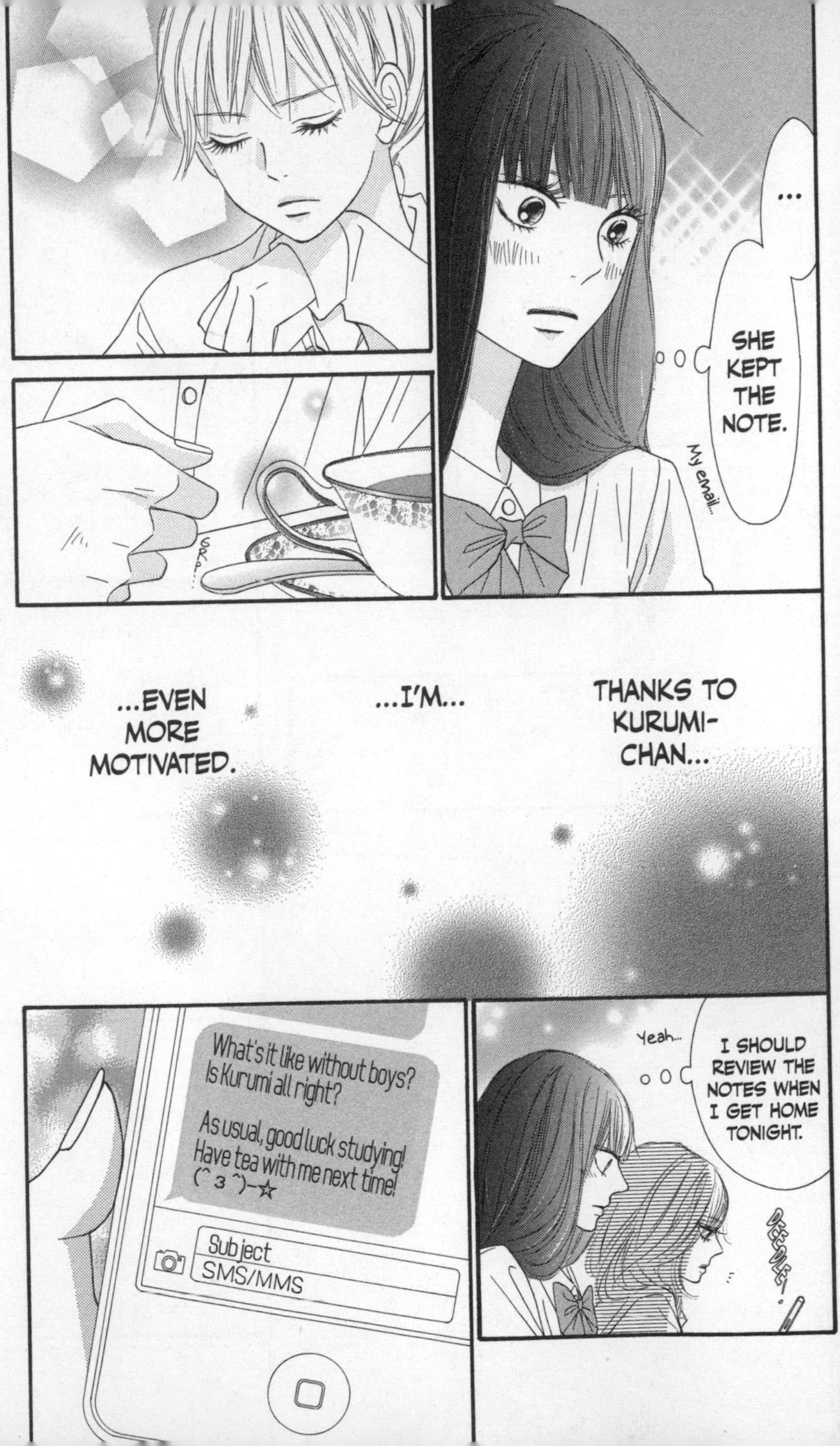
...
SHE KEPT THE NOTE.
My email...
ERP...
THANKS TO KURUMI-CHAN...
...I'M...
...EVEN MORE MOTIVATED.
Yeah...
I SHOULD REVIEW THE NOTES WHEN I GET HOME TONIGHT.
What's it like without boys? Is Kurumi all right?
As usual, good luck studying! Have tea with me next time! (^ 3 ^)-☆
Subject
SMS/MMS

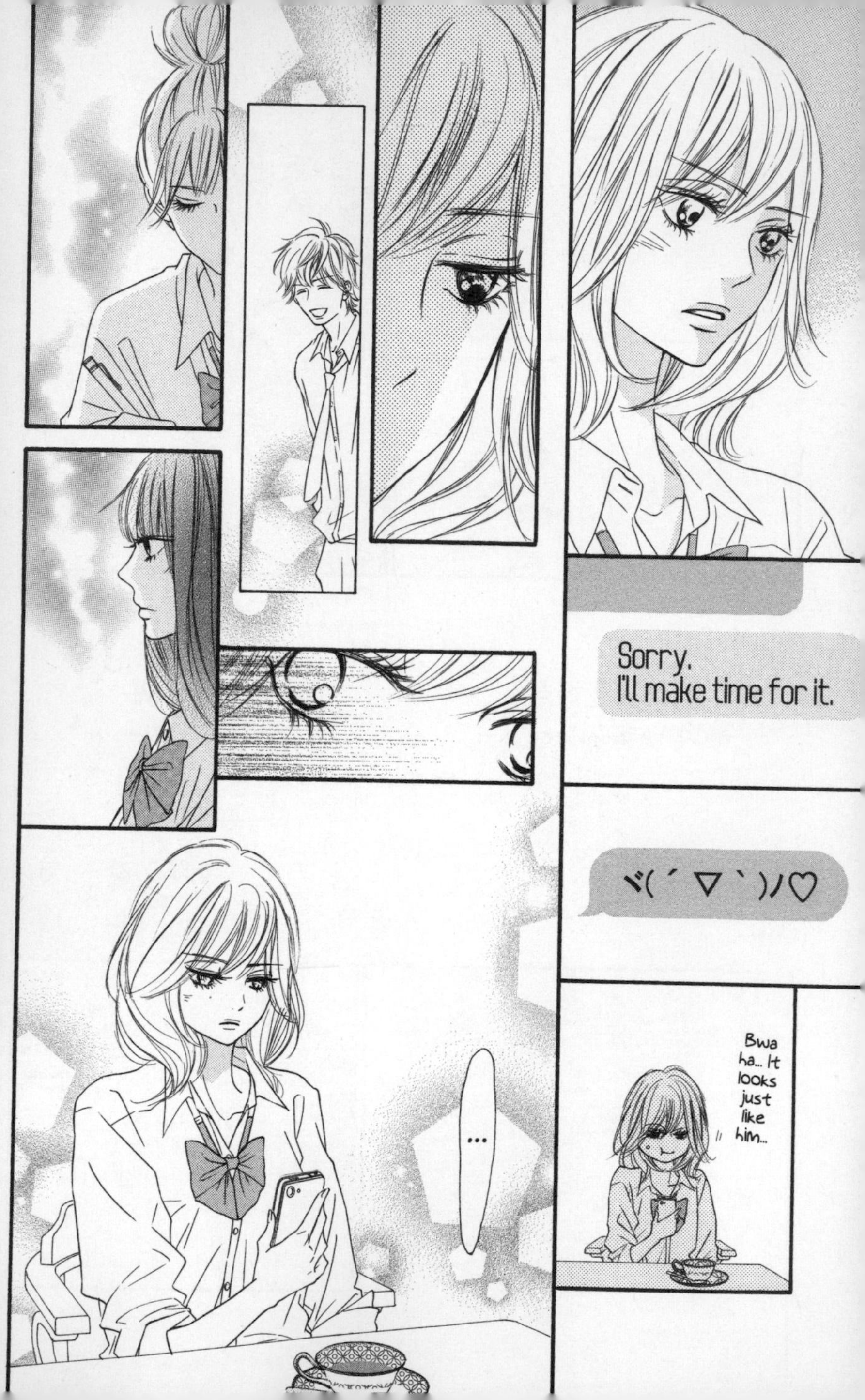
Sorry.
I'll make time for it.
ヾ(´▽`)ノ♡
Bwa ha... It looks just like him...
...

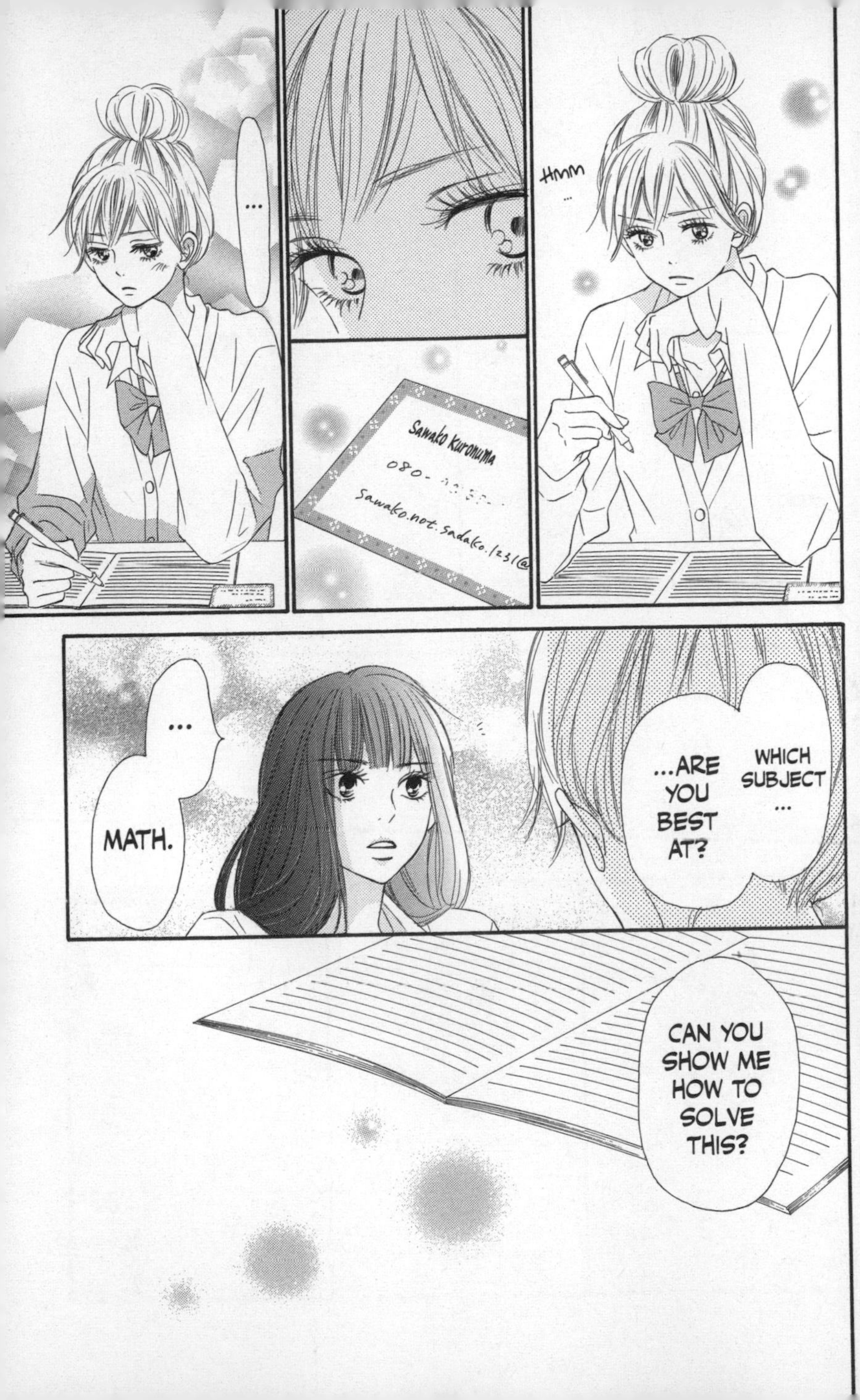

Hmm ...
Sawako Kuronuma
080-
sawako.not.sadako.1231@
...
WHICH SUBJECT ... ...ARE YOU BEST AT?
... MATH.
CAN YOU SHOW ME HOW TO SOLVE THIS?

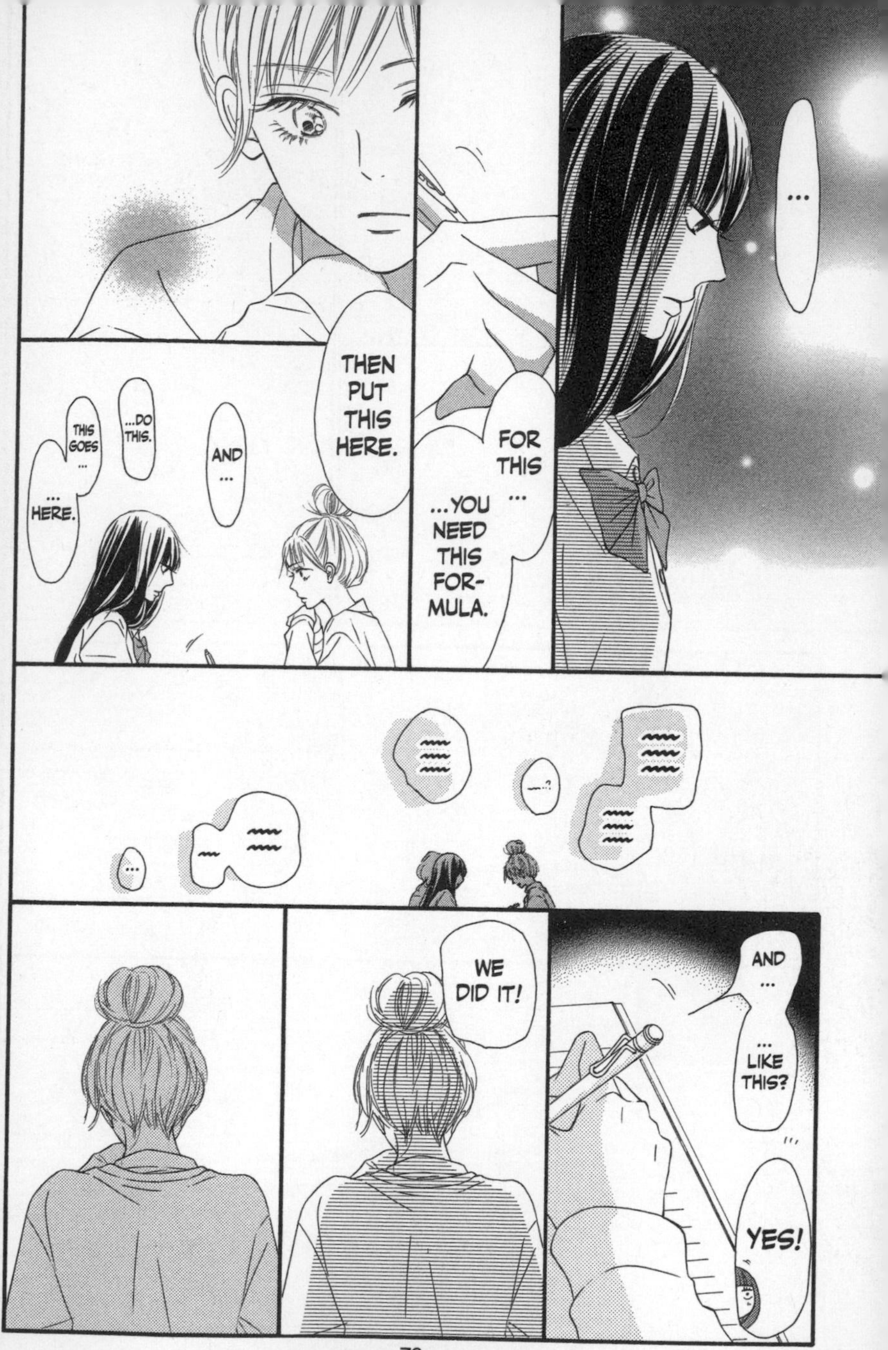
...
FOR THIS ...
...YOU NEED THIS FOR-MULA.
THEN PUT THIS HERE.
AND ...
...DO THIS.
THIS GOES ...
... HERE.
—?
...
AND ...
... LIKE THIS?
YES!
WE DID IT!

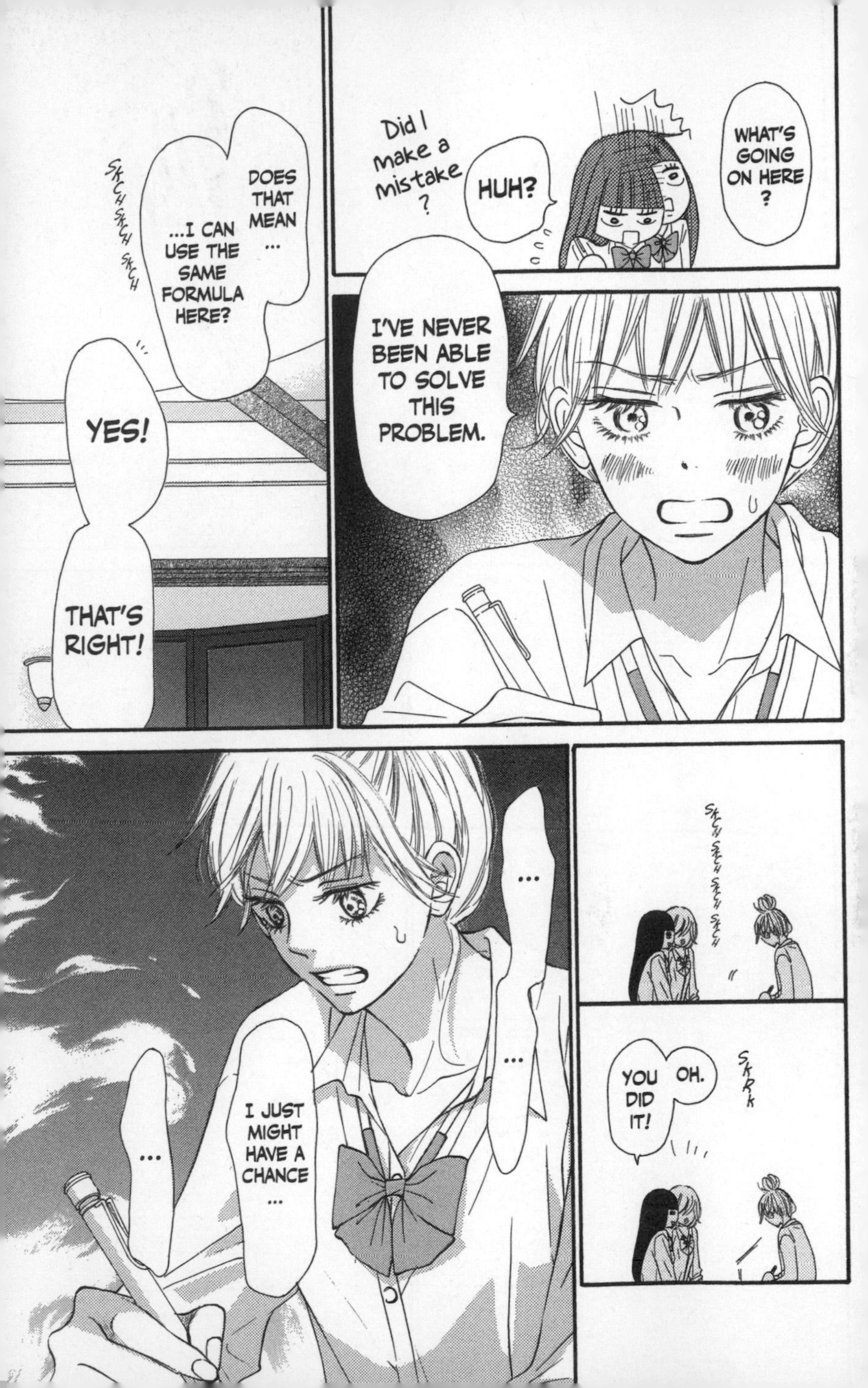
WHAT'S GOING ON HERE?
HUH?
Did I make a mistake?
I'VE NEVER BEEN ABLE TO SOLVE THIS PROBLEM.
DOES THAT MEAN...
...I CAN USE THE SAME FORMULA HERE?
SKCH SKCH SKCH
YES!
THAT'S RIGHT!
SKCH SKCH SKCH SKCH
OH.
YOU DID IT!
SKRK
...
...
I JUST MIGHT HAVE A CHANCE...
...

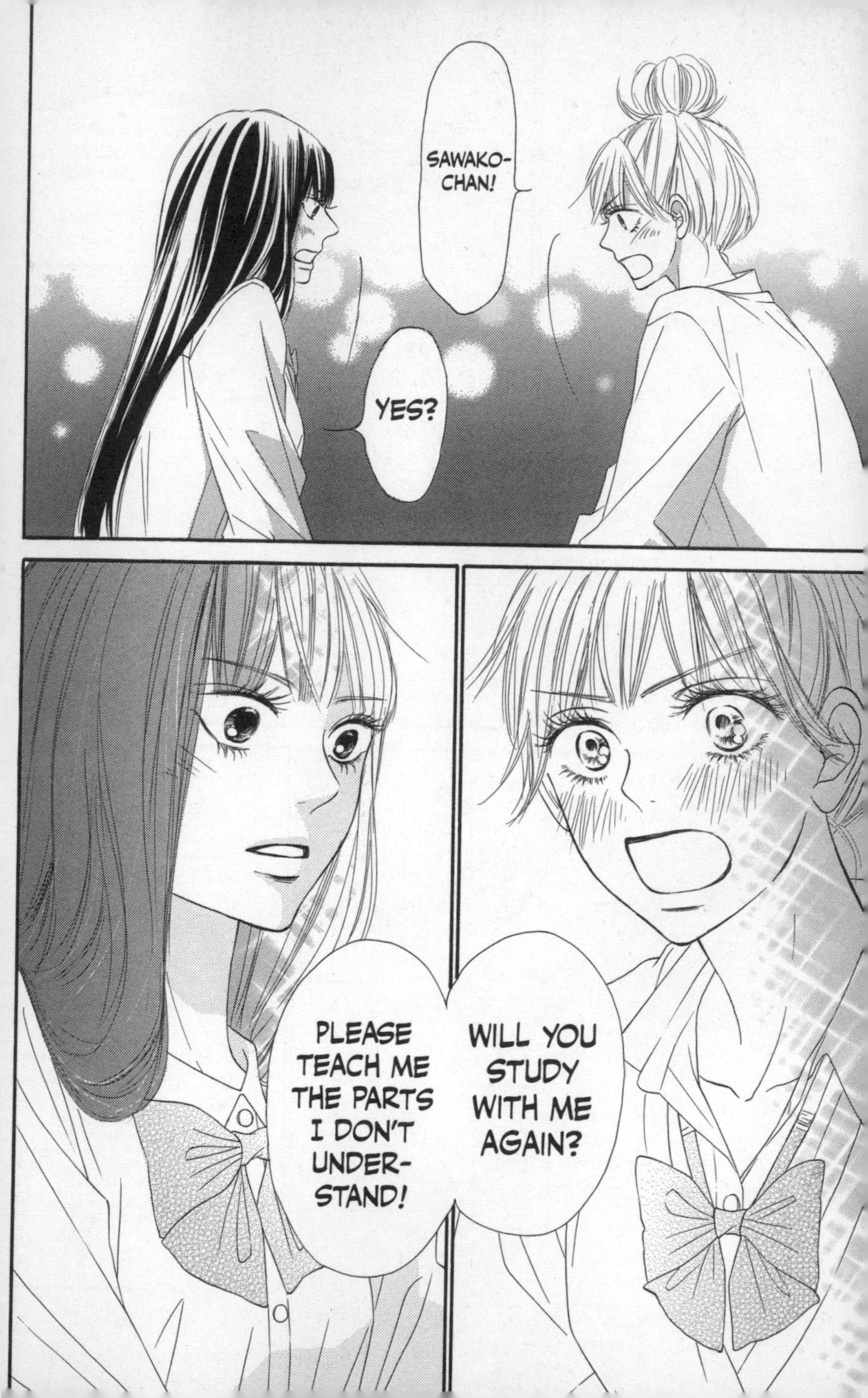
SAWAKO-CHAN!
YES?
WILL YOU STUDY WITH ME AGAIN?
PLEASE TEACH ME THE PARTS I DON'T UNDER-STAND!

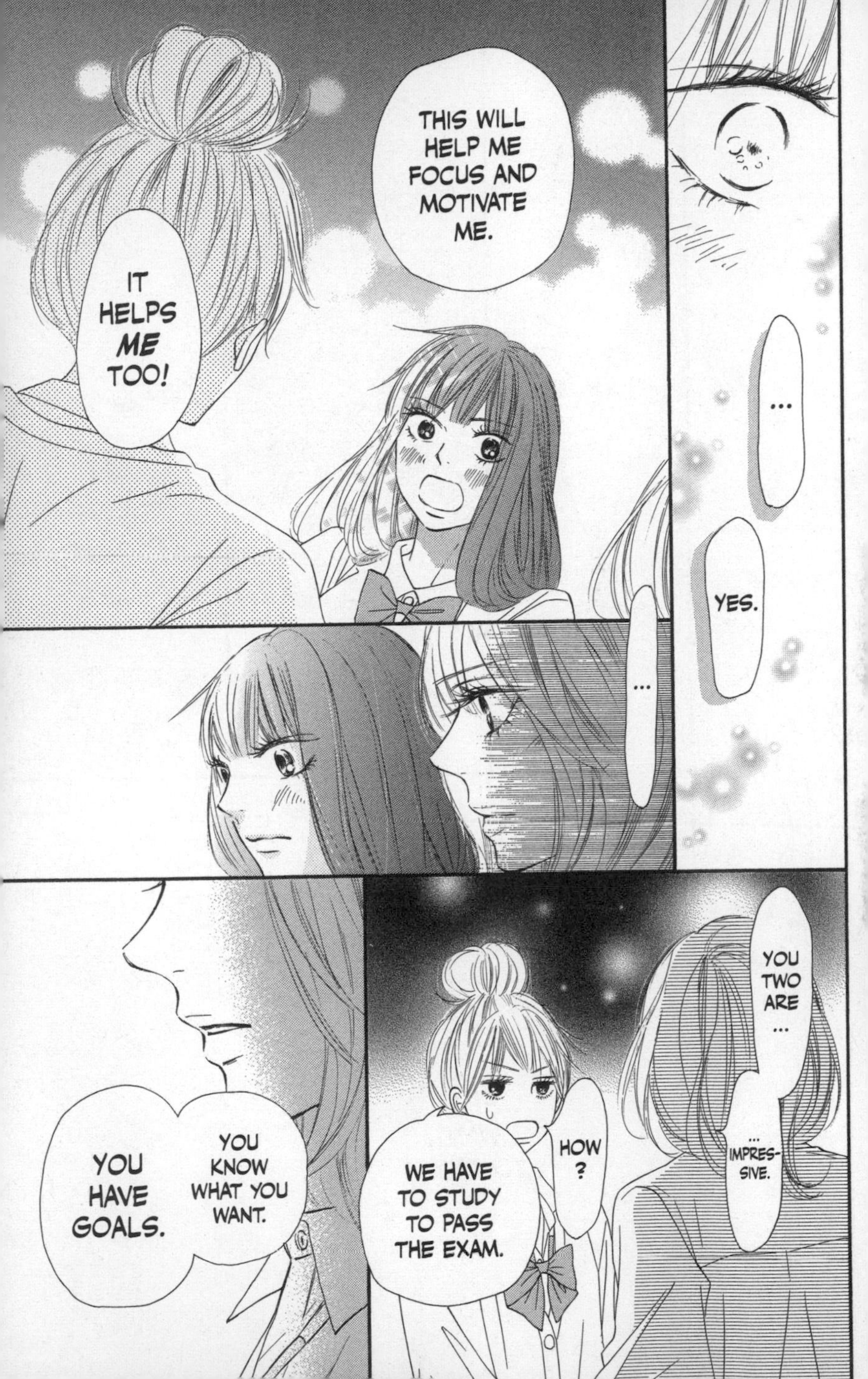
...
YES.
THIS WILL HELP ME FOCUS AND MOTIVATE ME.
IT HELPS *ME* TOO!
...
YOU TWO ARE ...
... IMPRES-SIVE.
HOW ?
WE HAVE TO STUDY TO PASS THE EXAM.
YOU KNOW WHAT YOU WANT.
YOU HAVE GOALS.

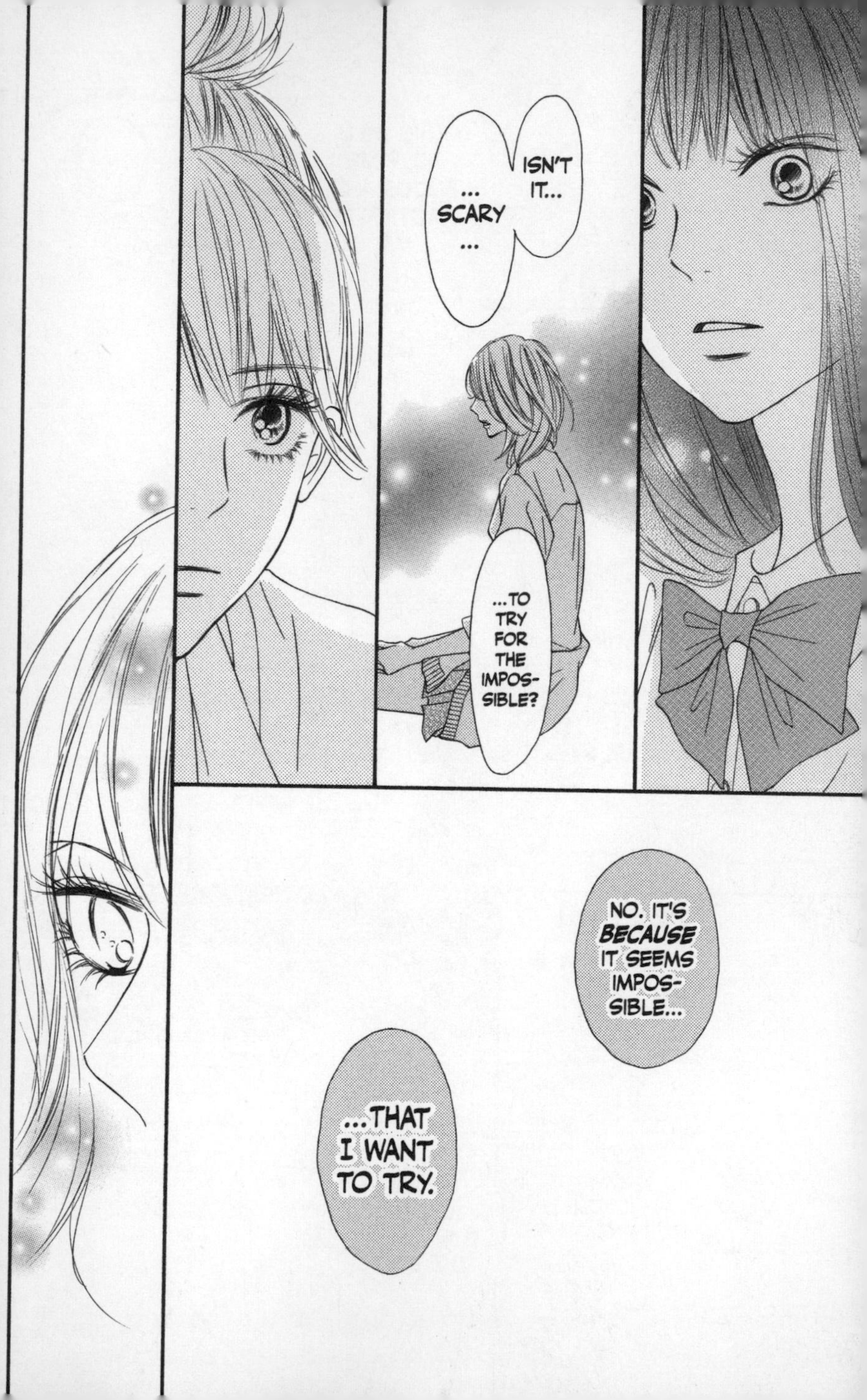
ISN'T IT...
...SCARY...
...TO TRY FOR THE IMPOSSIBLE?
NO. IT'S *BECAUSE* IT SEEMS IMPOSSIBLE...
...THAT I WANT TO TRY.

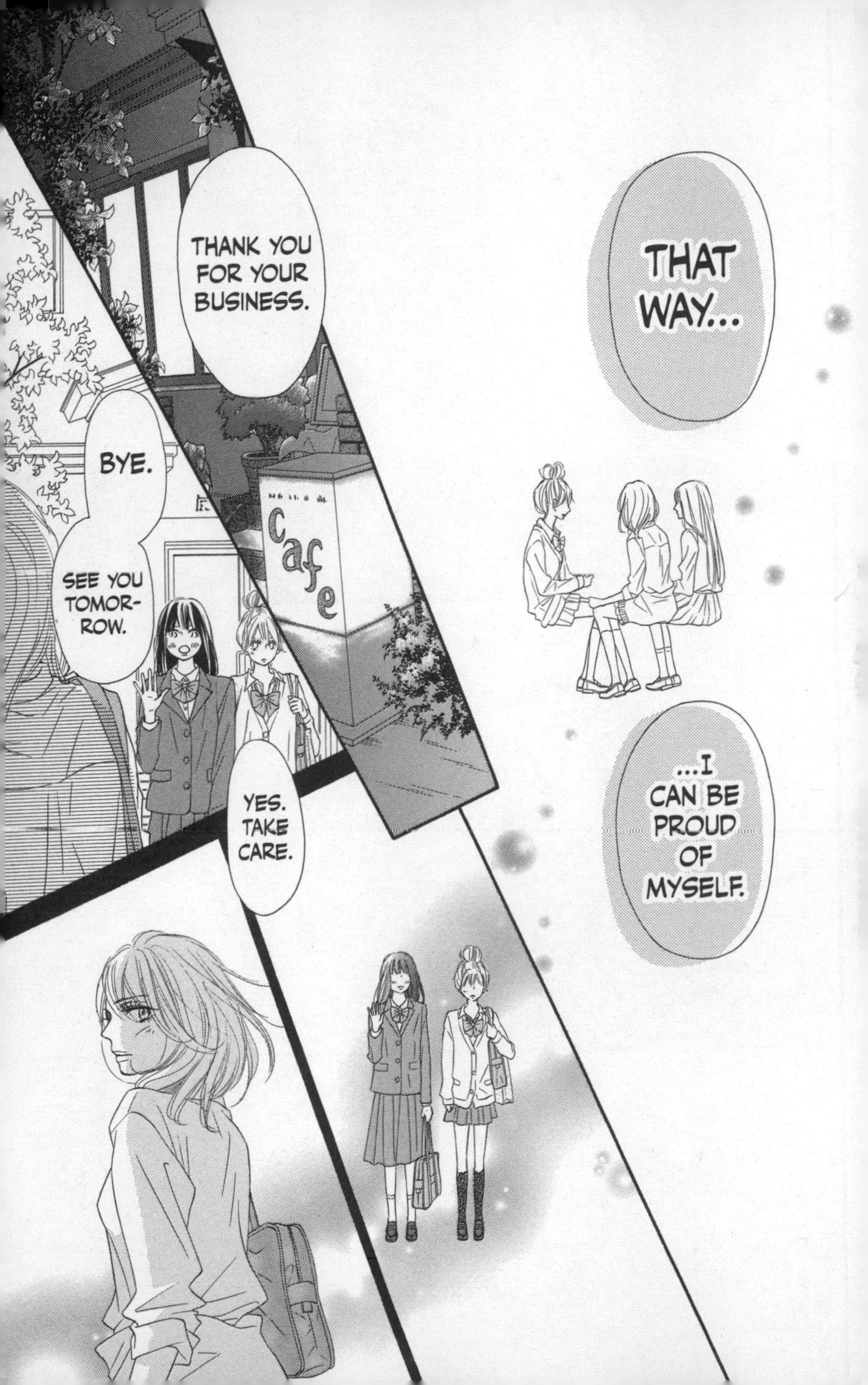
THAT WAY...
...I CAN BE PROUD OF MYSELF.
THANK YOU FOR YOUR BUSINESS.
cafe
BYE.
SEE YOU TOMORROW.
YES. TAKE CARE.

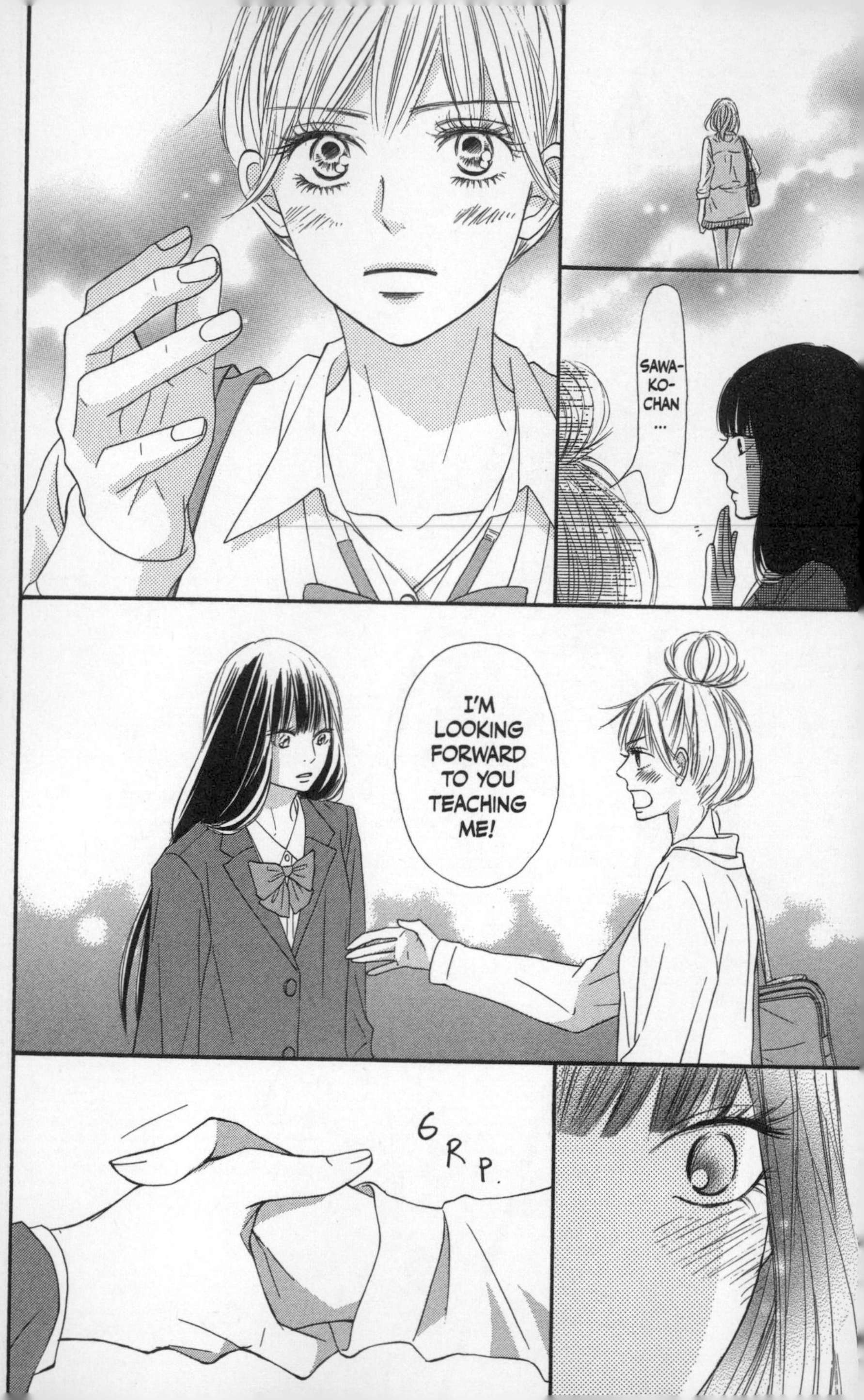
SAWAKO-CHAN...
I'M LOOKING FORWARD TO YOU TEACHING ME!
GRP.

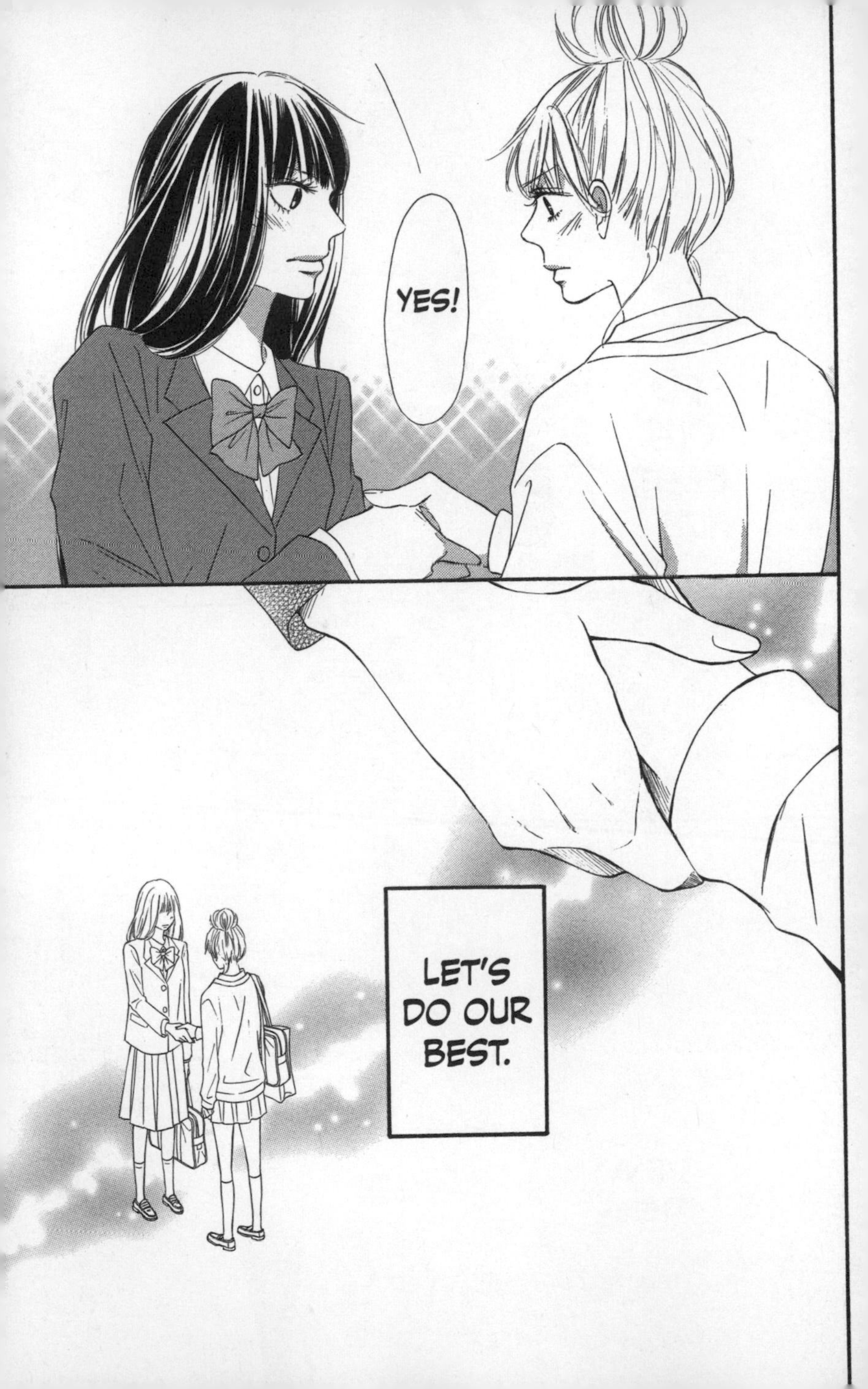
YES!
LET'S DO OUR BEST.

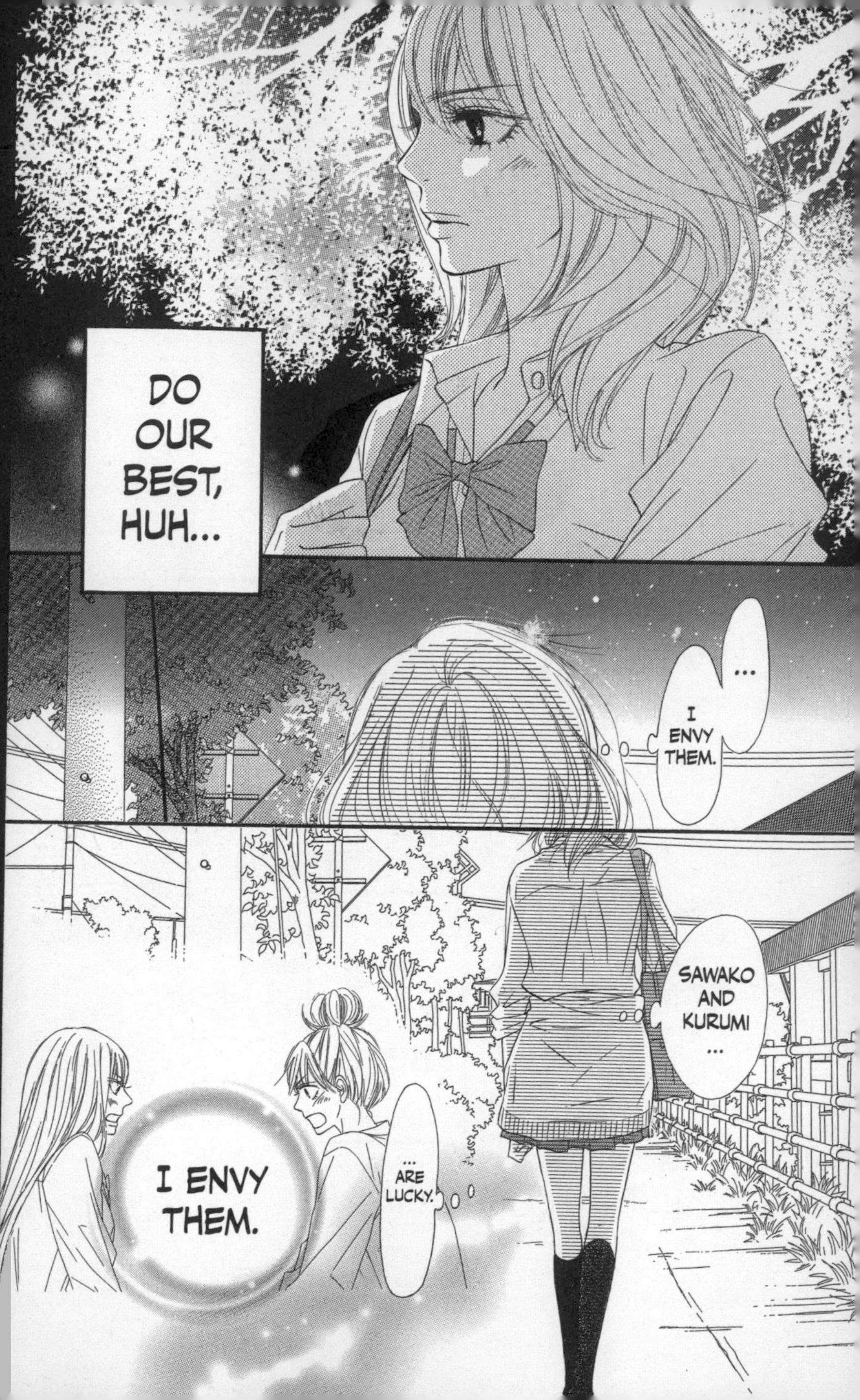
DO OUR BEST, HUH...
... I ENVY THEM.
SAWAKO AND KURUMI ...
... ARE LUCKY.
I ENVY THEM.

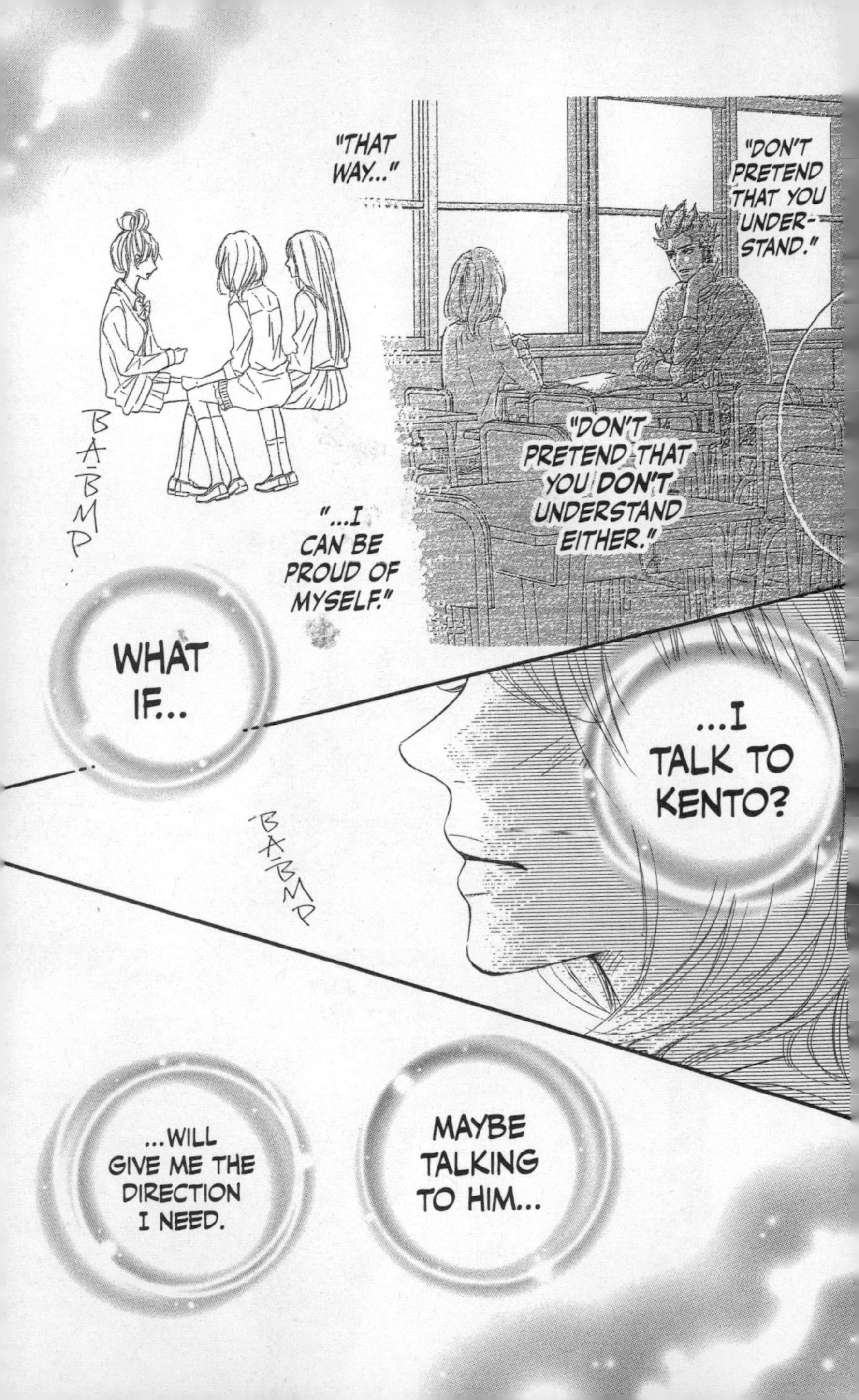
"DON'T PRETEND THAT YOU UNDER-STAND."
"DON'T PRETEND THAT YOU DON'T UNDERSTAND EITHER."
"THAT WAY..."
"...I CAN BE PROUD OF MYSELF."
BA-BAMP
WHAT IF...
...I TALK TO KENTO?
BA-BAMP
MAYBE TALKING TO HIM...
...WILL GIVE ME THE DIRECTION I NEED.

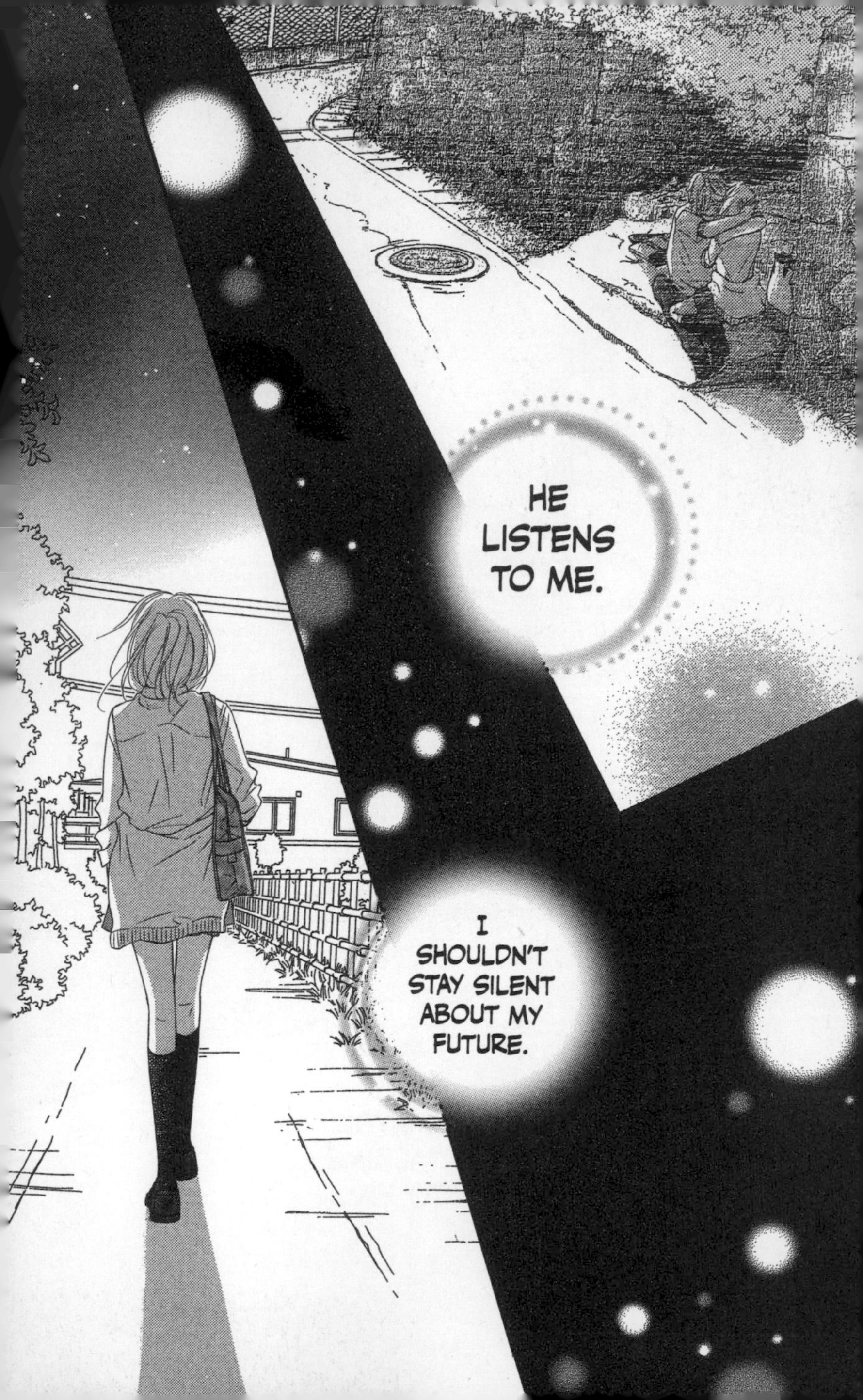
HE LISTENS TO ME.
I SHOULDN'T STAY SILENT ABOUT MY FUTURE.

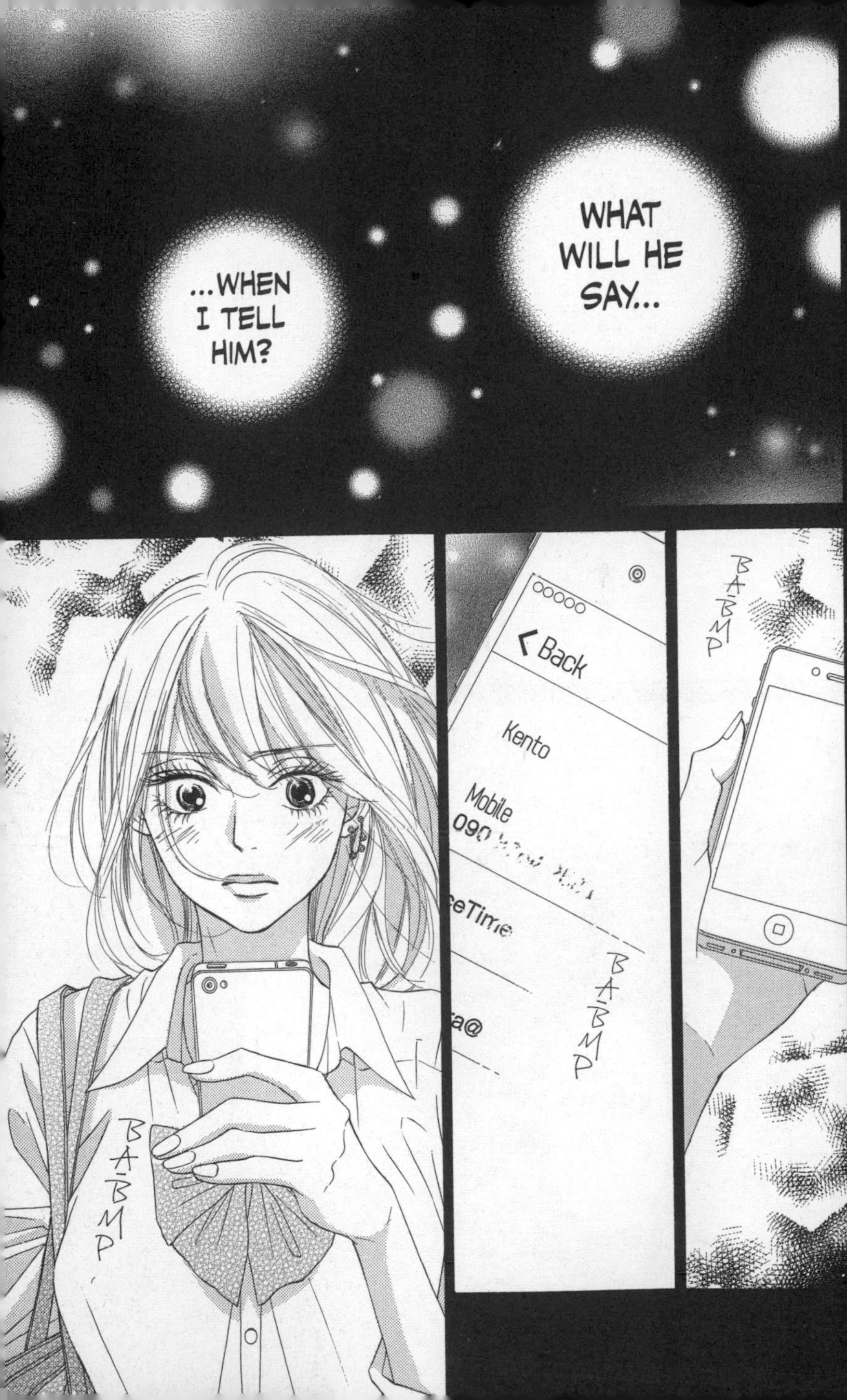
WHAT WILL HE SAY...
...WHEN I TELL HIM?
BA-BMP
Back
Kento
Mobile
BA-BMP
BA-BMP

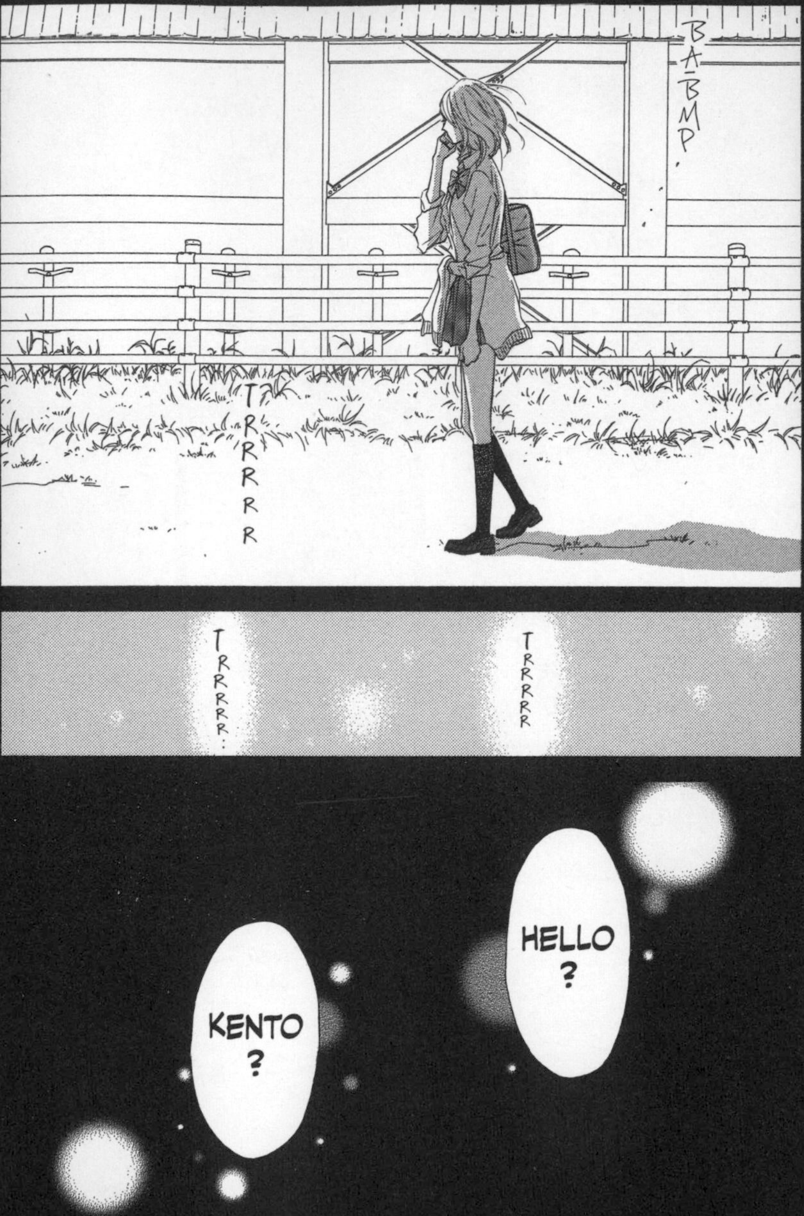
BA-BMP
TRRRRR
TRRRRR
TRRRRR...
HELLO?
KENTO?

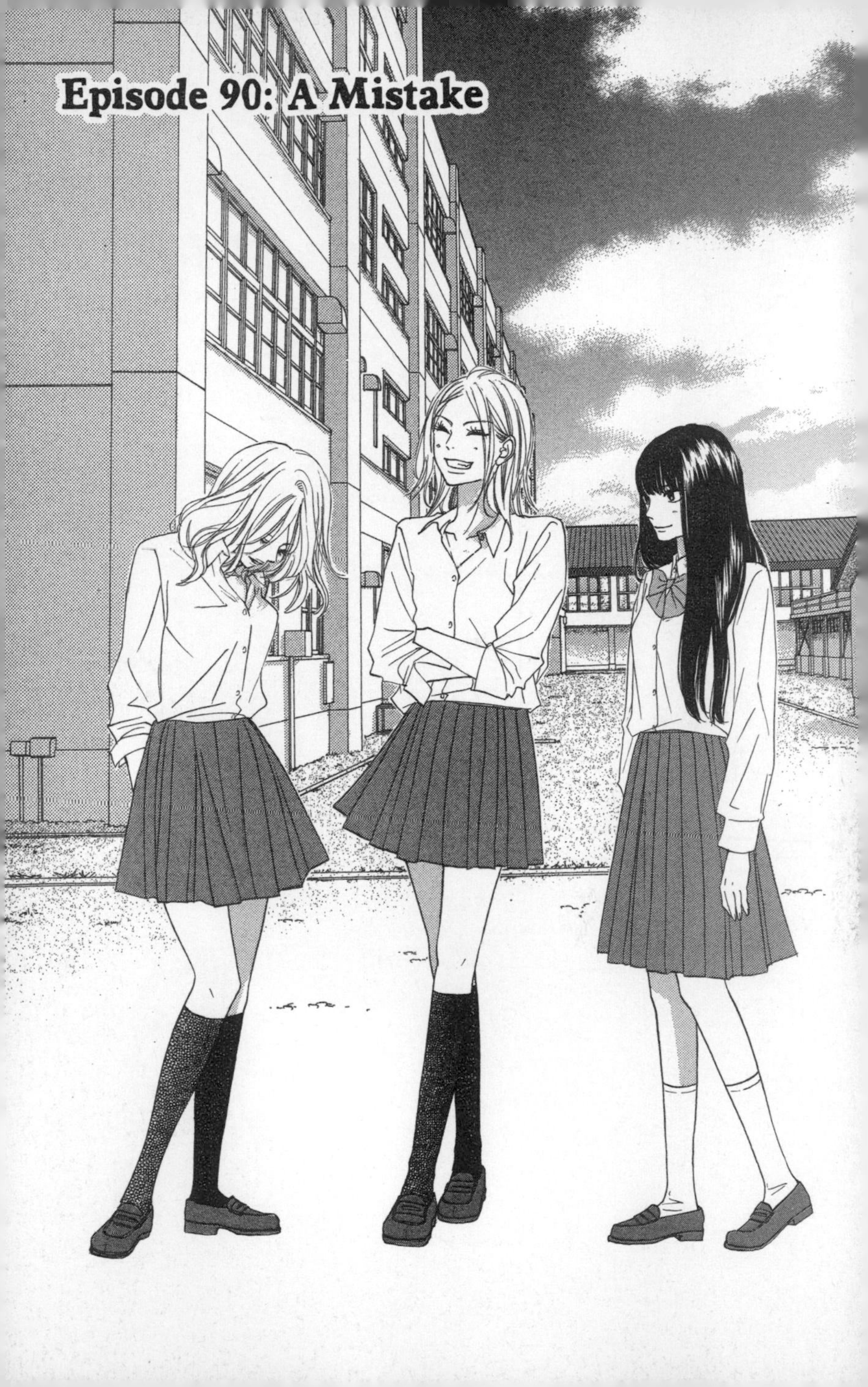
Episode 90: A Mistake

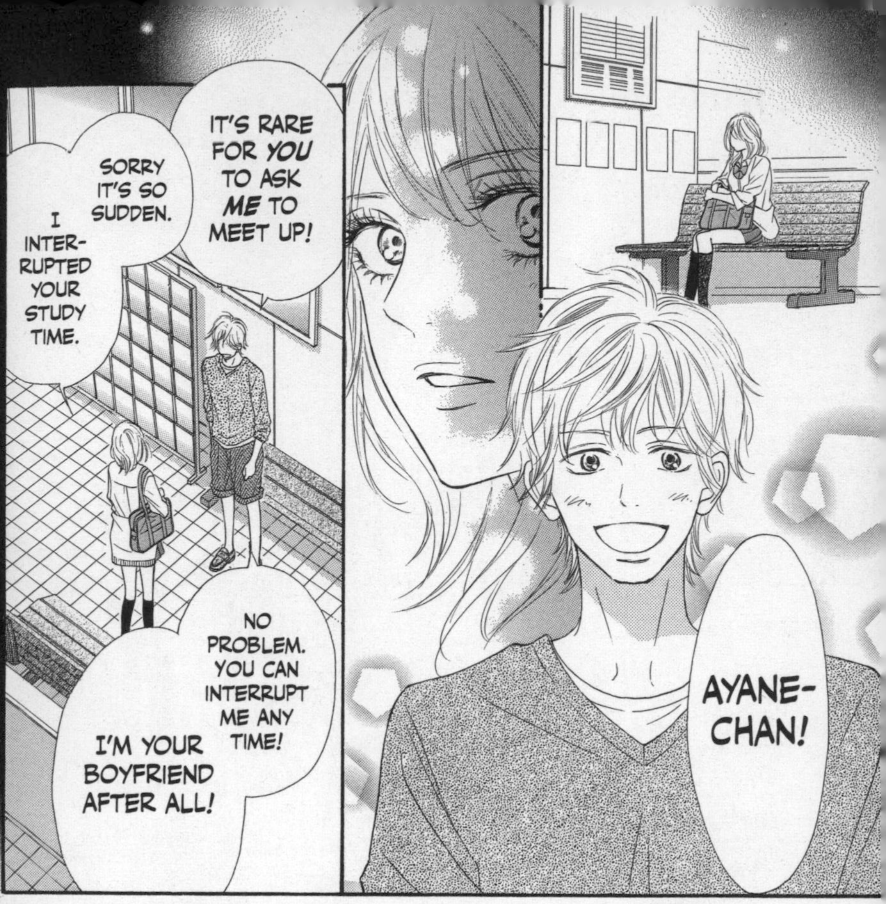
AYANE-CHAN!
IT'S RARE FOR *YOU* TO ASK *ME* TO MEET UP!
SORRY IT'S SO SUDDEN.
I INTERRUPTED YOUR STUDY TIME.
NO PROBLEM. YOU CAN INTERRUPT ME ANY TIME!
I'M YOUR BOYFRIEND AFTER ALL!

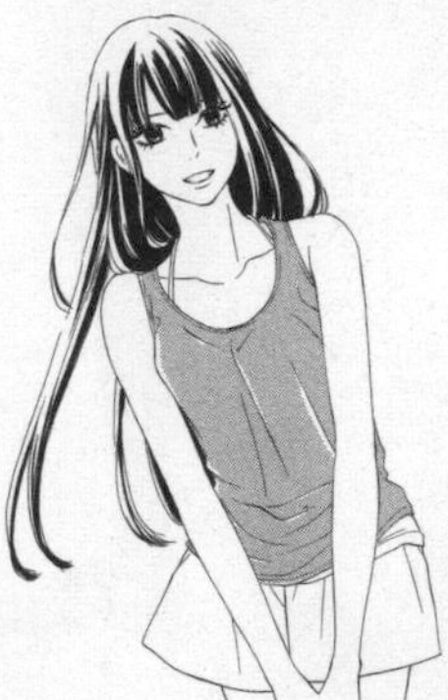

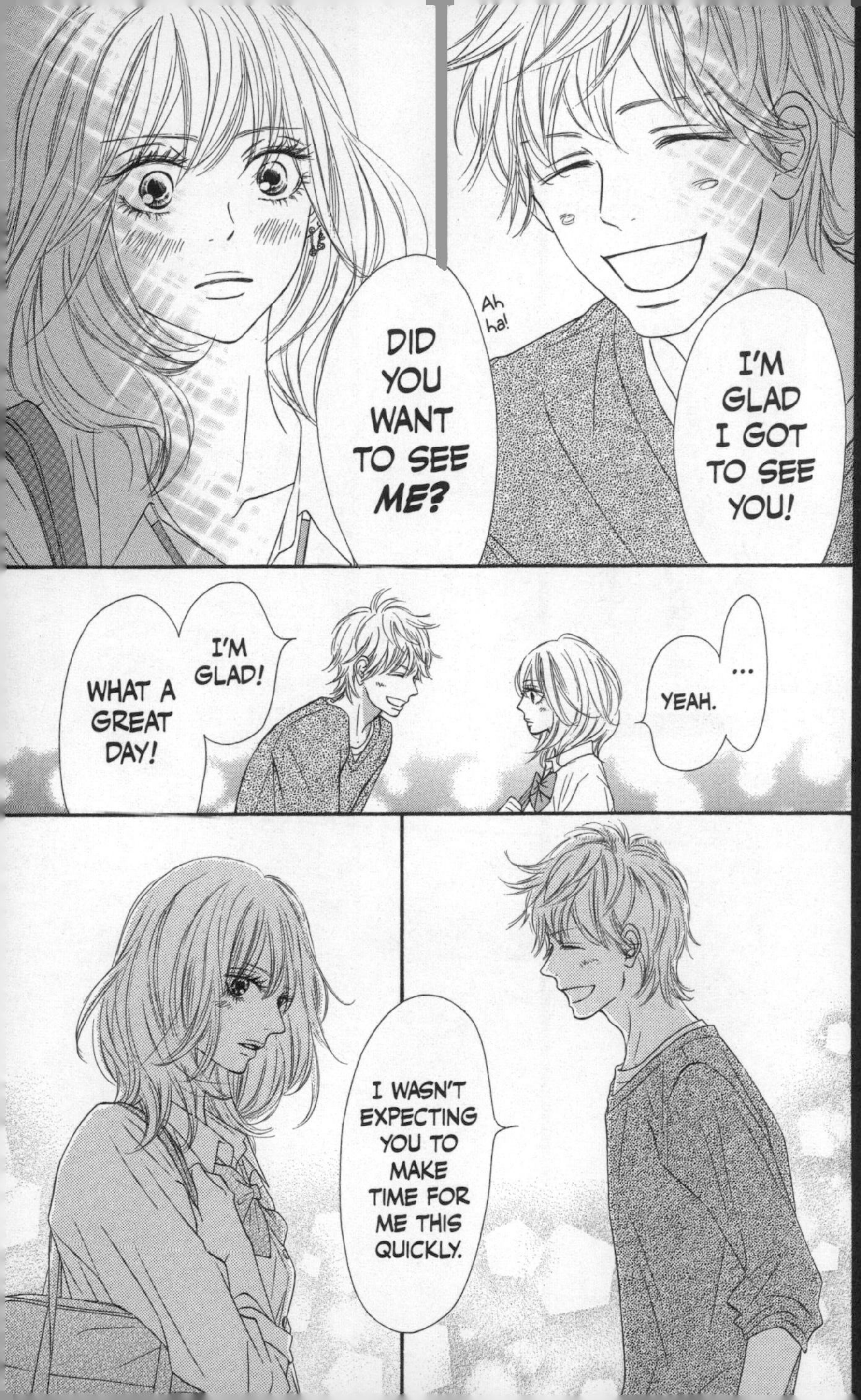
Ah ha!
I'M GLAD I GOT TO SEE YOU!
DID YOU WANT TO SEE ME?
... YEAH.
I'M GLAD! WHAT A GREAT DAY!
I WASN'T EXPECTING YOU TO MAKE TIME FOR ME THIS QUICKLY.

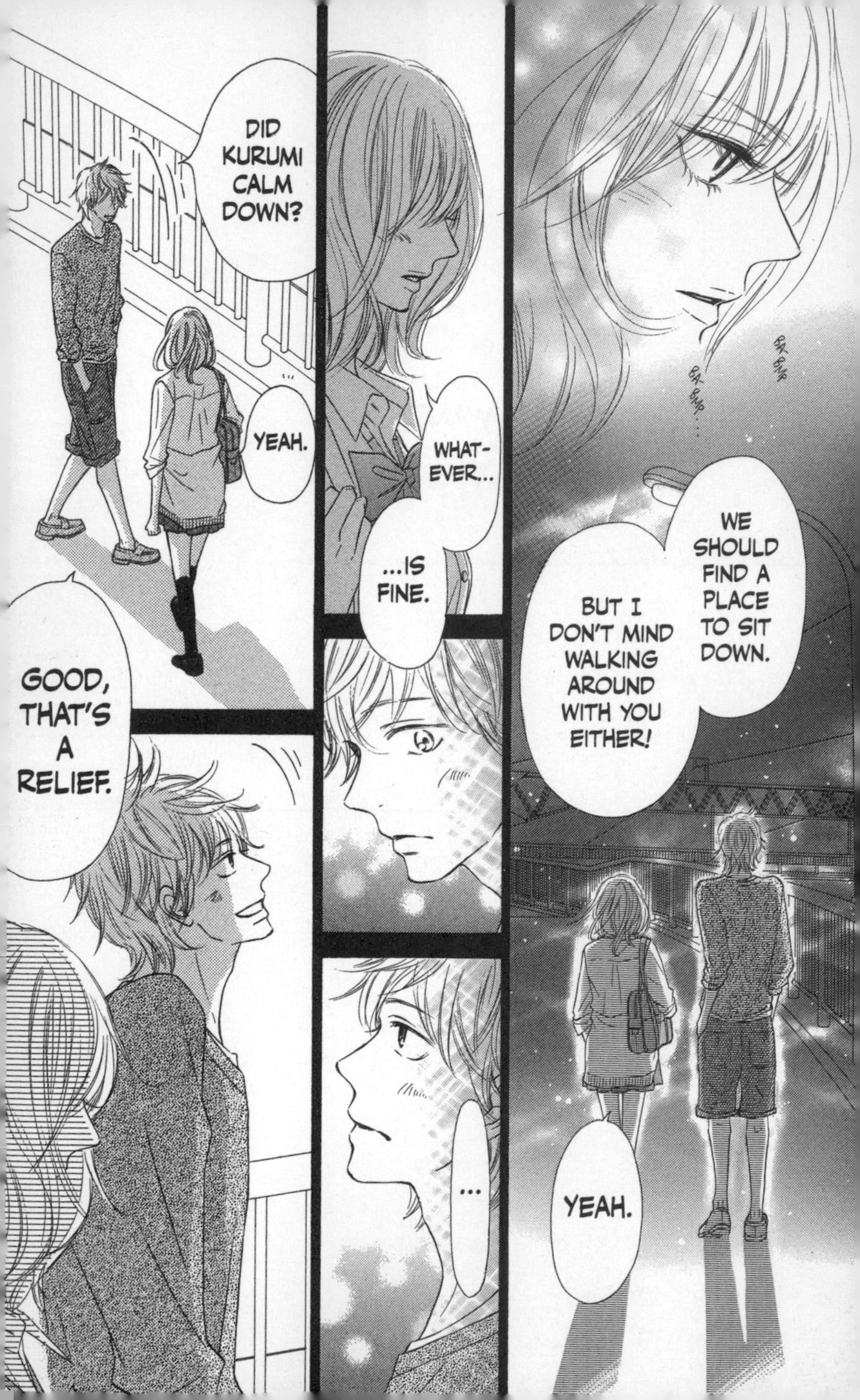
BA-BMP
BA-BMP...
WE SHOULD FIND A PLACE TO SIT DOWN.
BUT I DON'T MIND WALKING AROUND WITH YOU EITHER!
YEAH.
WHAT-EVER...
...IS FINE.
...
DID KURUMI CALM DOWN?
YEAH.
GOOD, THAT'S A RELIEF.

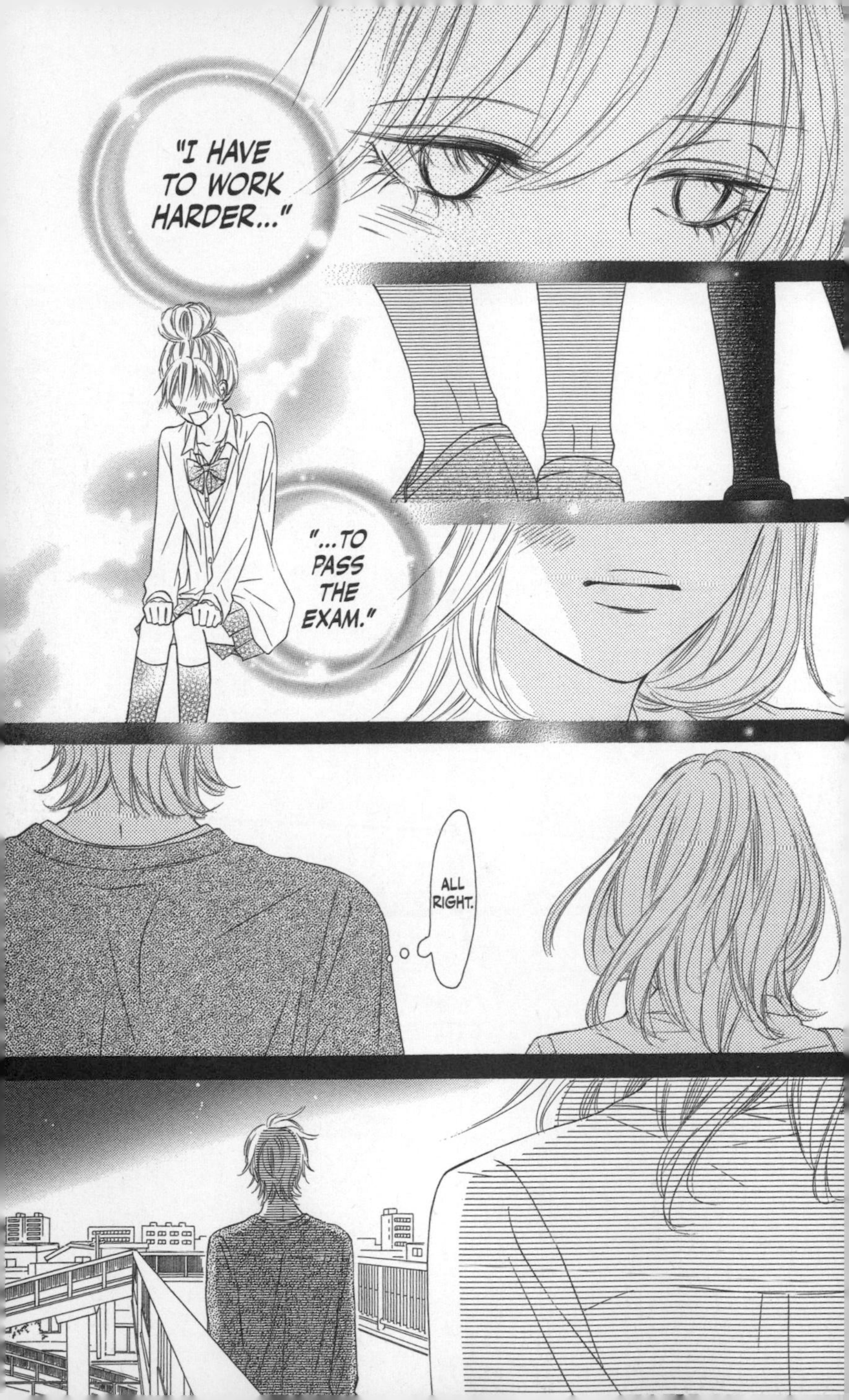
"I HAVE TO WORK HARDER..."
"...TO PASS THE EXAM."
ALL RIGHT.

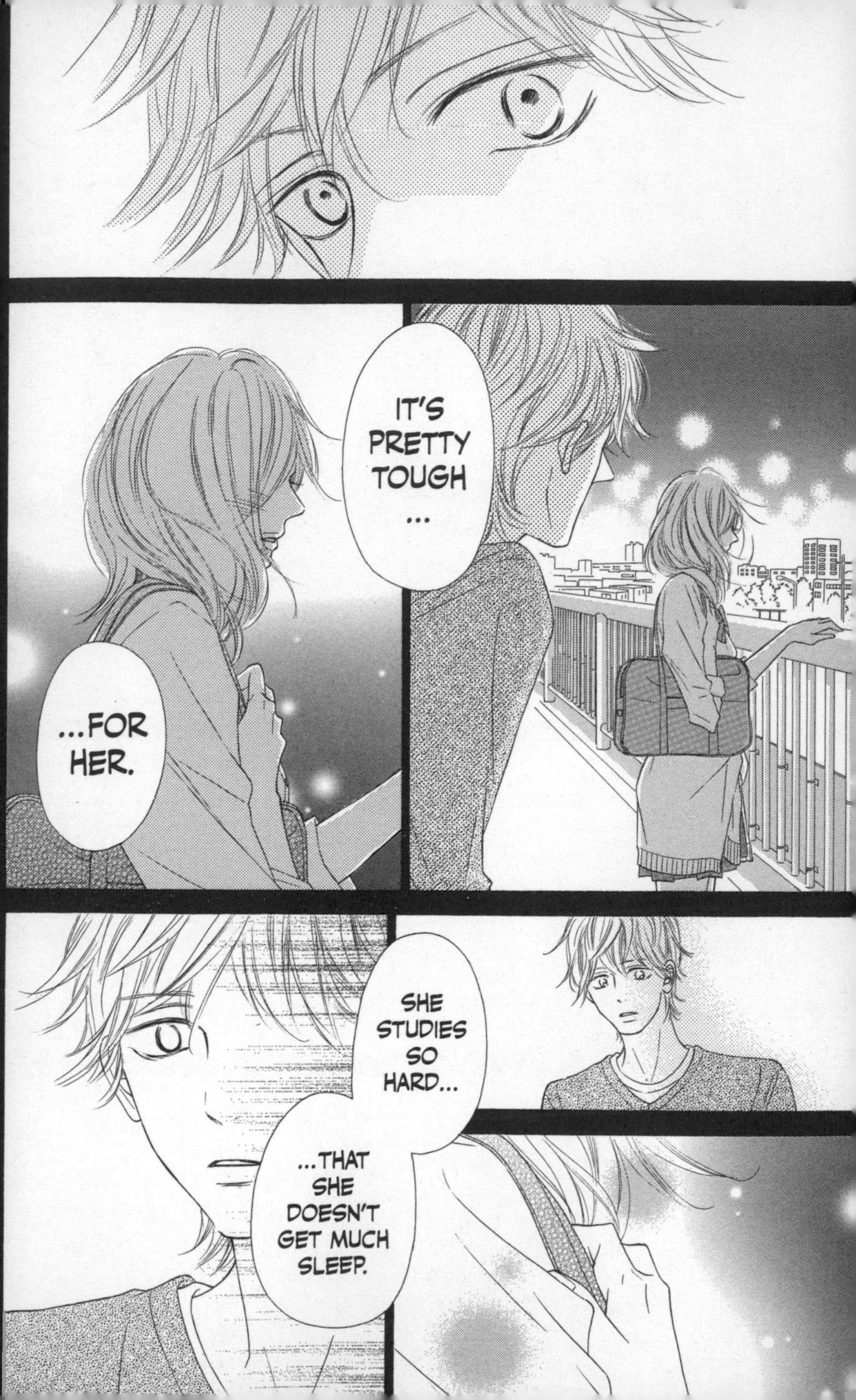
IT'S PRETTY TOUGH ...
...FOR HER.
SHE STUDIES SO HARD...
...THAT SHE DOESN'T GET MUCH SLEEP.

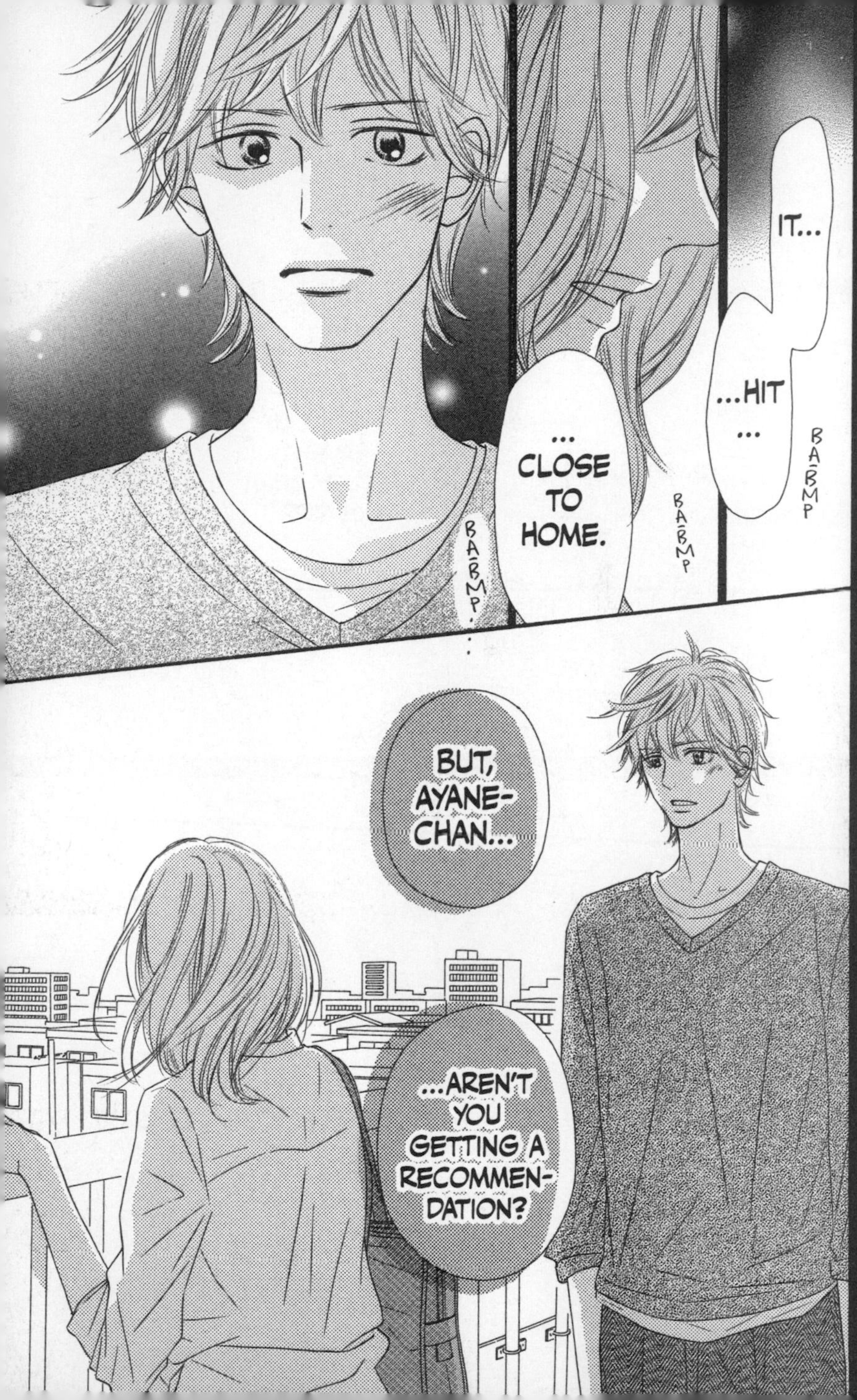
IT...
...HIT
...
BA-BMP
...
CLOSE
TO
HOME.
BA-BMP
BA-BMP...
BUT, AYANE-CHAN...
...AREN'T YOU GETTING A RECOMMEN-DATION?

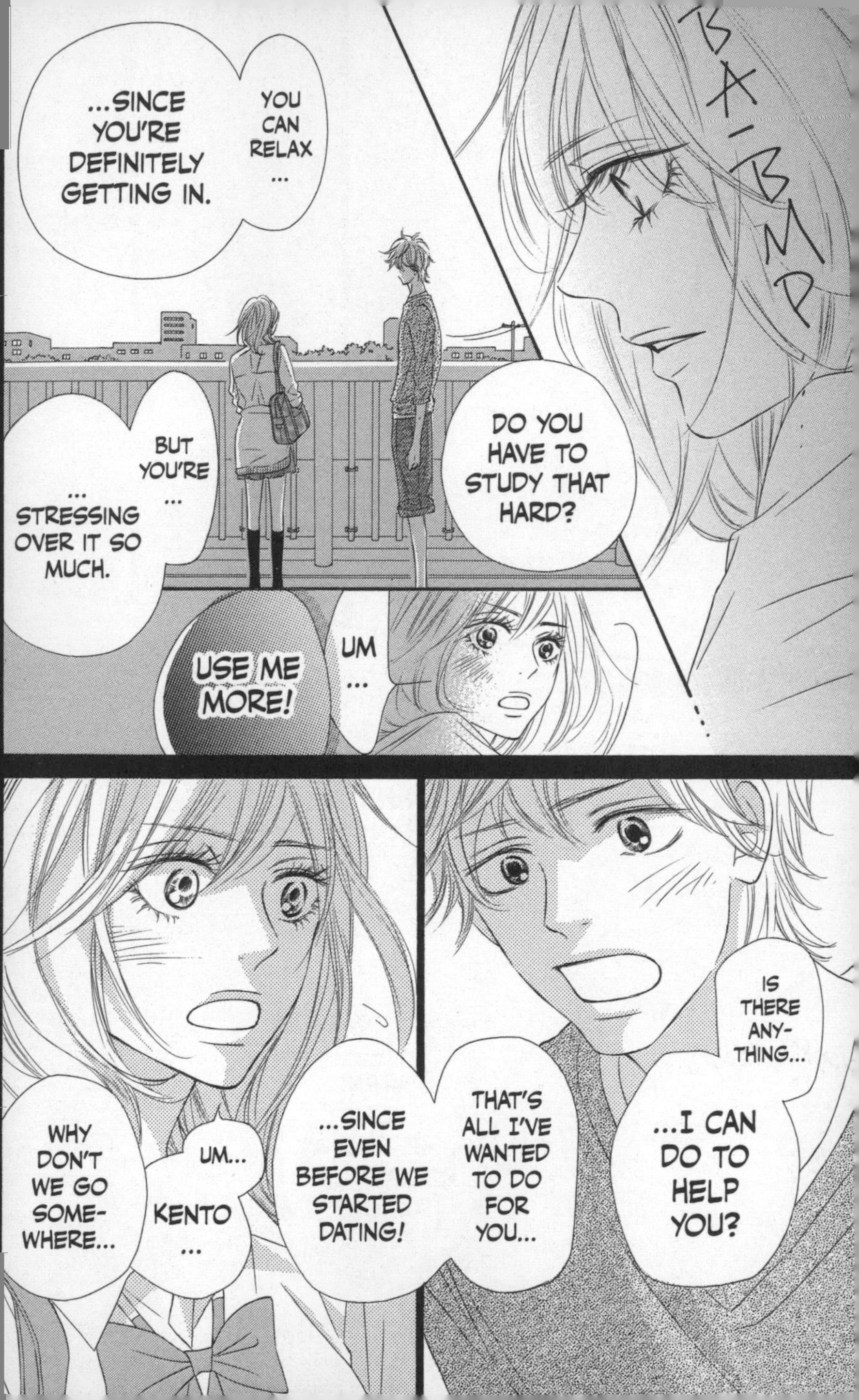
BA-BMP
YOU CAN RELAX ...
...SINCE YOU'RE DEFINITELY GETTING IN.
DO YOU HAVE TO STUDY THAT HARD?
BUT YOU'RE ...
... STRESSING OVER IT SO MUCH.
UM ...
USE ME MORE!
IS THERE ANY-THING...
...I CAN DO TO HELP YOU?
THAT'S ALL I'VE WANTED TO DO FOR YOU...
...SINCE EVEN BEFORE WE STARTED DATING!
UM... KENTO ...
WHY DON'T WE GO SOME-WHERE...

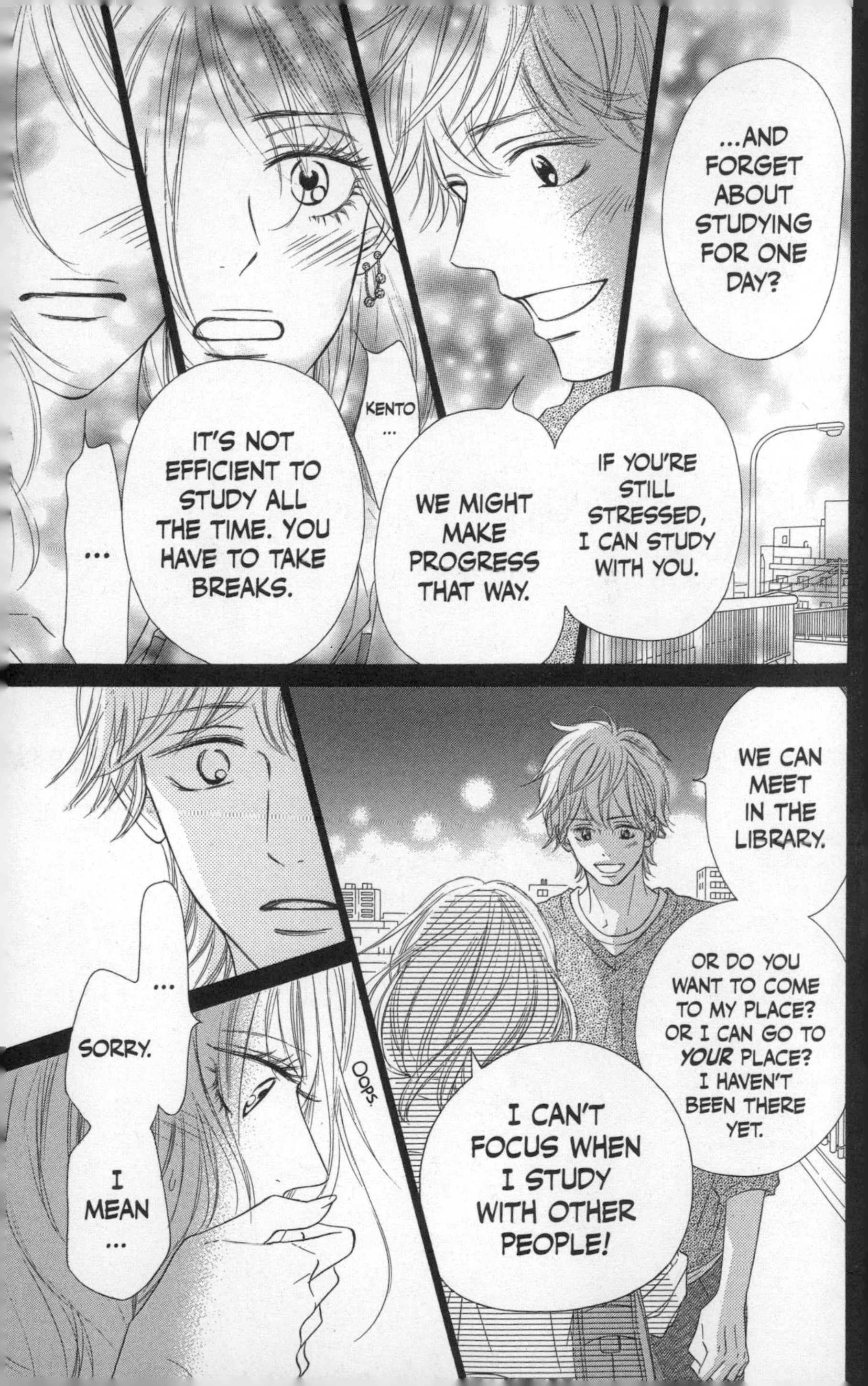
...AND FORGET ABOUT STUDYING FOR ONE DAY?
IF YOU'RE STILL STRESSED, I CAN STUDY WITH YOU.
WE MIGHT MAKE PROGRESS THAT WAY.
KENTO ...
IT'S NOT EFFICIENT TO STUDY ALL THE TIME. YOU HAVE TO TAKE BREAKS.
...
WE CAN MEET IN THE LIBRARY.
OR DO YOU WANT TO COME TO MY PLACE? OR I CAN GO TO *YOUR* PLACE? I HAVEN'T BEEN THERE YET.
I CAN'T FOCUS WHEN I STUDY WITH OTHER PEOPLE!
OOPS.
...
SORRY.
I MEAN ...

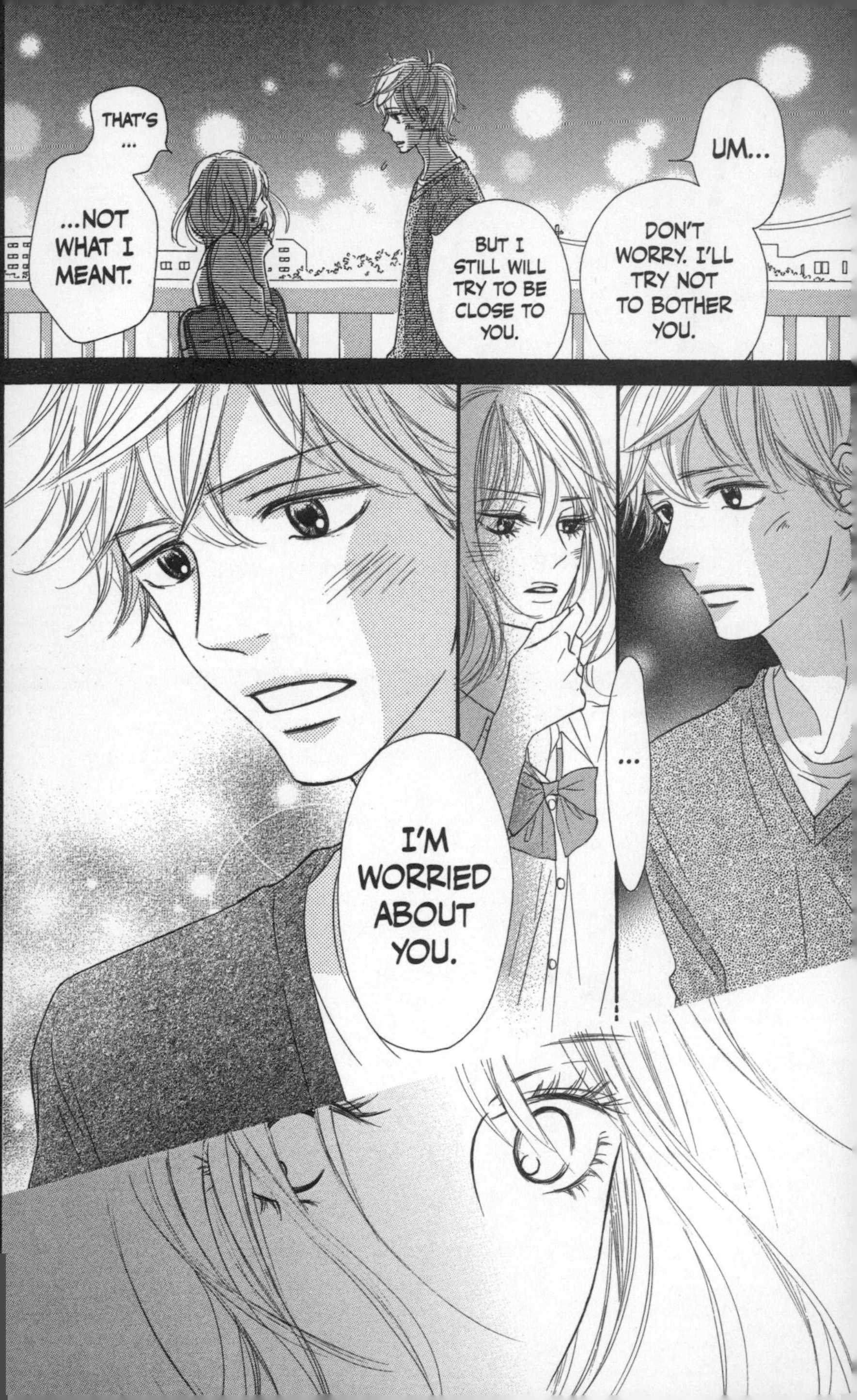
UM...
DON'T WORRY. I'LL TRY NOT TO BOTHER YOU.
BUT I STILL WILL TRY TO BE CLOSE TO YOU.
THAT'S ...
...NOT WHAT I MEANT.
...
I'M WORRIED ABOUT YOU.

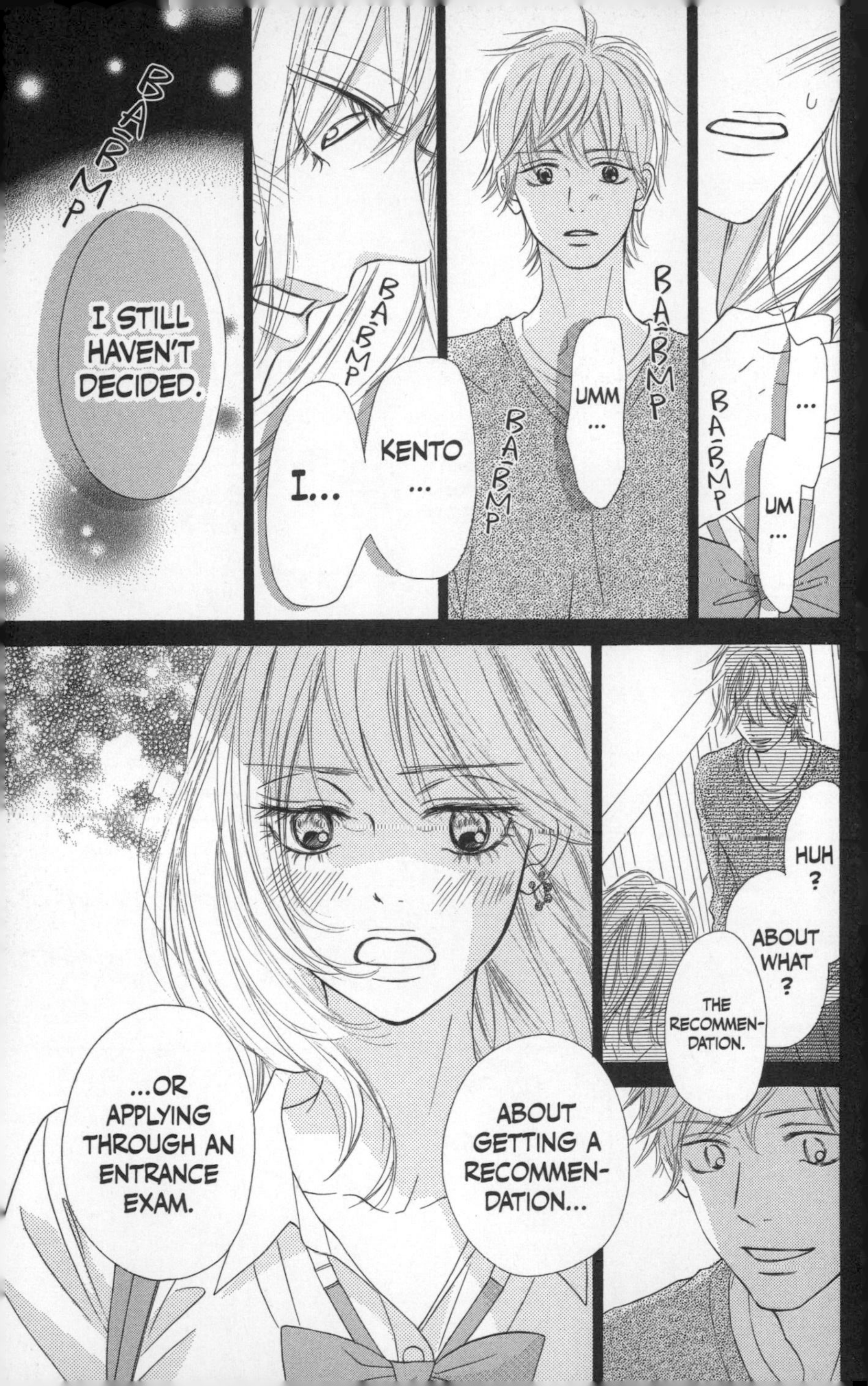
...
BA-BMP
UM ...
BA-BMP
UMM ...
BA-BMP
BA-BMP
KENTO ...
I...
BA-BMP
I STILL HAVEN'T DECIDED.
HUH?
ABOUT WHAT?
THE RECOMMENDATION.
ABOUT GETTING A RECOMMENDATION...
...OR APPLYING THROUGH AN ENTRANCE EXAM.

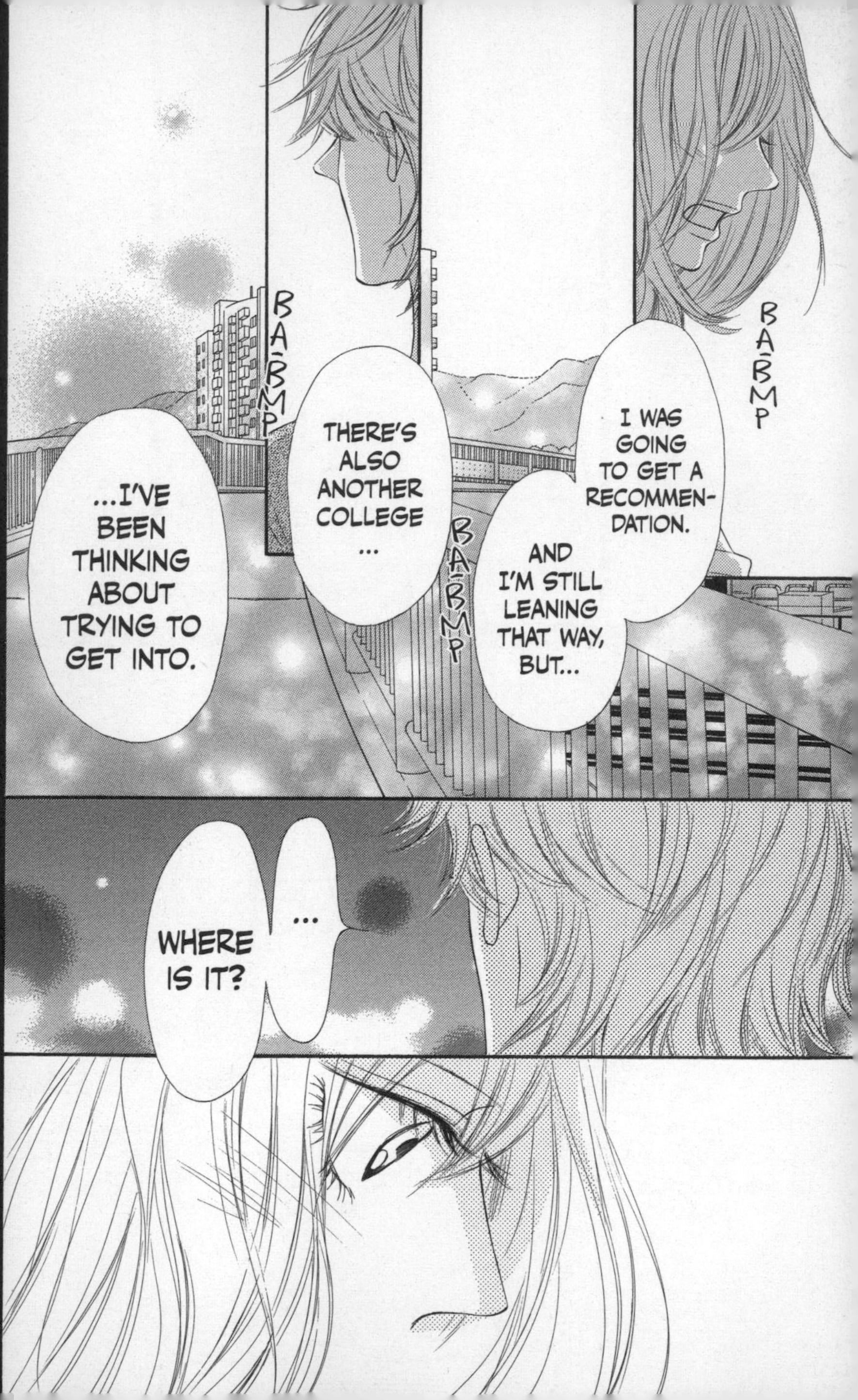
BA-BMP
I WAS GOING TO GET A RECOMMEN-DATION.
AND I'M STILL LEANING THAT WAY, BUT...
BA-BMP
THERE'S ALSO ANOTHER COLLEGE ...
BA-BMP
...I'VE BEEN THINKING ABOUT TRYING TO GET INTO.
...
WHERE IS IT?

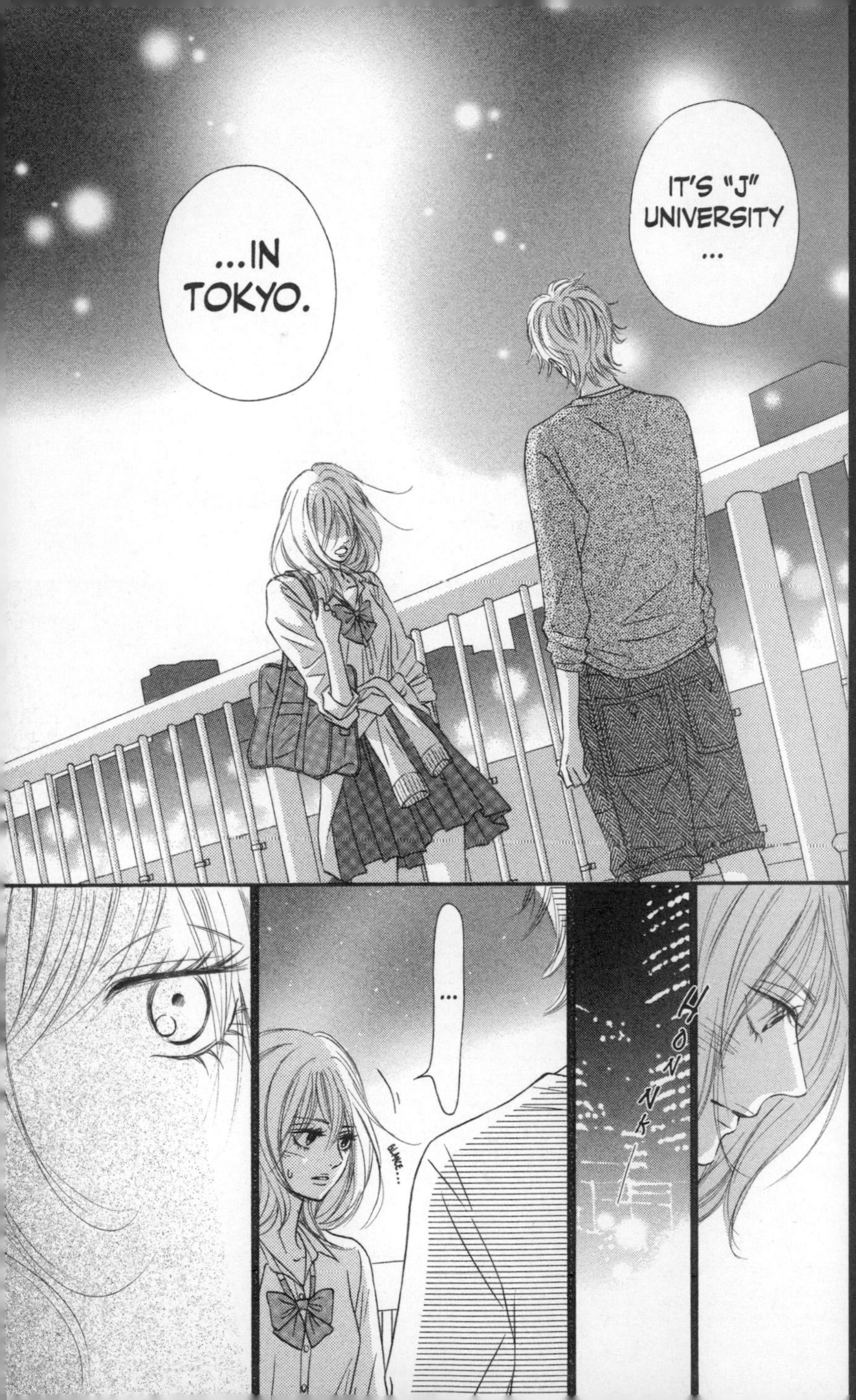
IT'S "J" UNIVERSITY ...
...IN TOKYO.
HONNNK—
...
GLANCE...

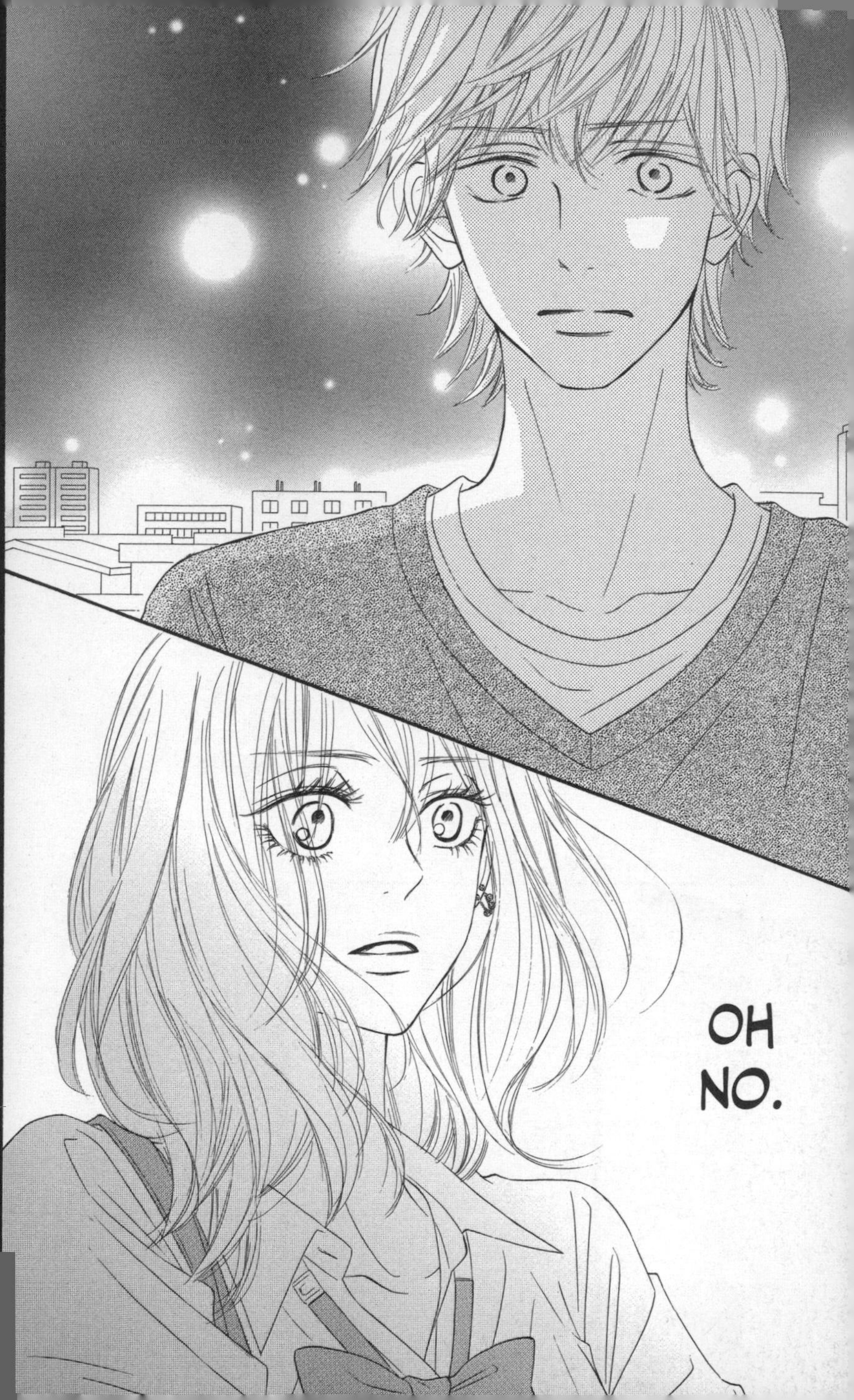
OH
NO.

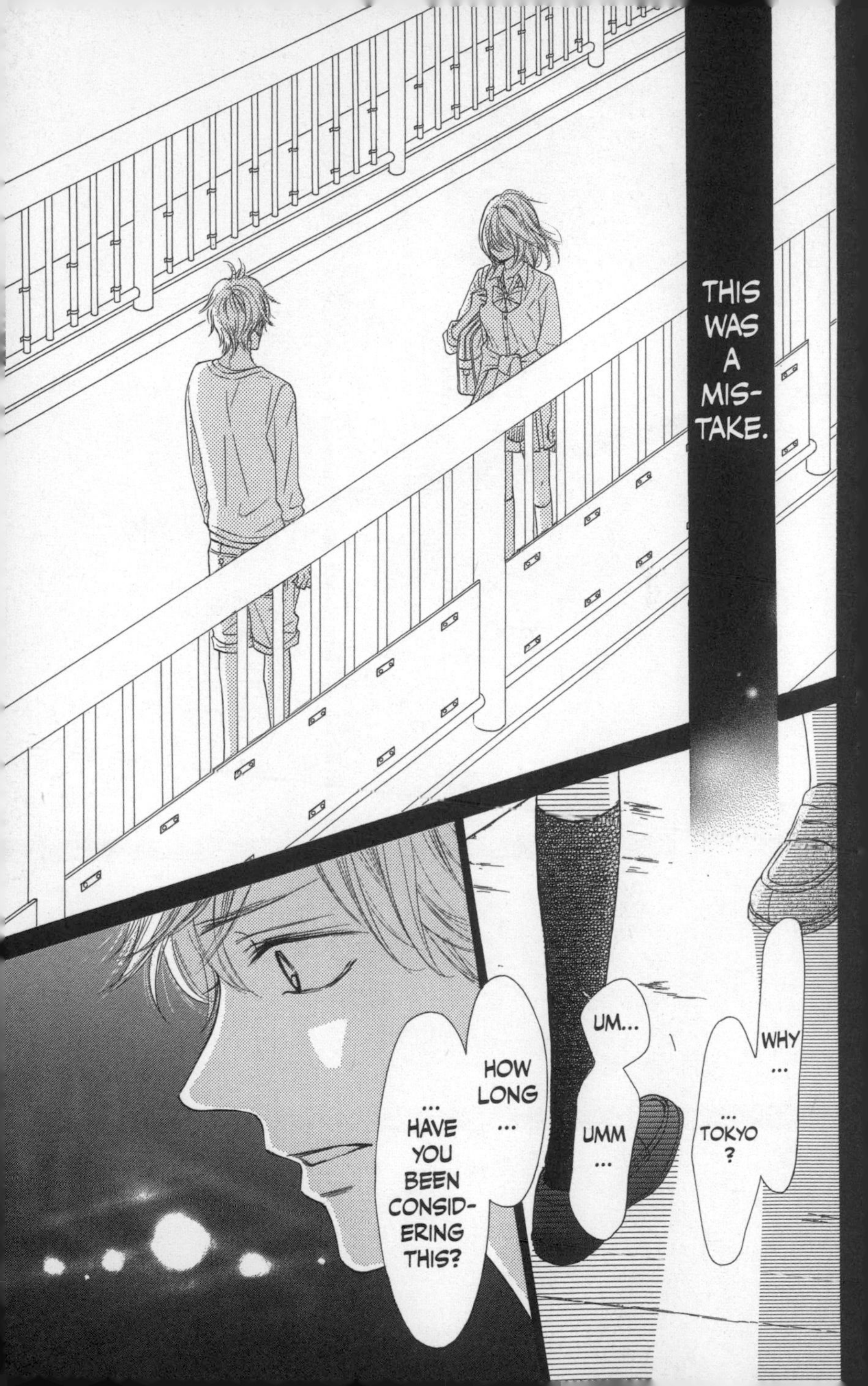
THIS WAS A MIS-TAKE.
WHY ... ... TOKYO ?
UM... UMM ...
HOW LONG ... ... HAVE YOU BEEN CONSID-ERING THIS?

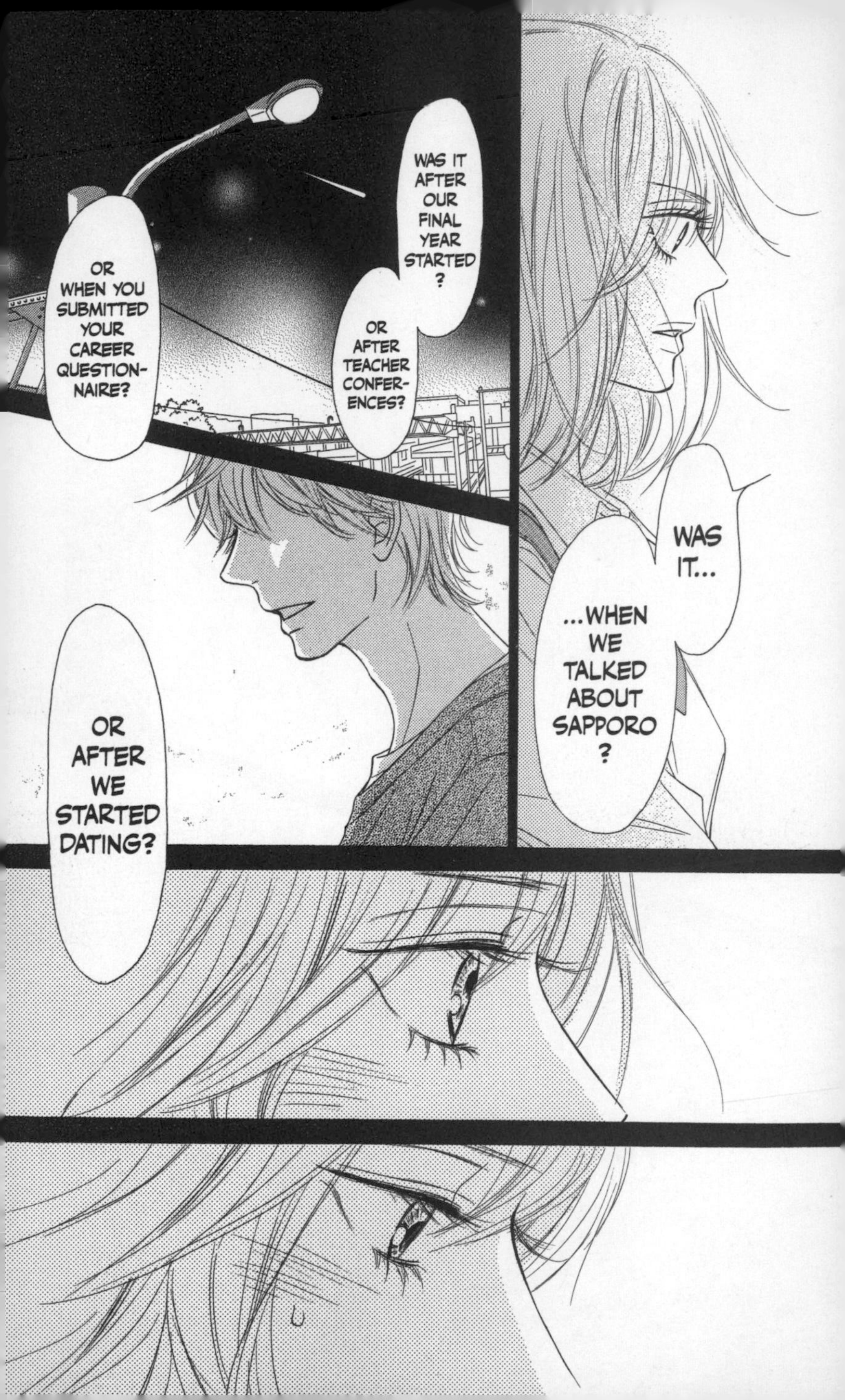
WAS IT...
...WHEN WE TALKED ABOUT SAPPORO?
WAS IT AFTER OUR FINAL YEAR STARTED?
OR AFTER TEACHER CONFERENCES?
OR WHEN YOU SUBMITTED YOUR CAREER QUESTIONNAIRE?
OR AFTER WE STARTED DATING?

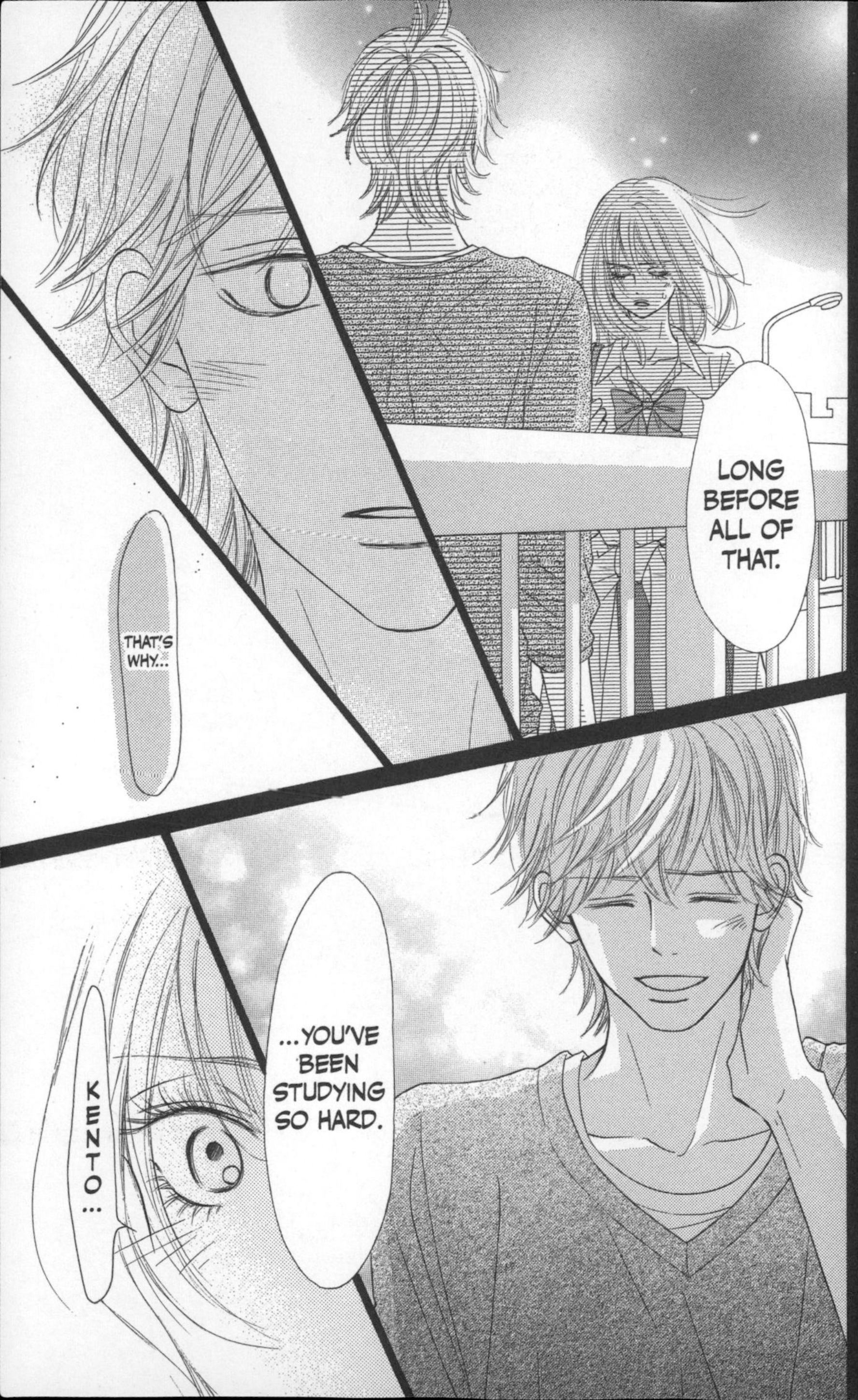
LONG BEFORE ALL OF THAT.
THAT'S WHY...
...YOU'VE BEEN STUDYING SO HARD.
KENTO...

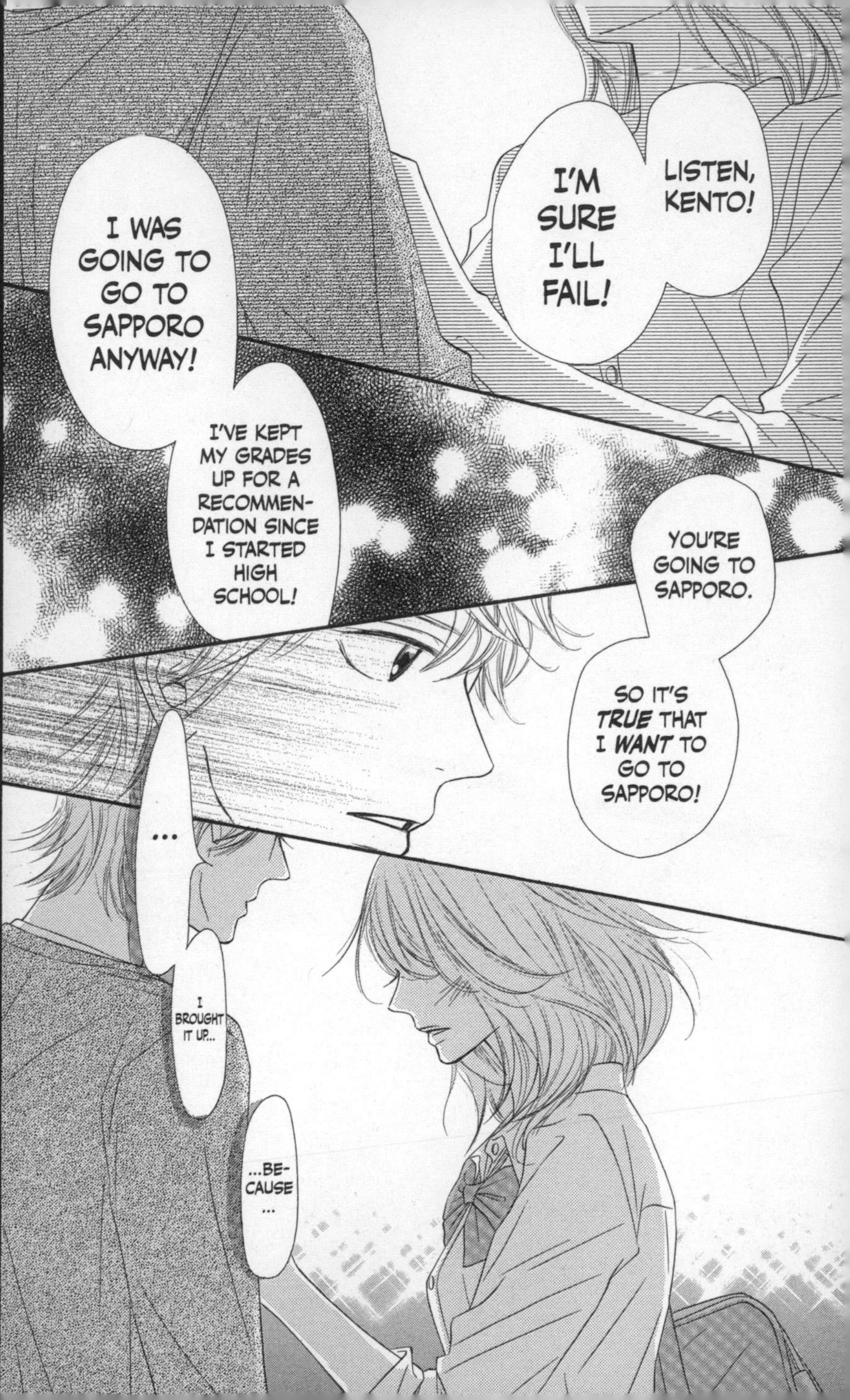
LISTEN, KENTO!
I'M SURE I'LL FAIL!
I WAS GOING TO GO TO SAPPORO ANYWAY!
I'VE KEPT MY GRADES UP FOR A RECOMMEN-DATION SINCE I STARTED HIGH SCHOOL!
YOU'RE GOING TO SAPPORO.
SO IT'S TRUE THAT I WANT TO GO TO SAPPORO!
...
I BROUGHT IT UP...
...BE-CAUSE ...

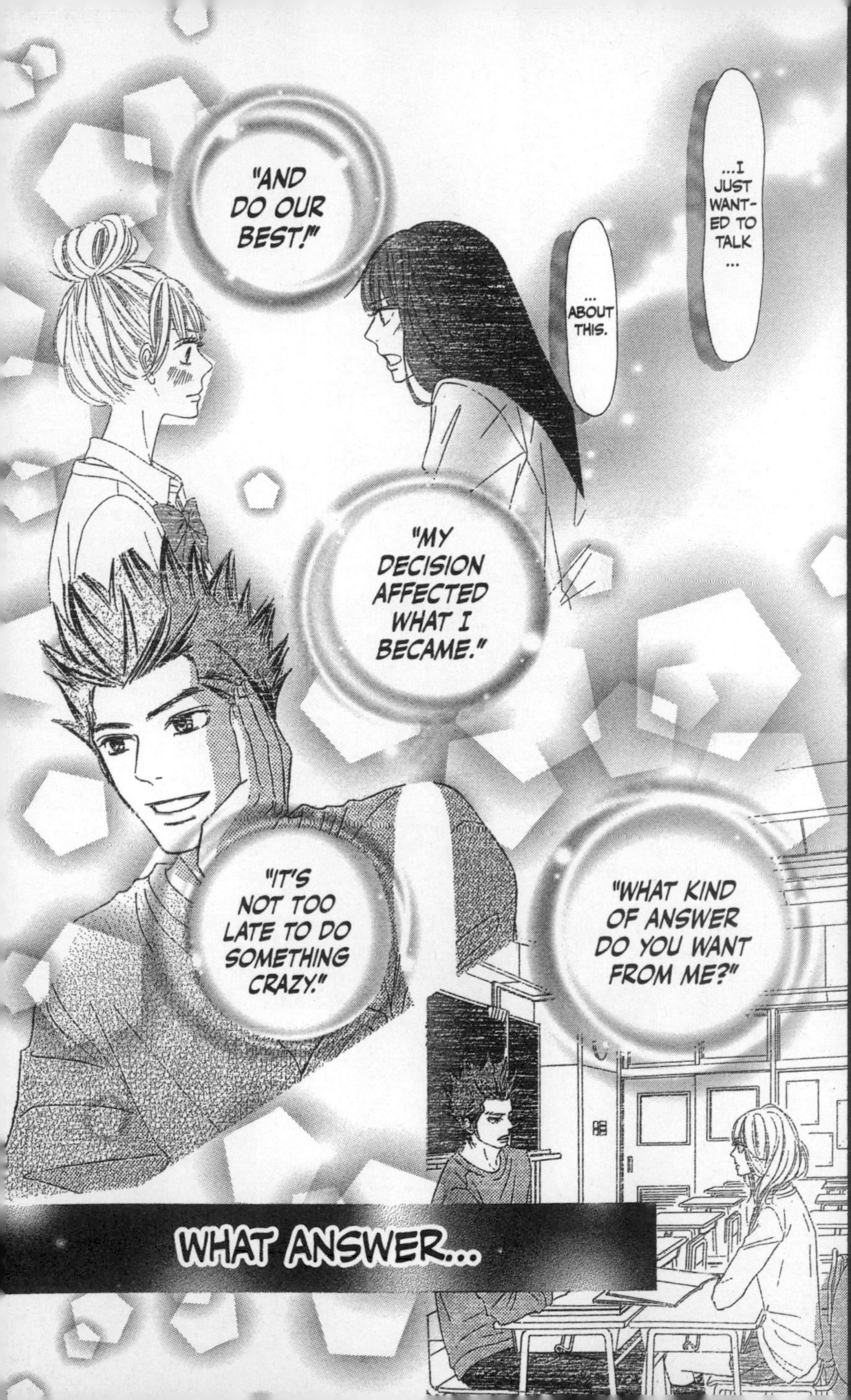
...I JUST WANTED TO TALK...
...ABOUT THIS.
"AND DO OUR BEST!"
"MY DECISION AFFECTED WHAT I BECAME."
"WHAT KIND OF ANSWER DO YOU WANT FROM ME?"
"IT'S NOT TOO LATE TO DO SOMETHING CRAZY."
WHAT ANSWER...

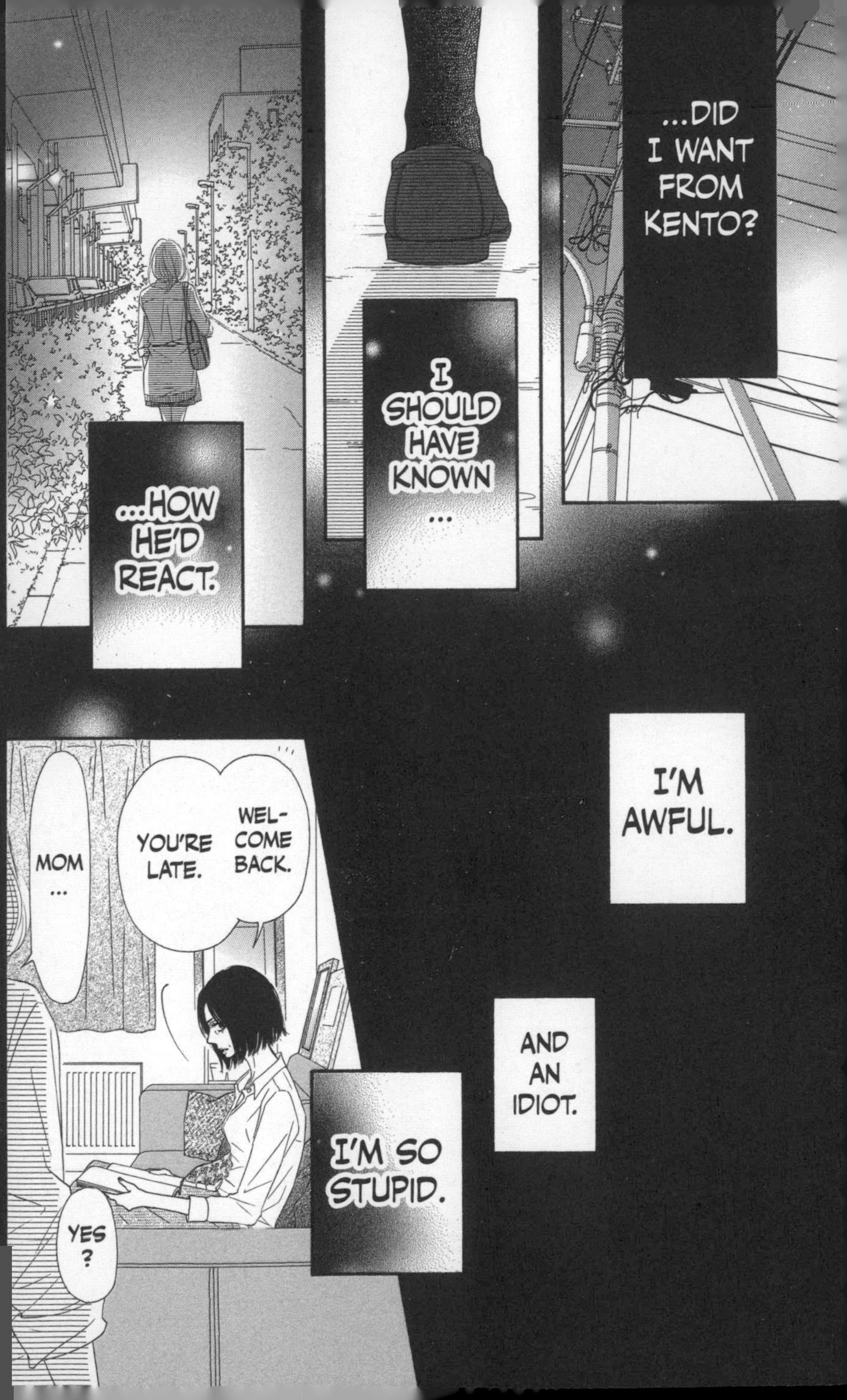
...DID I WANT FROM KENTO?
I SHOULD HAVE KNOWN ...
...HOW HE'D REACT.
I'M AWFUL.
AND AN IDIOT.
I'M SO STUPID.
WEL-COME BACK.
YOU'RE LATE.
MOM ...
YES ?

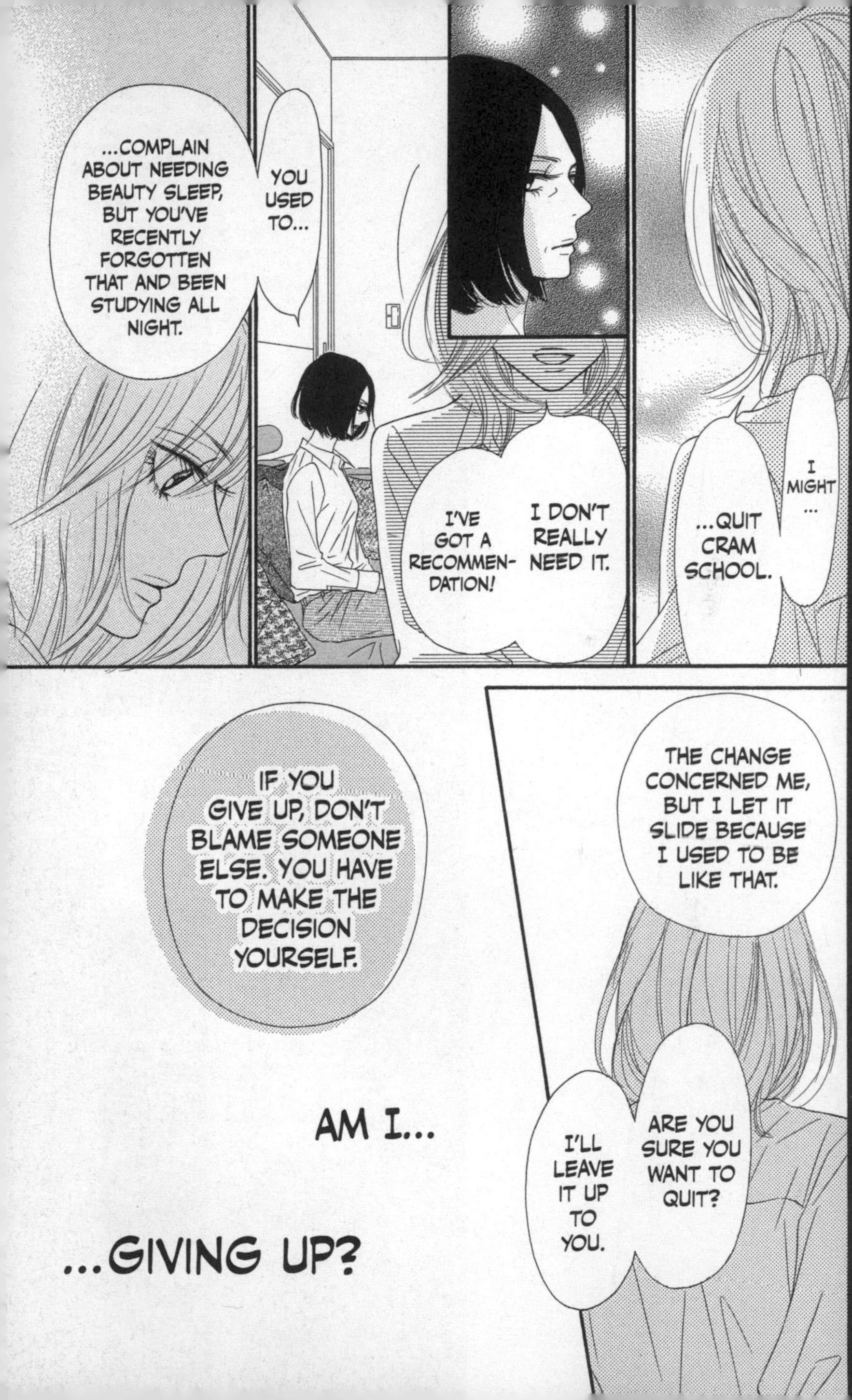
I MIGHT...
...QUIT CRAM SCHOOL.
I DON'T REALLY NEED IT.
I'VE GOT A RECOMMENDATION!
YOU USED TO...
...COMPLAIN ABOUT NEEDING BEAUTY SLEEP, BUT YOU'VE RECENTLY FORGOTTEN THAT AND BEEN STUDYING ALL NIGHT.
THE CHANGE CONCERNED ME, BUT I LET IT SLIDE BECAUSE I USED TO BE LIKE THAT.
ARE YOU SURE YOU WANT TO QUIT?
I'LL LEAVE IT UP TO YOU.
IF YOU GIVE UP, DON'T BLAME SOMEONE ELSE. YOU HAVE TO MAKE THE DECISION YOURSELF.
AM I...
...GIVING UP?

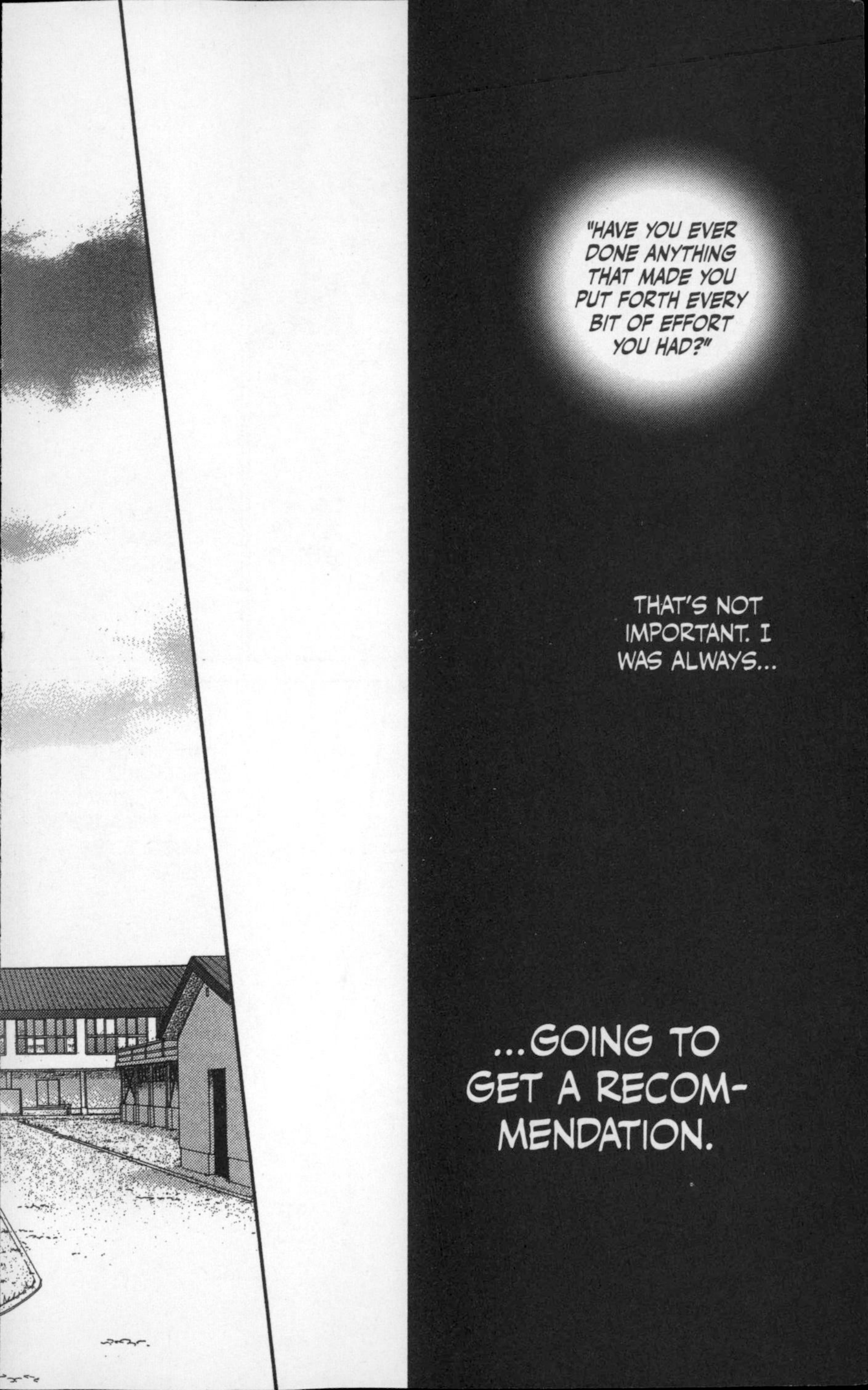
"HAVE YOU EVER DONE ANYTHING THAT MADE YOU PUT FORTH EVERY BIT OF EFFORT YOU HAD?"
THAT'S NOT IMPORTANT. I WAS ALWAYS...
...GOING TO GET A RECOM-MENDATION.

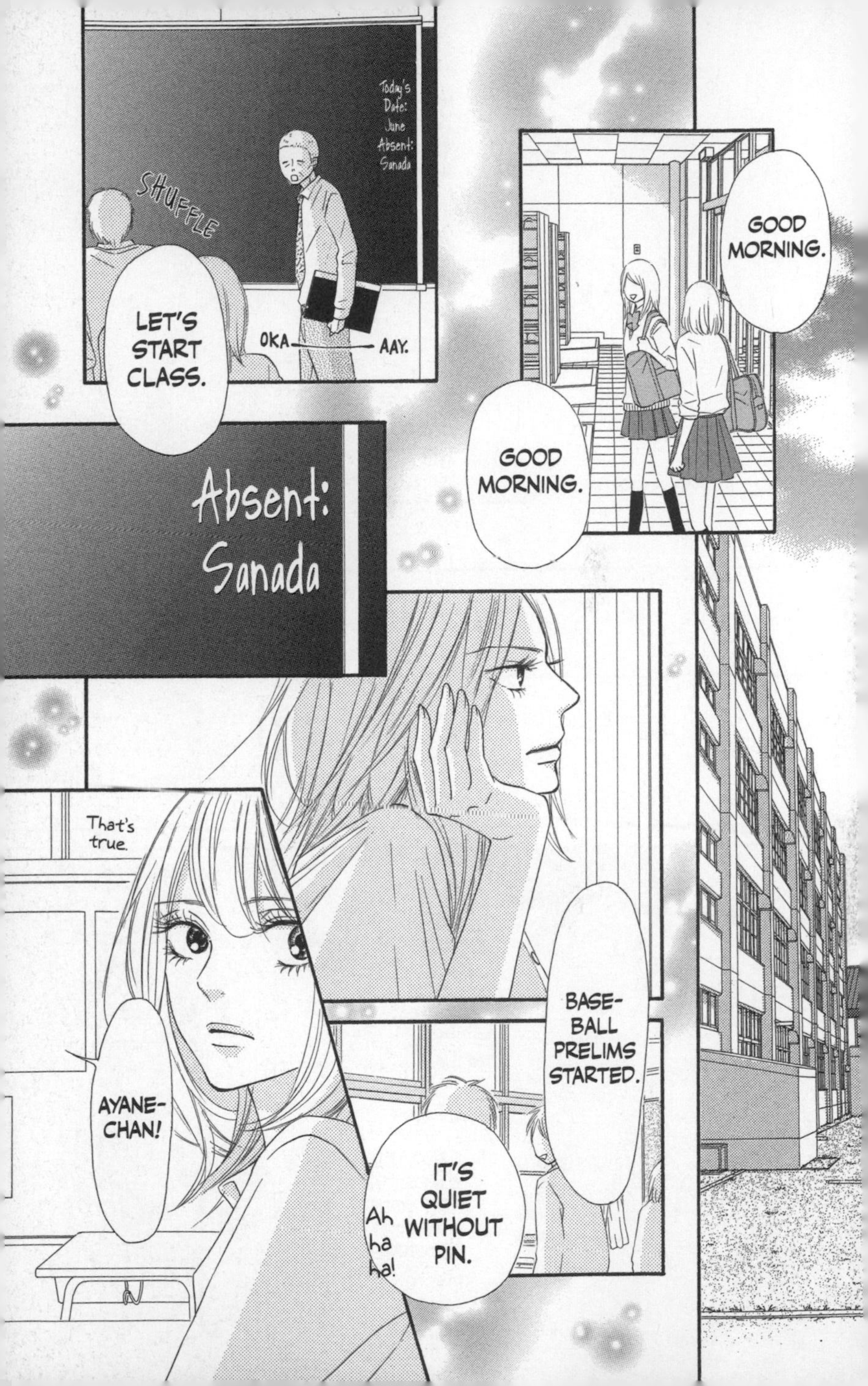
GOOD MORNING.
GOOD MORNING.
Today's Date: June Absent: Sanada
SHUFFLE
OKA— —AAY.
LET'S START CLASS.
Absent: Sanada
BASE-BALL PRELIMS STARTED.
IT'S QUIET WITHOUT PIN.
Ah ha ha!
That's true.
AYANE-CHAN!

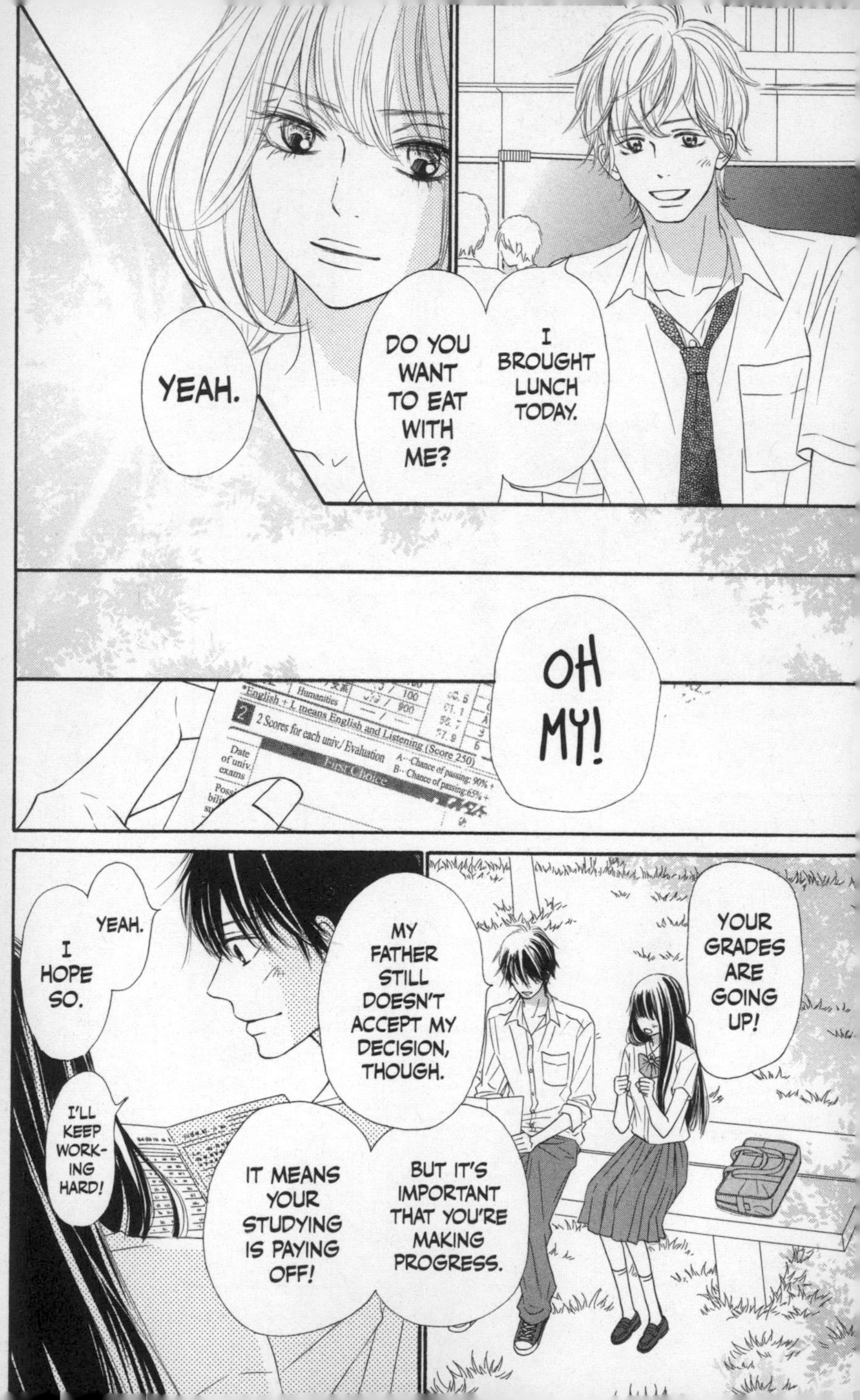
I BROUGHT LUNCH TODAY.
DO YOU WANT TO EAT WITH ME?
YEAH.
OH MY!
Humanities
*English + L means English and Listening (Score 250)
2 Scores for each univ./Evaluation
A···Chance of passing: 90% +
B···Chance of passing: 65% +
Date of univ. exams
First Choice
YOUR GRADES ARE GOING UP!
MY FATHER STILL DOESN'T ACCEPT MY DECISION, THOUGH.
BUT IT'S IMPORTANT THAT YOU'RE MAKING PROGRESS.
IT MEANS YOUR STUDYING IS PAYING OFF!
YEAH. I HOPE SO.
I'LL KEEP WORK-ING HARD!

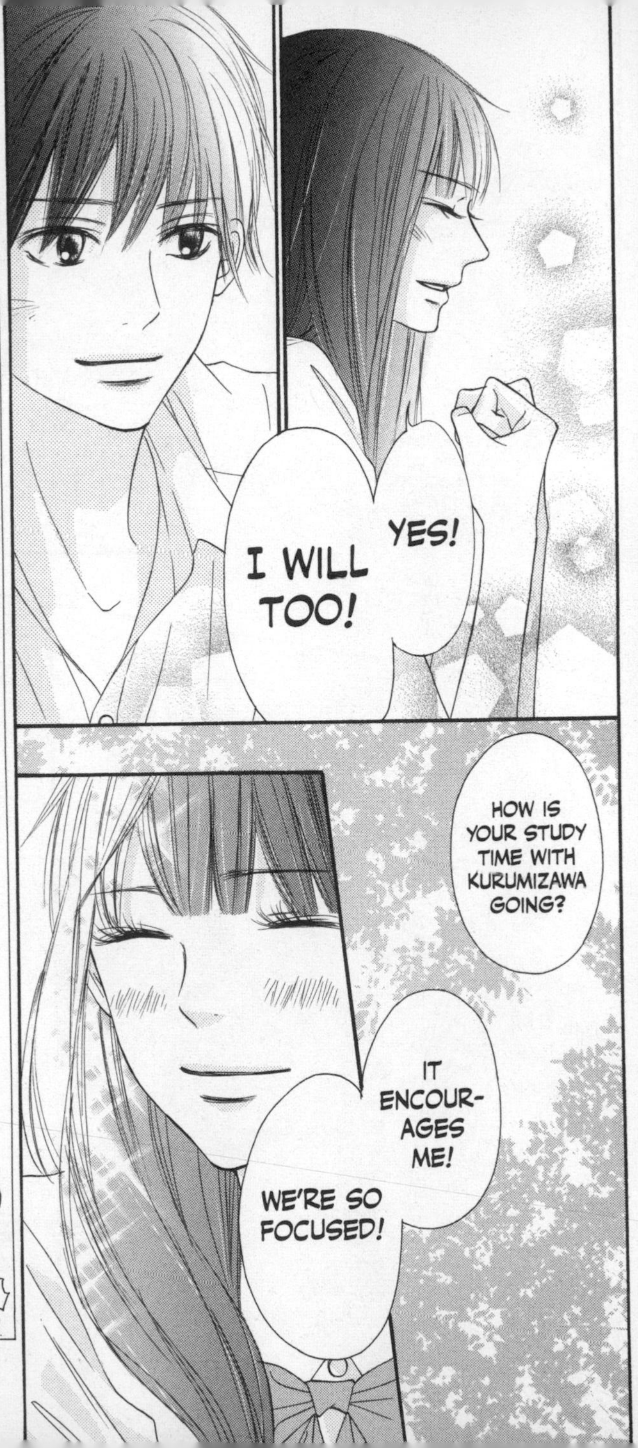
YES!
I WILL TOO!
HOW IS YOUR STUDY TIME WITH KURUMIZAWA GOING?
IT ENCOURAGES ME!
WE'RE SO FOCUSED!

KARUPIN on JAPAN 3

I couldn't wait for night...

4:00 PM

Rice porridge, chicken flakes and radish...

Who cares? It's dinner time! Let's eat!

CHOMP MNCH SNARF GOBBLE

But it wasn't enough!

But it's delicious!

Because I was hungry.

At work, I often skip lunch (especially when I have to think a lot...), so I don't really care about meals. I thought I would be okay because I was getting three meals, but it was hard.

I don't know why it was so hard. I couldn't write because my hands were shaking and I couldn't think about anything. I was just hungry!

Aha!

Have sugar!!

Hus-band

Sweet water tastes awesome!

Hot water with sugar.

I had two servings...

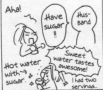

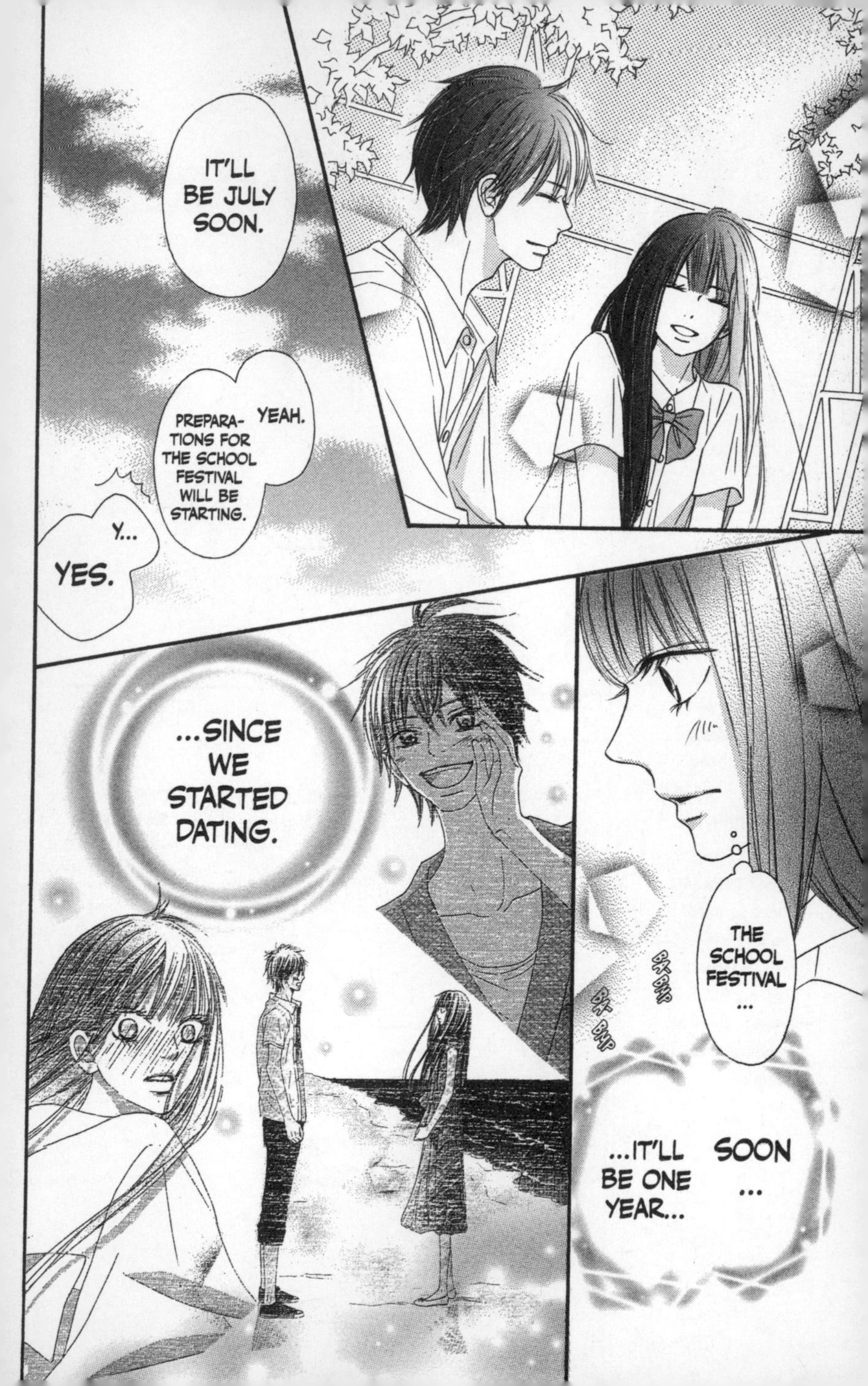
IT'LL BE JULY SOON.
YEAH.
PREPARATIONS FOR THE SCHOOL FESTIVAL WILL BE STARTING.
Y... YES.
THE SCHOOL FESTIVAL...
BK BMP BK BMP
SOON...
...IT'LL BE ONE YEAR...
...SINCE WE STARTED DATING.

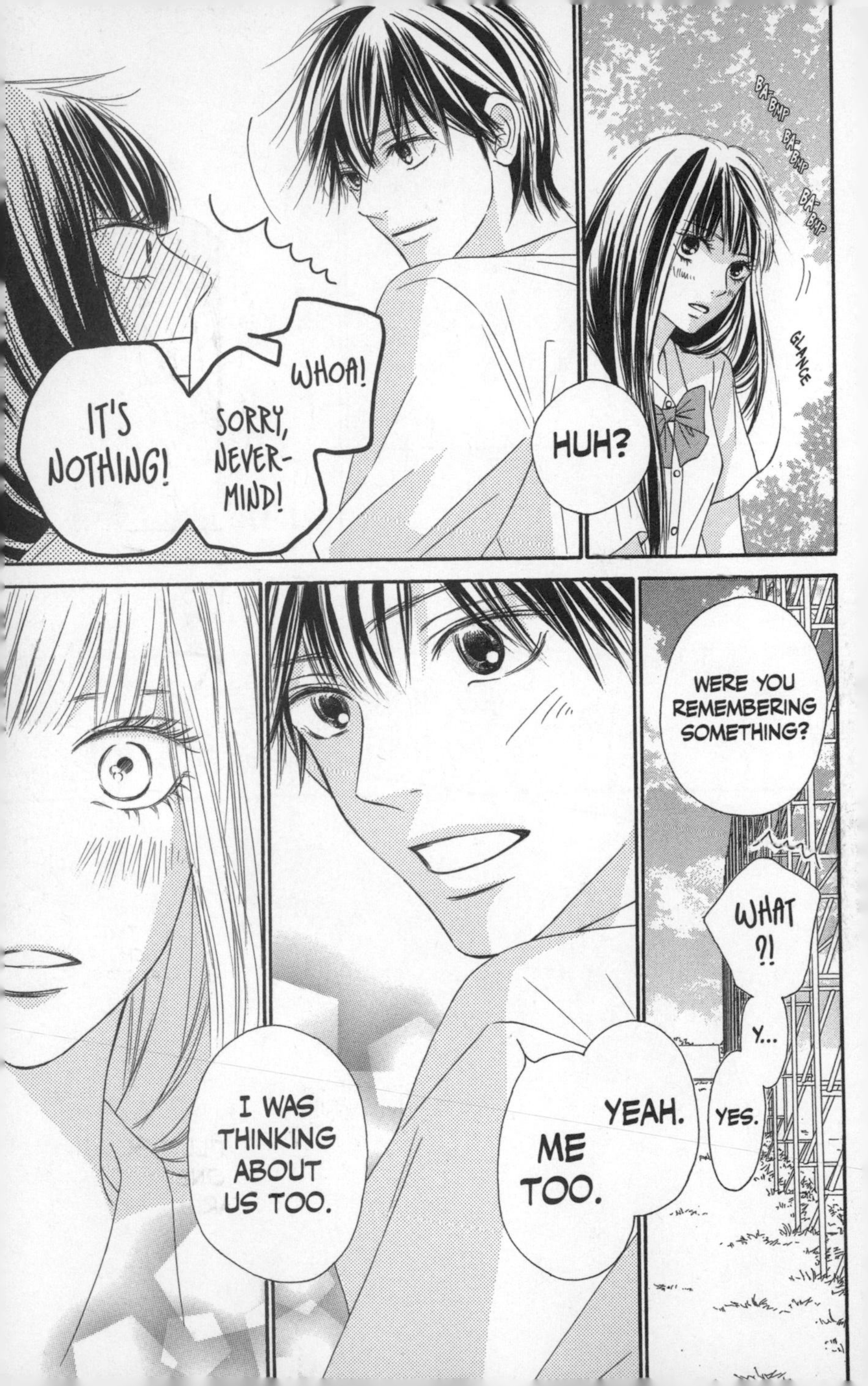
BA-BMP
BA-BMP
BA-BMP
GLANCE
HUH?
WHOA!
SORRY, NEVER-MIND!
IT'S NOTHING!
WERE YOU REMEMBERING SOMETHING?
WHAT?!
Y... YES.
YEAH.
ME TOO.
I WAS THINKING ABOUT US TOO.

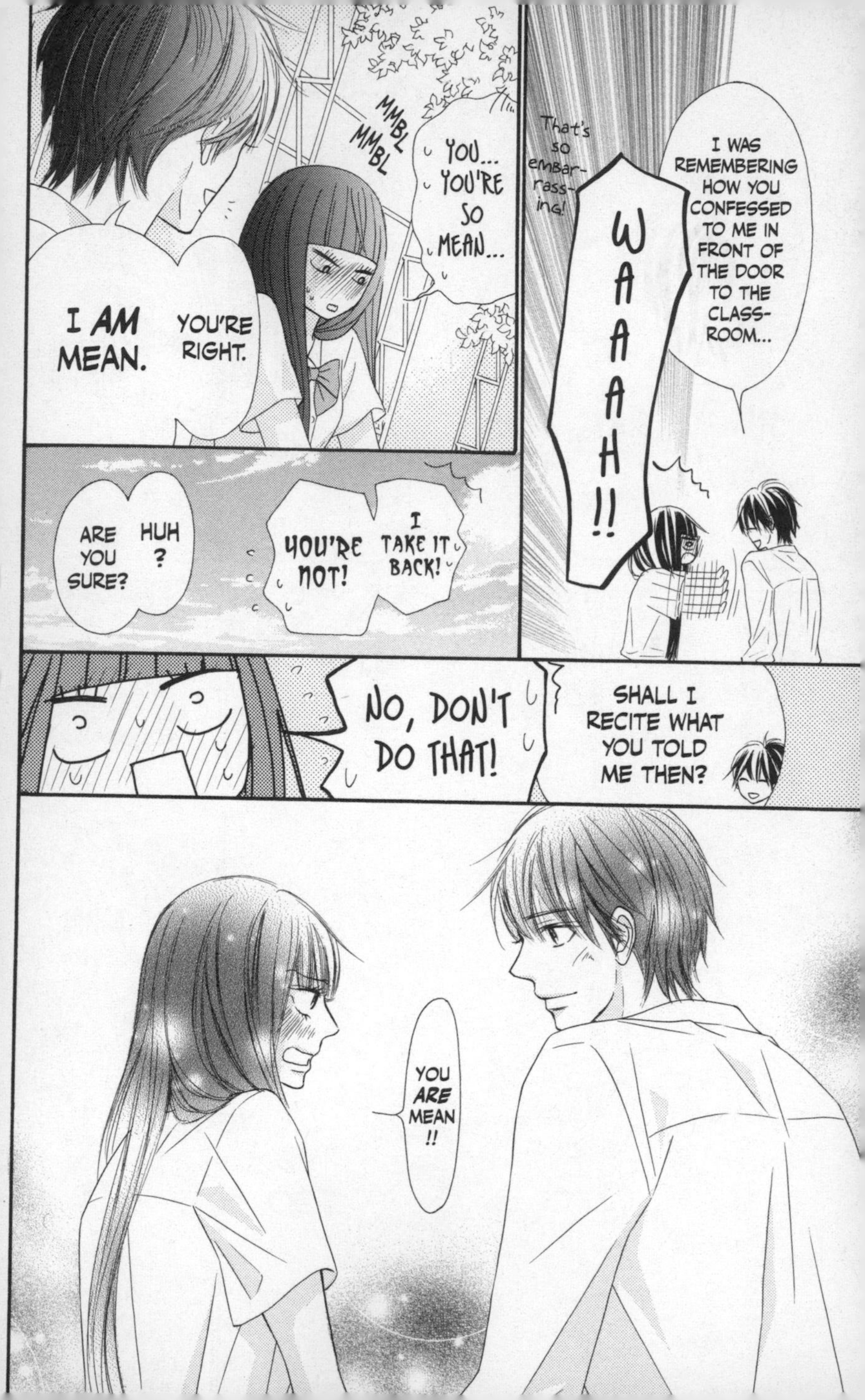
MMBL MMBL
YOU... YOU'RE SO MEAN...
YOU'RE RIGHT.
I AM MEAN.
I TAKE IT BACK!
YOU'RE NOT!
HUH?
ARE YOU SURE?
I WAS REMEMBERING HOW YOU CONFESSED TO ME IN FRONT OF THE DOOR TO THE CLASSROOM...
WAAAAH!!
That's so embarrassing!
SHALL I RECITE WHAT YOU TOLD ME THEN?
NO, DON'T DO THAT!
YOU ARE MEAN!!

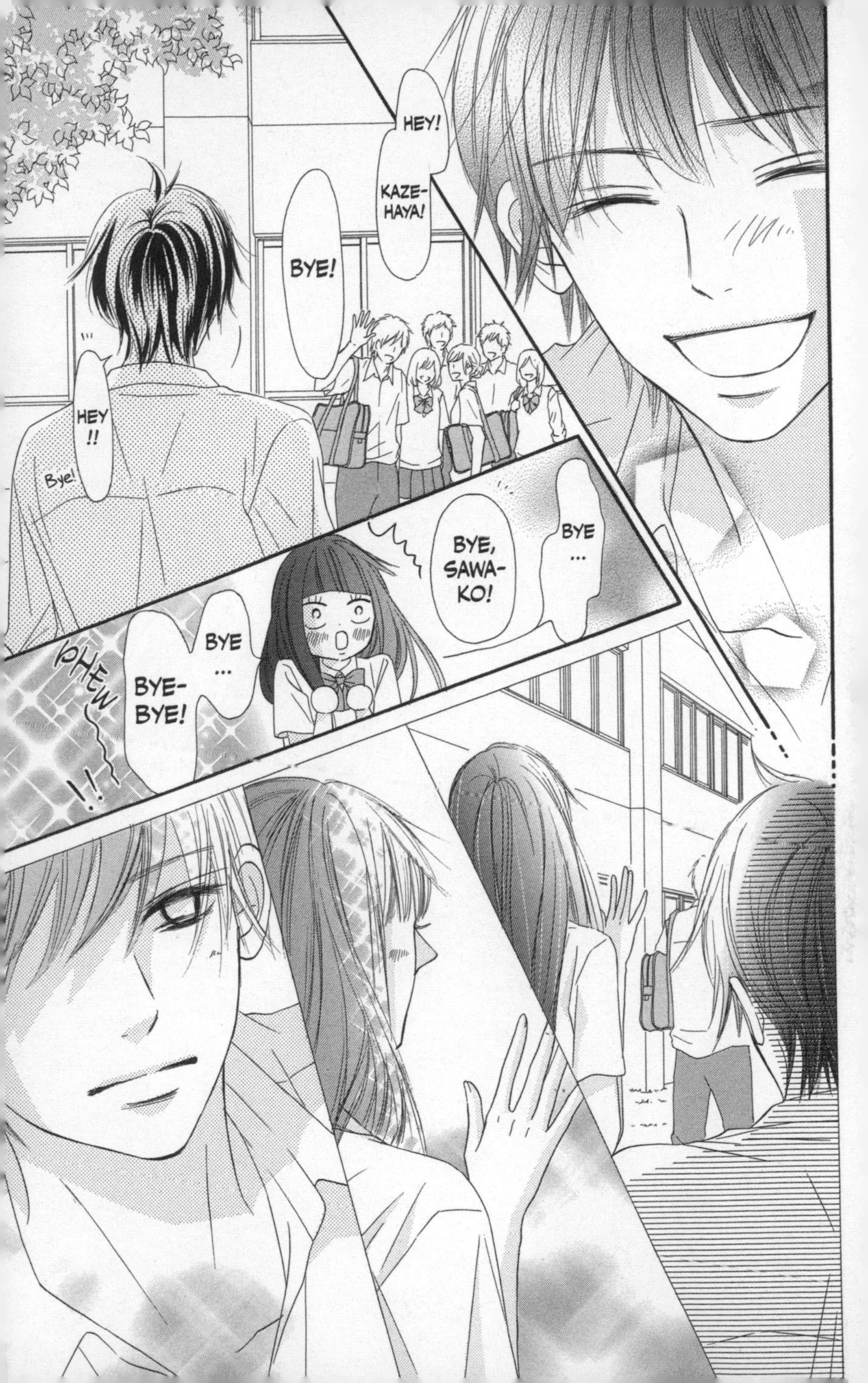

HEY! KAZE-HAYA!
BYE!
HEY !!
Bye!
BYE ...
BYE, SAWA-KO!
BYE ...
BYE-BYE!
PHEW~~!!

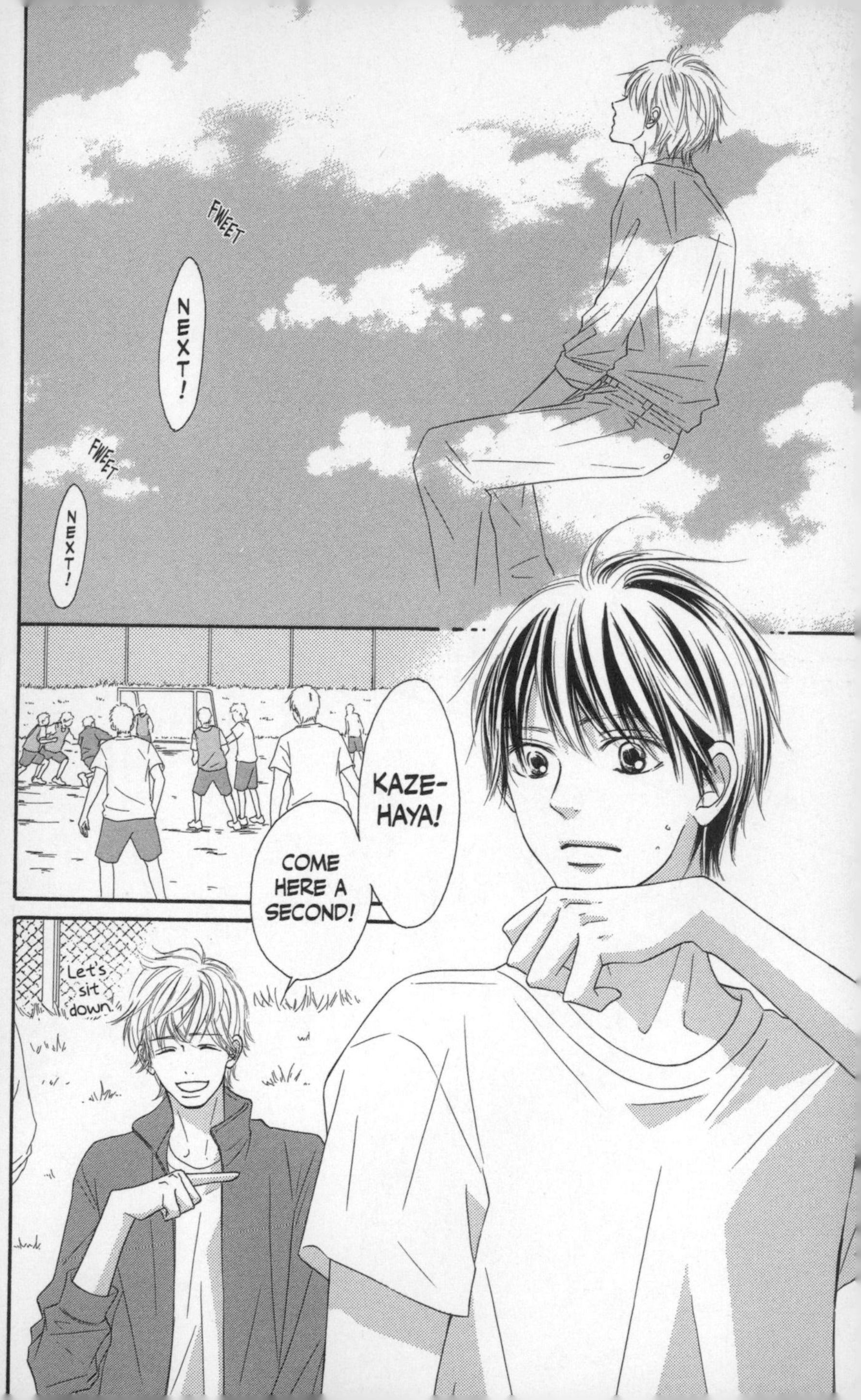
FWEET
NEXT!
FWEET
NEXT!
KAZE-HAYA!
COME HERE A SECOND!
Let's sit down.

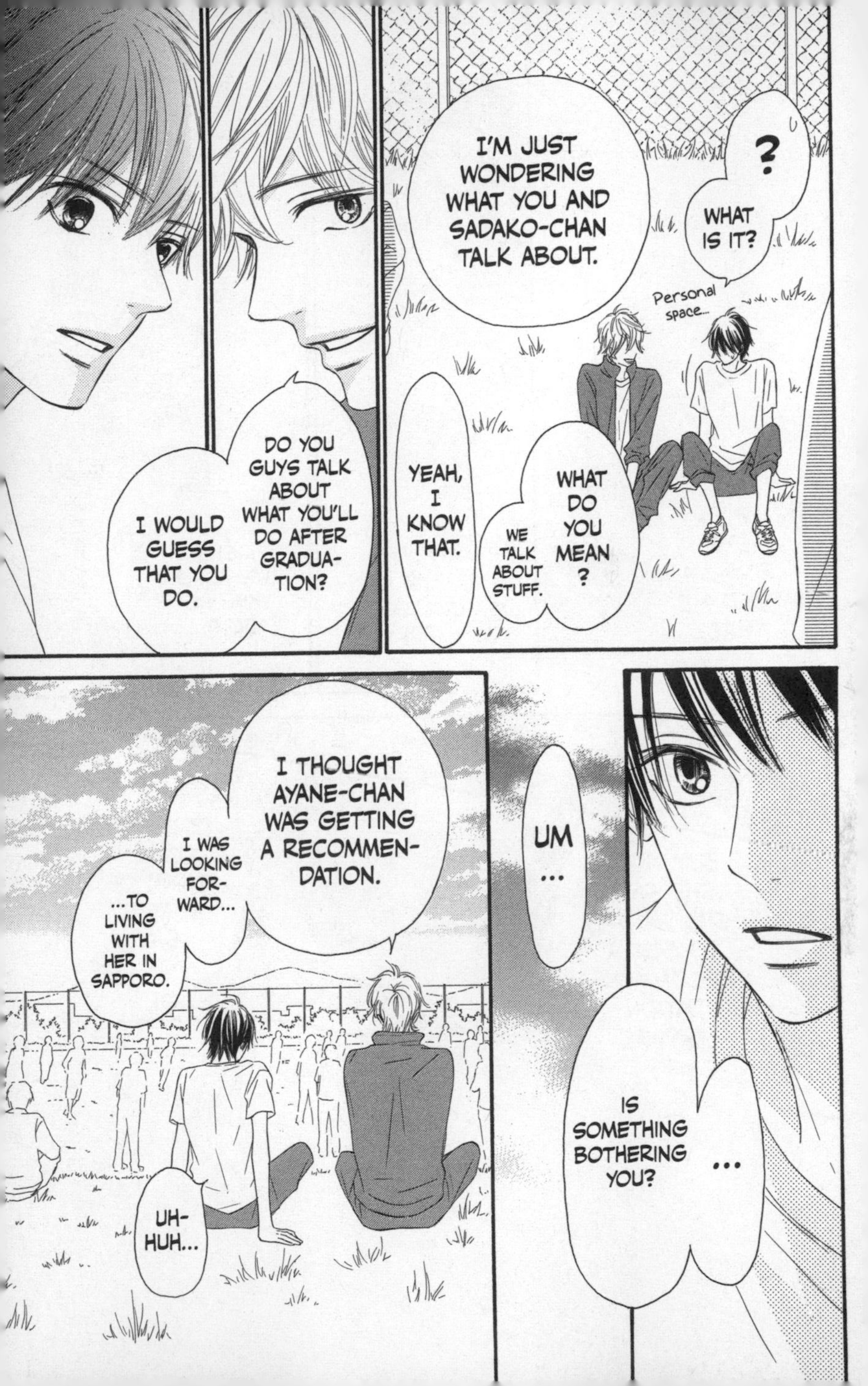
?
WHAT IS IT?
I'M JUST WONDERING WHAT YOU AND SADAKO-CHAN TALK ABOUT.
Personal space...
WHAT DO YOU MEAN?
WE TALK ABOUT STUFF.
YEAH, I KNOW THAT.
DO YOU GUYS TALK ABOUT WHAT YOU'LL DO AFTER GRADUATION?
I WOULD GUESS THAT YOU DO.
UM...
...
IS SOMETHING BOTHERING YOU?
I THOUGHT AYANE-CHAN WAS GETTING A RECOMMENDATION.
I WAS LOOKING FORWARD...
...TO LIVING WITH HER IN SAPPORO.
UH-HUH...

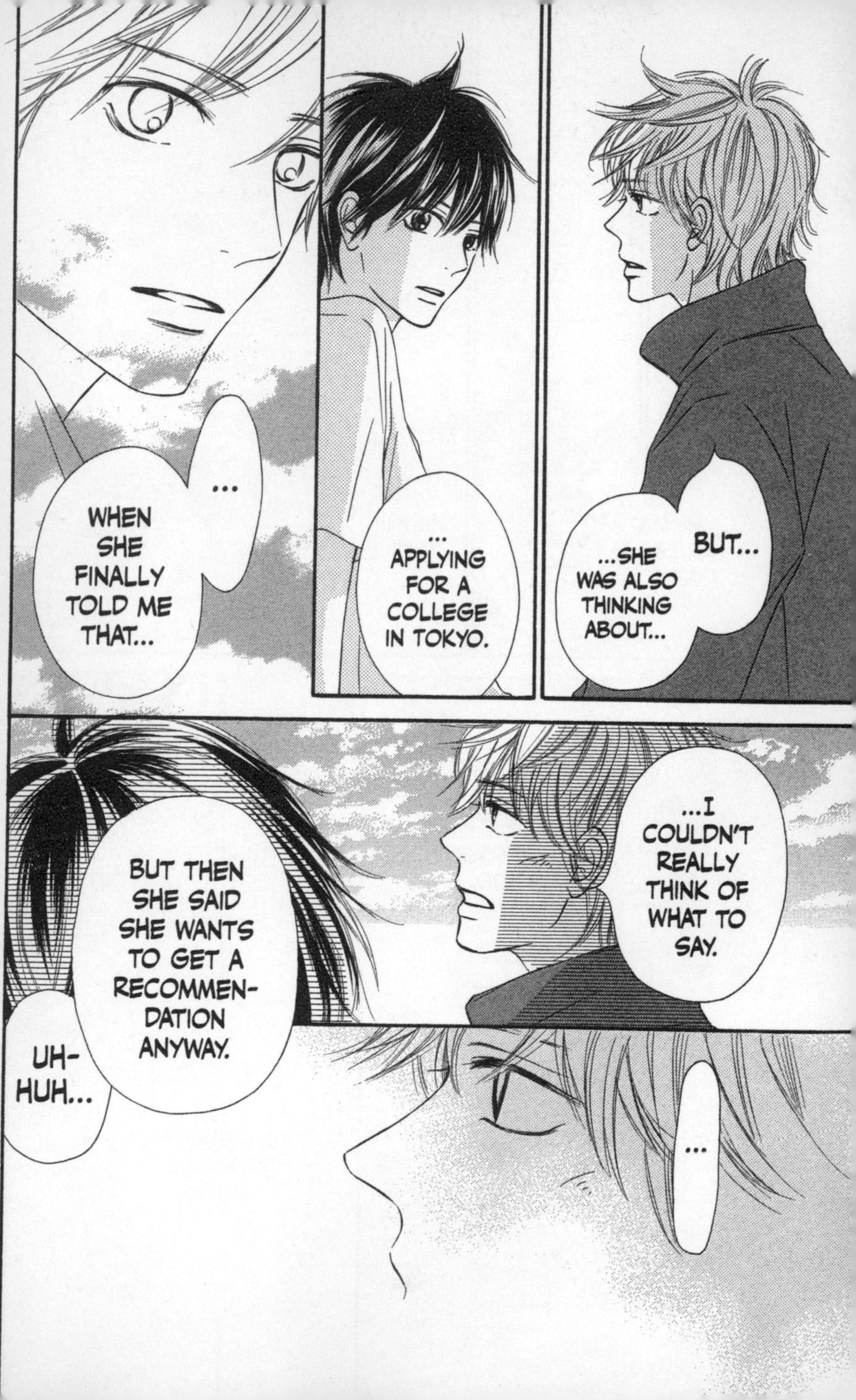
BUT...
...SHE WAS ALSO THINKING ABOUT...
... APPLYING FOR A COLLEGE IN TOKYO.
...
WHEN SHE FINALLY TOLD ME THAT...
...I COULDN'T REALLY THINK OF WHAT TO SAY.
BUT THEN SHE SAID SHE WANTS TO GET A RECOMMEN-DATION ANYWAY.
...
UH-HUH...

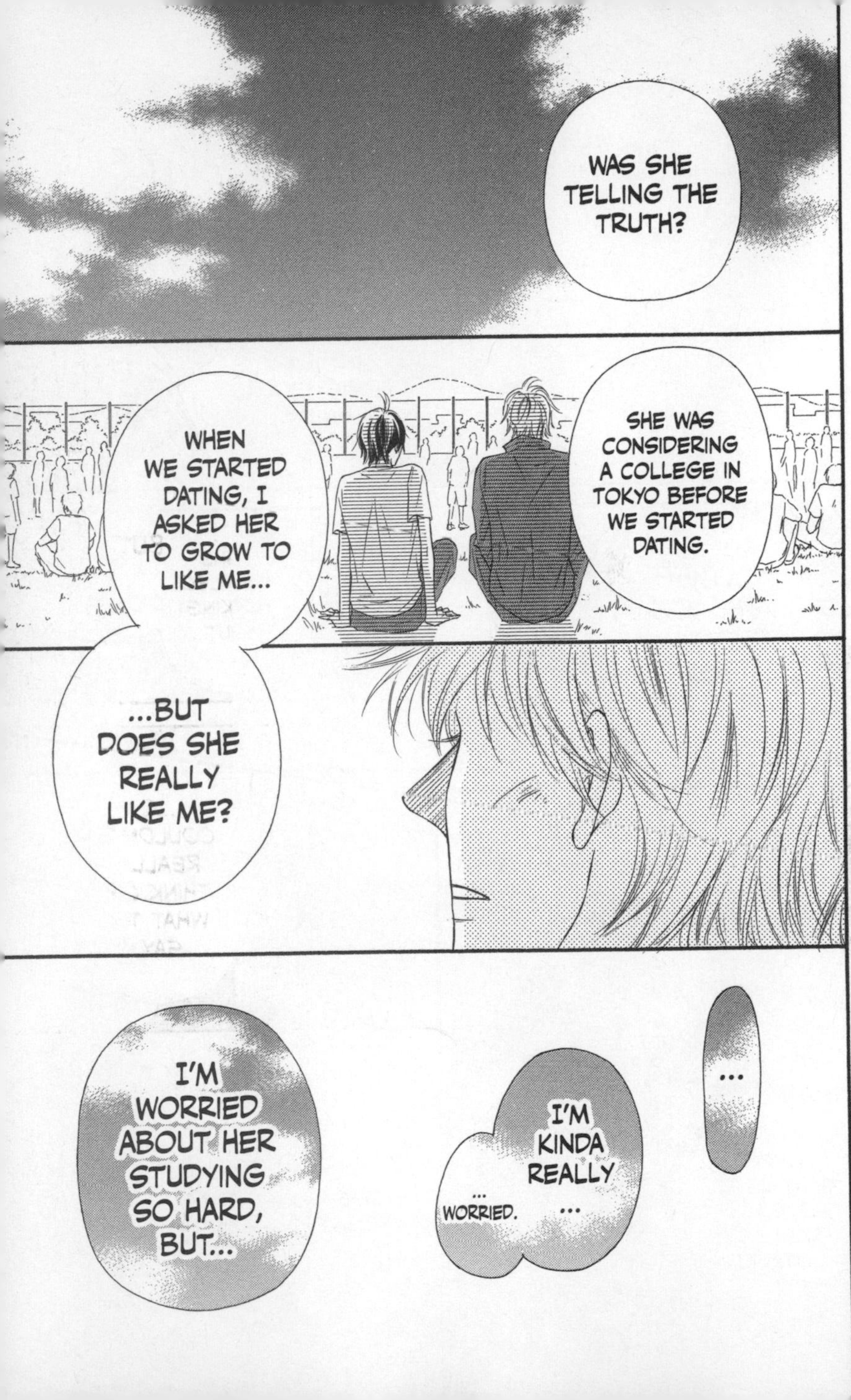
WAS SHE TELLING THE TRUTH?
SHE WAS CONSIDERING A COLLEGE IN TOKYO BEFORE WE STARTED DATING.
WHEN WE STARTED DATING, I ASKED HER TO GROW TO LIKE ME...
...BUT DOES SHE REALLY LIKE ME?
...
I'M KINDA REALLY ... ... WORRIED.
I'M WORRIED ABOUT HER STUDYING SO HARD, BUT...

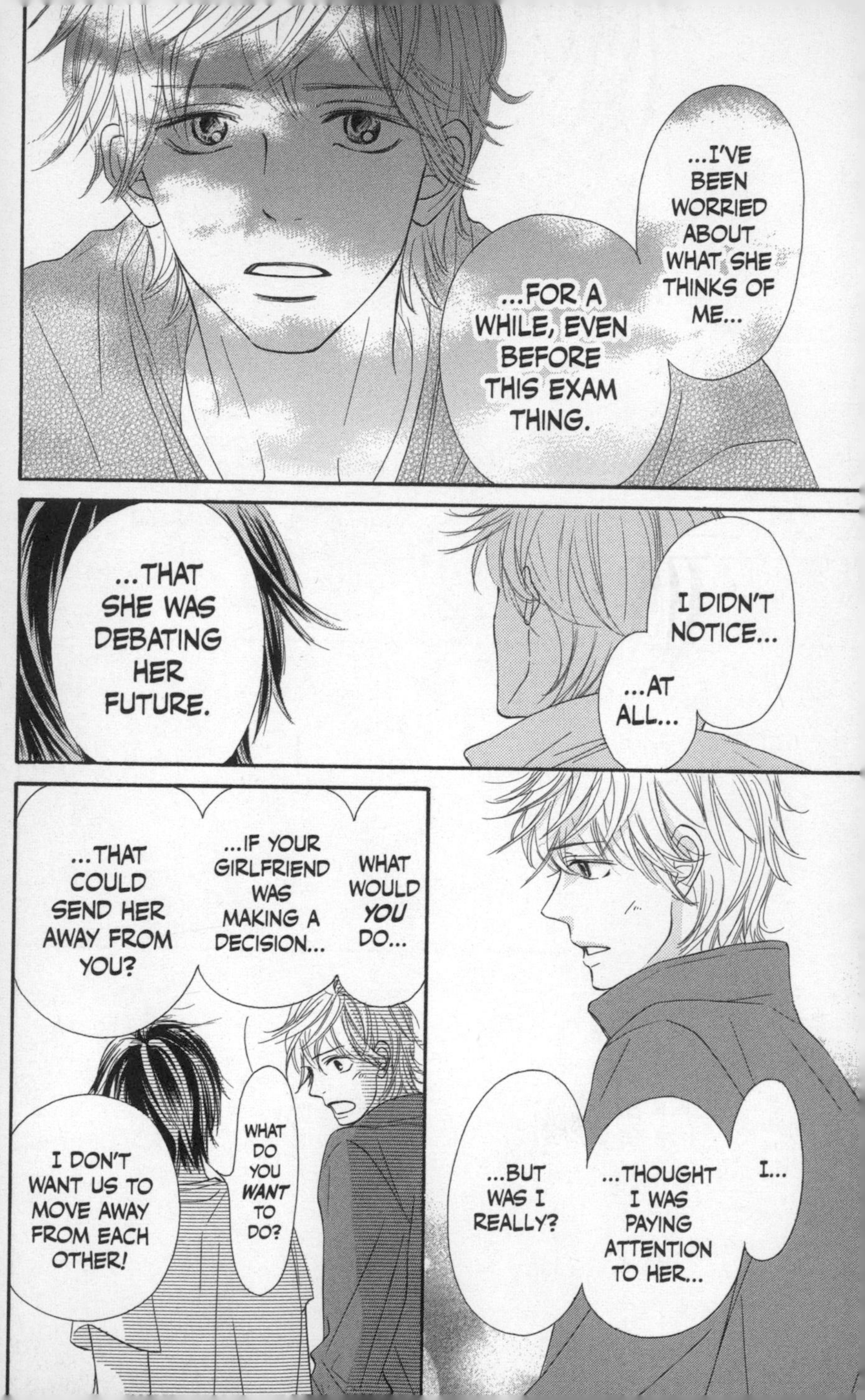
...I'VE BEEN WORRIED ABOUT WHAT SHE THINKS OF ME...
...FOR A WHILE, EVEN BEFORE THIS EXAM THING.
I DIDN'T NOTICE...
...AT ALL...
...THAT SHE WAS DEBATING HER FUTURE.
I...
...THOUGHT I WAS PAYING ATTENTION TO HER...
...BUT WAS I REALLY?
WHAT WOULD *YOU* DO...
...IF YOUR GIRLFRIEND WAS MAKING A DECISION...
...THAT COULD SEND HER AWAY FROM YOU?
WHAT DO YOU *WANT* TO DO?
I DON'T WANT US TO MOVE AWAY FROM EACH OTHER!

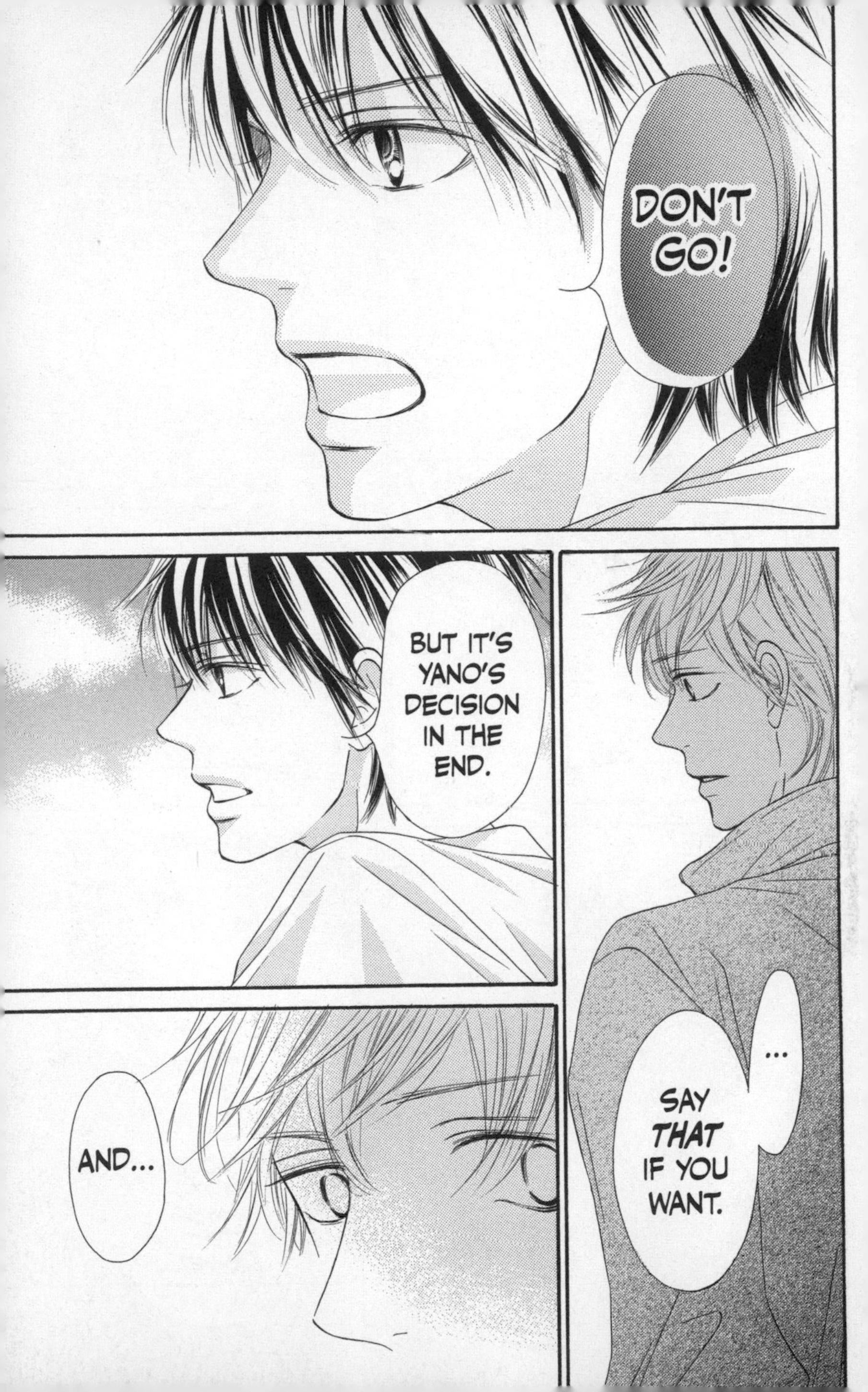
DON'T GO!
...
SAY *THAT* IF YOU WANT.
BUT IT'S YANO'S DECISION IN THE END.
AND...

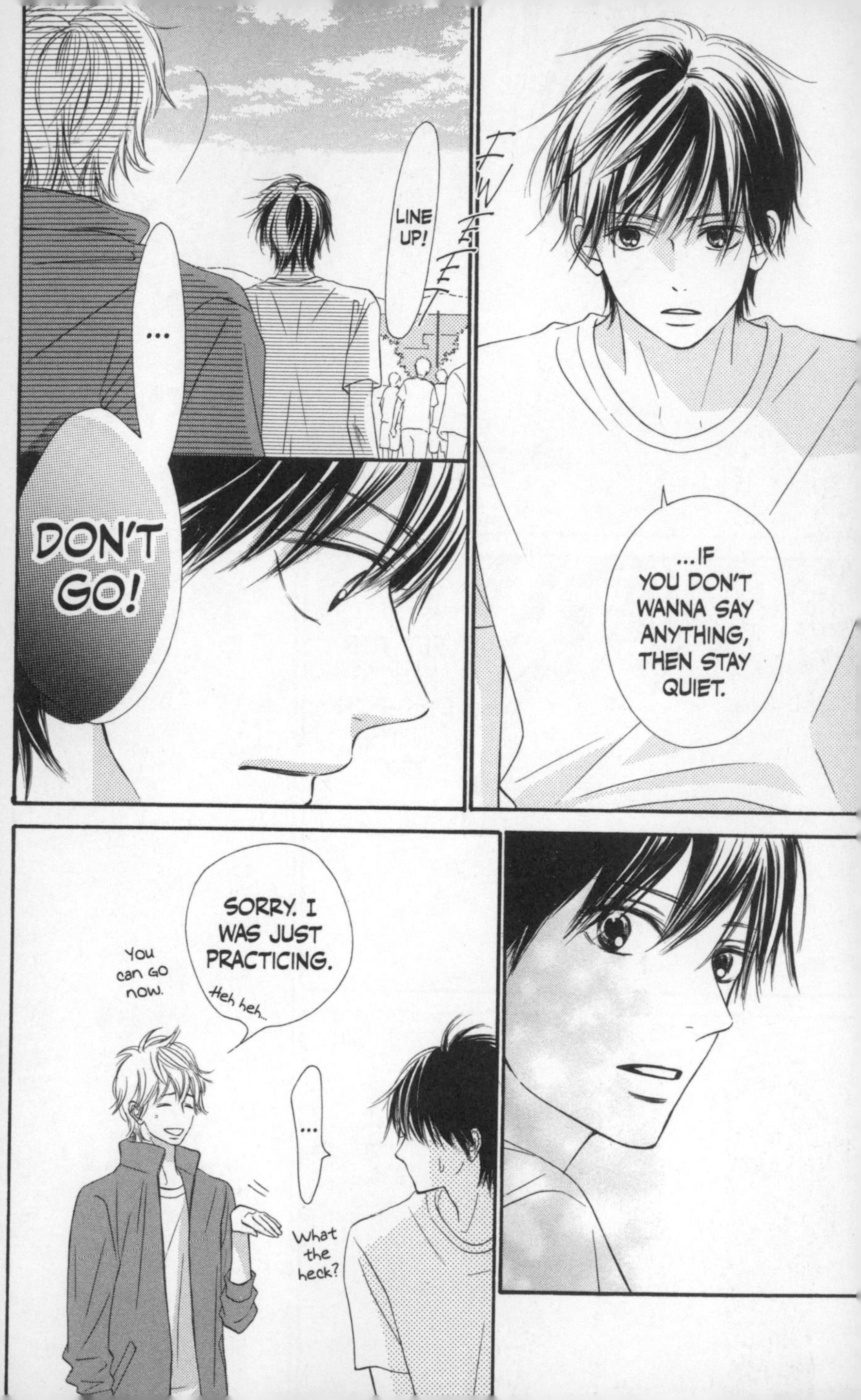
...IF YOU DON'T WANNA SAY ANYTHING, THEN STAY QUIET.
LINE UP!
FWEEEET
...
DON'T GO!
SORRY. I WAS JUST PRACTICING.
Heh heh...
You can go now.
...
What the heck?

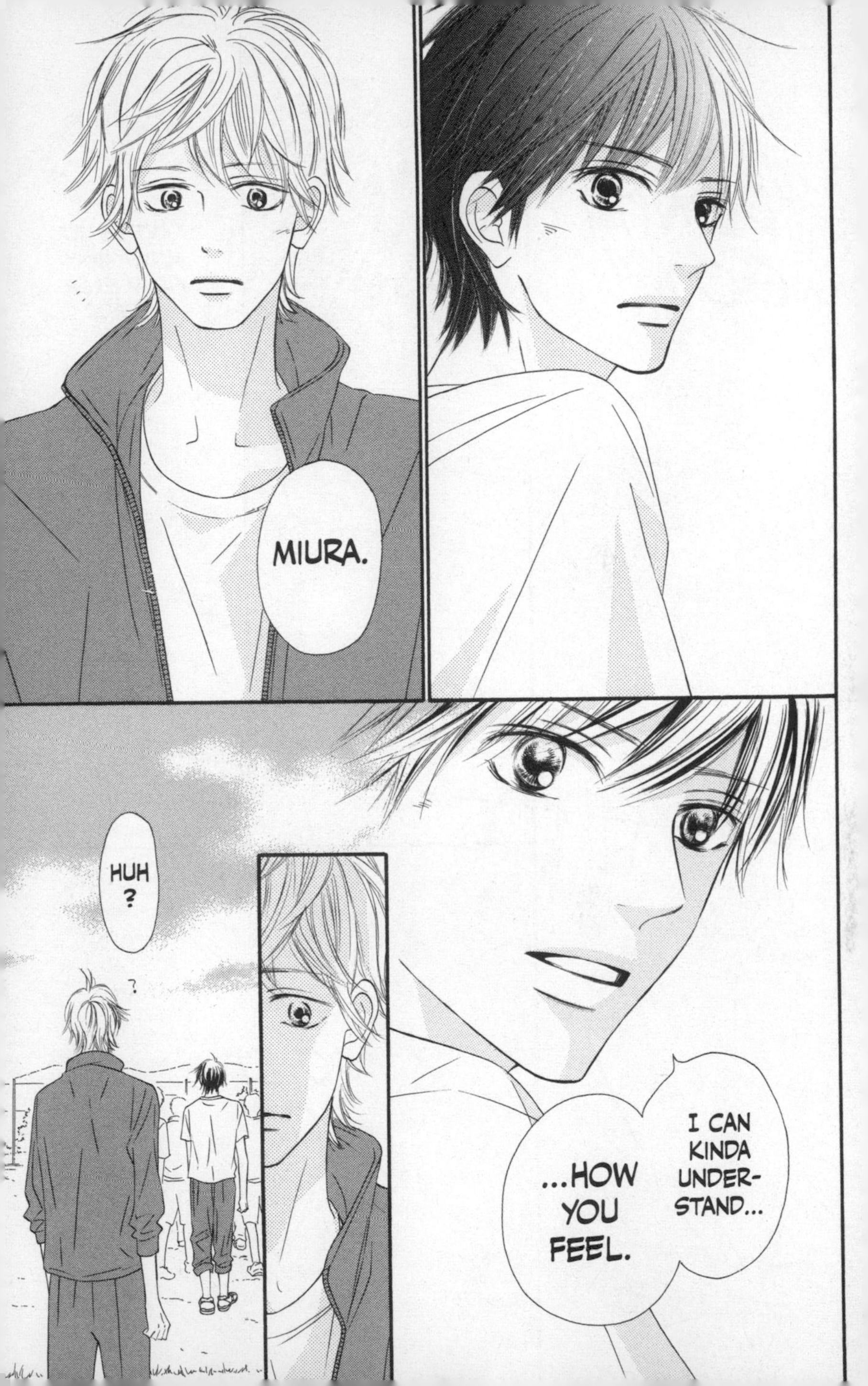
MIURA.
I CAN KINDA UNDER-STAND...
...HOW YOU FEEL.
HUH ?
?

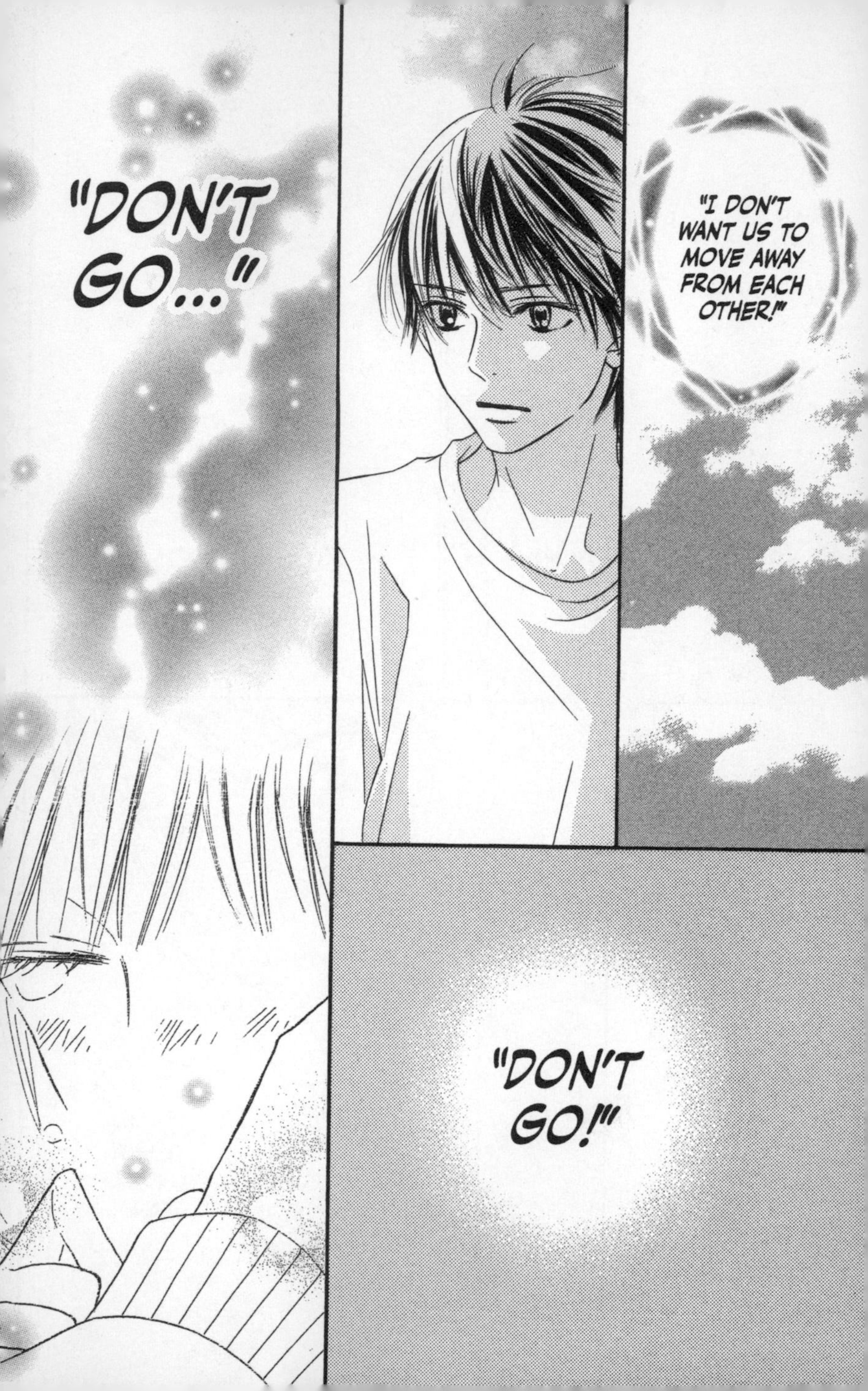
"I DON'T WANT US TO MOVE AWAY FROM EACH OTHER!"
"DON'T GO!"
"DON'T GO..."

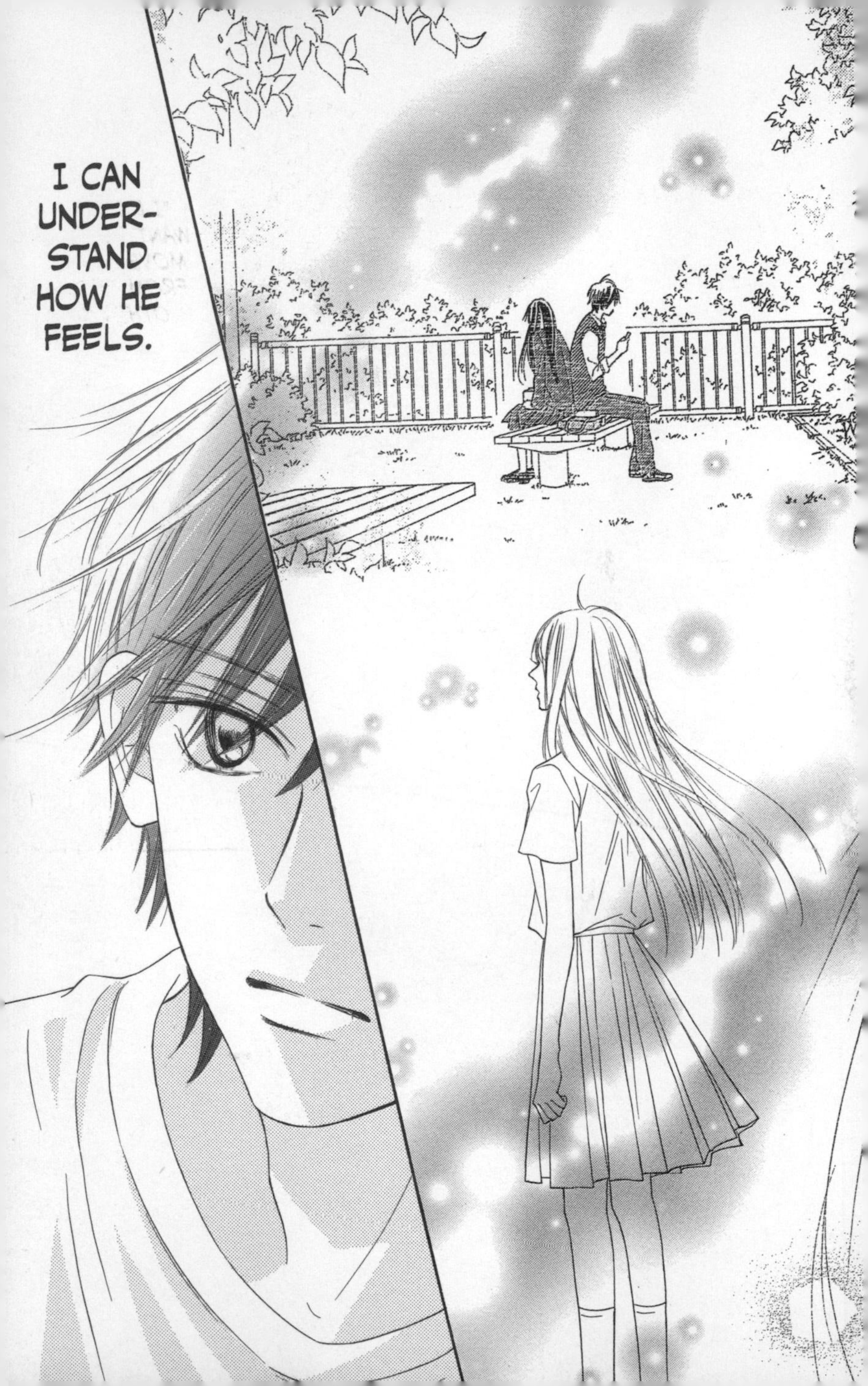
I CAN UNDER-STAND HOW HE FEELS.

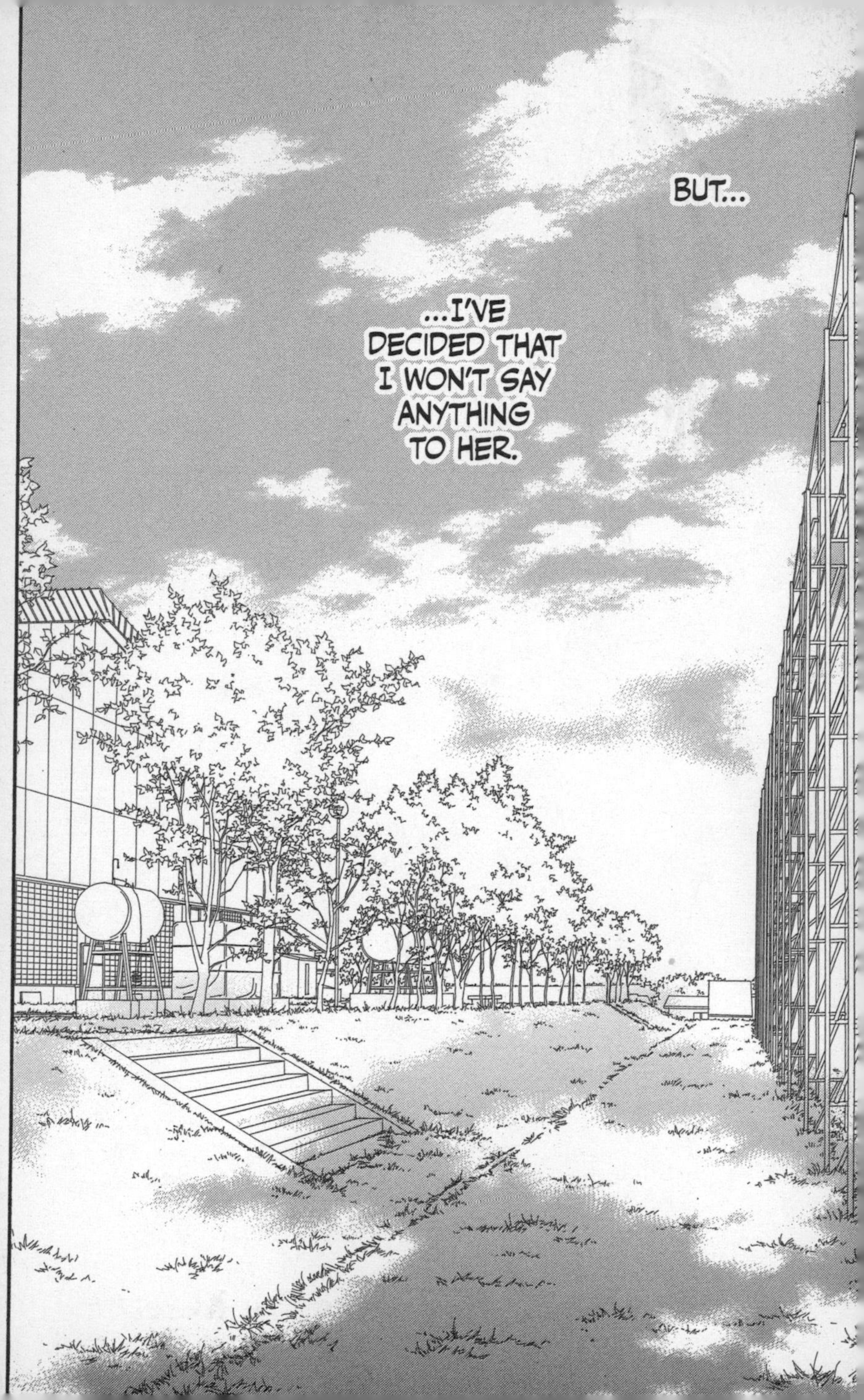
BUT...
...I'VE DECIDED THAT I WON'T SAY ANYTHING TO HER.

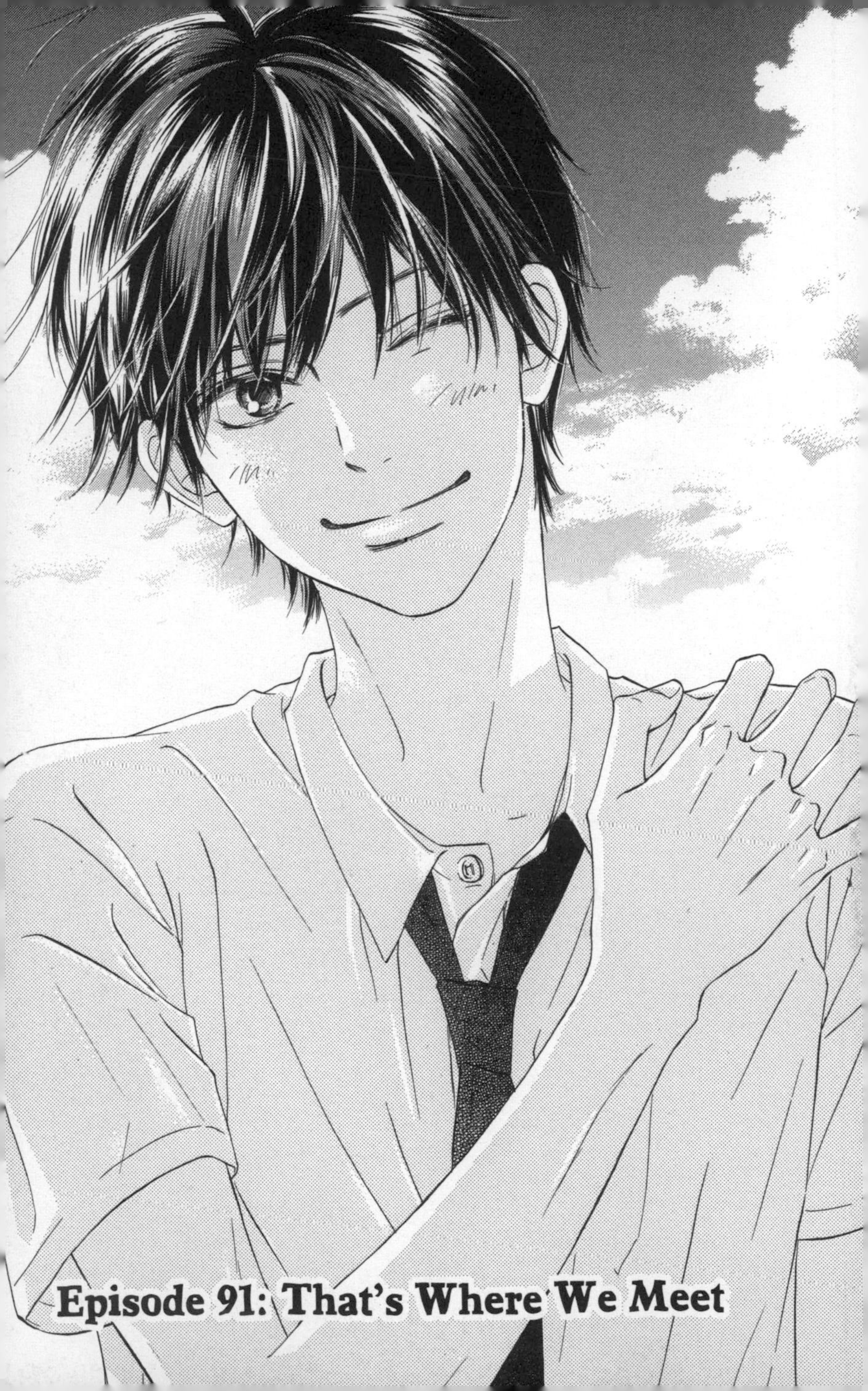
Episode 91: That's Where We Meet

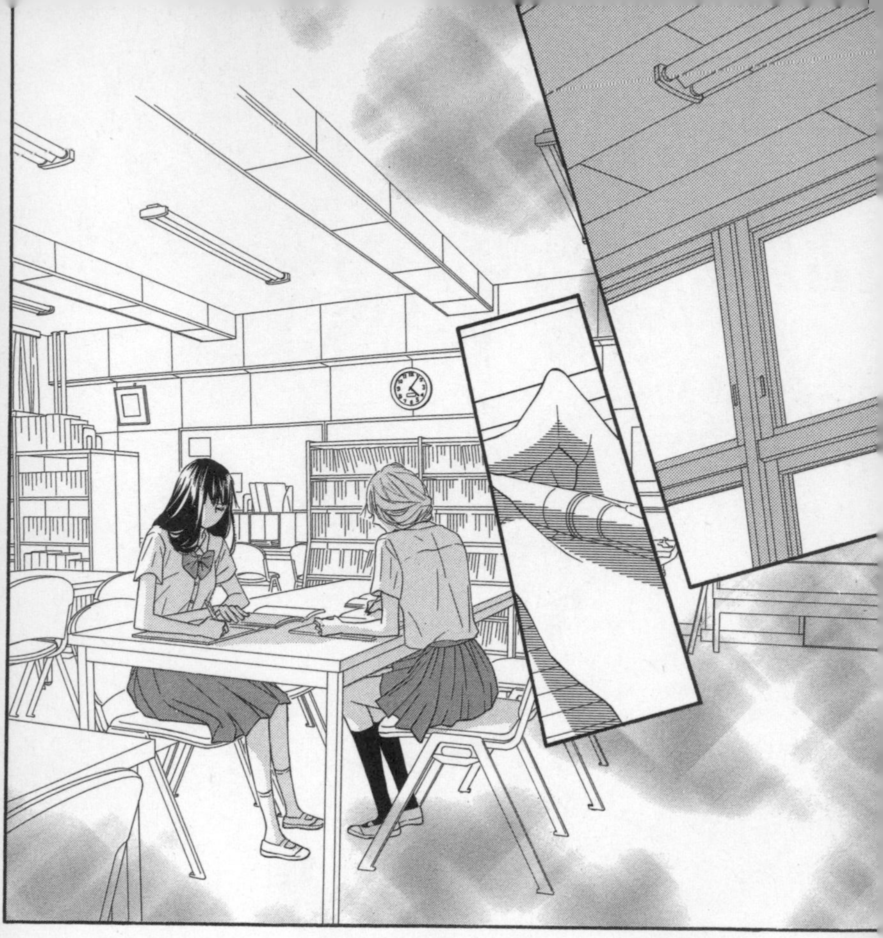
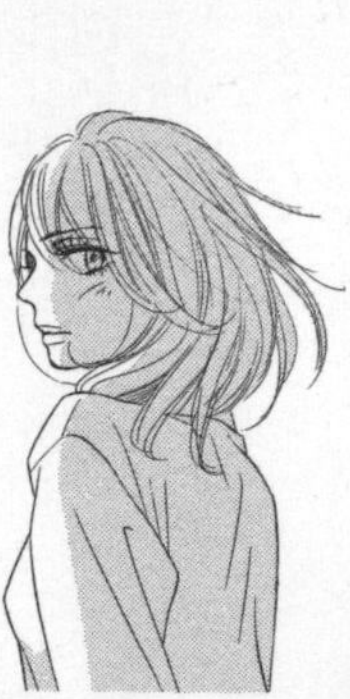

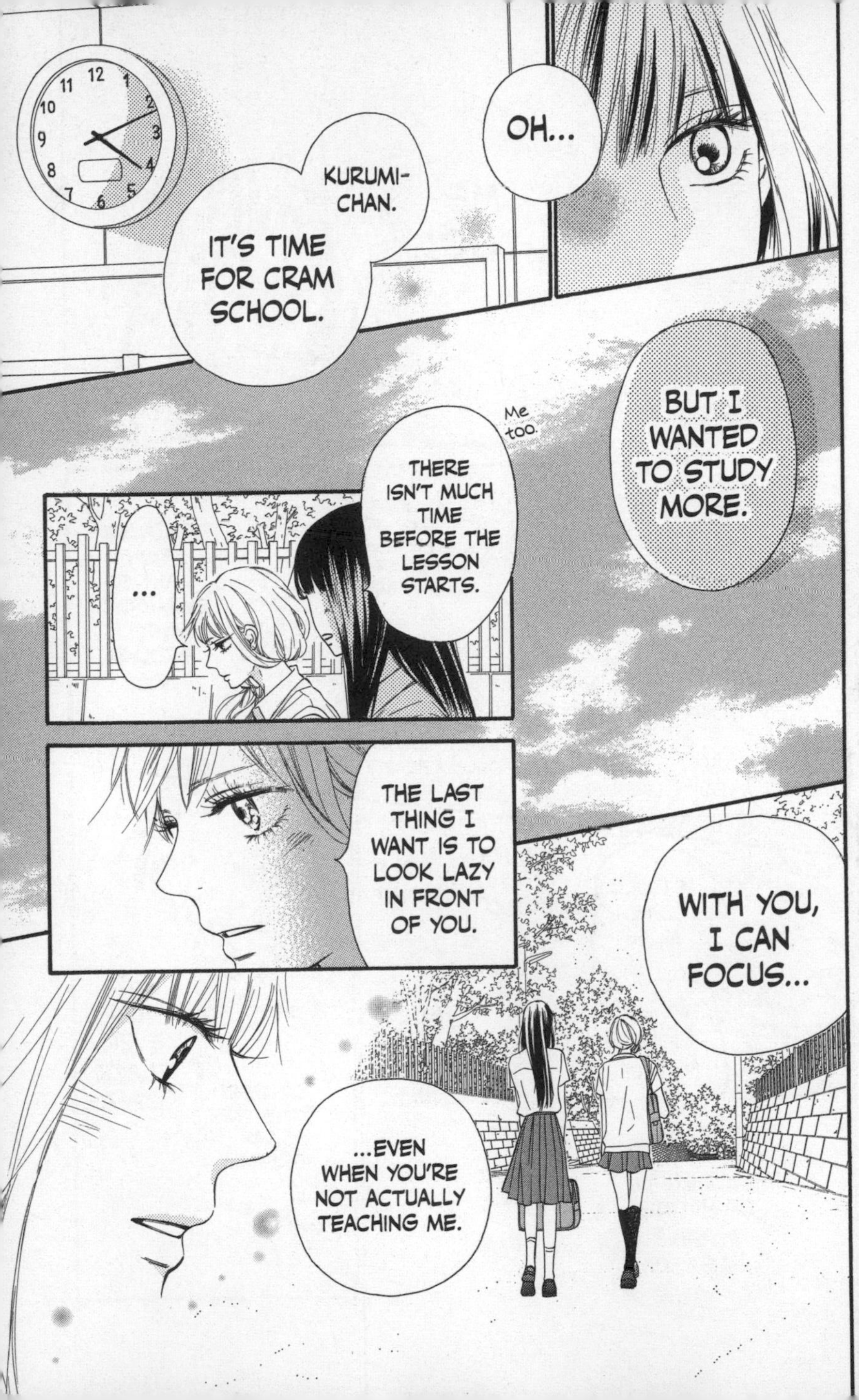
OH...
KURUMI-CHAN.
IT'S TIME FOR CRAM SCHOOL.
BUT I WANTED TO STUDY MORE.
Me too.
THERE ISN'T MUCH TIME BEFORE THE LESSON STARTS.
...
THE LAST THING I WANT IS TO LOOK LAZY IN FRONT OF YOU.
WITH YOU, I CAN FOCUS...
...EVEN WHEN YOU'RE NOT ACTUALLY TEACHING ME.

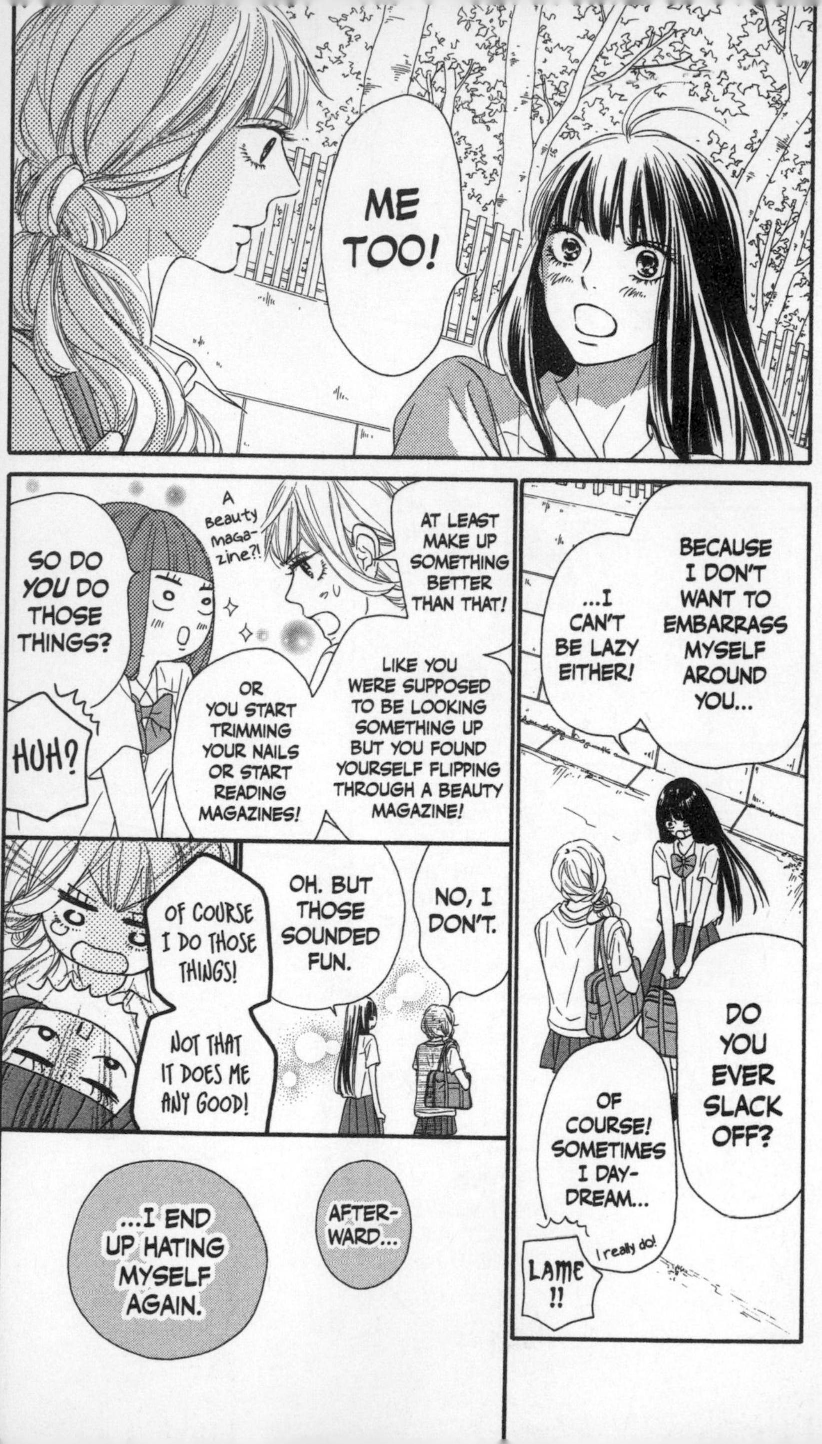
ME TOO!
BECAUSE I DON'T WANT TO EMBARRASS MYSELF AROUND YOU...
...I CAN'T BE LAZY EITHER!
DO YOU EVER SLACK OFF?
OF COURSE! SOMETIMES I DAY-DREAM...
I really do!
LAME!!
AT LEAST MAKE UP SOMETHING BETTER THAN THAT!
A Beauty Maga-zine?!
LIKE YOU WERE SUPPOSED TO BE LOOKING SOMETHING UP BUT YOU FOUND YOURSELF FLIPPING THROUGH A BEAUTY MAGAZINE!
OR YOU START TRIMMING YOUR NAILS OR START READING MAGAZINES!
SO DO *YOU* DO THOSE THINGS?
HUH?
NO, I DON'T.
OH. BUT THOSE SOUNDED FUN.
OF COURSE I DO THOSE THINGS!
NOT THAT IT DOES ME ANY GOOD!
AFTER-WARD...
...I END UP HATING MYSELF AGAIN.

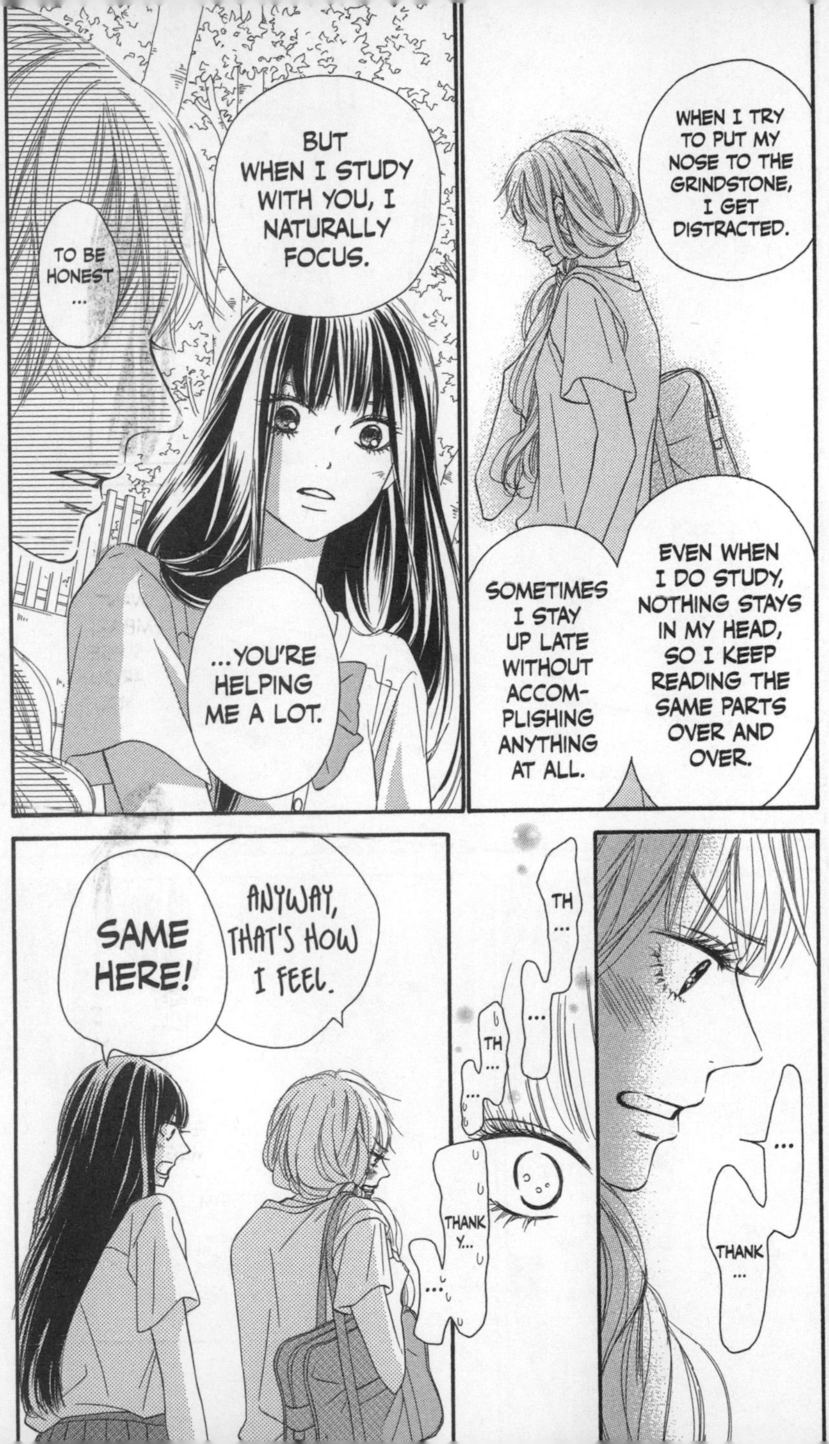
WHEN I TRY TO PUT MY NOSE TO THE GRINDSTONE, I GET DISTRACTED.
EVEN WHEN I DO STUDY, NOTHING STAYS IN MY HEAD, SO I KEEP READING THE SAME PARTS OVER AND OVER.
SOMETIMES I STAY UP LATE WITHOUT ACCOM-PLISHING ANYTHING AT ALL.
BUT WHEN I STUDY WITH YOU, I NATURALLY FOCUS.
TO BE HONEST ...
...YOU'RE HELPING ME A LOT.
...
THANK ...
TH ...
...
TH ...
...
THANK Y...
...
ANYWAY, THAT'S HOW I FEEL.
SAME HERE!

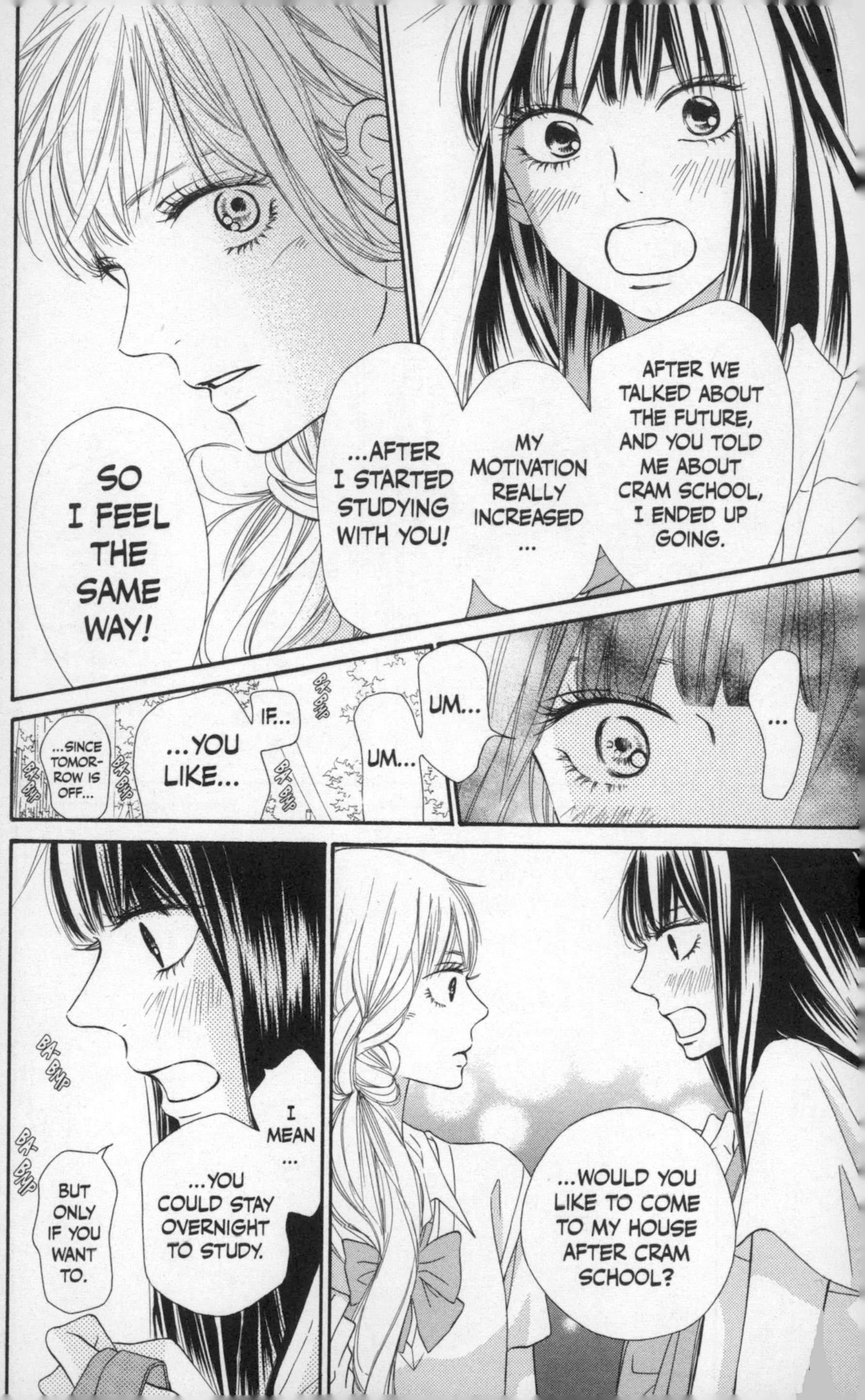
AFTER WE TALKED ABOUT THE FUTURE, AND YOU TOLD ME ABOUT CRAM SCHOOL, I ENDED UP GOING.
MY MOTIVATION REALLY INCREASED ...
...AFTER I STARTED STUDYING WITH YOU!
SO I FEEL THE SAME WAY!
...
UM...
UM...
BA-BMP
IF...
...YOU LIKE...
BA-BMP
BA-BMP
...SINCE TOMORROW IS OFF...
BA-BMP
...WOULD YOU LIKE TO COME TO MY HOUSE AFTER CRAM SCHOOL?
I MEAN ...
...YOU COULD STAY OVERNIGHT TO STUDY.
BUT ONLY IF YOU WANT TO.
BA-BMP
BA-BMP

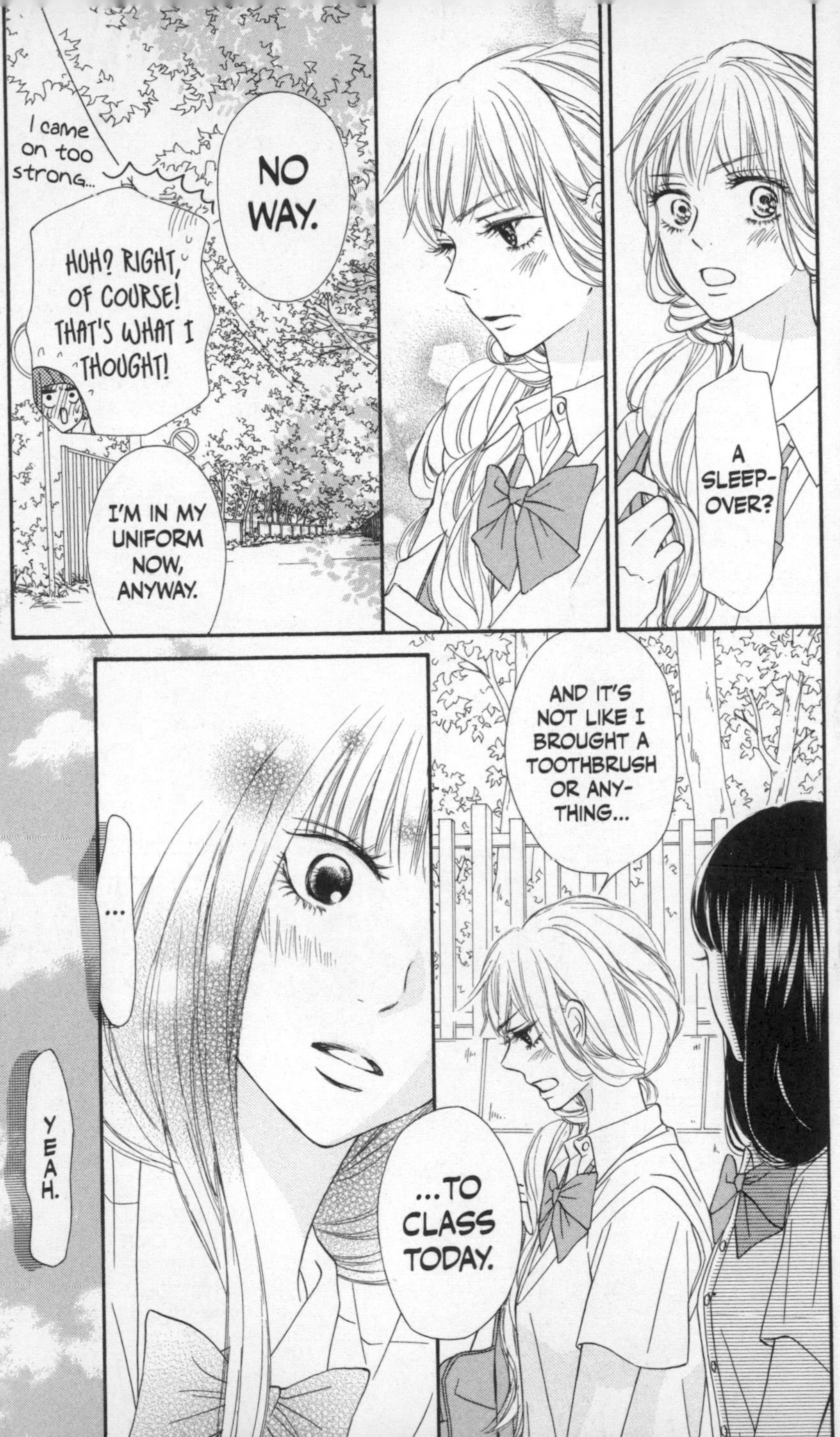
A SLEEP-OVER?
NO WAY.
I came on too strong...
HUH? RIGHT, OF COURSE! THAT'S WHAT I THOUGHT!
I'M IN MY UNIFORM NOW, ANYWAY.
AND IT'S NOT LIKE I BROUGHT A TOOTHBRUSH OR ANY-THING...
...TO CLASS TODAY.
...
YEAH.

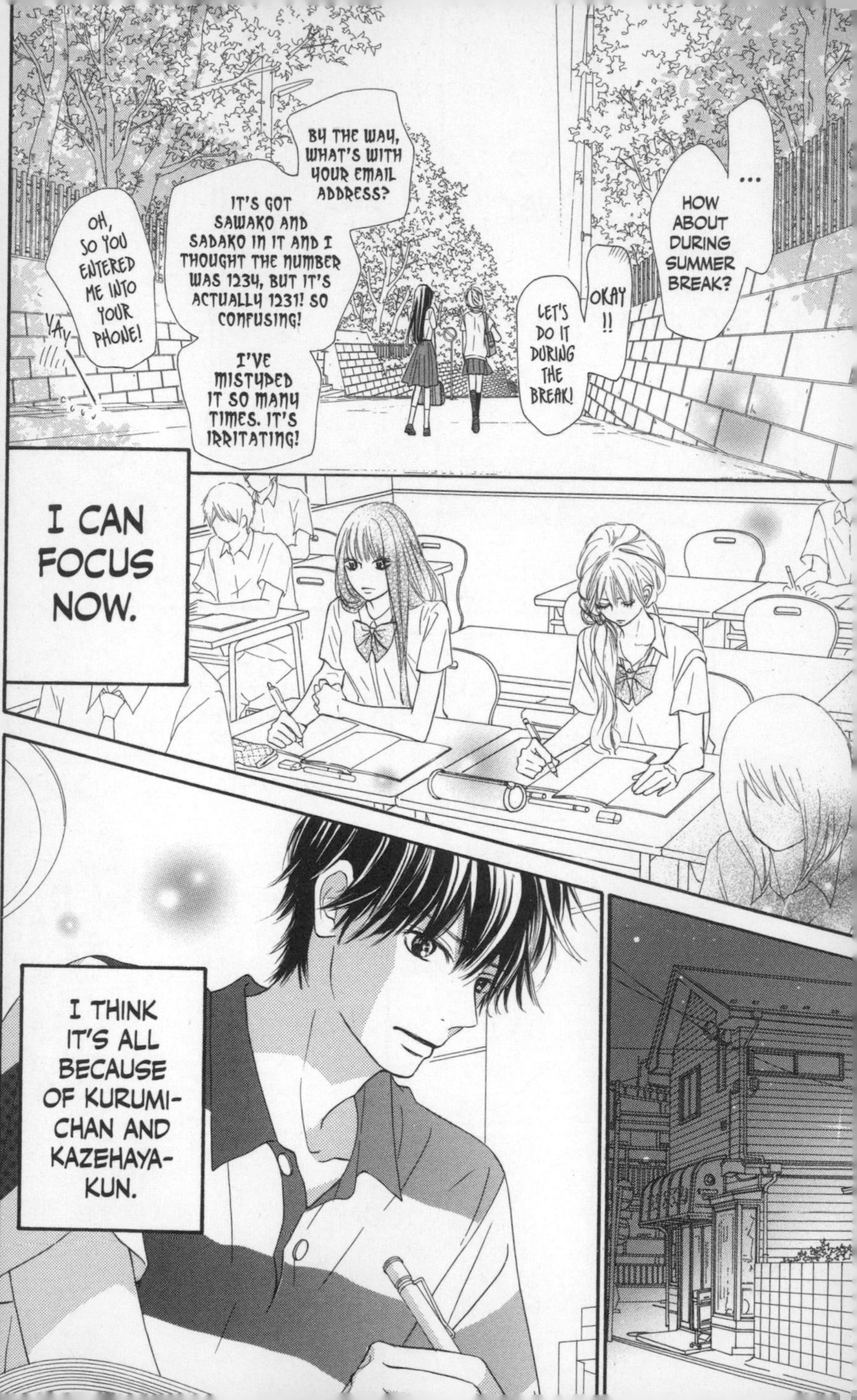
...
HOW ABOUT DURING SUMMER BREAK?
OKAY !!
LET'S DO IT DURING THE BREAK!
BY THE WAY, WHAT'S WITH YOUR EMAIL ADDRESS?
IT'S GOT SAWAKO AND SADAKO IN IT AND I THOUGHT THE NUMBER WAS 1234, BUT IT'S ACTUALLY 1231! SO CONFUSING!
I'VE MISTYPED IT SO MANY TIMES. IT'S IRRITATING!
OH, SO YOU ENTERED ME INTO YOUR PHONE!
YAY
I CAN FOCUS NOW.
I THINK IT'S ALL BECAUSE OF KURUMI-CHAN AND KAZEHAYA-KUN.

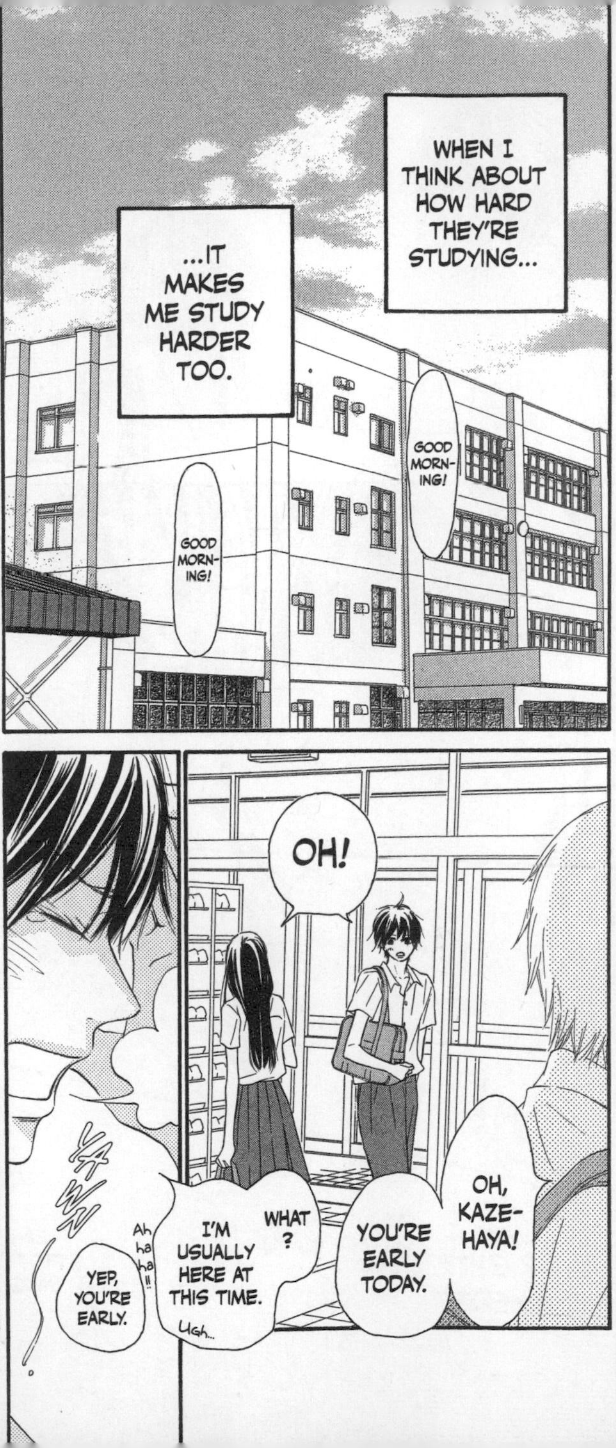
WHEN I THINK ABOUT HOW HARD THEY'RE STUDYING...
...IT MAKES ME STUDY HARDER TOO.
GOOD MORN-ING!
GOOD MORN-ING!
OH!
OH, KAZE-HAYA!
YOU'RE EARLY TODAY.
WHAT?
I'M USUALLY HERE AT THIS TIME.
Ugh...
Ah ha ha!!
YEP, YOU'RE EARLY.
YAWN

KARUPIN on JAPAN 4

Changing the topic...

Right now I have an old volume of my one-shots in front of me. I was curious, but afraid, to read the sidebars in it. I did it anyway. They're from the year 2002.

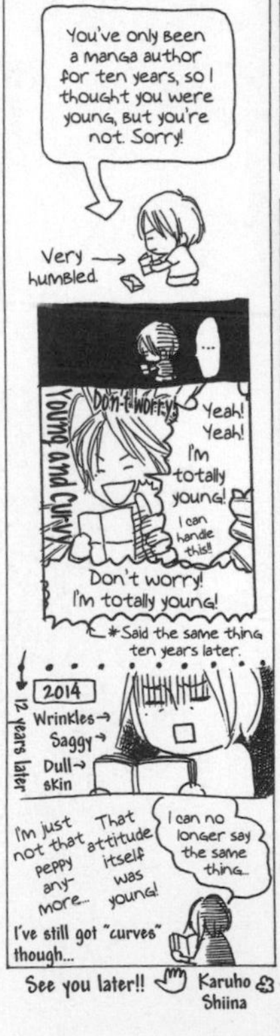
You've only been a manga author for ten years, so I thought you were young, but you're not. Sorry!
Very humbled.
...
Young and Curvy
Don't worry!
Yeah! Yeah! I'm totally young!
I can handle this!!
Don't worry! I'm totally young!
*Said the same thing ten years later.
2014
12 years later
Wrinkles
Saggy
Dull skin
I'm just not that peppy anymore...
That attitude itself was young!
I can no longer say the same thing.
I've still got "curves" though...

See you later!! Karuho Shiina

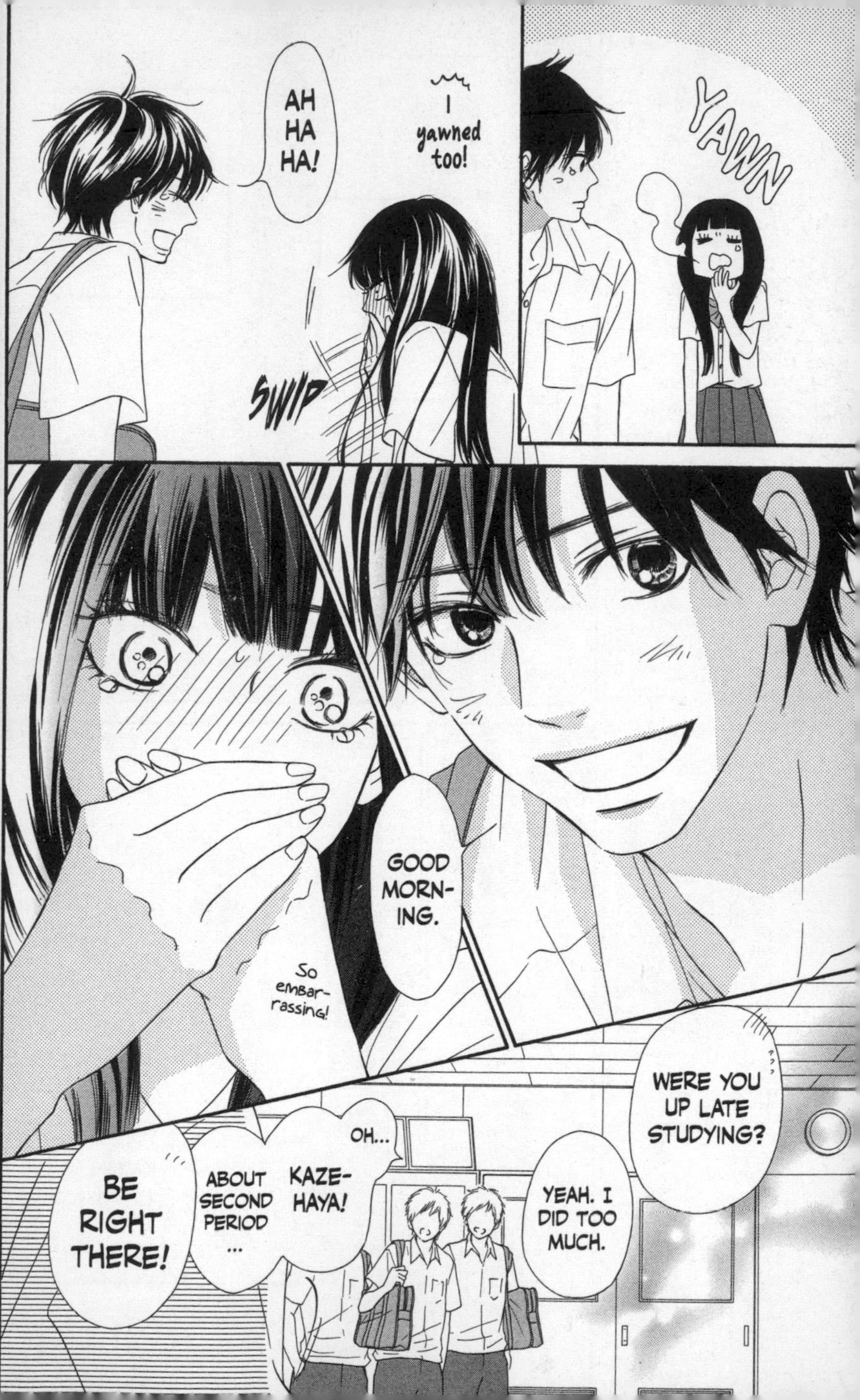
YAWN
I yawned too!
AH HA HA!
SWIP
GOOD MORNING.
So embarrassing!
WERE YOU UP LATE STUDYING?
YEAH. I DID TOO MUCH.
OH... KAZEHAYA!
ABOUT SECOND PERIOD ...
BE RIGHT THERE!

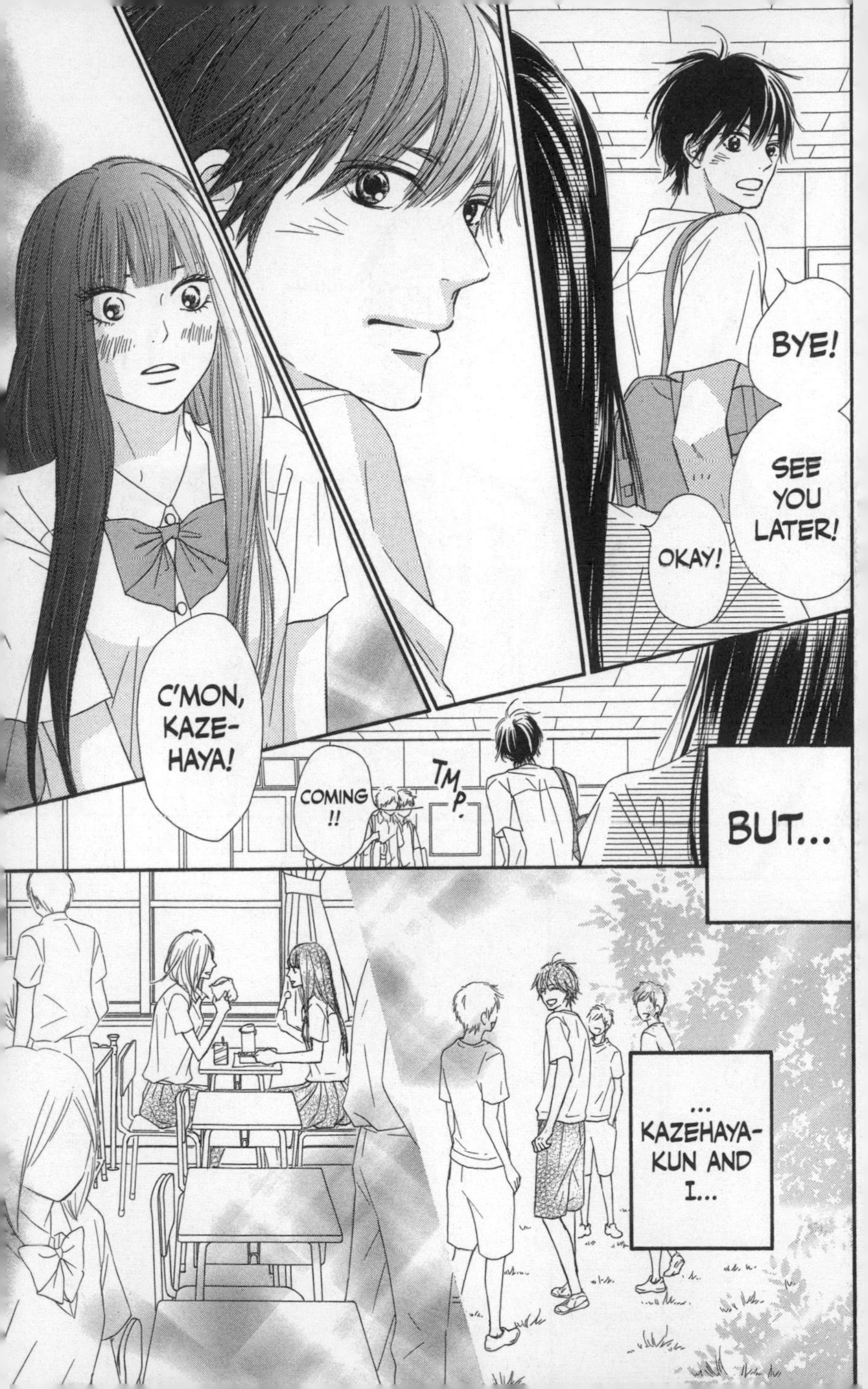
BYE!
SEE YOU LATER!
OKAY!
C'MON, KAZE-HAYA!
COMING!!
TMP.
BUT...
...KAZEHAYA-KUN AND I...

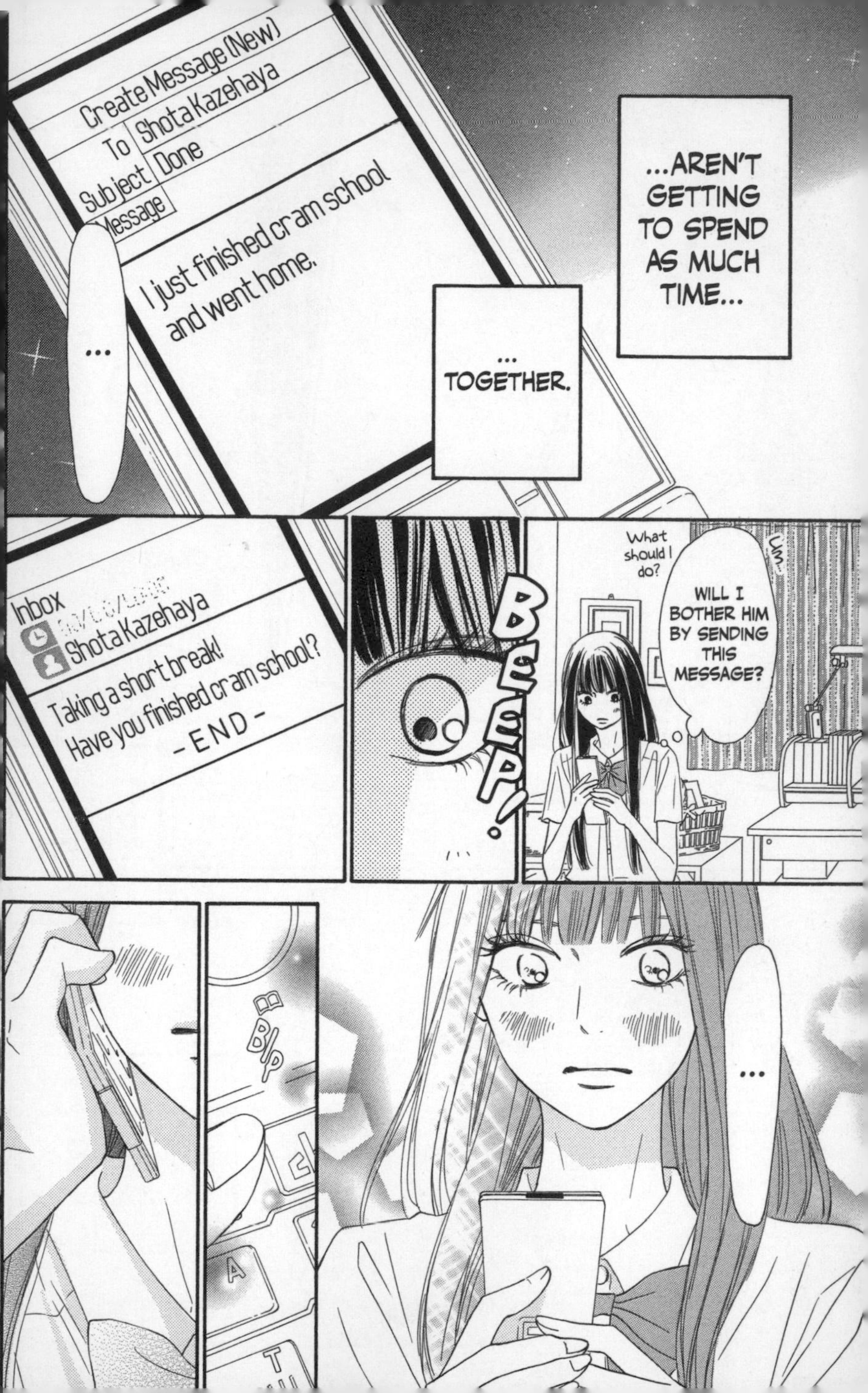
...AREN'T GETTING TO SPEND AS MUCH TIME...
... TOGETHER.
Create Message (New)
To Shota Kazehaya
Subject Done
Message
I just finished cram school and went home.
...
Um...
WILL I BOTHER HIM BY SENDING THIS MESSAGE?
What should I do?
BEEP!
Inbox
Shota Kazehaya
Taking a short break!
Have you finished cram school?
-END-
...
BIP

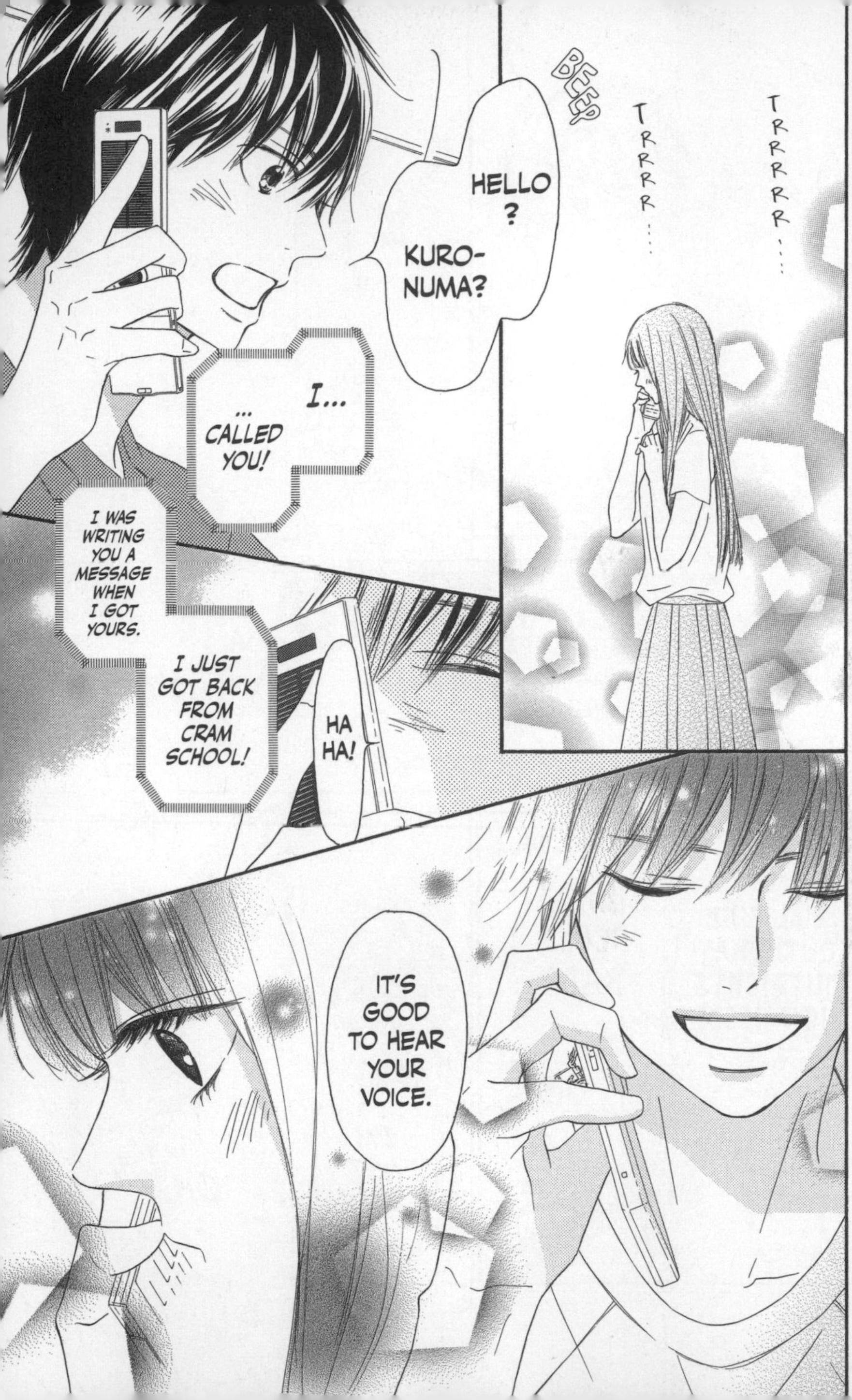
TRRRR...
TRRRR...
BEEP
HELLO?
KURO-NUMA?
I...
...CALLED YOU!
HA HA!
I WAS WRITING YOU A MESSAGE WHEN I GOT YOURS.
I JUST GOT BACK FROM CRAM SCHOOL!
IT'S GOOD TO HEAR YOUR VOICE.

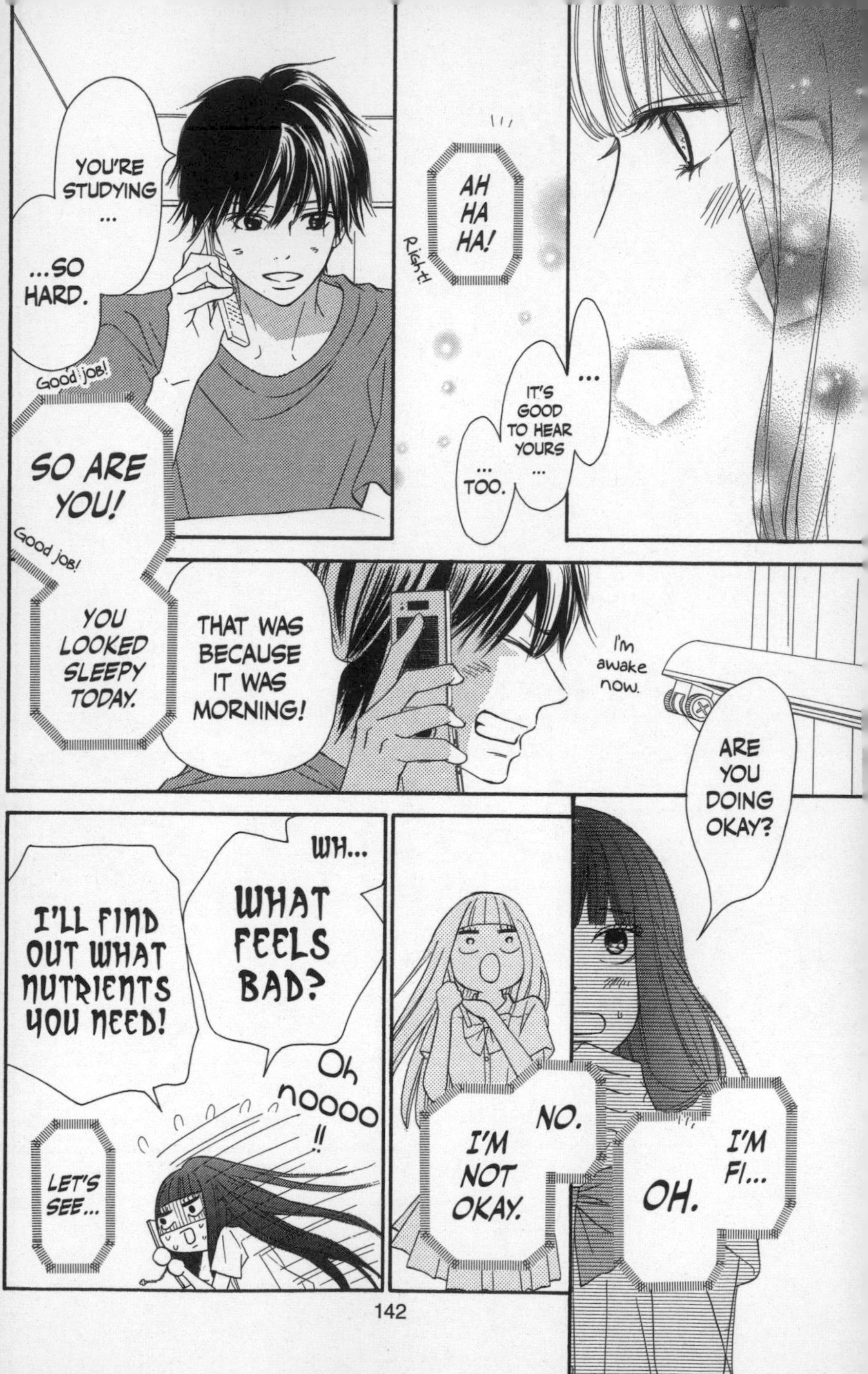
...
It's good to hear yours...
...too.
AH HA HA!
Right!
You're studying...
...so hard.
Good job!
So are you!
Good job!
You looked sleepy today.
That was because it was morning!
I'm awake now.
Are you doing okay?
I'm fi...
Oh.
No. I'm not okay.
Wh...
What feels bad?
I'll find out what nutrients you need!
Oh noooo!!
Let's see...

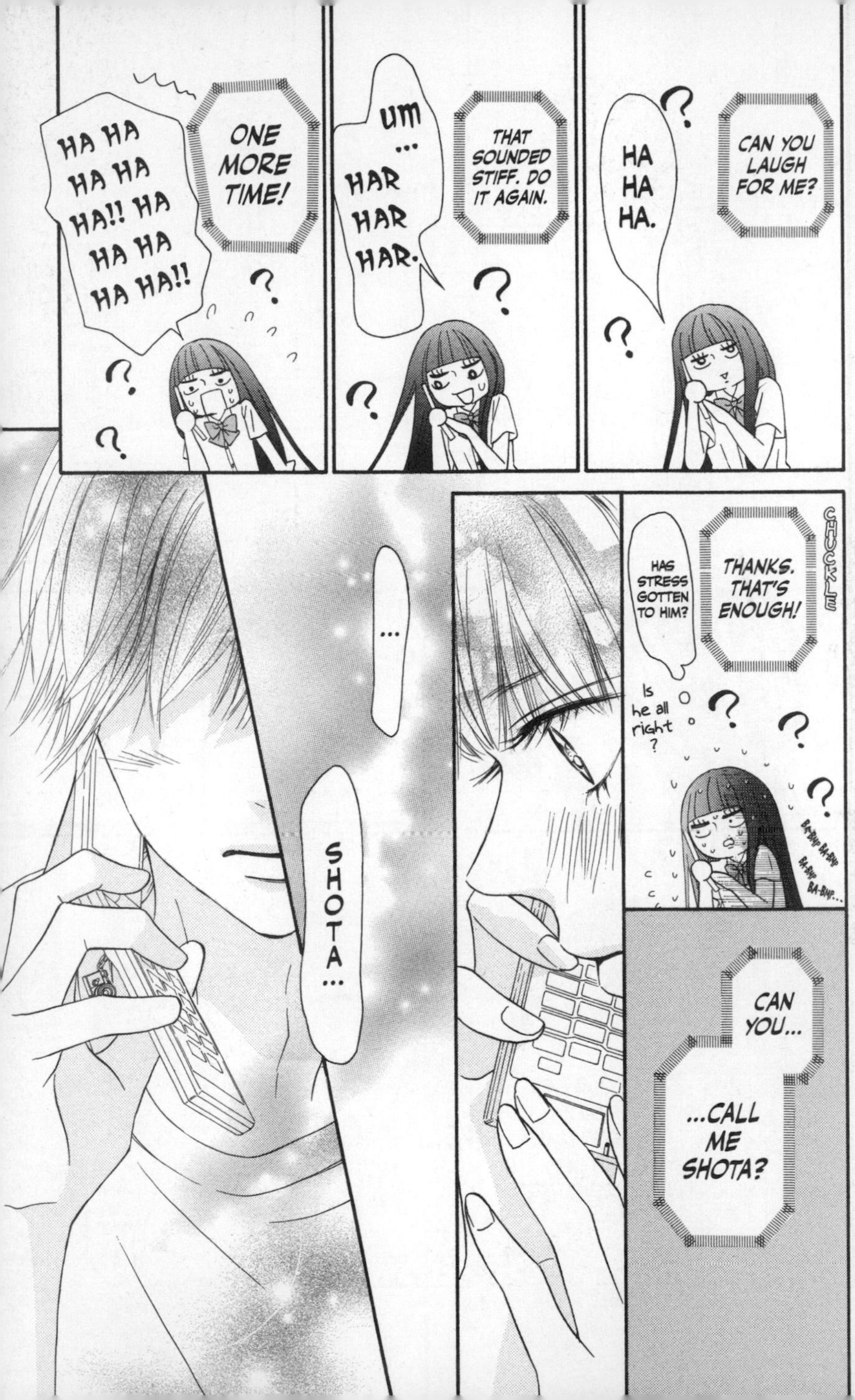
CAN YOU LAUGH FOR ME?
HA HA HA.
THAT SOUNDED STIFF. DO IT AGAIN.
UM... HAR HAR HAR.
ONE MORE TIME!
HA HA HA HA HA!! HA HA HA HA HA!!
CHUCKLE
THANKS. THAT'S ENOUGH!
HAS STRESS GOTTEN TO HIM?
Is he all right?
BA-BMP BA-BMP BA-BMP BA-BMP...
CAN YOU...
...CALL ME SHOTA?
...
SHOTA...

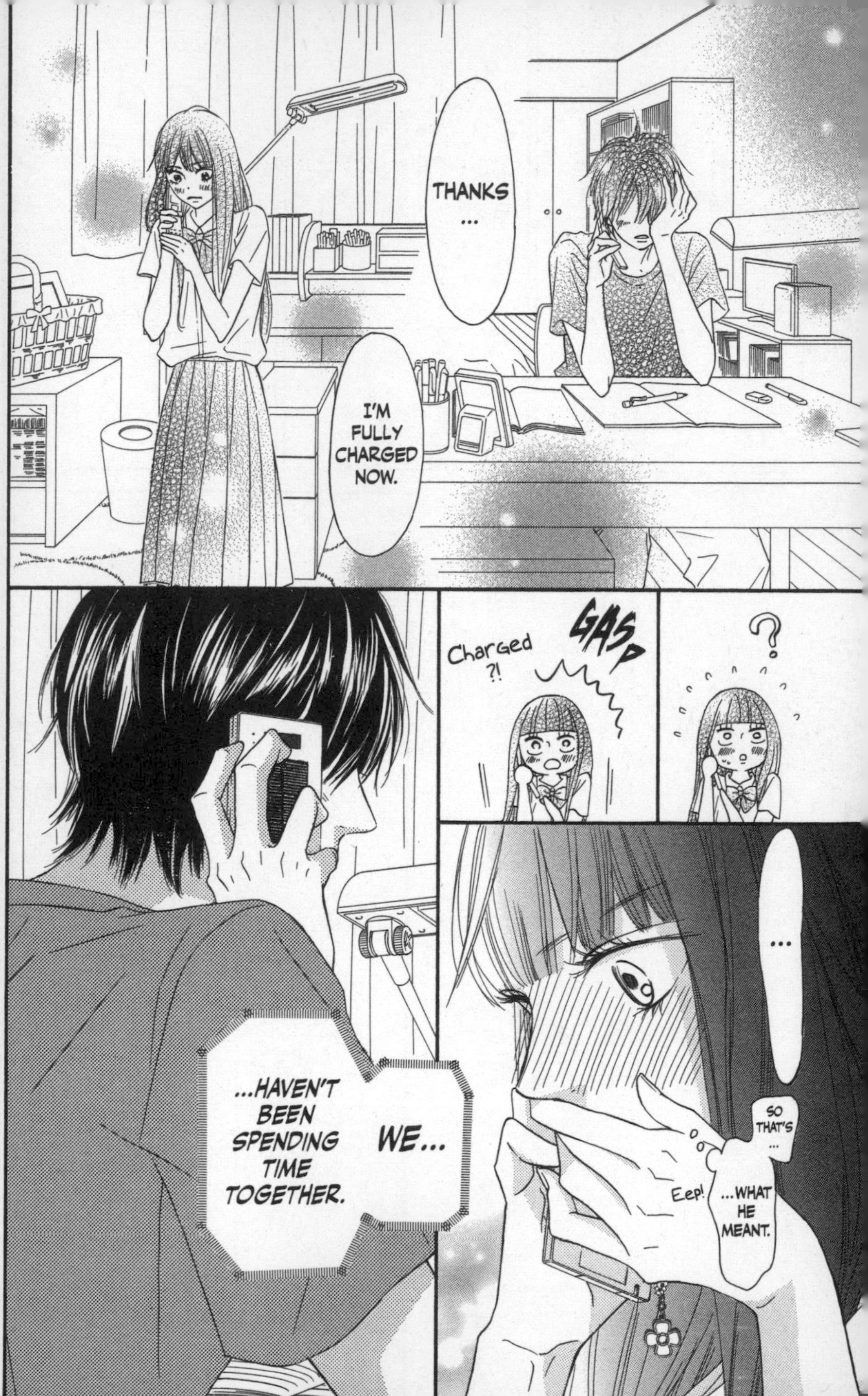
THANKS ...
I'M FULLY CHARGED NOW.
?
GASP
Charged ?!
...
SO THAT'S ...
...WHAT HE MEANT.
Eep!
WE...
...HAVEN'T BEEN SPENDING TIME TOGETHER.

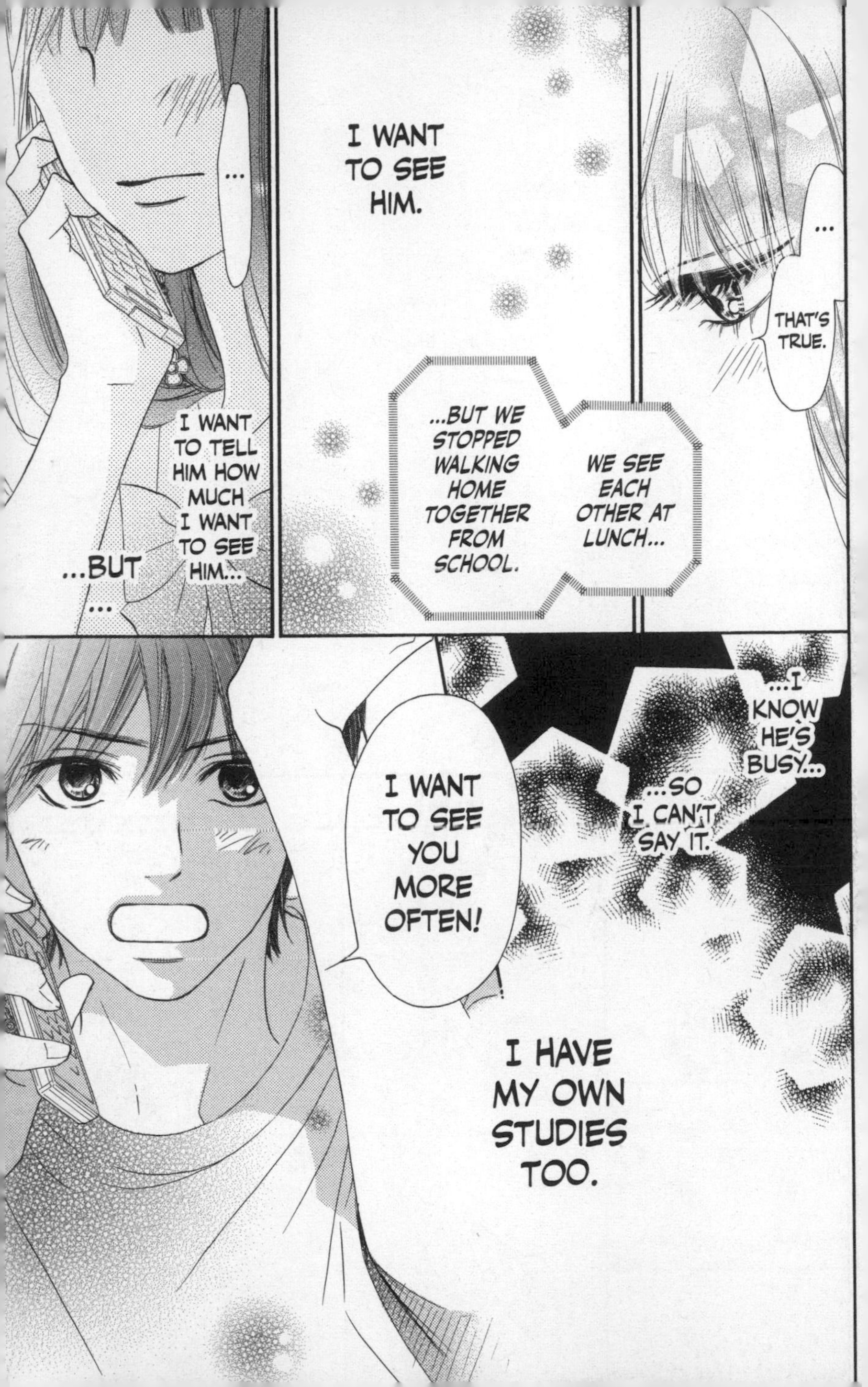
...
THAT'S TRUE.
I WANT TO SEE HIM.
WE SEE EACH OTHER AT LUNCH...
...BUT WE STOPPED WALKING HOME TOGETHER FROM SCHOOL.
...
I WANT TO TELL HIM HOW MUCH I WANT TO SEE HIM...
...BUT
...
...I KNOW HE'S BUSY...
...SO I CAN'T SAY IT.
I WANT TO SEE YOU MORE OFTEN!
I HAVE MY OWN STUDIES TOO.

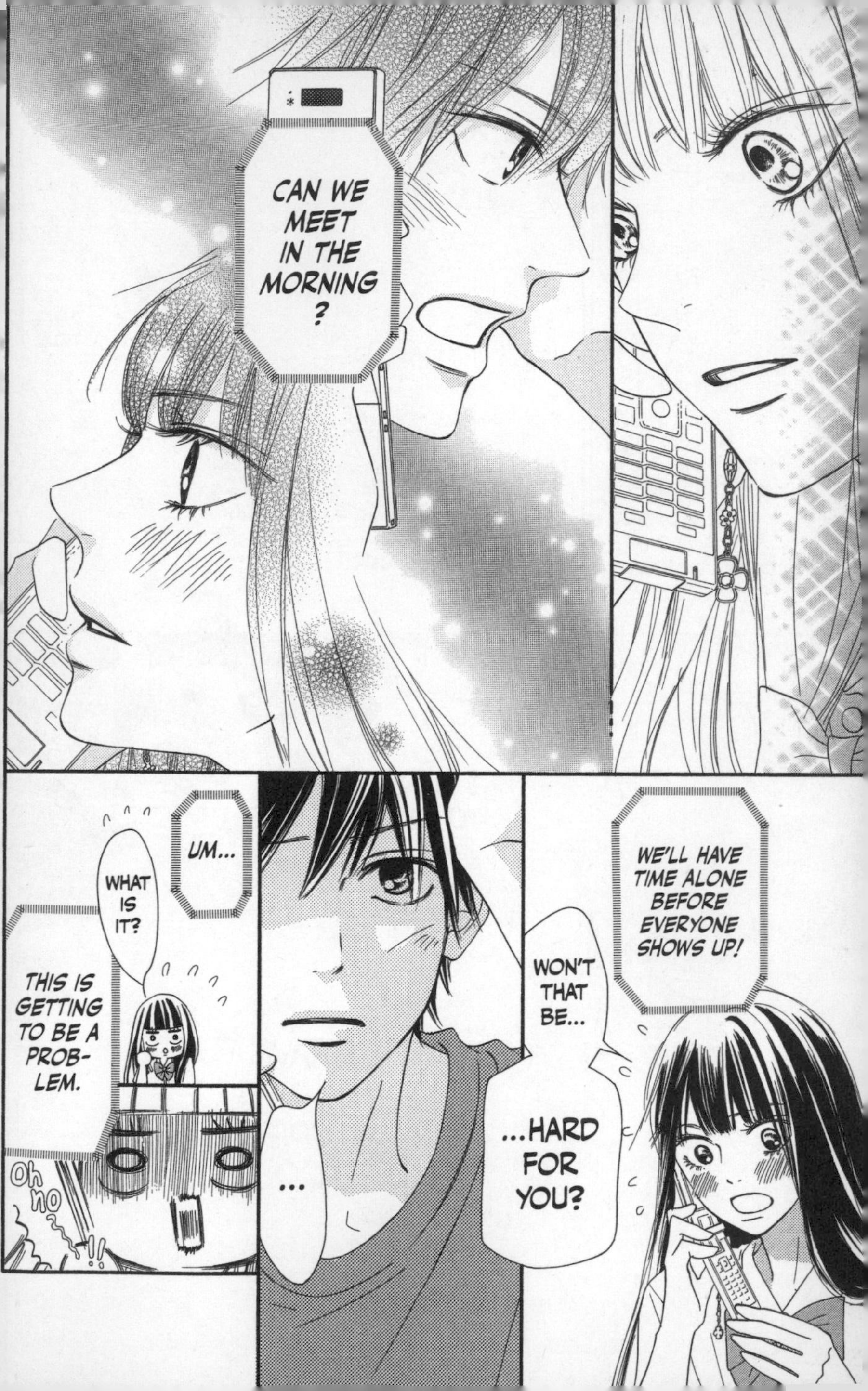
CAN WE MEET IN THE MORNING?
WE'LL HAVE TIME ALONE BEFORE EVERYONE SHOWS UP!
WON'T THAT BE...
...HARD FOR YOU?
UM...
...
WHAT IS IT?
THIS IS GETTING TO BE A PROB-LEM.
Oh no~!!

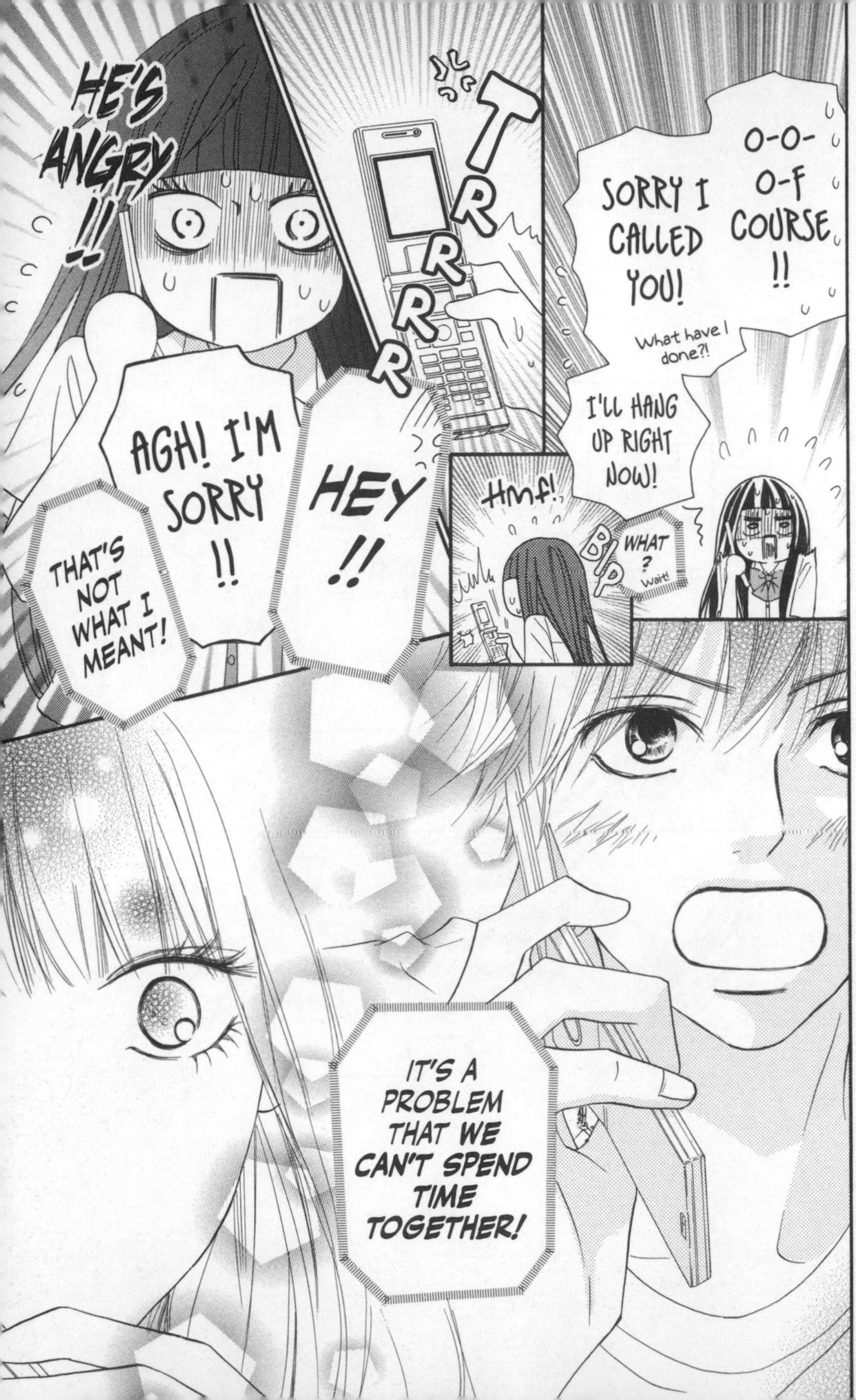
O-O-O-F COURSE!!
SORRY I CALLED YOU!
What have I done?!
I'LL HANG UP RIGHT NOW!
Hmf!
BIP
WHAT? Wait!
TRRRR
HE'S ANGRY!!
HEY!!
AGH! I'M SORRY!!
THAT'S NOT WHAT I MEANT!
IT'S A PROBLEM THAT WE CAN'T SPEND TIME TOGETHER!

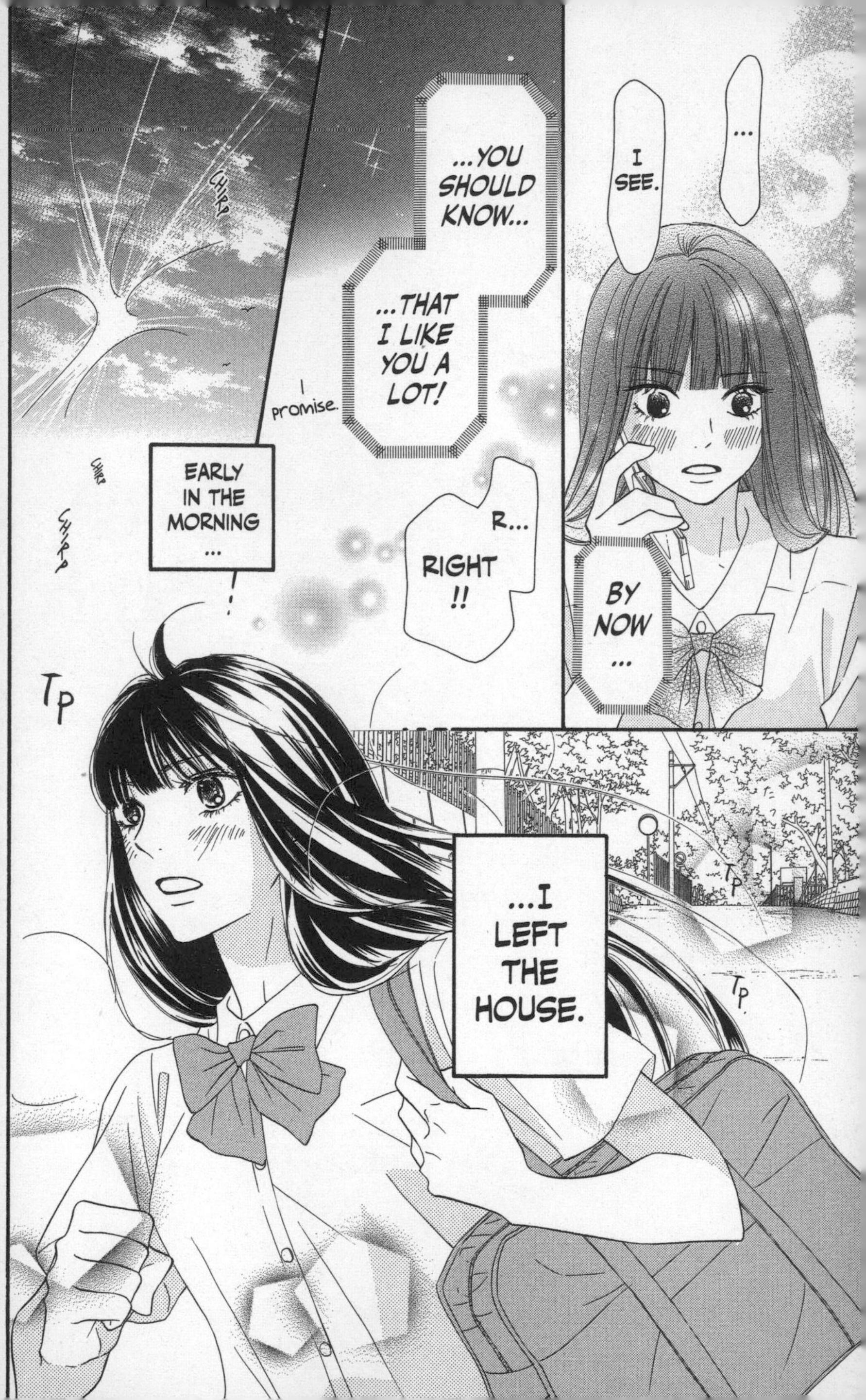
...
I SEE.
BY NOW ...
...YOU SHOULD KNOW...
...THAT I LIKE YOU A LOT!
R... RIGHT !!
I promise.
CHIRP
CHIRP
CHIRP
EARLY IN THE MORNING ...
...I LEFT THE HOUSE.
TP
TP
TP

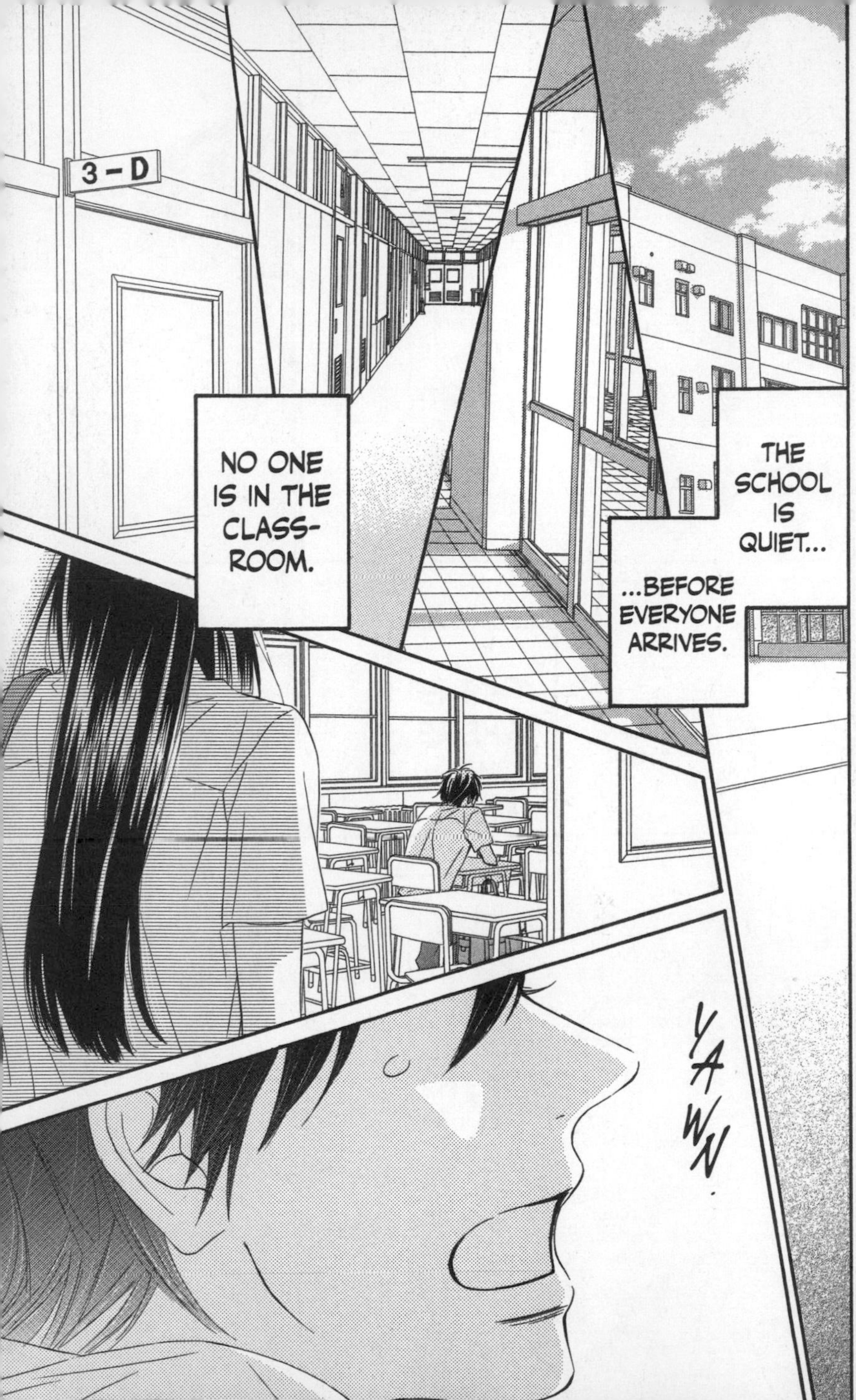
THE SCHOOL IS QUIET...
...BEFORE EVERYONE ARRIVES.
3-D
NO ONE IS IN THE CLASS-ROOM.
YAWN.

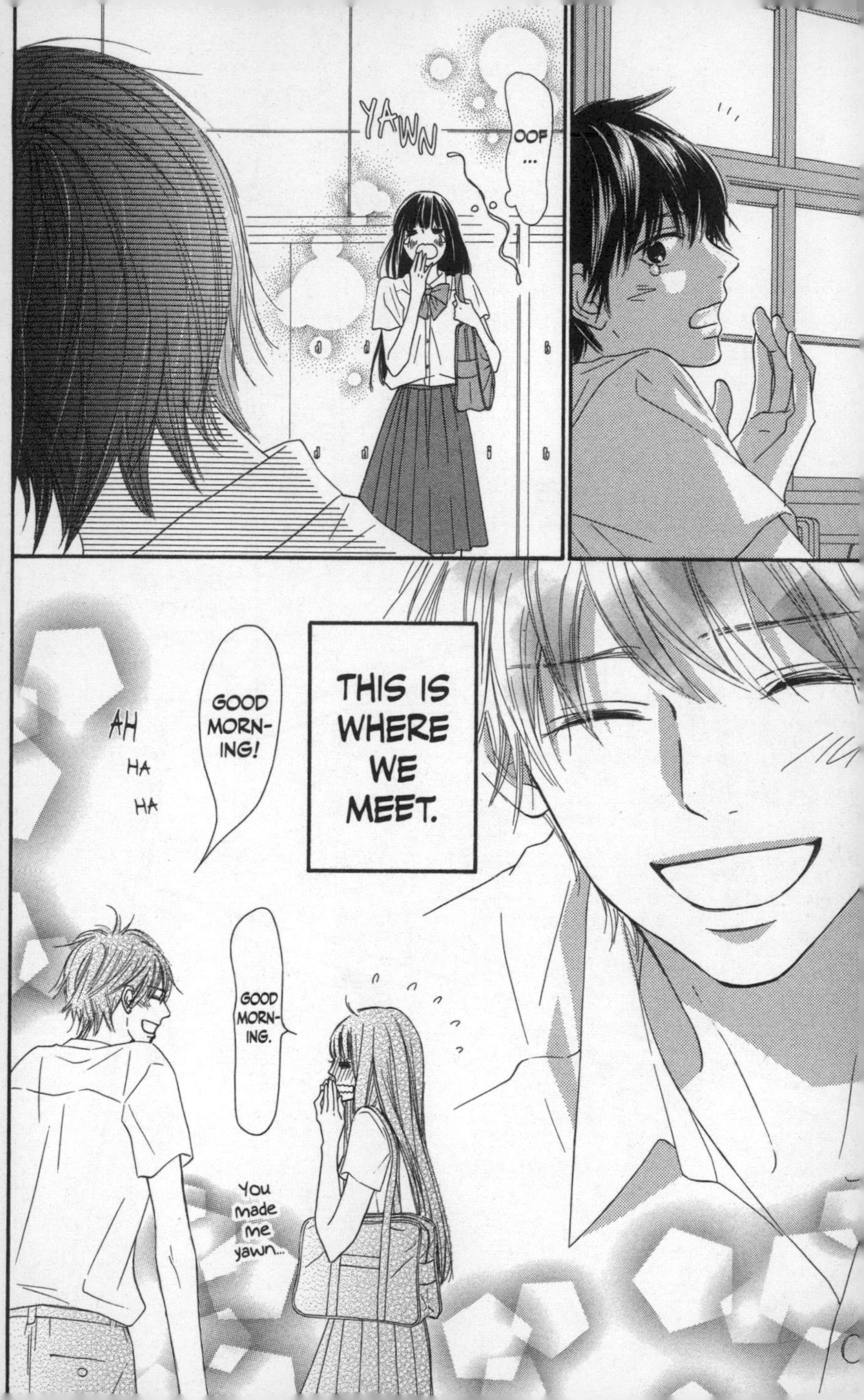
OOF ...
YAWN
THIS IS WHERE WE MEET.
GOOD MORNING!
AH HA HA
GOOD MORNING.
You made me yawn...

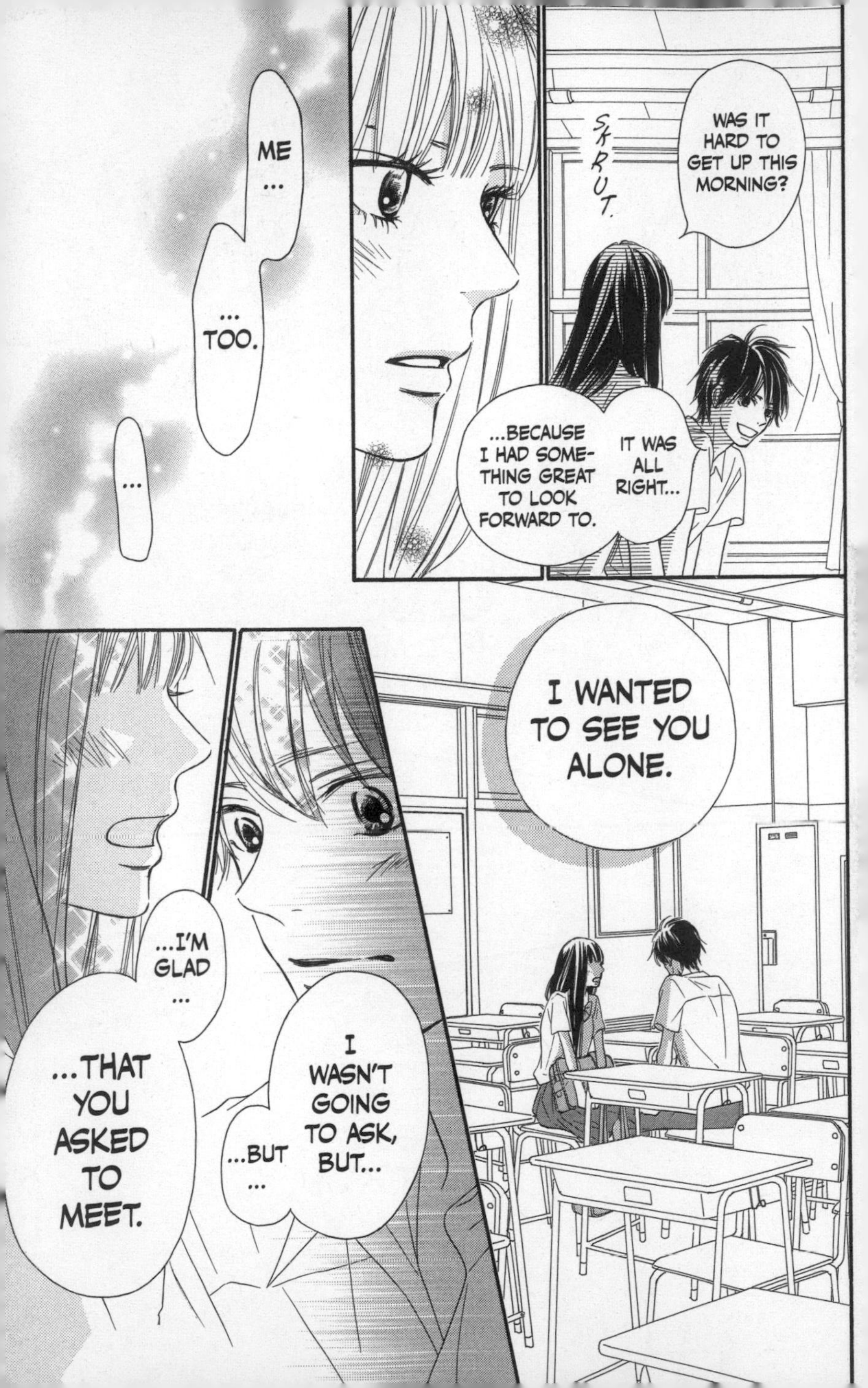
WAS IT HARD TO GET UP THIS MORNING?
SKRUT.
IT WAS ALL RIGHT...
...BECAUSE I HAD SOME-THING GREAT TO LOOK FORWARD TO.
ME ...
... TOO.
...
I WANTED TO SEE YOU ALONE.
I WASN'T GOING TO ASK, BUT...
...BUT ...
...I'M GLAD ...
...THAT YOU ASKED TO MEET.

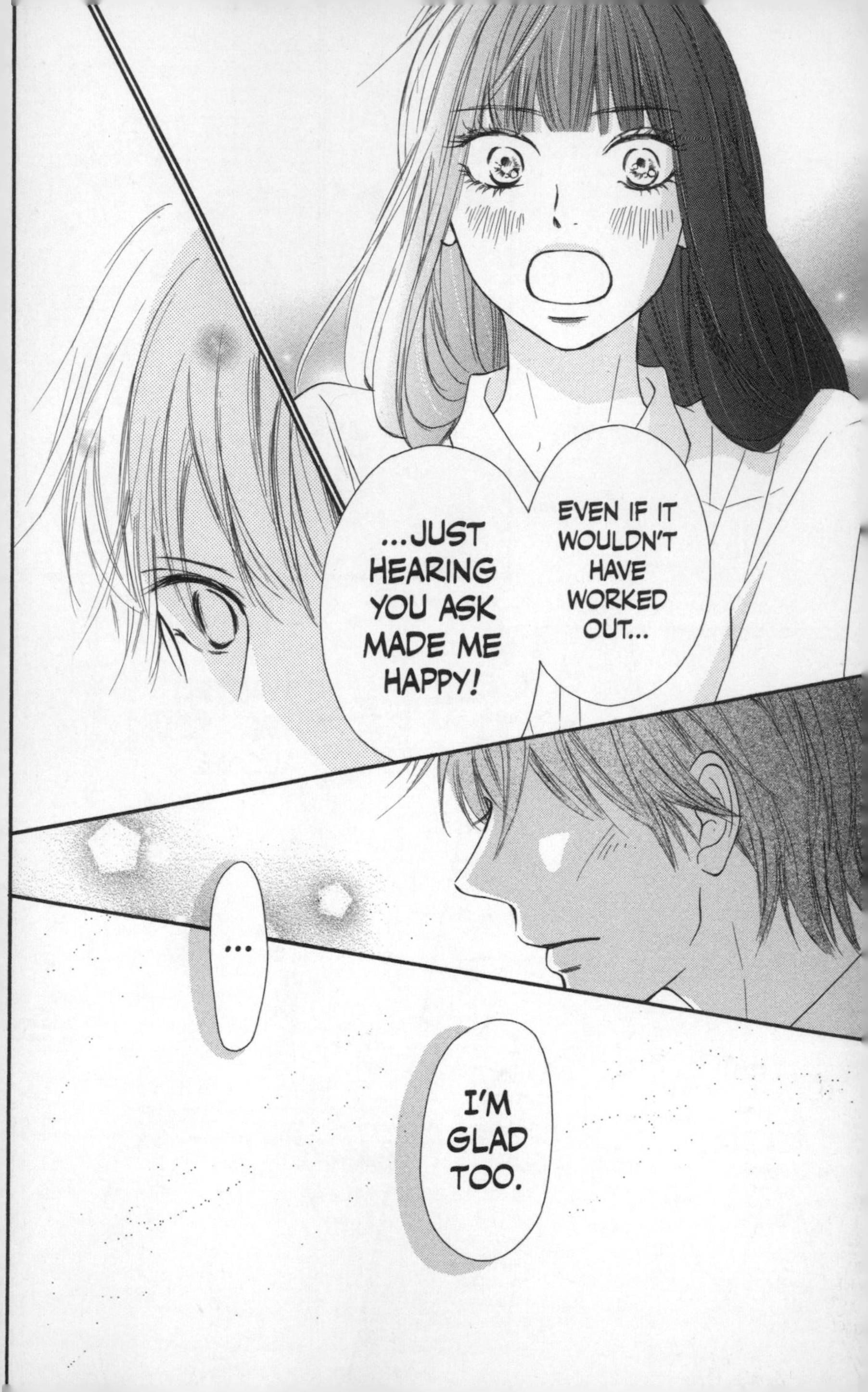
EVEN IF IT WOULDN'T HAVE WORKED OUT...
...JUST HEARING YOU ASK MADE ME HAPPY!
...
I'M GLAD TOO.

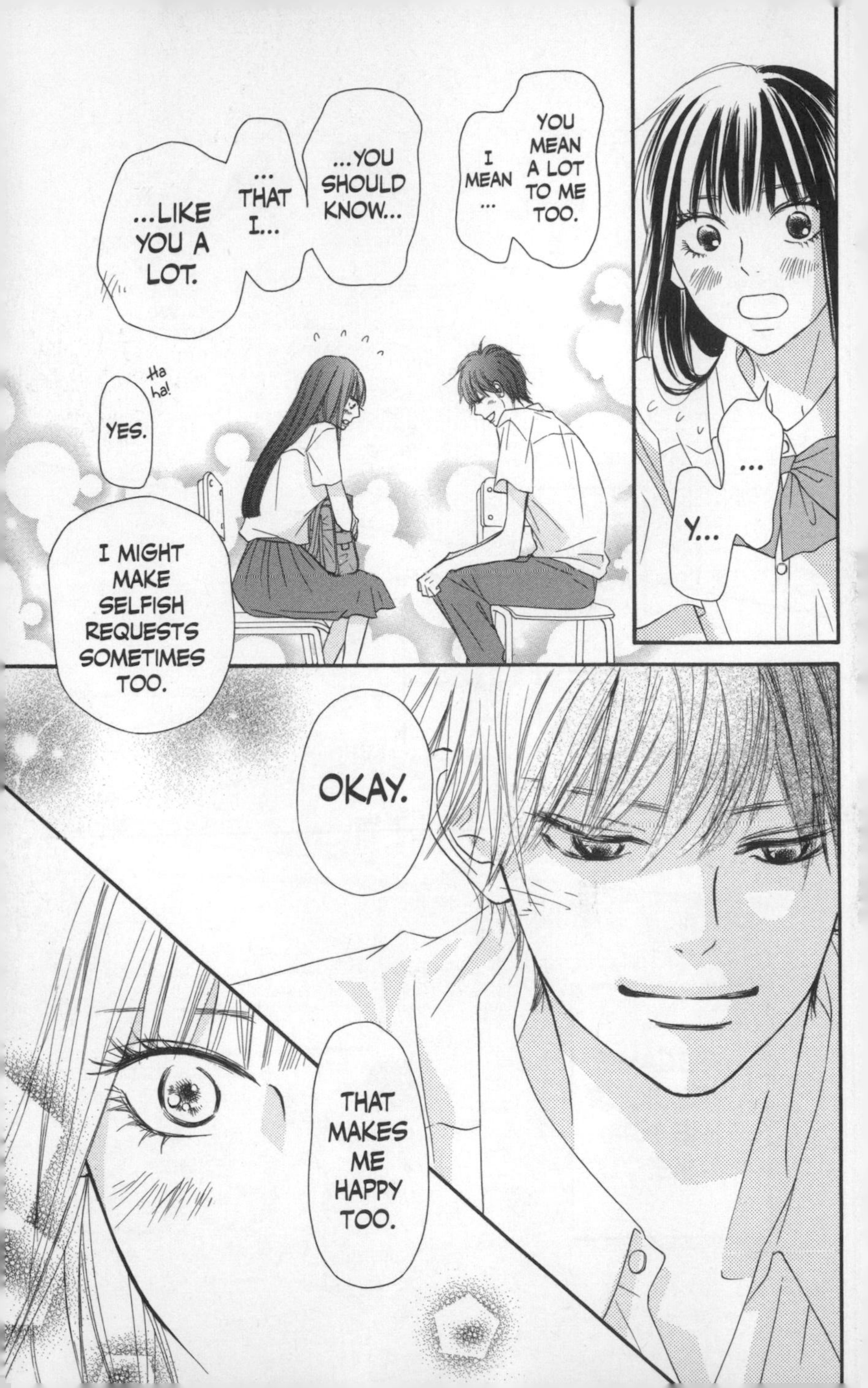

... Y...
YOU MEAN A LOT TO ME TOO.
I MEAN ...
...YOU SHOULD KNOW...
... THAT I...
...LIKE YOU A LOT.
Ha ha!
YES.
I MIGHT MAKE SELFISH REQUESTS SOMETIMES TOO.
OKAY.
THAT MAKES ME HAPPY TOO.

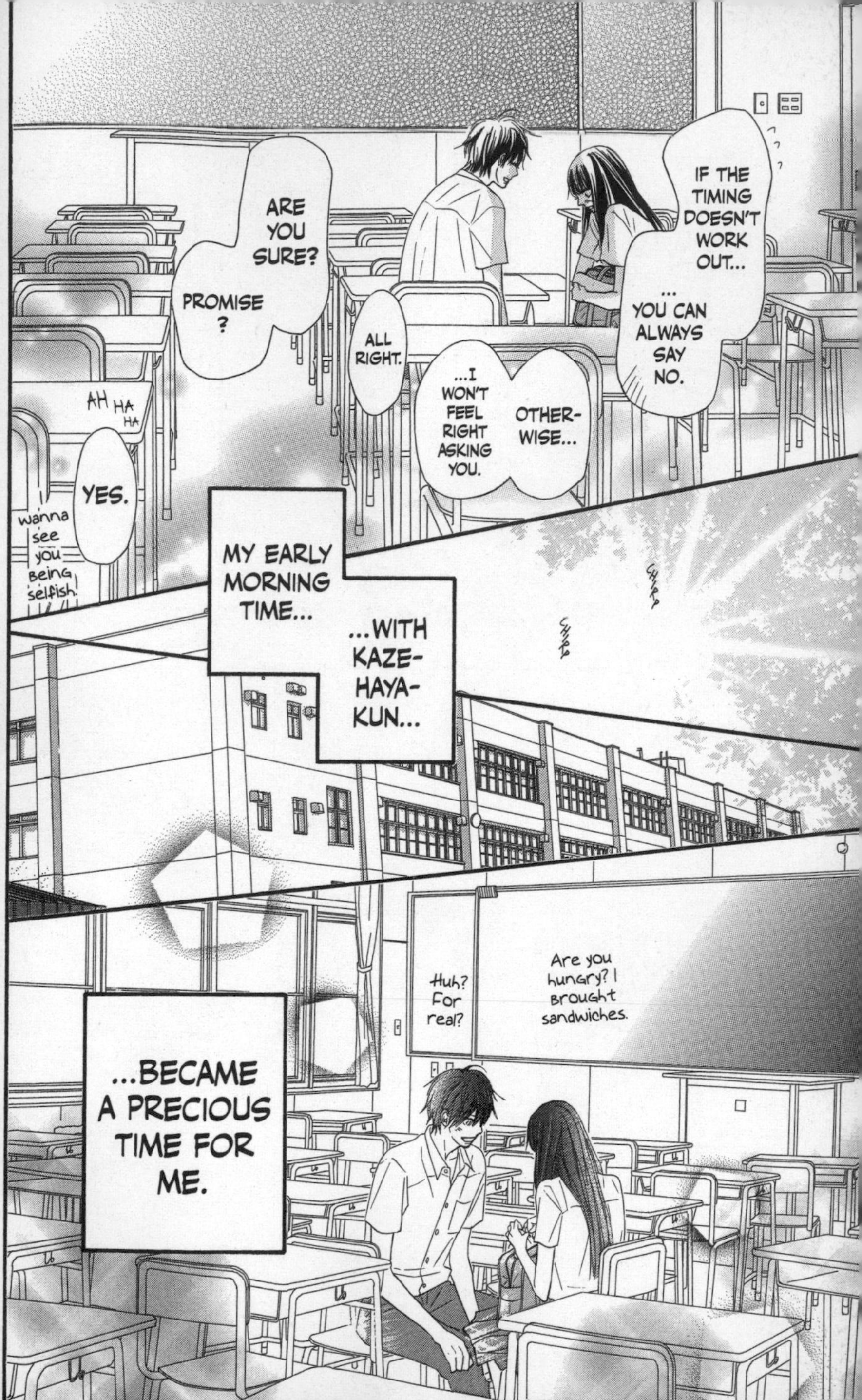
IF THE TIMING DOESN'T WORK OUT...
...YOU CAN ALWAYS SAY NO.
OTHER-WISE...
...I WON'T FEEL RIGHT ASKING YOU.
ALL RIGHT.
ARE YOU SURE?
PROMISE?
AH HA HA
YES.
I wanna see you being selfish!
CHIRP
CHIRP
MY EARLY MORNING TIME...
...WITH KAZE-HAYA-KUN...
Are you hungry? I brought sandwiches.
Huh? For real?
...BECAME A PRECIOUS TIME FOR ME.

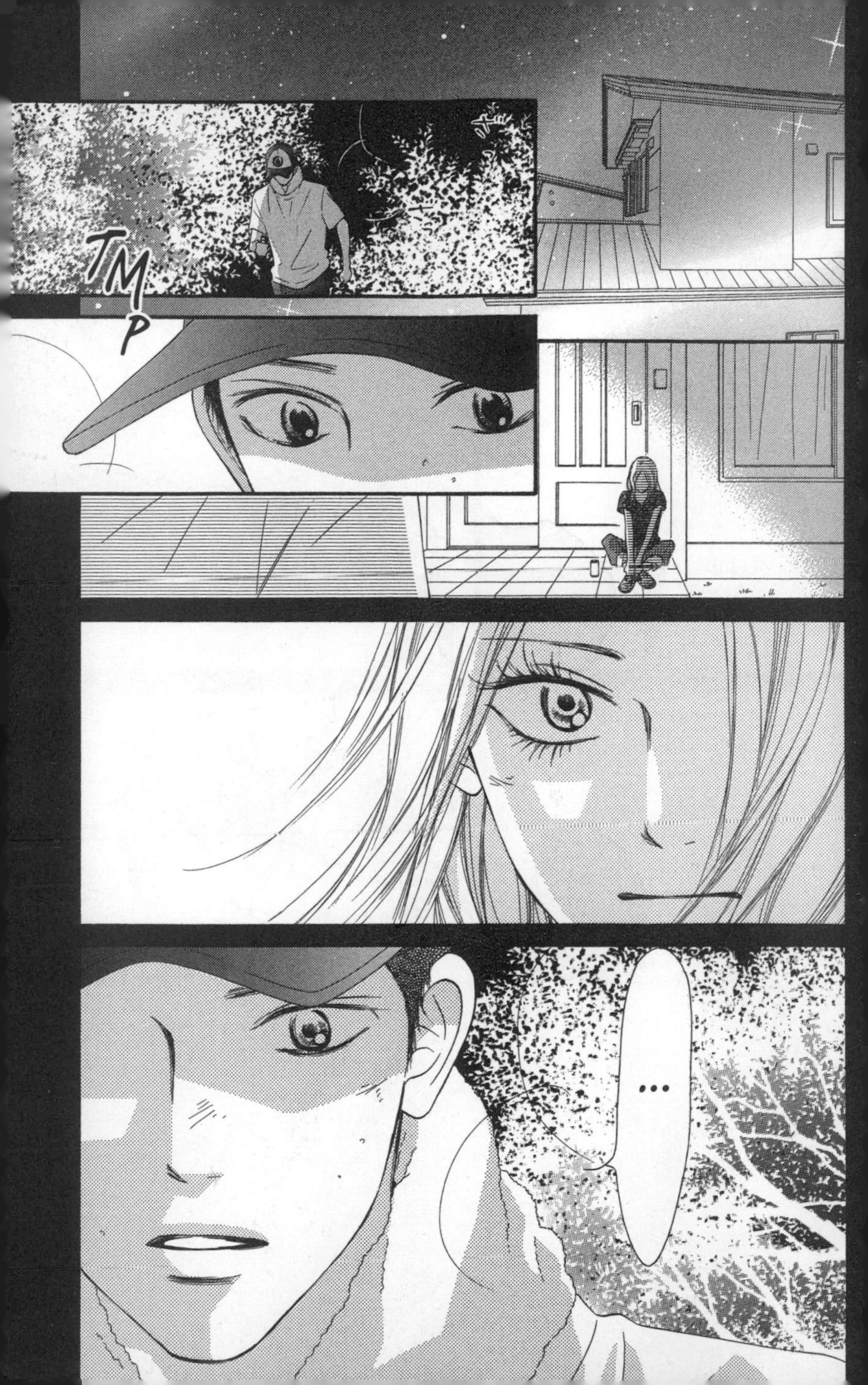
TMP
TMP
...

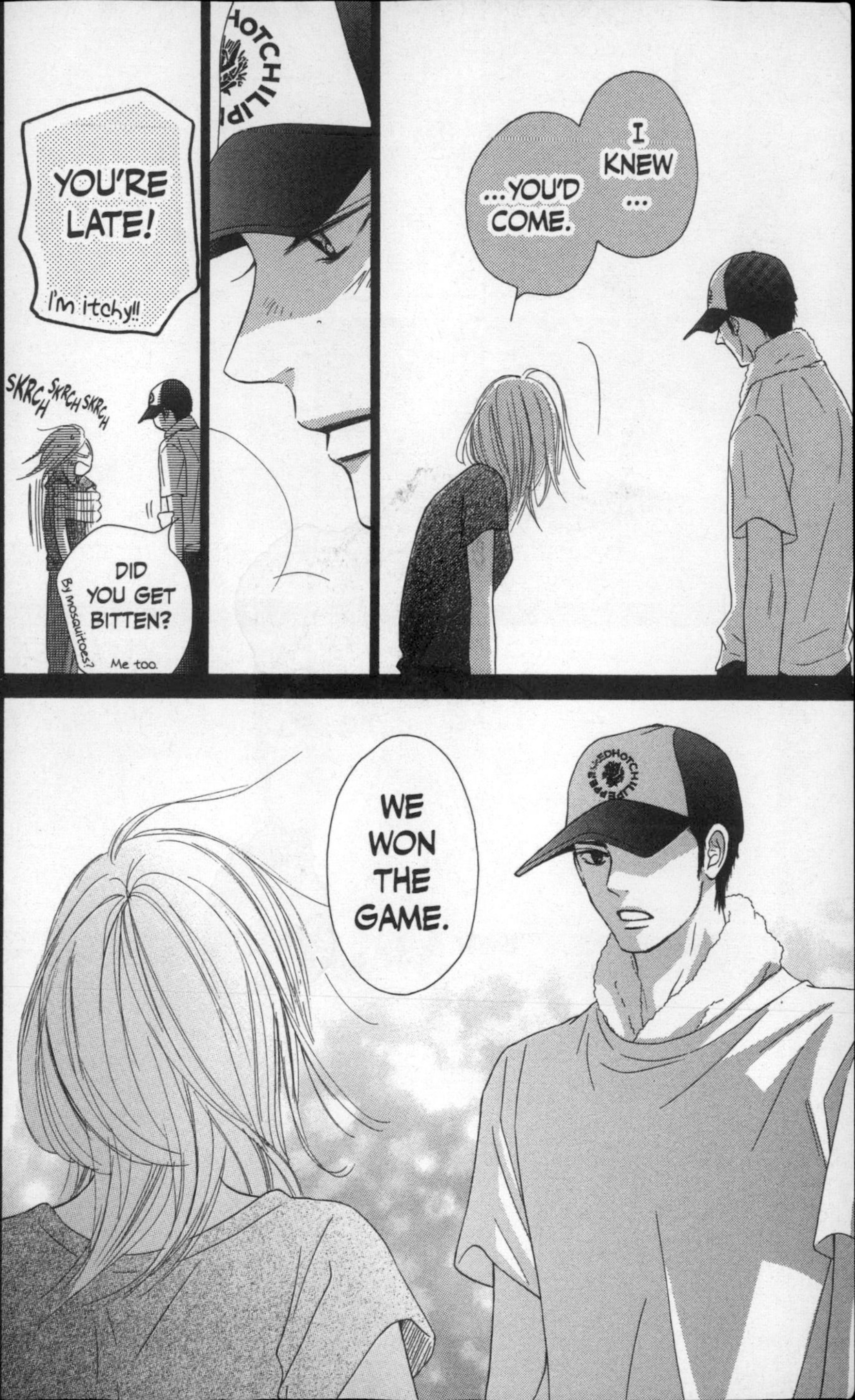
I KNEW...
...YOU'D COME.
YOU'RE LATE!
I'm itchy!!
SKRCH SKRCH SKRCH
DID YOU GET BITTEN?
By mosquitoes?
Me too.
WE WON THE GAME.

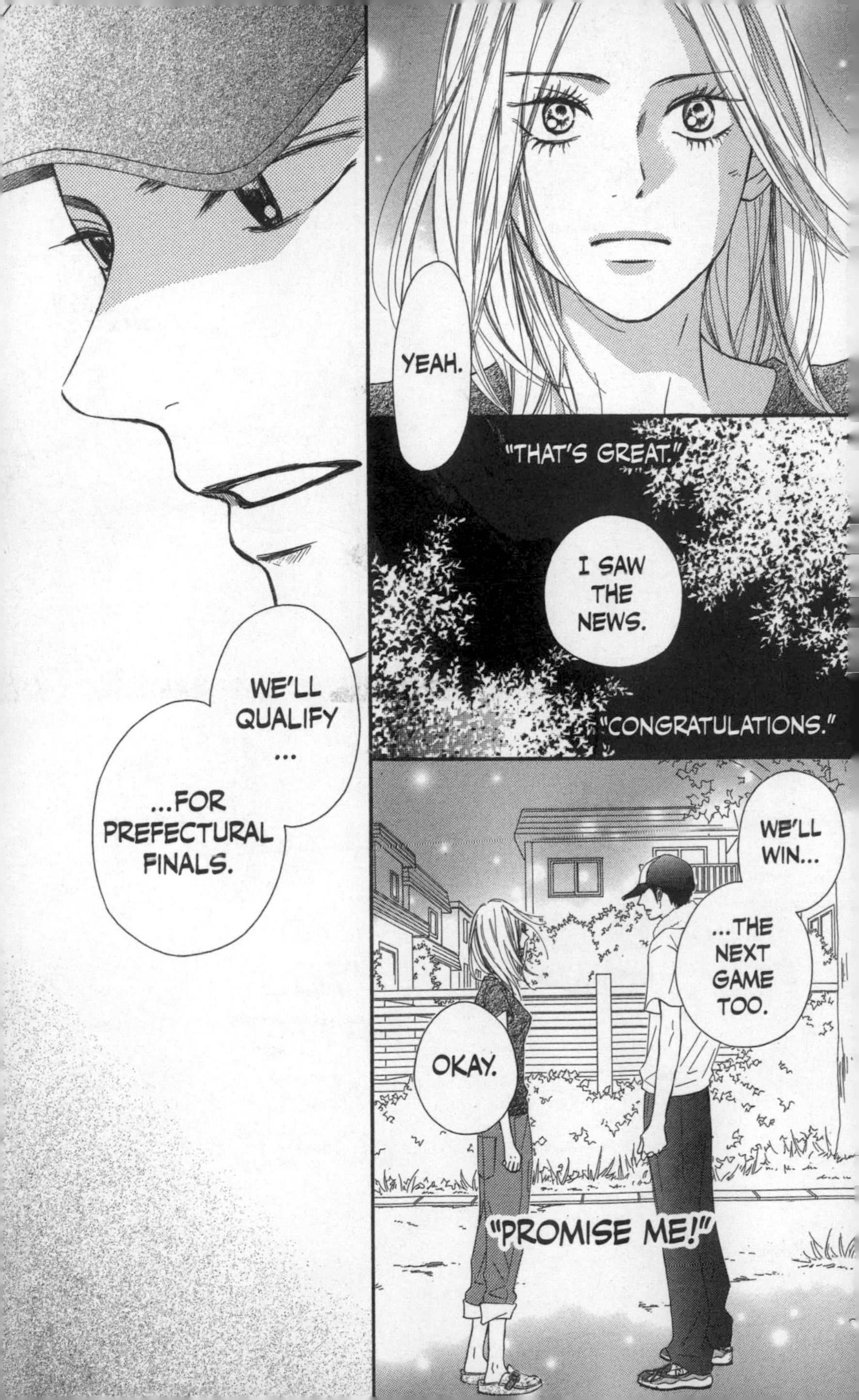
YEAH.
"THAT'S GREAT."
I SAW THE NEWS.
"CONGRATULATIONS."
WE'LL WIN...
...THE NEXT GAME TOO.
OKAY.
"PROMISE ME!"
WE'LL QUALIFY ...
...FOR PREFECTURAL FINALS.

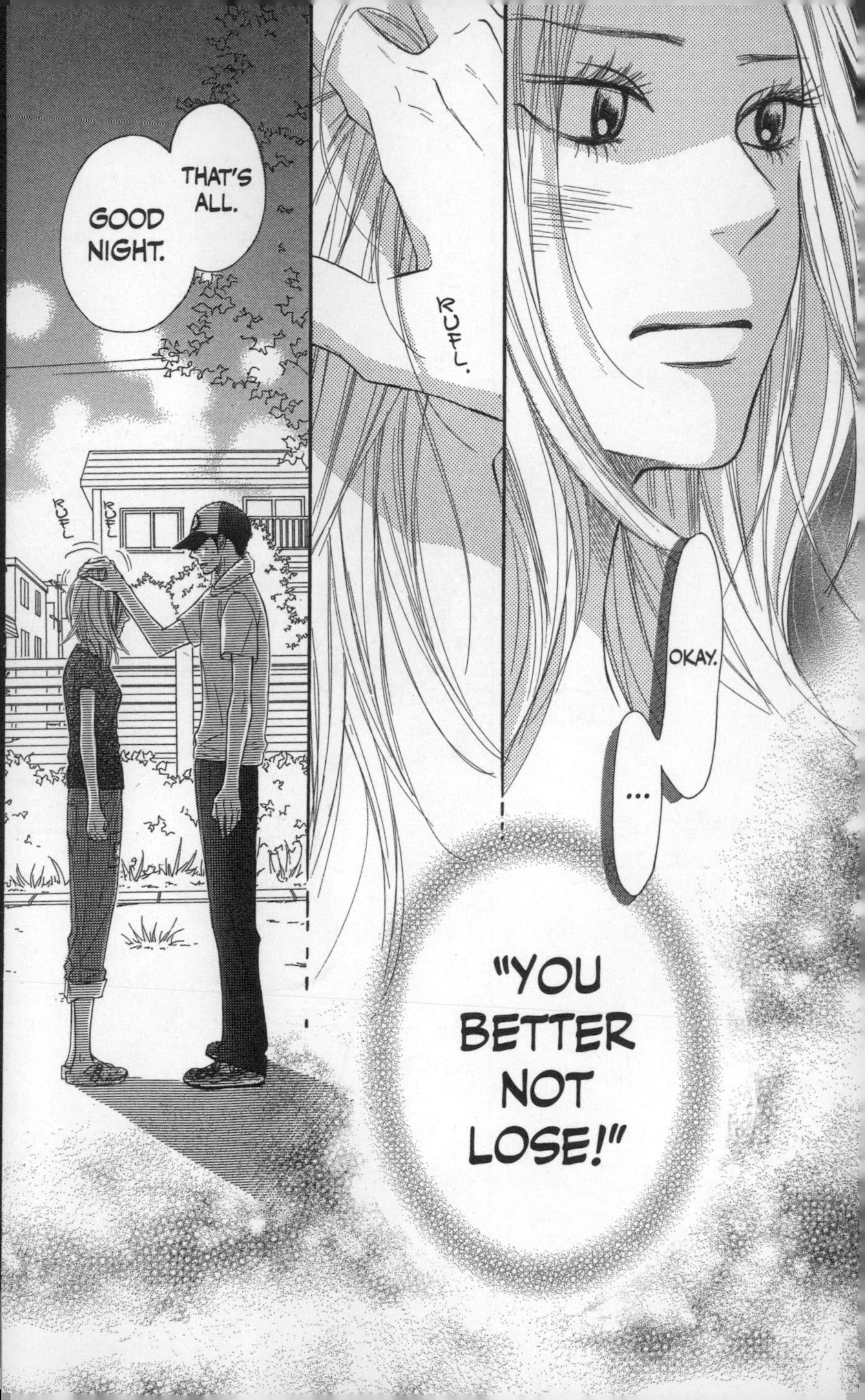
OKAY.
...
RUFL.
THAT'S ALL.
GOOD NIGHT.
RUFL
RUFL
"YOU BETTER NOT LOSE!"

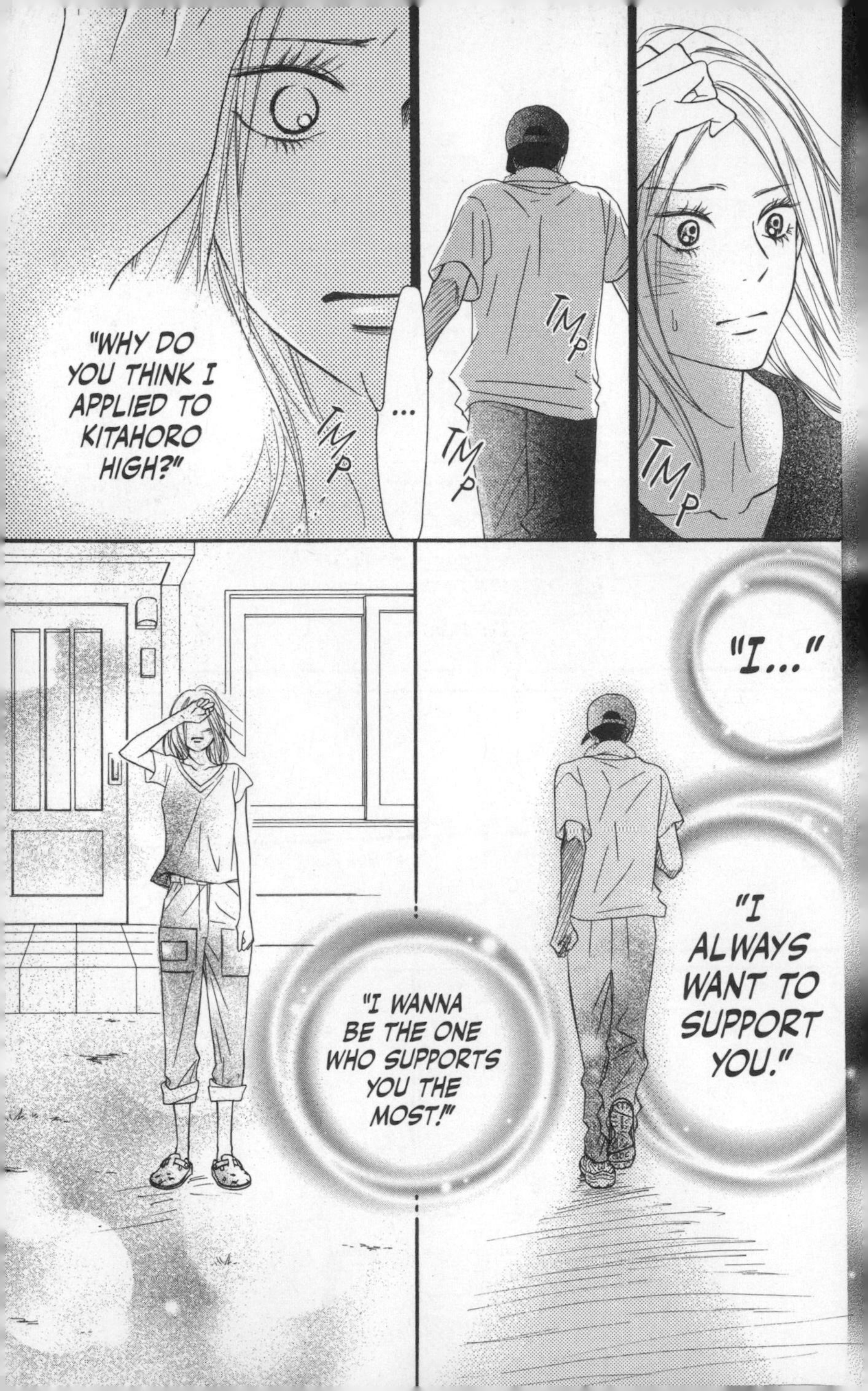
TMP
TMP
TMP
...
"WHY DO YOU THINK I APPLIED TO KITAHORO HIGH?"
TMP
"I..."
"I ALWAYS WANT TO SUPPORT YOU."
"I WANNA BE THE ONE WHO SUPPORTS YOU THE MOST!"

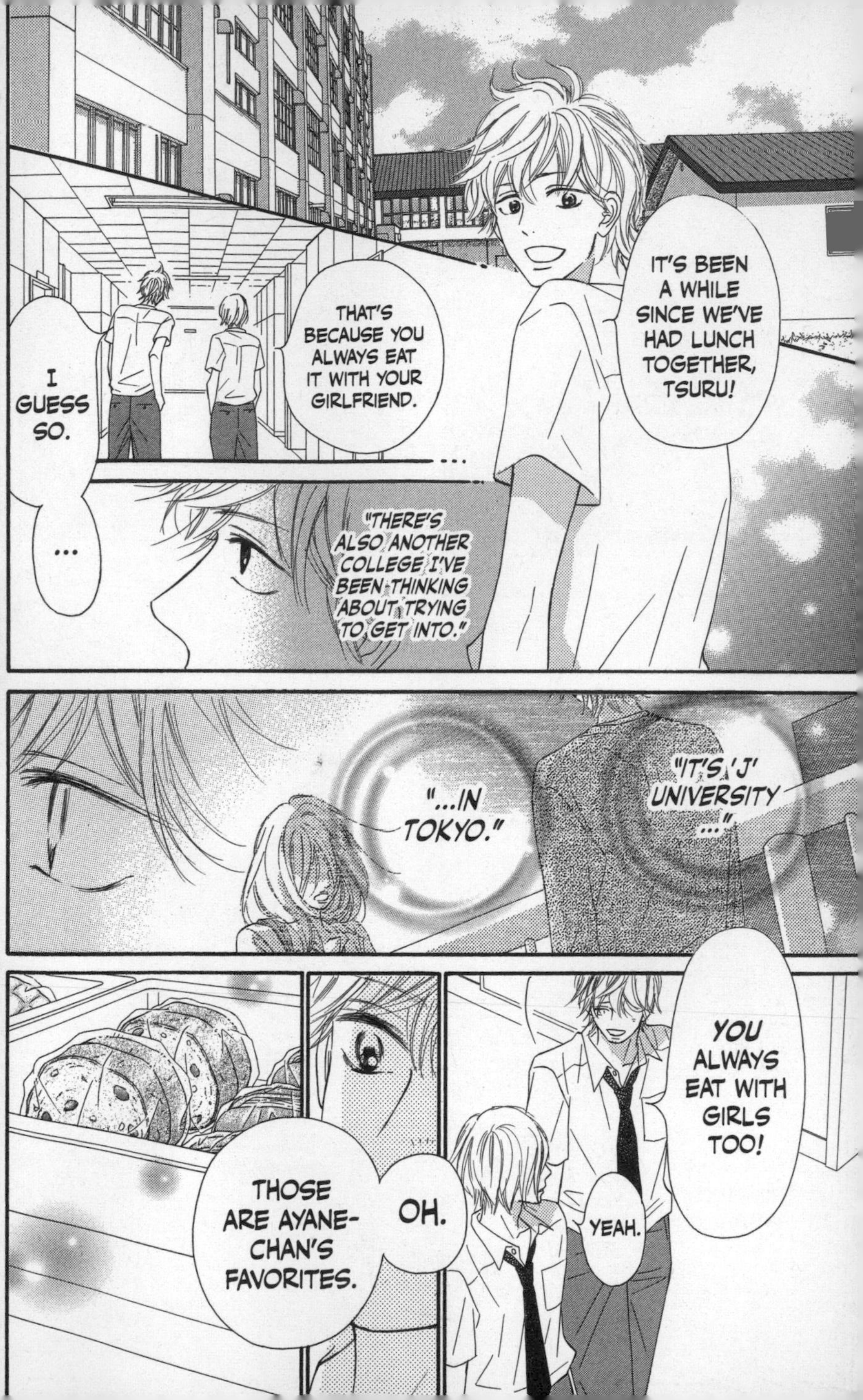
IT'S BEEN A WHILE SINCE WE'VE HAD LUNCH TOGETHER, TSURU!
THAT'S BECAUSE YOU ALWAYS EAT IT WITH YOUR GIRLFRIEND.
I GUESS SO.
...
...
"THERE'S ALSO ANOTHER COLLEGE I'VE BEEN THINKING ABOUT TRYING TO GET INTO."
"IT'S 'J' UNIVERSITY ..."
"...IN TOKYO."
YOU ALWAYS EAT WITH GIRLS TOO!
YEAH.
OH.
THOSE ARE AYANE-CHAN'S FAVORITES.

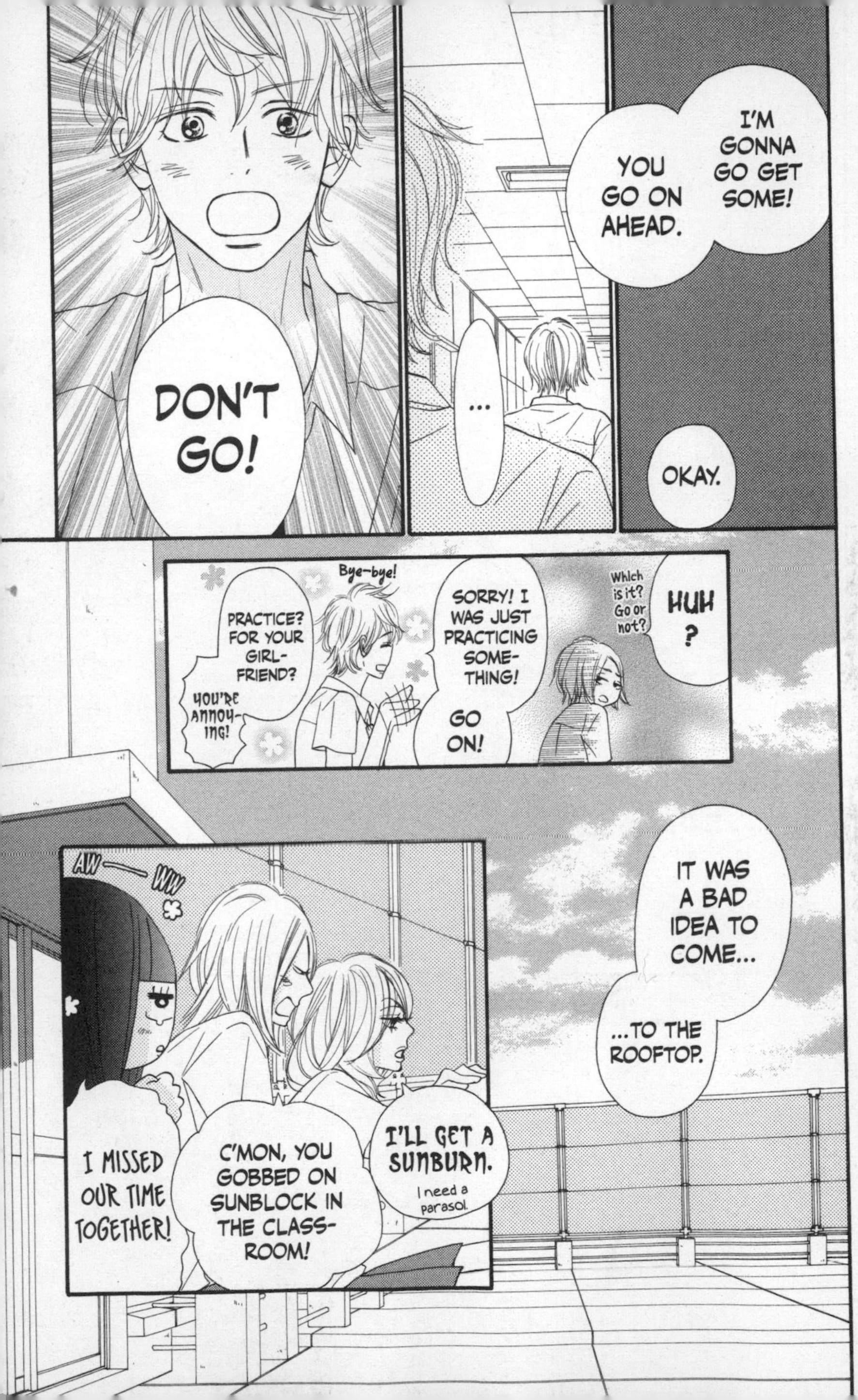
I'M GONNA GO GET SOME!
YOU GO ON AHEAD.
OKAY.
...
DON'T GO!
HUH ?
Which is it? Go or not?
SORRY! I WAS JUST PRACTICING SOME-THING!
GO ON!
Bye-bye!
PRACTICE? FOR YOUR GIRL-FRIEND?
YOU'RE ANNOY-ING!
IT WAS A BAD IDEA TO COME...
...TO THE ROOFTOP.
AW—WW
I'LL GET A SUNBURN.
I need a parasol.
C'MON, YOU GOBBED ON SUNBLOCK IN THE CLASS-ROOM!
I MISSED OUR TIME TOGETHER!

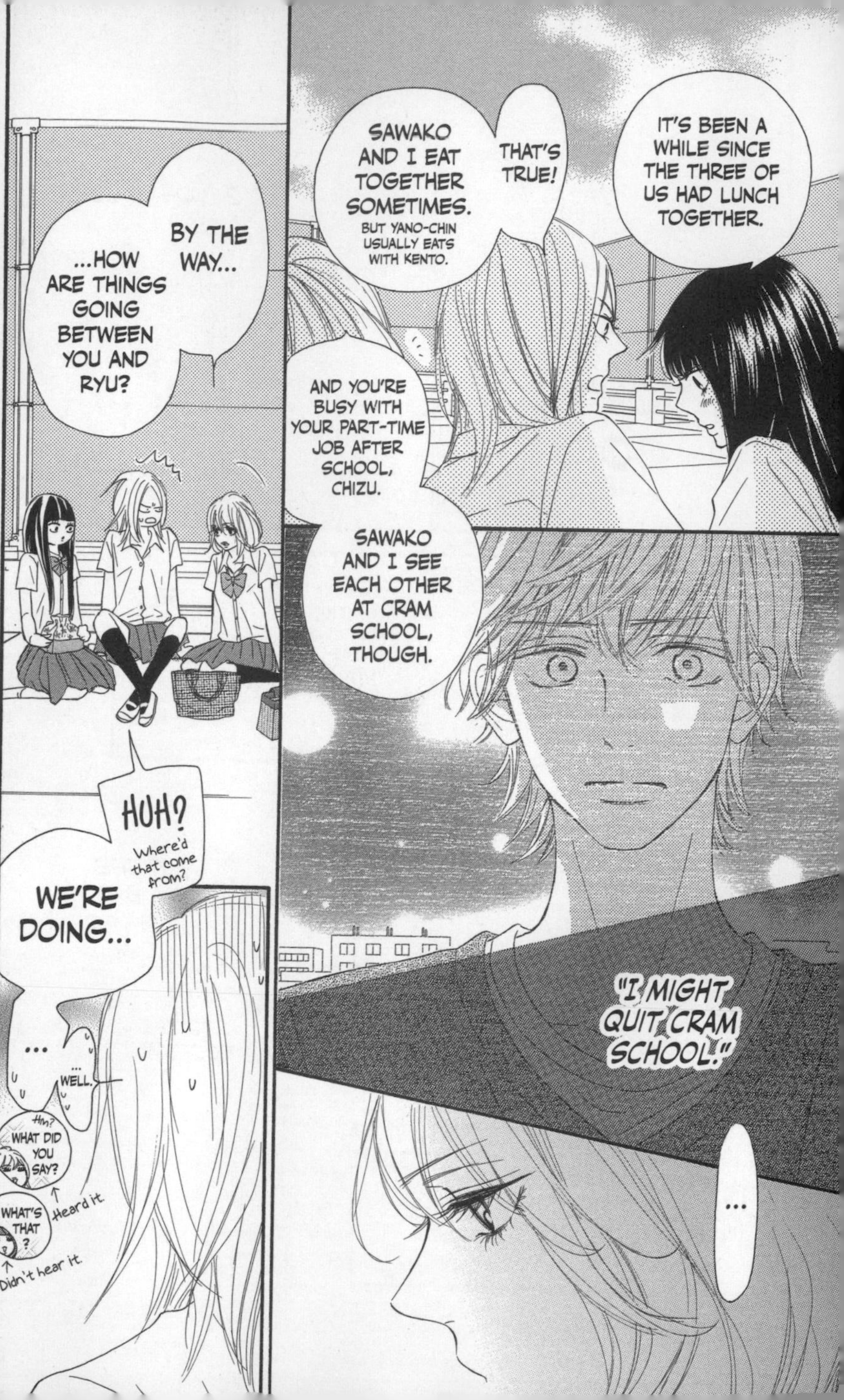
IT'S BEEN A WHILE SINCE THE THREE OF US HAD LUNCH TOGETHER.
THAT'S TRUE!
SAWAKO AND I EAT TOGETHER SOMETIMES.
BUT YANO-CHIN USUALLY EATS WITH KENTO.
AND YOU'RE BUSY WITH YOUR PART-TIME JOB AFTER SCHOOL, CHIZU.
SAWAKO AND I SEE EACH OTHER AT CRAM SCHOOL, THOUGH.
"I MIGHT QUIT CRAM SCHOOL."
...
BY THE WAY...
...HOW ARE THINGS GOING BETWEEN YOU AND RYU?
HUH?
Where'd that come from?
WE'RE DOING...
...
...WELL.
Hm? WHAT DID YOU SAY?
Heard it.
WHAT'S THAT?
Didn't hear it.

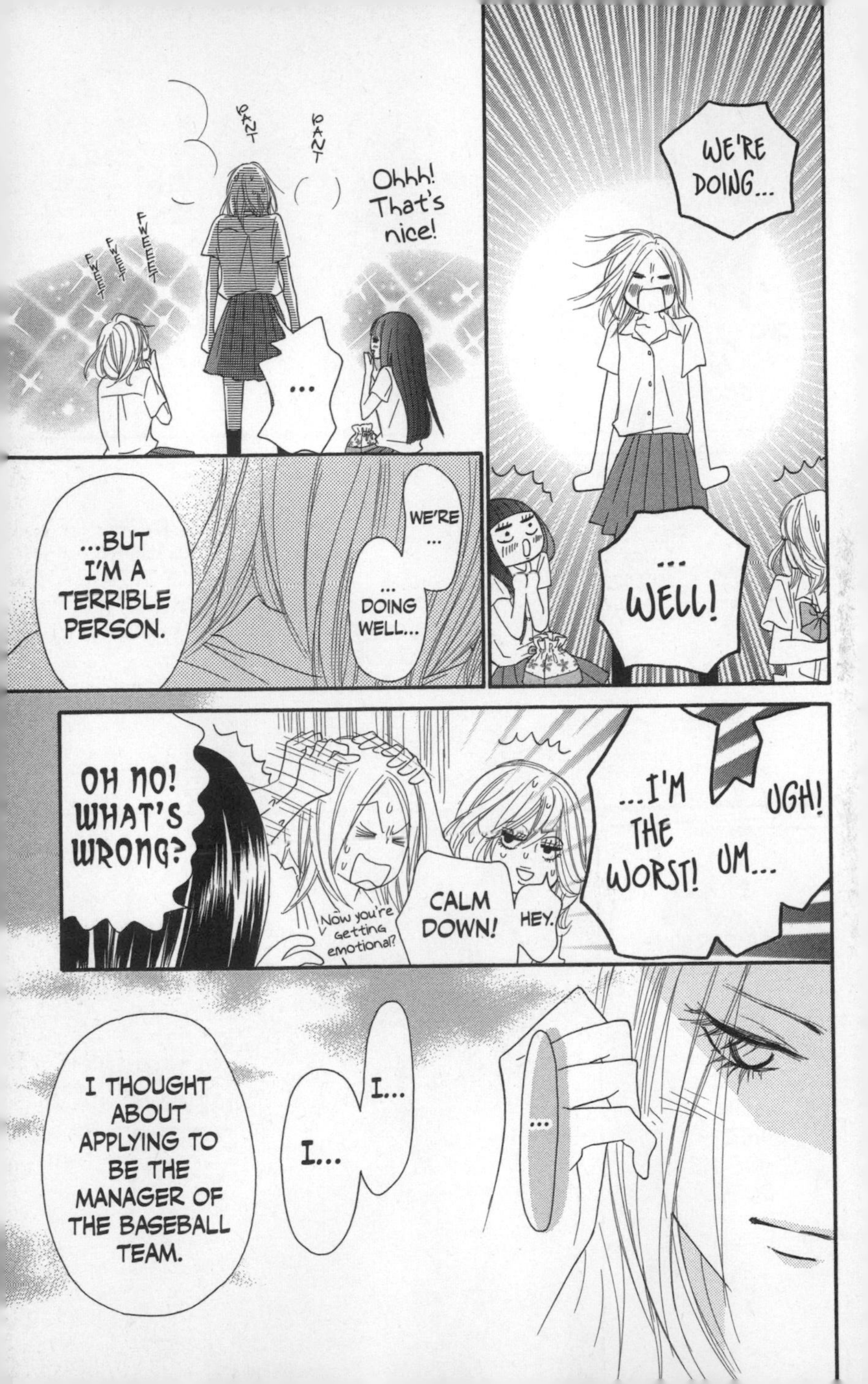
WE'RE DOING...
... WELL!
PANT
PANT
Ohhh! That's nice!
FWEEET
FWEET
FWEET
...
WE'RE ... ... DOING WELL...
...BUT I'M A TERRIBLE PERSON.
UGH! UM...
...I'M THE WORST!
HEY.
CALM DOWN!
Now you're getting emotional?
OH NO! WHAT'S WRONG?
...
I...
I...
I THOUGHT ABOUT APPLYING TO BE THE MANAGER OF THE BASEBALL TEAM.

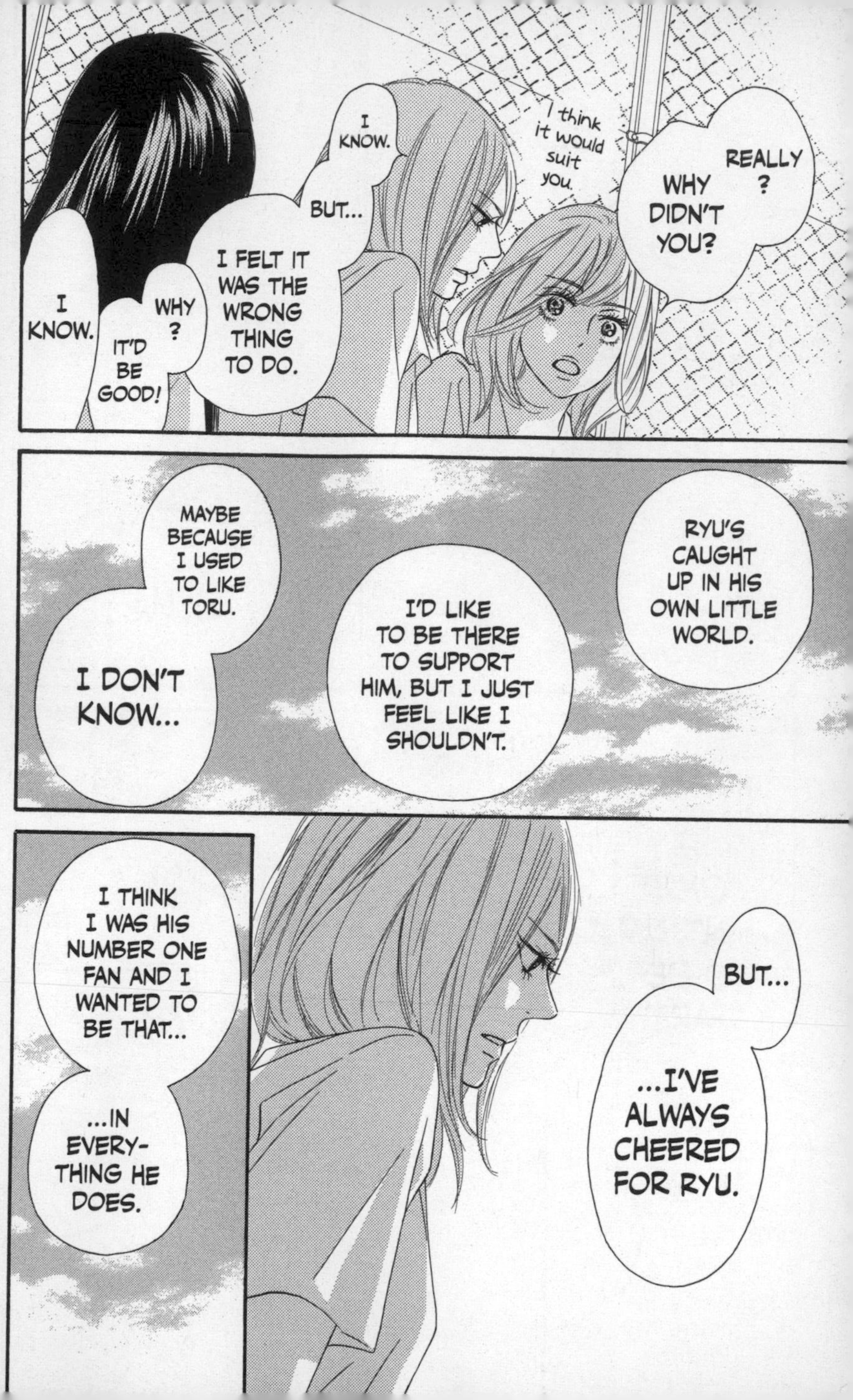
REALLY? WHY DIDN'T YOU?
I think it would suit you.
I KNOW.
BUT...
I FELT IT WAS THE WRONG THING TO DO.
WHY? IT'D BE GOOD!
I KNOW.
RYU'S CAUGHT UP IN HIS OWN LITTLE WORLD.
I'D LIKE TO BE THERE TO SUPPORT HIM, BUT I JUST FEEL LIKE I SHOULDN'T.
MAYBE BECAUSE I USED TO LIKE TORU.
I DON'T KNOW...
BUT...
...I'VE ALWAYS CHEERED FOR RYU.
I THINK I WAS HIS NUMBER ONE FAN AND I WANTED TO BE THAT...
...IN EVERY-THING HE DOES.

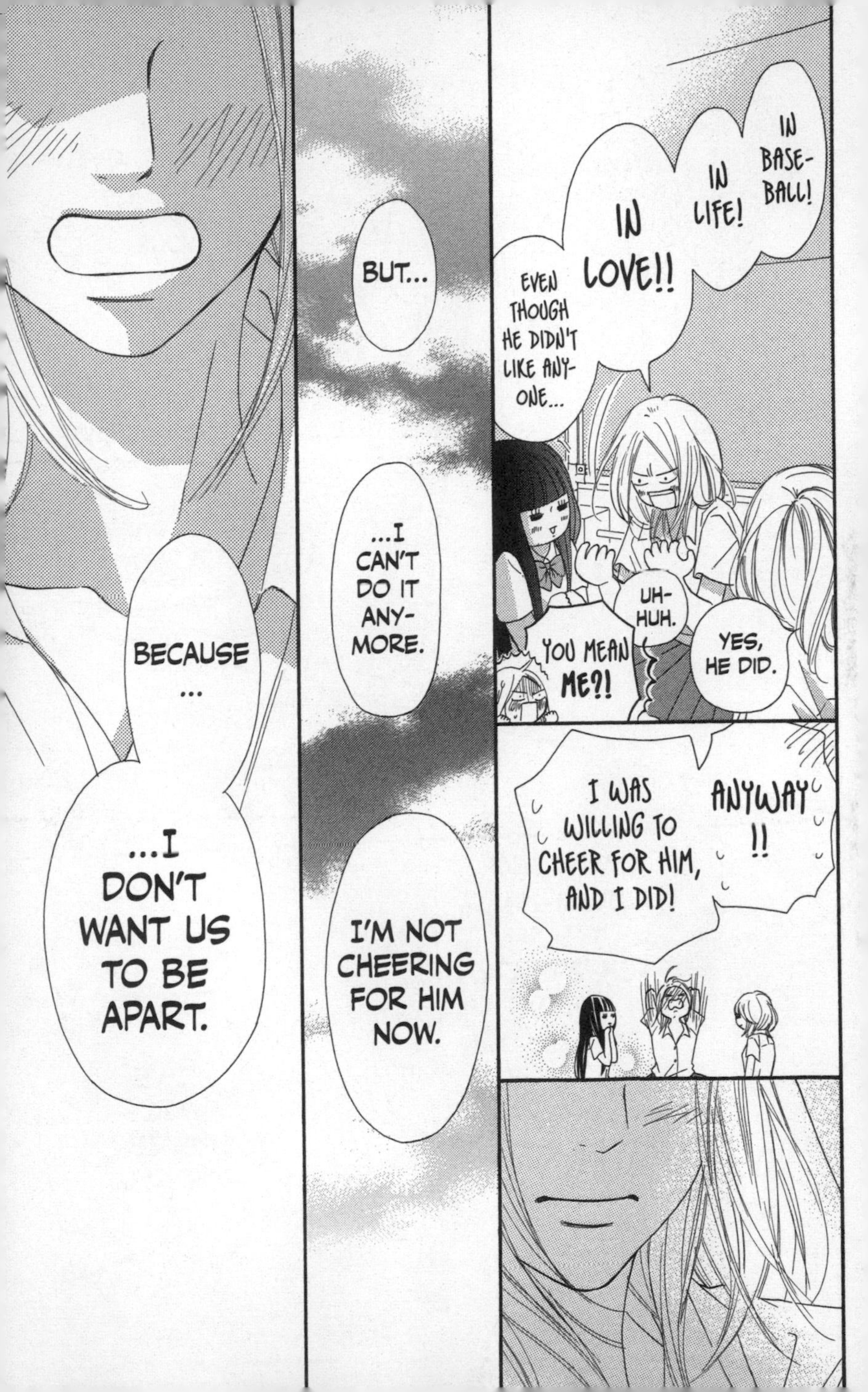
IN BASE-BALL!
IN LIFE!
IN LOVE!!
EVEN THOUGH HE DIDN'T LIKE ANY-ONE...
YES, HE DID.
UH-HUH.
YOU MEAN ME?!
ANYWAY!!
I WAS WILLING TO CHEER FOR HIM, AND I DID!
BUT...
...I CAN'T DO IT ANY-MORE.
I'M NOT CHEERING FOR HIM NOW.
BECAUSE ...
...I DON'T WANT US TO BE APART.

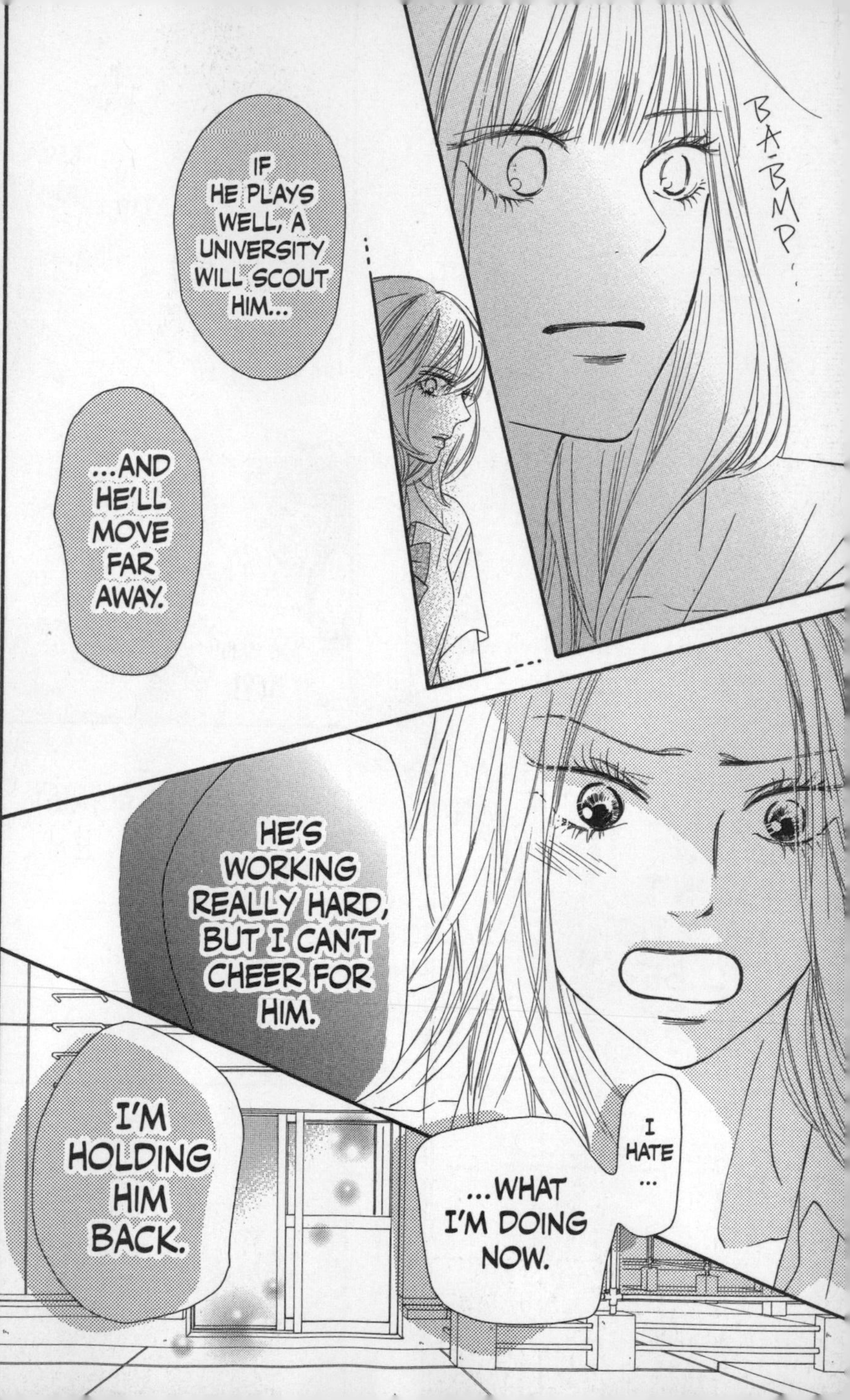
BA-BMP
IF HE PLAYS WELL, A UNIVERSITY WILL SCOUT HIM...
...AND HE'LL MOVE FAR AWAY.
HE'S WORKING REALLY HARD, BUT I CAN'T CHEER FOR HIM.
I HATE...
...WHAT I'M DOING NOW.
I'M HOLDING HIM BACK.

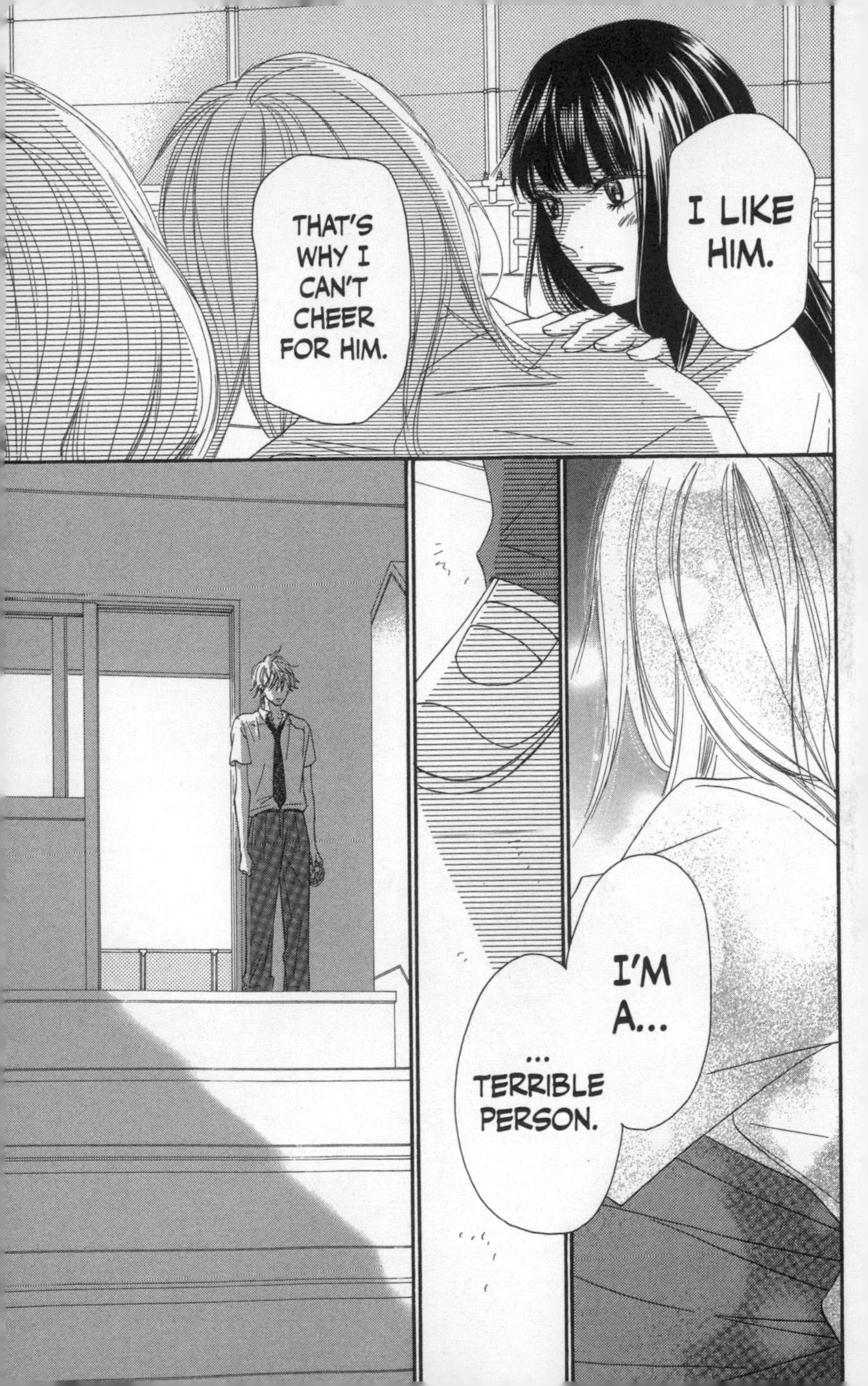
I LIKE HIM.
THAT'S WHY I CAN'T CHEER FOR HIM.
I'M A...
...TERRIBLE PERSON.

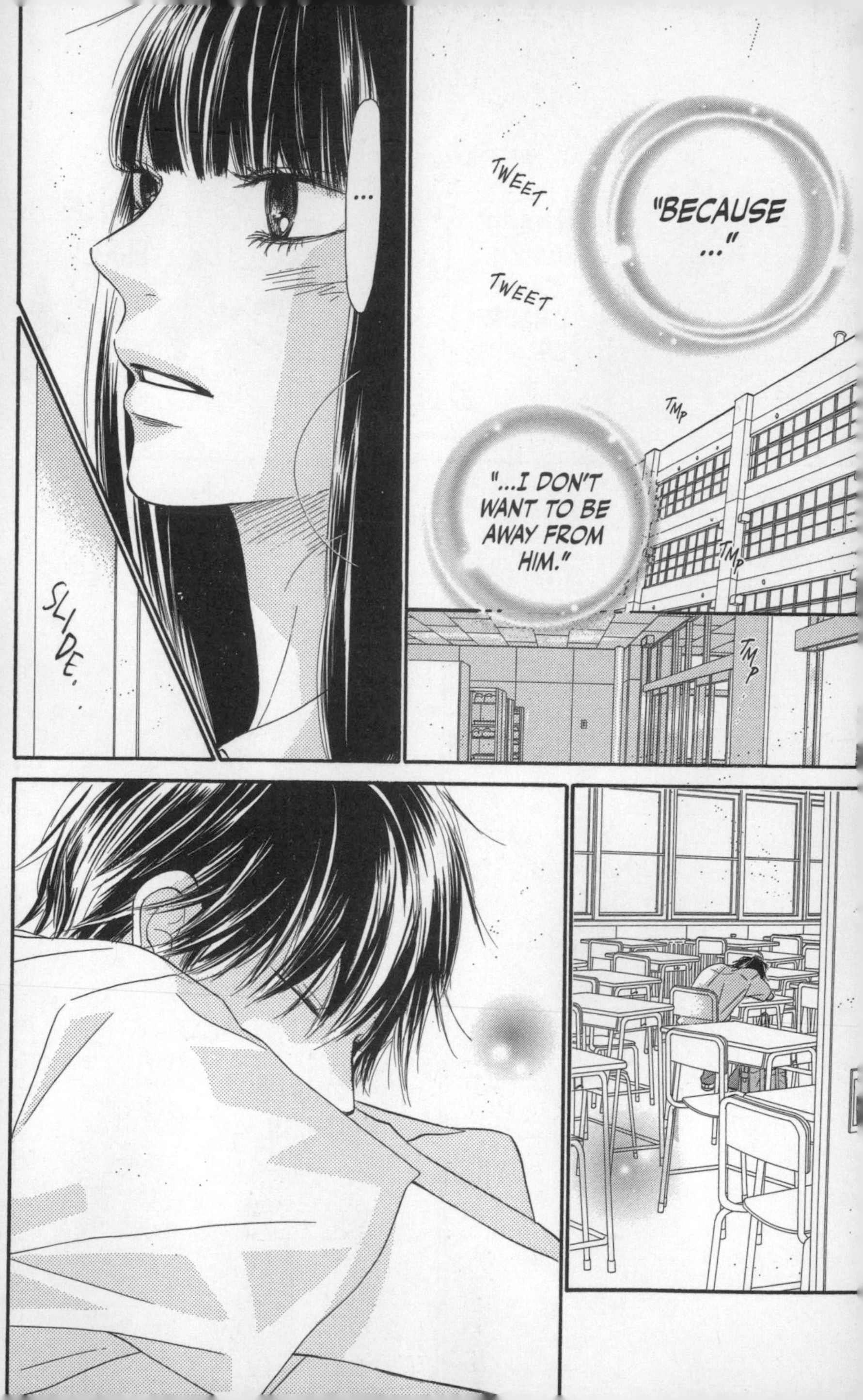
TWEET.
TWEET...
"BECAUSE ..."
TMP
"...I DON'T WANT TO BE AWAY FROM HIM."
TMP
TMP
...
SLIDE.

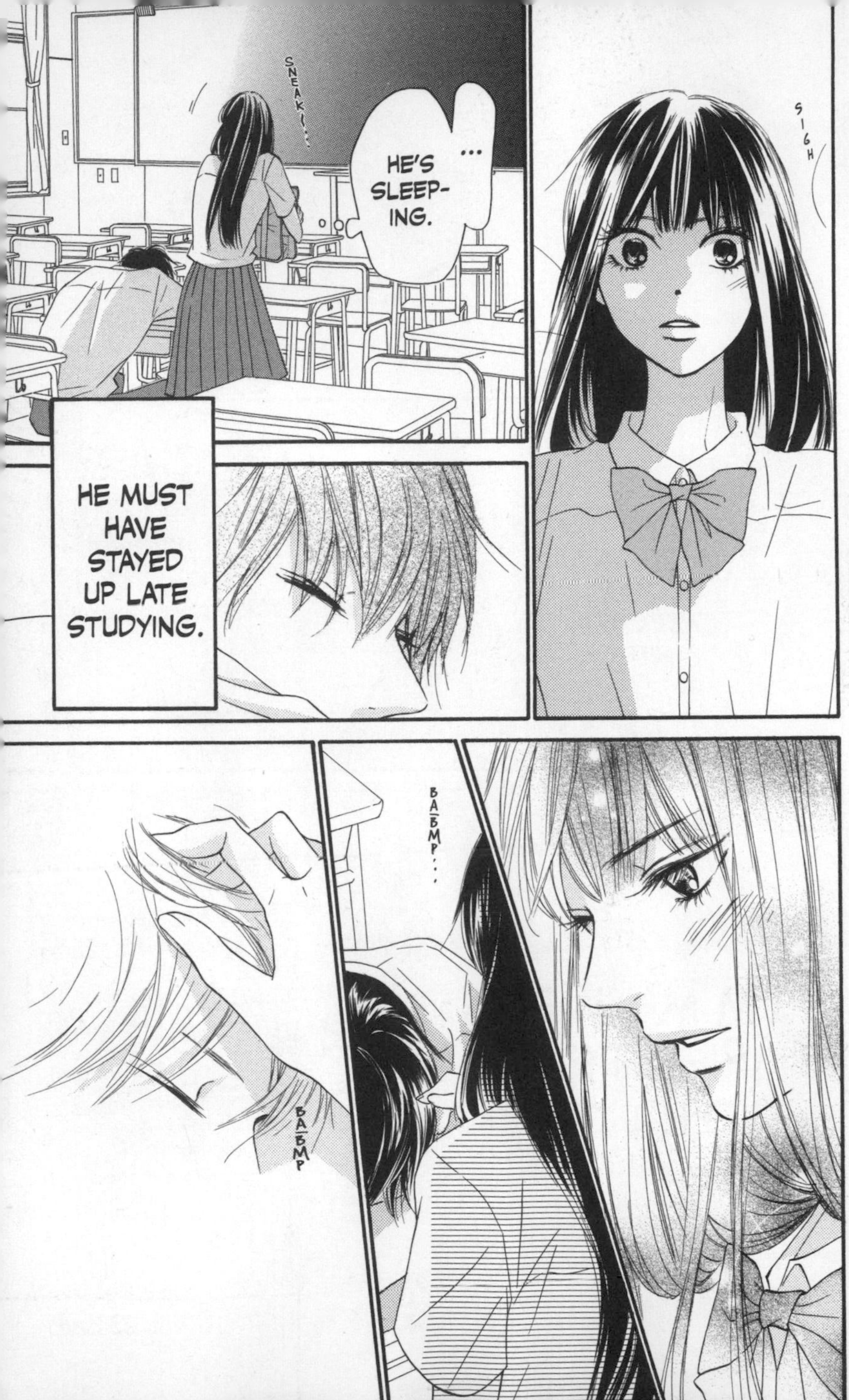
SIGH
SNEAK...
...
HE'S SLEEPING.
HE MUST HAVE STAYED UP LATE STUDYING.
BA-BMP...
BA-BMP

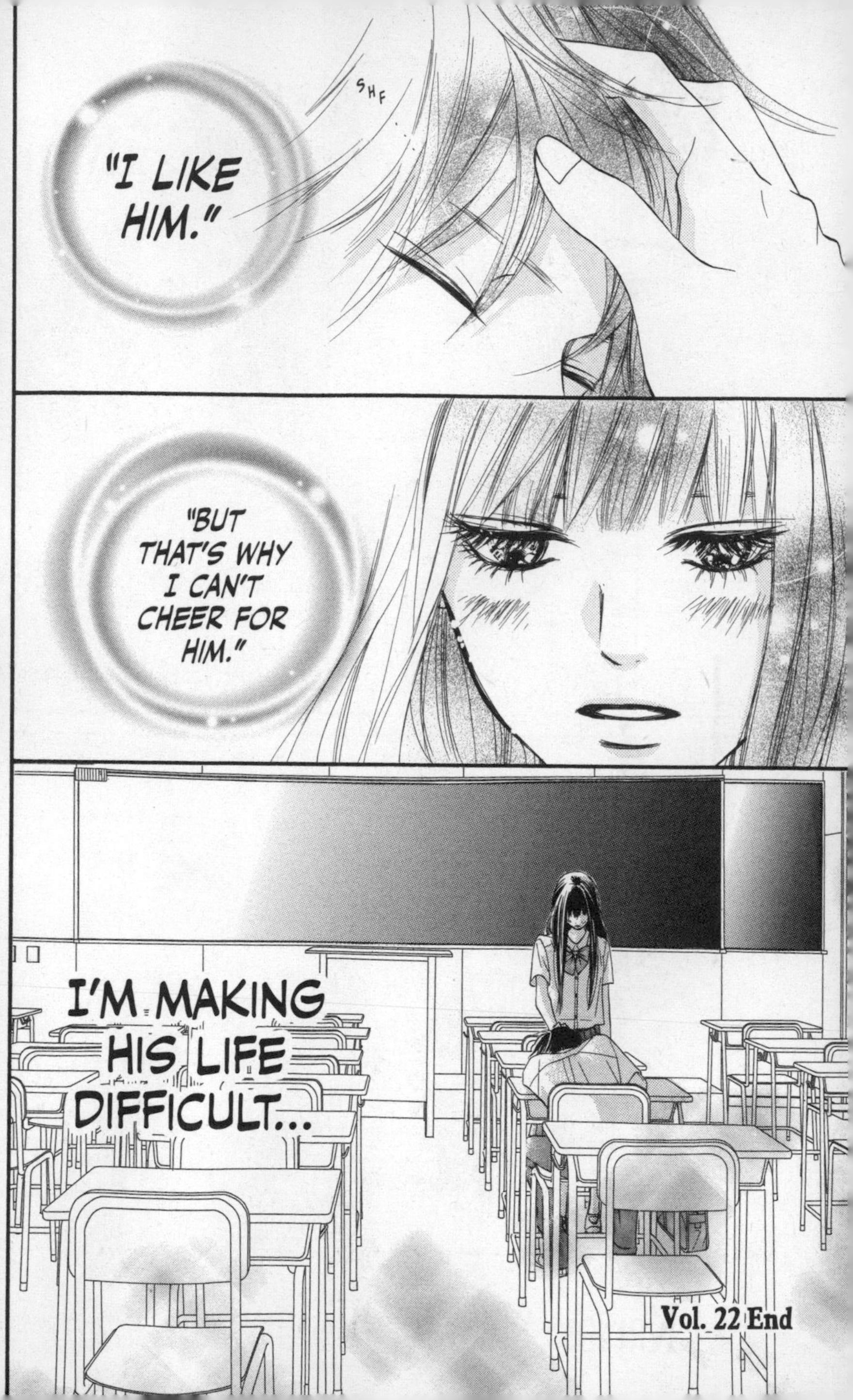
SHF
"I LIKE HIM."
"BUT THAT'S WHY I CAN'T CHEER FOR HIM."
I'M MAKING HIS LIFE DIFFICULT...
Vol. 22 End

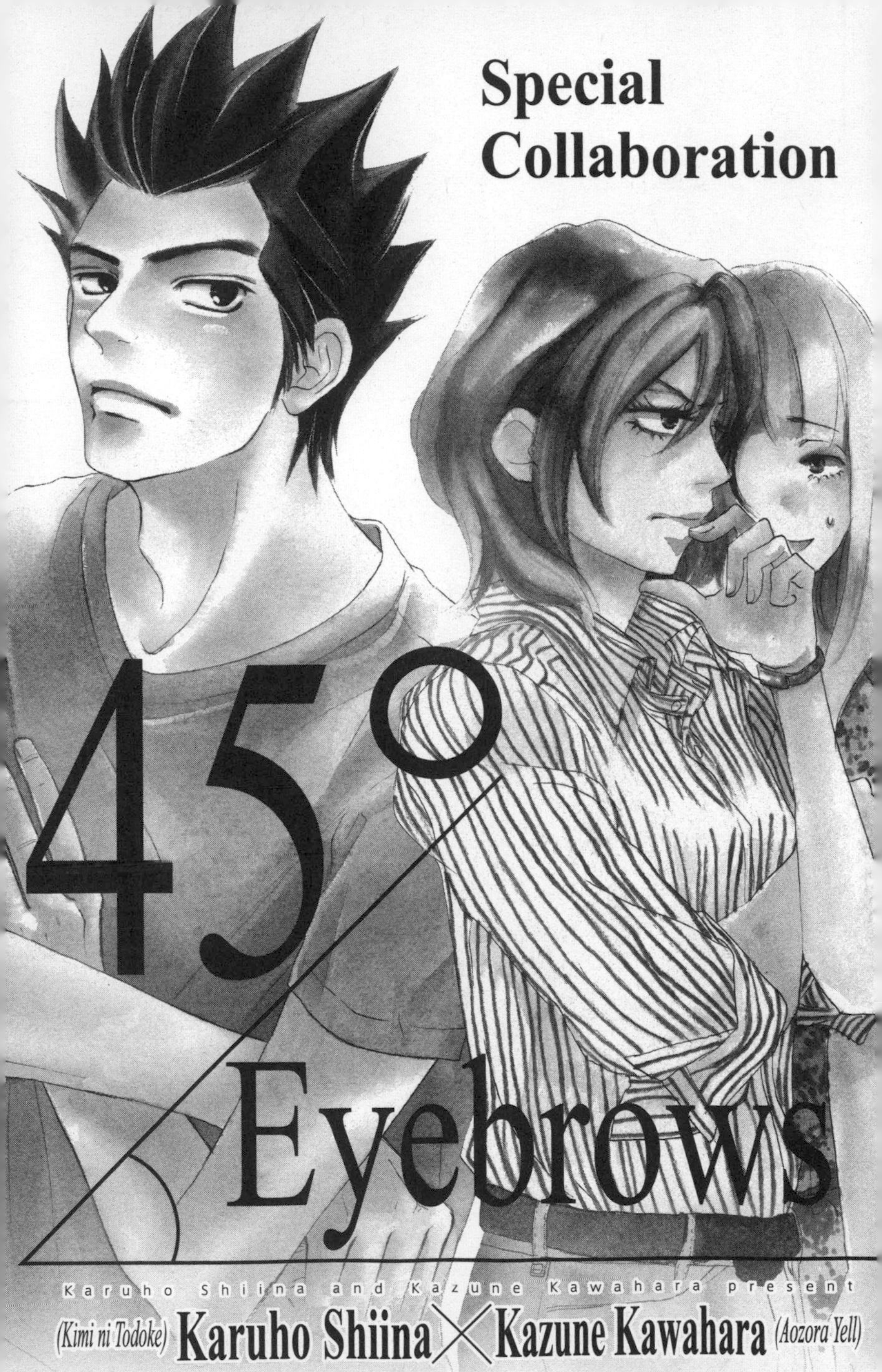
Special Collaboration
45°
Eyebrows

Karuho Shiina and Kazune Kawahara present

(Kimi ni Todoke) **Karuho Shiina** × **Kazune Kawahara** (Aozora Yell)

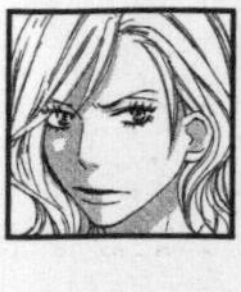

Yoko Sugimura
(from *Aozora Yell*)
Band teacher. She's very strict.

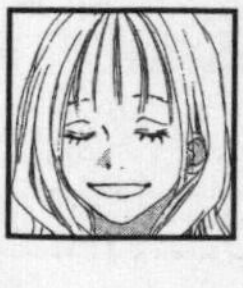

Nanako Maki
(from *Aozora Yell*)
Assistant band teacher. She's very kind.

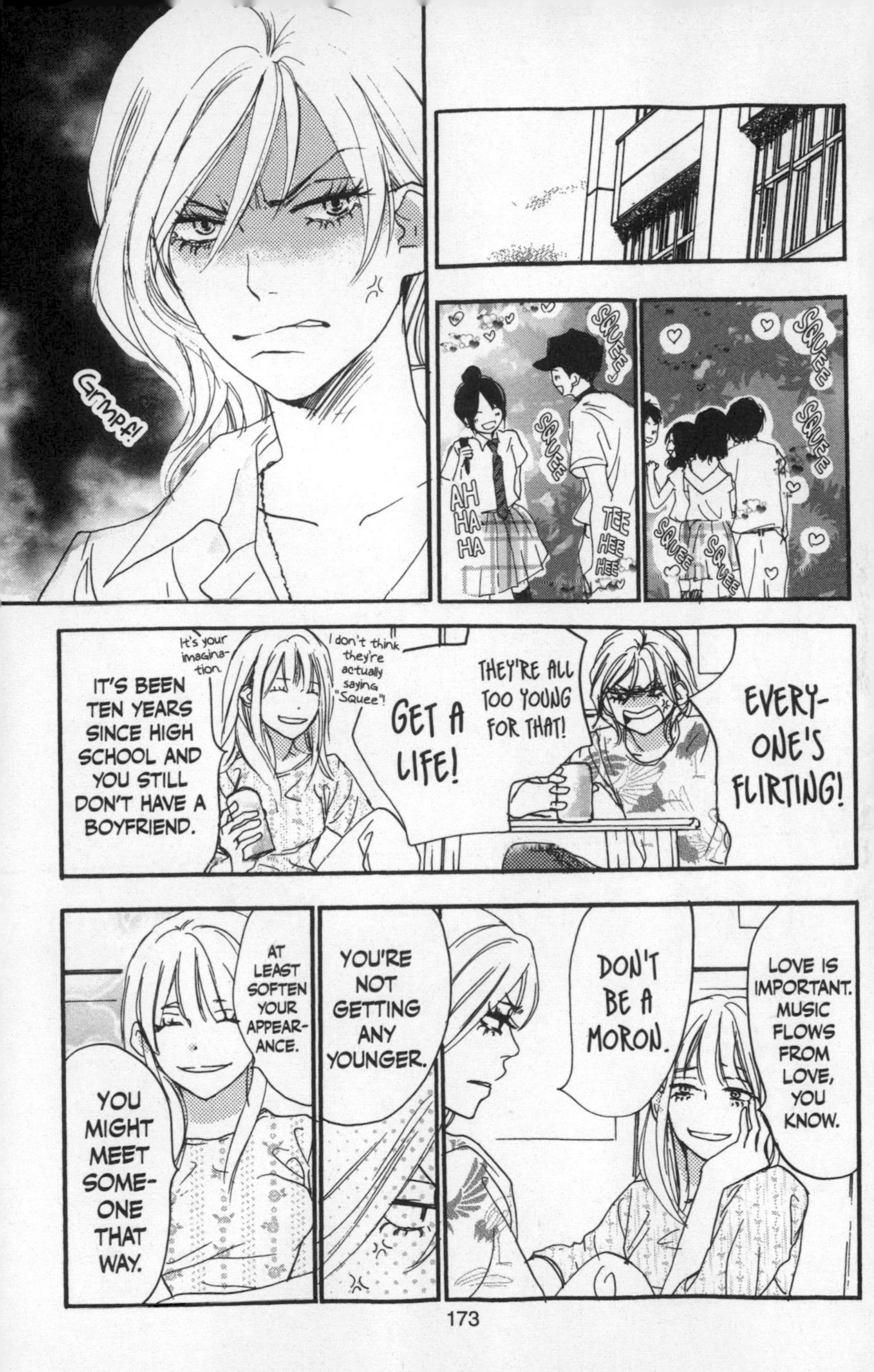

SQUEEE
SQUEE
SQUEE
SQUEE
SQUEE
SQUEE
AH HA HA
TEE HEE HEE
Grmpf!
EVERY-ONE'S FLIRTING!
THEY'RE ALL TOO YOUNG FOR THAT!
GET A LIFE!
I don't think they're actually saying "Squee"!
It's your imagination.
IT'S BEEN TEN YEARS SINCE HIGH SCHOOL AND YOU STILL DON'T HAVE A BOYFRIEND.
LOVE IS IMPORTANT. MUSIC FLOWS FROM LOVE, YOU KNOW.
DON'T BE A MORON.
YOU'RE NOT GETTING ANY YOUNGER.
AT LEAST SOFTEN YOUR APPEARANCE.
YOU MIGHT MEET SOME-ONE THAT WAY.

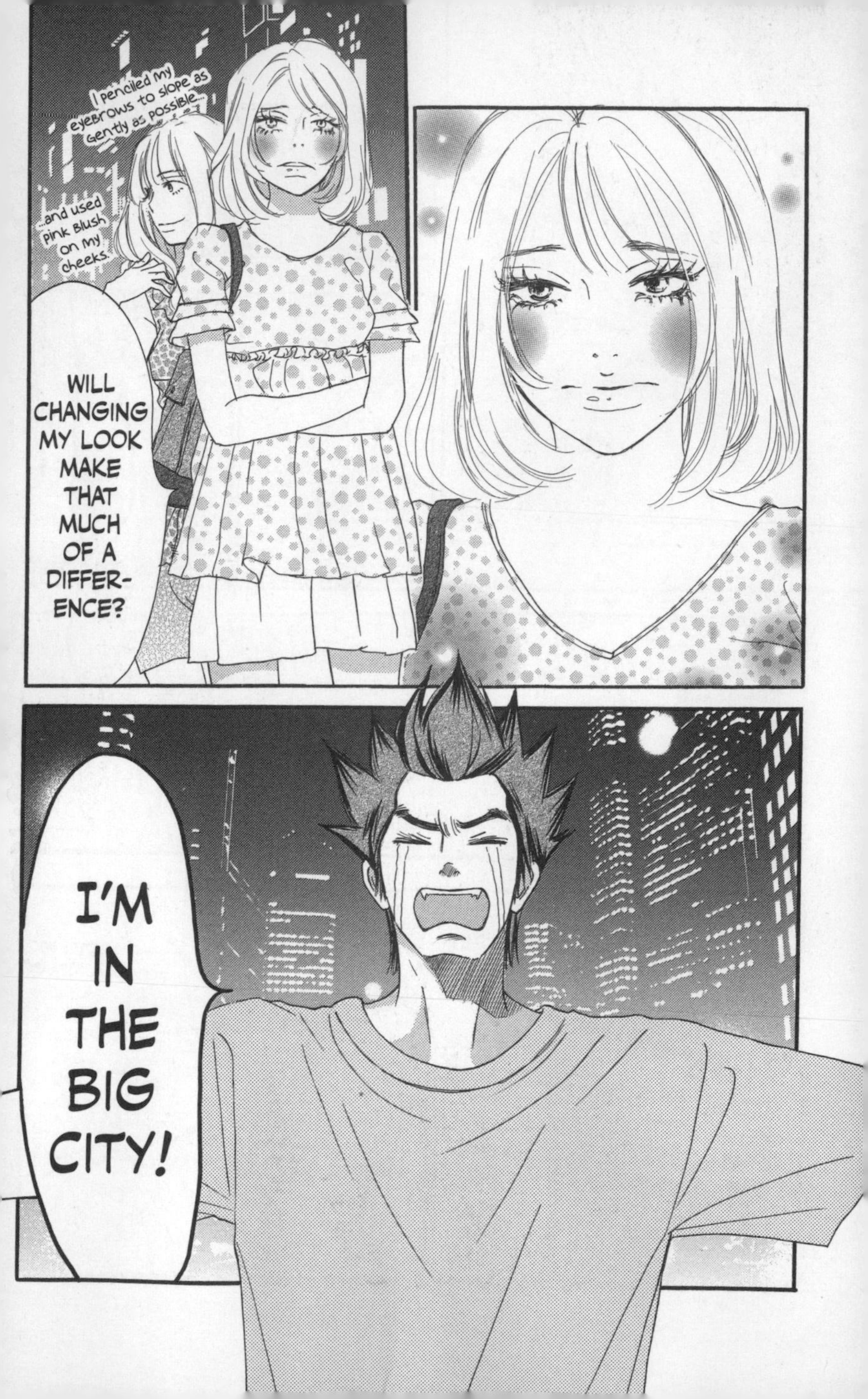
I penciled my eyebrows to slope as gently as possible...
...and used pink blush on my cheeks.
WILL CHANGING MY LOOK MAKE THAT MUCH OF A DIFFER-ENCE?
I'M IN THE BIG CITY!

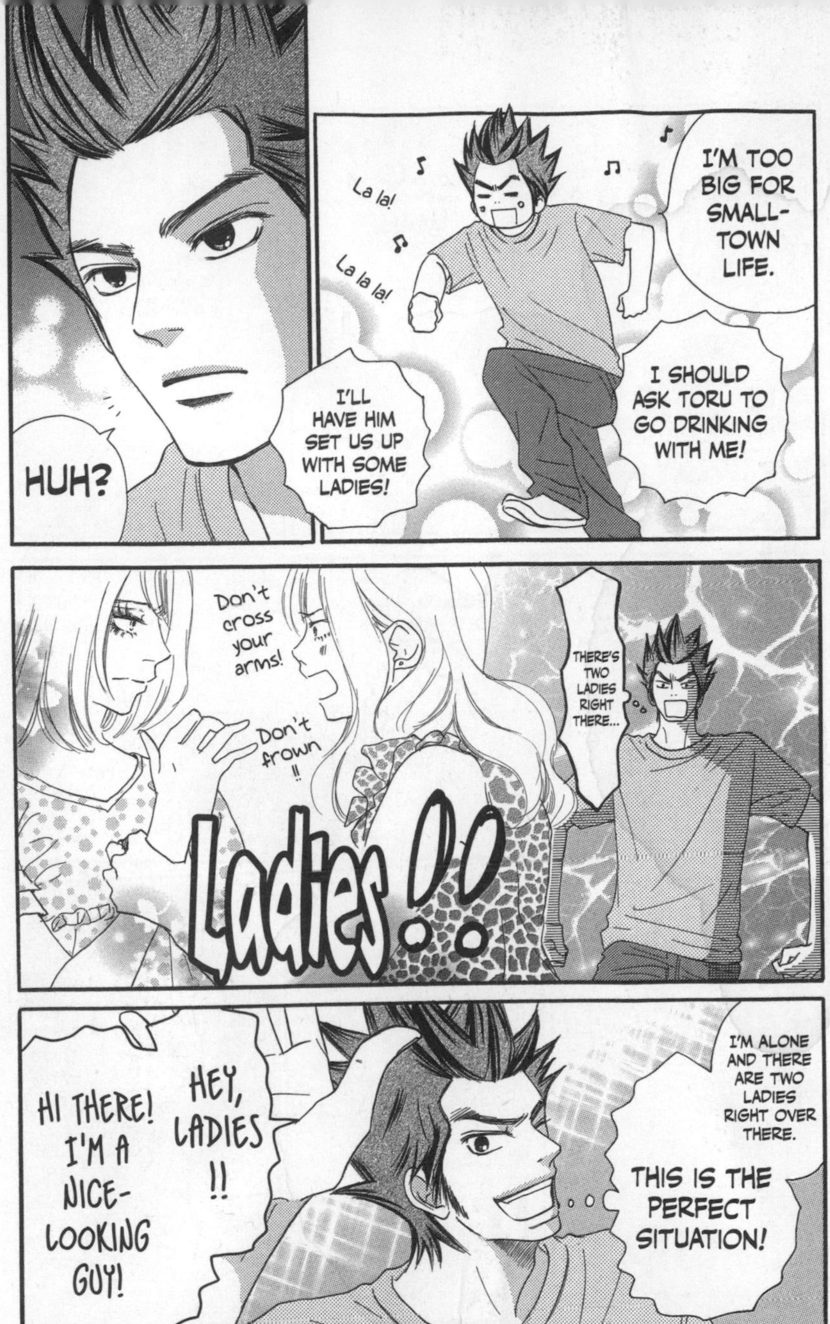
I'M TOO BIG FOR SMALL-TOWN LIFE.
La la!
La la la!
I SHOULD ASK TORU TO GO DRINKING WITH ME!
I'LL HAVE HIM SET US UP WITH SOME LADIES!
HUH?
THERE'S TWO LADIES RIGHT THERE...
Don't cross your arms!
Don't frown!!
Ladies!!
I'M ALONE AND THERE ARE TWO LADIES RIGHT OVER THERE.
THIS IS THE PERFECT SITUATION!
HEY, LADIES!!
HI THERE! I'M A NICE-LOOKING GUY!

HERE COMES SOME GUY!
A LADIES' MAN!
WINK WINK WINK
I'm a fast wink-er!
GOOD EVE-NING.
Hey...
Huh?
I'M 29 YEARS OLD.
WHAT A WEIRD REPLY.
YOU'RE OLDER THAN I AM.
THAT'S PERFECT!
ZOOM
LET'S DRINK! WHERE DO YOU WANNA GO?
SO HOW OLD ARE YOU?
WHAT DO YOU MEAN BY PER-FECT?
WHY DOES... ...YOKO CARE ABOUT HIS AGE?
ME? I'M YOUNG!
HMM ...
B-cup...
Oh! E-cup?!

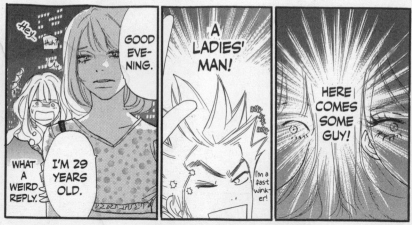

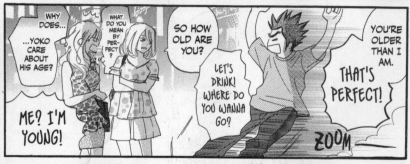

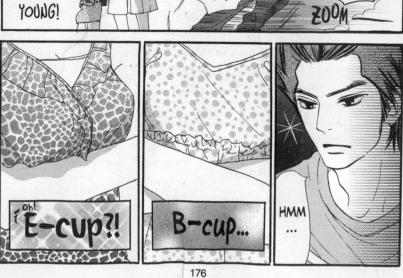

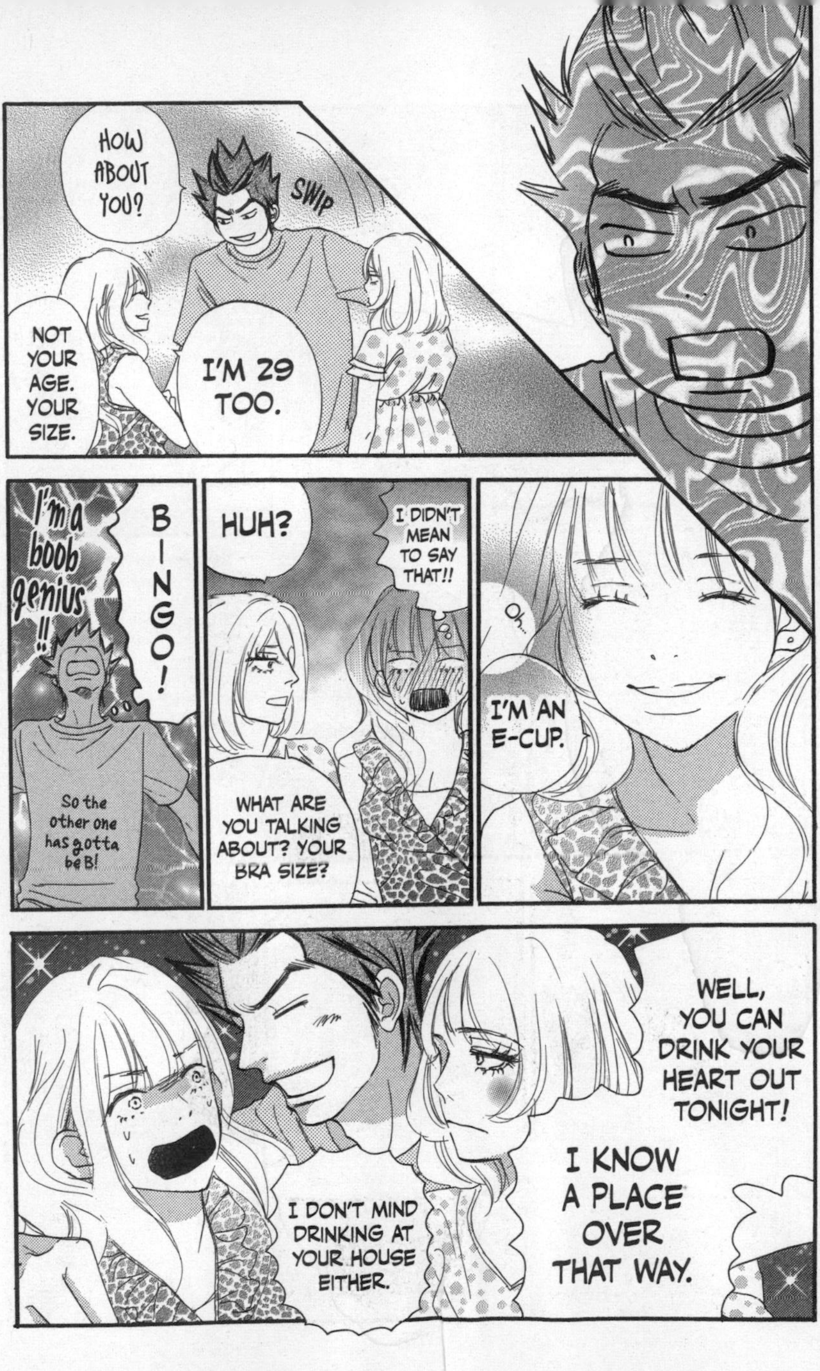
HOW ABOUT YOU?
SWIP
I'M 29 TOO.
NOT YOUR AGE. YOUR SIZE.
Oh...
I'M AN E-CUP.
I DIDN'T MEAN TO SAY THAT!!
HUH?
WHAT ARE YOU TALKING ABOUT? YOUR BRA SIZE?
BINGO!
I'm a boob genius!!
So the other one has gotta be B!
WELL, YOU CAN DRINK YOUR HEART OUT TONIGHT!
I KNOW A PLACE OVER THAT WAY.
I DON'T MIND DRINKING AT YOUR HOUSE EITHER.

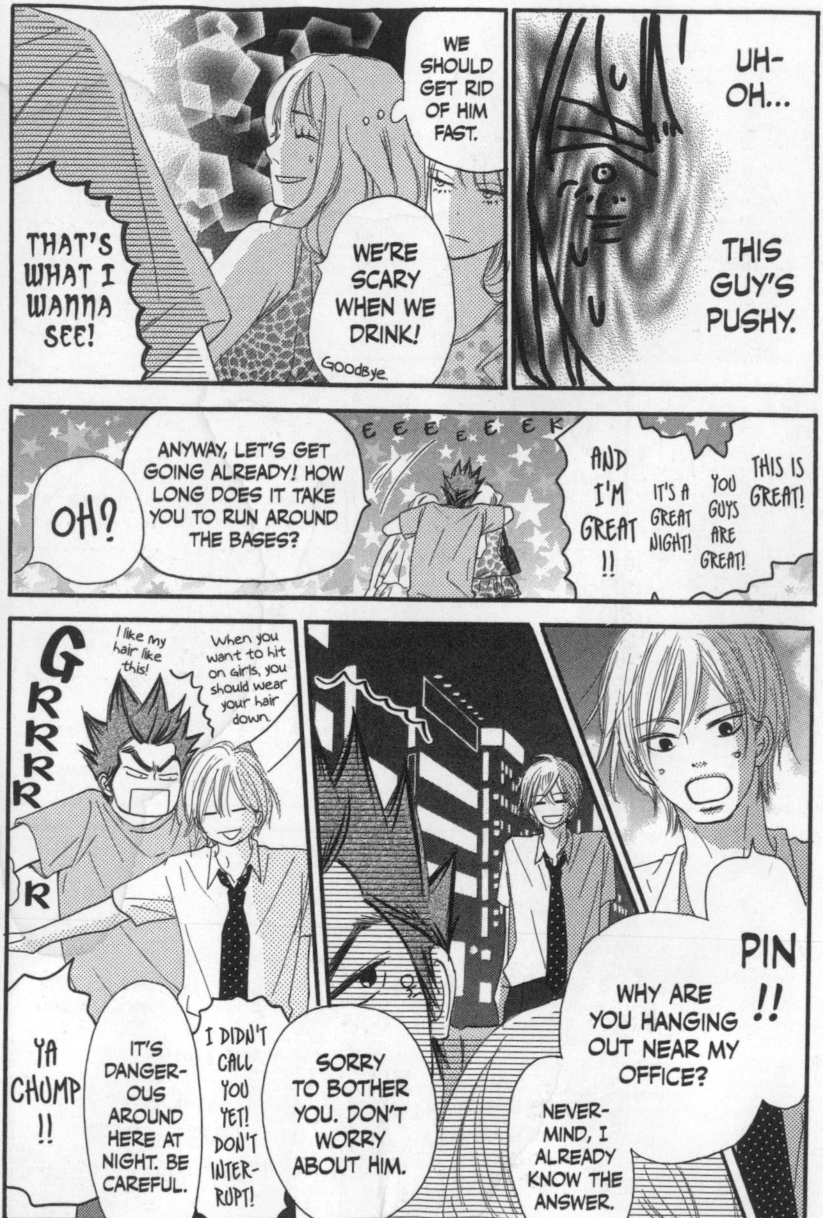
UH-OH...
THIS GUY'S PUSHY.
WE SHOULD GET RID OF HIM FAST.
WE'RE SCARY WHEN WE DRINK!
GoodBye.
THAT'S WHAT I WANNA SEE!
THIS IS GREAT!
YOU GUYS ARE GREAT!
IT'S A GREAT NIGHT!
AND I'M GREAT!!
EEEEEEK
ANYWAY, LET'S GET GOING ALREADY! HOW LONG DOES IT TAKE YOU TO RUN AROUND THE BASES?
OH?
PIN!!
WHY ARE YOU HANGING OUT NEAR MY OFFICE?
NEVER-MIND, I ALREADY KNOW THE ANSWER.
SORRY TO BOTHER YOU. DON'T WORRY ABOUT HIM.
When you want to hit on girls, you should wear your hair down.
I like my hair like this!
GRRRRR
I DIDN'T CALL YOU YET! DON'T INTER-RUPT!
IT'S DANGER-OUS AROUND HERE AT NIGHT. BE CAREFUL.
YA CHUMP!!

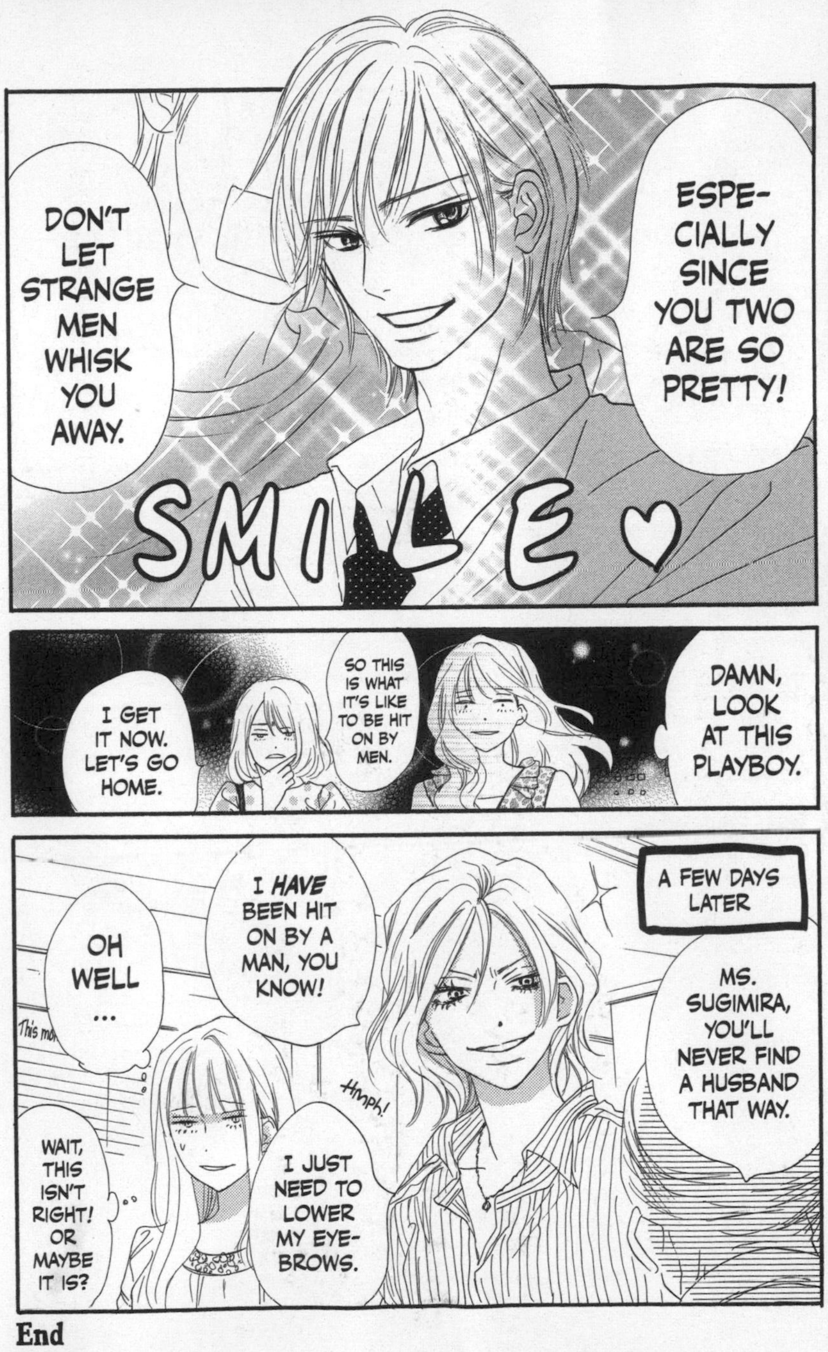
ESPE-CIALLY SINCE YOU TWO ARE SO PRETTY!
DON'T LET STRANGE MEN WHISK YOU AWAY.
SMILE ♥
DAMN, LOOK AT THIS PLAYBOY.
SO THIS IS WHAT IT'S LIKE TO BE HIT ON BY MEN.
I GET IT NOW. LET'S GO HOME.
A FEW DAYS LATER
MS. SUGIMIRA, YOU'LL NEVER FIND A HUSBAND THAT WAY.
I *HAVE* BEEN HIT ON BY A MAN, YOU KNOW!
OH WELL ...
Hmph!
I JUST NEED TO LOWER MY EYE-BROWS.
WAIT, THIS ISN'T RIGHT! OR MAYBE IT IS?

End

From me (the editor) to you (the reader).

Here are some Japanese culture explanations that will help you better understand the references in the *Kimi ni Todoke* world.

Honorifics:
When saying someone's name in Japanese, a suffix is often attached to indicate how familiar the speaker is with the person. Some are more polite and respectful, while others are endearing. Calling someone by just their first name is the most informal.
-kun is used for young men or boys, usually someone you are familiar with.
-chan is used for young women, girls or young children and can be used as a term of endearment.
-san is used for someone you respect or are not close to, or to be polite.

Page 72, rakugo:
The traditional Japanese storytelling form that Sawako mastered for the school trip. A lone storyteller sits on a stage with just a fan and a cloth as props and proceeds to relate a comedic story. The performer voices all the characters.

Page 179, playboy:
A boy who is *charai* (we've translated it as "playboy") is flashy and smooth-talking, but also frivolous and superficial. People often use this word to describe Kento.

I went to a high school baseball game
for research. The players and all their
teammates who were cheering got all fired
up. You can't help but admire people who
are really passionate about whatever it is
they do.

--Karuho Shiina

Karuho Shiina was born and raised in
Hokkaido, Japan. Though *Kimi ni Todoke*
is only her second series following many
one-shot stories, it has already racked
up accolades from various "Best Manga
of the Year" lists. Winner of the 2008
Kodansha Manga Award for the shojo
category, *Kimi ni Todoke* also placed
fifth in the first-ever Manga Taisho
(Cartoon Grand Prize) contest in 2008. In
Japan, an animated TV series debuted in
October 2009, and a live-action film was
released in 2010.

Kimi ni Todoke
VOL. 22

Shojo Beat Edition

STORY AND ART BY
KARUHO SHIINA

Translation/Ari Yasuda, HC Language Solutions, Inc.
Touch-up Art & Lettering/Vanessa Satone
Design/Nozomi Akashi
Editor/Marlene First

KIMI NI TODOKE © 2005 by Karuho Shiina
All rights reserved. First published in Japan in 2005 by SHUEISHA Inc.,
Tokyo. English translation rights arranged by SHUEISHA Inc.

Printed in the U.S.A.

Published by VIZ Media, LLC
P.O. Box 77010
San Francisco, CA 94107

10 9 8 7 6 5 4 3 2 1
First printing, September 2015

Surprise!

You may be reading the wrong way!

It's true: In keeping with the original Japanese comic format, this book reads from right to left—so action, sound effects, and word balloons are completely reversed. This preserves the orientation of the original artwork—plus, it's fun! Check out the diagram shown here to get the hang of things, and then turn to the other side of the book to get started!

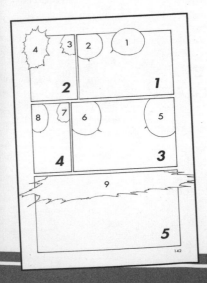